ROYAL COMMISSION ON THE PRESS

CHAIRMAN: PROFESSOR O R McGREGOR

Attitudes to the Press

A Report by Social and Community Planning Research

Research Series 3

Presented to Parliament by Command of Her Majesty
July 1977

LONDON
HER MAJESTY'S STATIONERY OFFICE
£5·50 net

Cmnd. 6810-3

Foreword by the Chairman

1. The present Royal Commission on the Press was set up in 1974 with the following terms of reference:

To inquire into the factors affecting the maintenance of the independence, diversity and editorial standards of newspapers and periodicals, and the public's freedom of choice of newspapers and periodicals, nationally, regionally and locally, with particular reference to:

  (a) the economics of newspaper and periodical publishing and distribution;

  (b) the interaction of the newspaper and periodical interests held by the companies concerned with their other interests and holdings, within and outside the communications industry;

  (c) management and labour practices and relations in the newspaper and periodical industry;

  (d) conditions and security of employment in the newspaper and periodical industry;

  (e) the distribution and concentration of ownership of the newspaper and periodical industry, and the adequacy of existing law in relation thereto;

  (f) the responsibilities, constitution and functioning of the Press Council;

and to make recommendations.

2. The Royal Commission took evidence from a large number of organisations and individuals, and commissioned work by a number of organisations and individuals with special knowledge in appropriate fields of interests. Jean Morton-Williams, Richard Stowell and Douglas Wood of Social and Community Planning Research (SCPR) here report the findings of three opinion surveys.

3. In the first survey, over two thousand members of the general public in Great Britain were interviewed and asked about their use of, and attitudes towards, the national and provincial press. The demographic characteristics of the sample are so similar to those of the population of Great Britain as to indicate that the results are representative of the population as a whole. The Commission set great store by this and the results have been drawn on in our discussions and in our Report. The second survey covered a sample of 350 people who held positions of influence in local communities. Their consumption of, and involvement in, local news would, we believed, allow a closer study to be made of the performance of the provincial press than was possible

in the survey of the general public. The results of these surveys taken together provide an illuminating account of the attitudes of readers to the newspapers they buy, and the uses to which they put them. We hope that by publishing these reports, we shall help those concerned with the provincial press, and provide information which has hitherto been lacking.

4. The other survey was of editors and journalists, and it was carried out by post. The questionnaires for each were identical in the questions they asked on matters of opinion and differed only in the background information required. We were surprised and disappointed that, despite assurances that confidentiality would be respected and that individuals would not be identifiable, many of those approached refused to take part in the survey. It was also unfortunate that the list from which the sample of journalists was chosen was out of date. The result was a response rate of 63% of editors which, if rather low, was nevertheless acceptable and of 43% of senior journalists. It was judged that this was too low to be relied on statistically, although the results which relate to questions of opinion have been recorded in the report for comparison with the views of editors.

5. A further survey by SCPR, on the training of journalists, is not included in this volume but is published in summary form as an appendix to the Royal Commission's Final Report.

6. Any views expressed in this volume are those of the authors alone and are not necessarily shared by the Royal Commission.

O R McGregor

June 1977

Contents

	Page
Part 1: The Attitudes of the General Public	1
Introduction	3
Conclusions	7

Main Findings
1. Newspaper Reading, Television Watching and Radio Listening ... 11
2. News Interests and Sources ... 27
3. What People Read in Regional and Local Newspapers ... 44
4. Attitudes to Newspapers ... 52
5. Ownership and Choice ... 86
6. Letters to the Editor ... 93
7. Other Topics of Enquiry ... 97

APPENDICES
Appendix 1: Scotland and the *Sunday Post* ... 105
Appendix 2: Sampling and Fieldwork ... 113
Appendix 3: The Questionnaire ... 117

PART 2: The Attitudes of People in Influential Positions

Introduction ... 143

Conclusions ... 145

Main Findings
1. Survey Method ... 151
2. A Profile of the "Influential" Sample ... 156
3. Consumers of News ... 161
4. The Role and Importance of the Regional Press ... 175
5. Standards in the Regional Press ... 187
6. Does the Provincial Press cover all Sections of the Community Fairly ... 211
7. Competition in the Provincial Press ... 223
8. Other Topics of Enquiry ... 230

Page

APPENDICES

Appendix 1: Response by Type of Respondent 239
Appendix 2: Response by Town/Type of Respondent 241
Appendix 3: The Questionnaires 247

PART 3: Postal Survey among Editors and Journalists

Summary 279

Introduction 287

Editor's Responsibilities, Conditions of Work and Career Background ... 293

Editors' Opinions on Some Major Issues 323

The Views of Senior Journalists 333

APPENDICES

Appendix 1: Further Details of the Sampling Method 351
Appendix 2: Response Rate Analyses 353
Appendix 3: The Questionnaires 355

List of Tables

		Page
1.001	Daily newspaper readership by type of newspaper	14
1.002	Daily newspaper readership by type (*Daily Record* treated as a regional morning)	14
1.003	Overlap of readership between types of newspaper	15
1.004	Duplication ratios of regular readership of types of newspaper	15
1.005	Overlap of readership between types of newspaper (*Daily Record* treated as a regional morning)	16
1.006	Duplication ratios of regular readership of types of newspaper (*Daily Record* treated as a regional morning)	16
1.007	Readership of other dailies by readership of regional mornings	16
1.008	Readership of local weeklies by readership of evenings	17
1.009	Readership of daily newspapers by region	18
1.010	Readership of regional and local newspapers by region	18
1.011	Newspaper readership by sex and age	19
1.012	Newspaper readership by occupation	20
1.013	Newspaper readership by socio-economic group of household	20
1.014	Identification with political parties	21
1.015	Party identification and union membership by newspaper readership	21
1.016	Regular readers of individual national mornings	22
1.017	Readership profiles of the larger national mornings	22–23
1.018	Time spent reading newspapers	23
1.019	Time spent reading individual national mornings	24
1.020	Time spent watching TV and listening to the radio	24
1.021	Frequency of exposure to TV and radio news	25
1.022	Frequent exposure to TV and radio news by social group	26
1.023	Frequent exposure to TV and radio news by readership of daily newspapers	26
1.024	Strong interest in different types of news	27
1.025	Interest in general and political news	29
1.026	Interest in general and political news by social group	30
1.027	Interest in general and political news by newspaper readership	30

		Page
1.028	Useful sources for keeping up to date with general and political news	31
1.029	Interest in trade union and business news	32
1.030	Interest in trade union and business news by occupation	32
1.031	Interest in trade union and business news by newspaper readership	33
1.032	Useful sources for keeping up to date with trade union and business news	33
1.033	Interest in news about sport and leisure interests	34
1.034	Interest in news about sport by newspaper readership	34
1.035	Useful sources for keeping up to date with news about sport	35
1.036	Interest in news about leisure interests by social group	35
1.037	Interest in news about leisure interests by newspaper readership	36
1.038	Useful sources for keeping up to date with news about leisure interests	36
1.039	Interest in local and regional news	37
1.040	Rank ordering of interest in different types of news	37
1.041	Interest in local and regional news by social group	38
1.042	Interest in local and regional news by region	38
1.043	Interest in local and regional news by newspaper readership	39
1.044	Useful sources for keeping up to date with local and regional news	39
1.045	Types of news for which different media are seen as useful sources	40
1.046	Main problems of respondents' districts	41
1.047	Main problems of respondents' districts by region	42
1.048	Main problems of respondents' district by respondents' political views	42
1.049	Sources of information on main problem of district	43
1.050	Mention of local newspapers as a source of information on main district problem by nature of main problem	43
1.051	Main items read in regional and local newspapers	44
1.052	Awareness of content of regional and local newspapers	45
1.053	Items read in regional and local newspapers	46
1.054	Ranking of items read in regional and local newspapers	47
1.055	Ranking of items read in local newspapers by sex	48
1.056	Ranking of items read in local newspapers by age	49
1.057	Items read in provincial evenings by circulation	50
1.058	Opinions on depth of news coverage in the regional and local press	58
1.059	Opinions on depth of news coverage in national and local newspapers	58

		Page
1.060	Opinions on depth of news coverage in provincial evenings by circulation	59
1.061	Opinions on reporting standard of provincial evenings by ownership	60
1.062	Opinions on content of national and local newspapers	60
1.063	Opinions on news and advertising content of provincial evenings by circulation	61
1.064	Opinions on approach to news of national and local newspapers	62
1.065	Opinions on approach to news of provincial evenings by circulation	63
1.066	Opinions on interest in ordinary people's problems of national and local newspapers	64
1.067	Attachment to national and local newspapers	65
1.068	Attachment to provincial evenings by circulation and ownership	66
1.069	Opinions on fairness of coverage of points of view of national and local newspapers	67
1.070	Opinions on fear of advertisers among national and local newspapers	67
1.071	Opinions on readiness of national and local newspapers to criticise those who deserve it	68
1.072	Opinions on readiness of provincial evenings to criticise those who deserve it by ownership and circulation	68
1.073	Opinions on parties supported by different types of newspaper ...	69
1.074	Opinions on parties supported by particular national newspapers	69
1.075	Opinions on parties supported by provincial evenings by ownership and circulation	70
1.076	Opinions on parties supported by provincial evenings by main owners	70
1.077	Opinions on parties supported by local weeklies by ownership ...	71
1.078	Opinions on parties supported by evenings and weeklies by political views of respondent	72
1.079	Opinions on parties supported by evenings and weeklies among very strong supporters of the main parties	72
1.080	Opinions of unfairness of coverage of political parties by type of newspaper	73
1.081	Opinions on unfairness of coverage of political parties by individual national mornings	74
1.082	Opinions on unfairness of coverage of political parties by local newspapers by political views of respondent	75
1.083	Opinions on unfairness of coverage of political parties by local newspapers among very strong supporters of the main parties	75
1.084	Opinions on fullness of coverage of industrial disputes by type of newspaper	76

		Page
1.085	Opinions of fullness of coverage of industrial disputes in provincial evenings by ownership and circulation	77
1.086	Opinions of fullness of coverage of industrial disputes in provincial evenings by main owners	77
1.087	Opinions on fullness of coverage of industrial disputes in local newspapers by political views of respondents and by union membership	78
1.088	Attention paid to the views of community groups in the regional and local press	80
1.089	Attention paid to the views of community groups in local newspapers by ownership	81–82
1.090	Attention paid to the views of community groups in local newspapers by political views of respondents	83
1.091	Attention given to main district problem by regional and local newspapers	84
1.092	Attention given to main district problem in provincial evenings by circulation	84
1.093	Awareness of ownership of provincial evening newspapers by ownership	87
1.094	Awareness of ownership of provincial evenings by main owner groups	88
1.095	Awareness of ownership of local weeklies by ownership	88
1.096	Awareness of group connections of provincial evening newspapers by ownership	89
1.097	Awareness of group connections of provincial evening newspapers by main groups	89
1.098	Awareness of group connections of local weekly newspapers by ownership	90
1.099	Numbers of evening newspapers circulating by area	90
1.100	Attitudes to choice in evening newspapers by political view ...	91
1.101	Perceived benefits of choice by whether choice available and by region	92
1.102	Time since last letter sent to the newspapers	93
1.103	Profile of those who write letters to the newspapers	94
1.104	Type of newspaper last written to	95
1.105	Type of newspaper last written to by whether letter was published	95
1.106	Chances of publication of letters by type of newspaper written to	96
1.107	National mornings people would want to keep	98
1.108	Claimed readership of national mornings	98
1.109	Ratios of wish to keep newspapers to newspaper readership ...	99
1.110	Claimed awareness of the Press Council and its functions... ...	101
1.111	Opinions on function of Press Council	101

		Page
1.112	Profile of people claiming to know what the Press Council does	102
2.001	Age of respondents in the "influential" sample	156
2.002	Socio-economic grouping of councillors and lay trade union officials	157
2.003	Terminal education age	158
2.004	Length of association with the county	158
2.005	Membership of local organisations	159
2.006	Trade union membership and activity	159
2.007	Political view of respondents	160
2.008	Regular readership of national daily newspapers	162
2.009	Number of national newspapers titles read or looked at at least once a week or more often	162
2.010	Occasional and regular readership of national daily newspapers	163
2.011	Readership of the provincial and local press	164
2.012	Overlap of regular readership of daily newspapers	165
2.013	Overlap in claimed regular readership of the national and provincial press	166
2.014	The duplication of regular readership of the different types of newspaper	166
2.015	Readership of national mornings and provincial evenings by readers and non-readers of regional morning newspapers	167
2.016	Readership of local weeklies by readers and non-readers of provincial evening newspapers	167
2.017	Average time spent reading each issue of newspapers read regularly	168
2.018	Hours spent watching TV and listening to radio on an average weekday	169
2.019	Listening to news bulletins on radio and television	169
2.020	Number of different national daily newspapers read or looked at in an average week	170
2.021	Readership of national dailies	171
2.022	Readership of provincial newspapers	171
2.023	Overlap in regular readership within the provincial press	172
2.024	Time spent reading each issue (on average) of provincial newspapers	173
2.025	The importance of newspapers in keeping the "influential" sample "up to date and well informed"	177
2.026	Relative importance of media in keeping the "influential" sample "up to date and well informed"	177
2.027	Relative importance of media in keeping "influential" groups "up to date and well informed"	178

                                                                    Page

2.028	"It helps me to understand how what is happening in the country will affect my interests in the area" … … … …	179
2.029	How respondents came to know of the issues and problems they considered to be important in their districts … … …	180
2.030	Perceptions of news coverage by types of newspaper … …	180
2.031	"I would miss it a lot if it stopped being published" … …	181
2.032	"Reading it is always enjoyable" … … … … …	181
2.033	Reasons given for not reading regional morning or evening newspapers more than once a week … … … …	182
2.034	Perceived influence of types of newspaper on their readers …	183
2.035	The importance of the provincial press for presenting the point of view of respondents' party group/company/trade union to the public in the area … … … … … …	184
2.036	Provincial press presentation of the points of view of respondents' company, union district or party group … …	184–185
2.037	Causes of satisfaction or dissatisfaction with provincial press presentation of respondents' points of view … … …	185
2.038	"It gives a good service to its advertisers" … … …	186
2.039	General rating of the quality of provincial newspapers: a comparison of newspaper types … … … … …	189
2.040	General rating of the quality of provincial newspapers: a comparison between "influential" groups … … …	189
2.041	Changes in the quality of provincial newspapers in recent years	190
2.042	Some specific opinions of standards in the provincial press …	191
2.043	General standards in the provincial press: the opinions of "influentials" and the general public … … … …	192
2.044	Perceptions of sensationalism in newspapers of different types	193
2.045	Specific aspects of editorial standards in the provincial press …	193
2.046	Most important local issue … … … … … …	194
2.047	Attention given to the important problems of the area by the provincial press … … … … … … …	195
2.048	Provincial press treatment of particular topics: a comparison of newspaper types … … … … … … …	196
2.049	Provincial press treatment of particular topics: the views of different groups … … … … … … …	197
2.050	Topic treated least well by the provincial press: the views of different groups … … … … … … …	197
2.051	Reasons given for bad treatment of topics … … …	198
2.052	Approaches made to the provincial press … … … …	200
2.053	Reasons given for never speaking to the provincial press …	200
2.054	Responsibility for contacts with the press … … …	201
2.055	How approaches are made to the provincial press … …	201

		Page
2.056	Provincial papers containing recent articles on issues in which respondents were involved/particularly interested	202
2.057	Articles in the provincial press on issues in which respondents were involved	203
2.058	Respondents' opinions of articles on issues/events in which they were involved	204
2.059	Comments made on articles of recent interest by topic area	205
2.060	The accuracy, fairness and amount of coverage in articles of particular interest in the provincial press	205
2.061	Reasons for faults in recent articles appearing in the provincial press	206
2.062	Respondents' opinions of present relations with the provincial press	207
2.063	Complaints against the provincial press	208
2.064	Had respondents ever felt like complaining about anything that appeared in the papers they read?	209
2.065	Reasons for respondents' complaints to newspapers	209
2.066	The result of most recent complaints made by respondents	209
2.067	The direction of complaints made and the outcome of complaints	210
2.068	Fairness of coverage by type of newspaper	213
2.069	Fairness of coverage in the provincial press: the views of different respondents	213
2.070	People the provincial press often pays too much attention to when reporting on controversial local issues	214
2.071	People the provincial press pays too little attention to when reporting on controversial local issues	215
2.072	Provincial press treatment of local council activities: the different views of Conservative and Labour supporters	216
2.073	Provincial press treatment of the activities of the Conservative and Labour Parties on the Council: a comparison of newspaper allegiances	217
2.074	Provincial press support for the political parties	217
2.075	Regional morning and provincial evening press support for the political parties	218
2.076	Parties to which the provincial press does not give fair coverage	219
2.077	Press reporting of disagreements between employers and unions: a comparison between newspaper types	220
2.078	Provincial daily press reporting of disagreements between employers and unions: a comparison between types of respondent	220
2.079	Provincial press reporting of disagreements between employers and unions: a comparison between trade union members and non-members	221

		Page
2.080	Provincial press comments on disagreements between employers and unions ...	221
2.081	Press comments on disagreements between employers and unions: a comparison between types of newspaper	222
2.082	Provincial press reporting of industrial relations ...	222
2.083	Awareness of who owns the provincial press	224
2.084	Respondents' knowledge of which other newspapers circulating in the area are owned by the company owning papers they read	225
2.085	Do people benefit from a choice of provincial newspapers: the view of those who do have a choice and the view of those who don't	225
2.086	Benefits from a choice of evening newspapers	226
2.087	Circulation figures for provincial daily newspapers read by respondents	227
2.088	The relationship between ownership and circulation in the provincial daily press	227
2.089	General rating of the quality of provincial newspapers: a comparison of types of ownership and of circulation ...	227
2.090	A comparison of standards in the provincial daily press by newspaper size and ownership	228
2.091	Claimed awareness of the Press Council and of its function	230
2.092	The performance of the Press Council	231
2.093	Opinions of the functioning of the Press Council	231
2.094	National mornings people would want to keep ...	232
2.095	National mornings people would want to keep by extent of readership ...	233
2.096	Threats to the freedom of the press	234
2.097	Threats to the freedom of the press: the view of different groups	235
3.001	Sex and age of editors responding by type of publication	294
3.002	Number of publications worked on by editors	294
3.003	Publications worked on by editors in addition to their main publication ...	295
3.004	Details of types of publication worked on in total by editors classified according to type of main publication worked on ...	296
3.005	Approximate circulation of publications edited ...	296
3.006	(A) Proportion working in company that is part of a group by type of publication	297
	(B) Group belonged to	297
3.007	Length of time (a) in present company and (b) in present position	298
3.008	Number of journalists working under respondent	299
3.009	Responsibility (a) for hiring, (b) for firing staff ...	299

		Page
3.010	Responsibility (a) for setting the editorial budget, (b) for controlling the spending of the editorial budget	300
3.011	Amount of time spent by editors in three main aspects of work	301
3.012	Mean percentage of time spent on three main aspects of work by type of publication and group membership	302
3.013	Hours worked in the last week by editors	302
3.014	Average hours worked last week by type of publication ...	303
3.015	Contracts of employment, notice and pension schemes	304
3.016	Proportion doing other paid work in addition to employment as an editor:	
	(a) By type of publication	304
	(b) By group membership and number of journalists working under editor	305
3.017	Sources of income and amount (total sample)	306
3.018	Income from other journalistic activities	306
3.019	Union membership among editors:	
	(a) By type of newspaper	308
	(b) By group membership and number of journalists ...	308
3.020	Age finishing full-time education and qualifications obtained ...	309
3.021	Training as a journalist	310
3.022	Age entering journalism and previous employment	311
3.023	Previous contacts with journalism and father's occupation ...	312
3.024	First job in journalism by type of current publication	313
3.025	Proportion who were never a trainee journalist by type of current publication	314
3.026	Age that became a senior journalist and whether took proficiency test	314
3.027	First job as a senior journalist	314
3.028	How much editors enjoy their present work as a journalist ...	316
3.029	What editors like and dislike about working in journalism ...	317
3.030	Whether expects to continue in journalism or expects to change	318
3.031	Journalism as a career: ratings on conditions of work	319
3.032	Journalism as a career: ratings on enjoyment of the work ...	320
3.033	Journalism as a career: ratings on its influence in the community	321
3.034	Threats to the freedom of the press	324
3.035	Undesirable pressures perceived by editors on their work ...	325
3.036	How editors voted in the last three General Elections	326
3.037	Views on the Press Council	327
3.038	Importance attached to being censured by Press Council ...	328
3.039	Views on diversity of opinion represented by the national press	328
3.040	Views on different aspects of press concentration	329

		Page
3.041	Positions favoured in the field of press monopoly law	330
3.042	Editors' views on state assistance to the press	332
3.043	Sex and age of senior journalists replying to survey	333
3.044	How much journalists enjoy their present work as journalists ...	334
3.045	What journalists like and dislike about working in journalism ...	335
3.046	Whether journalists expect to continue in journalism	336
3.047	Journalism as a career: ratings on conditions of work by journalists	338
3.048	Journalism as a career: ratings on enjoyment of the work ...	339
3.049	Journalism as a career: ratings on its influence in the community	340
3.050	Threats to the freedom of the press	341
3.051	Undesirable pressures perceived by journalists on their work ...	341
3.052	How journalists voted in the last three General Elections ...	342
3.053	Newspaper journalists' comparison of their own views with those of their publication	342
3.054	Views on the Press Council	343
3.055	Importance attached to being censured by Press Council ...	343
3.056	Views on diversity of opinion represented by the national press	344
3.057	Views on different aspects of press concentration	345
3.058	Positions favoured in the field of press monopoly law	345
3.059	Journalists' views on state assistance to the press	347

General Introduction

This report covers studies of the attitudes to the press of editors, journalists and readers carried out by Social and Community Planning Research and its associated fieldwork and data processing organisation, the Centre for Sample Surveys Ltd at the request of the Royal Commission on the Press.

The Commission intended that the study of readers should concentrate on attitudes to the regional and local press. Specifically, it was intended that the study should investigate:

(a) the roles that the regional and local press play in relation to other media;

(b) the adequacy with which the regional press is seen as fulfilling these roles;

(c) the relationship between people's attitudes to regional and local newspapers and different types of newspaper ownership.

It is clear, however, that attitudes to the regional and local press only wholly make sense in the context of attitudes to the rest of the press and of attitudes to other media. Hence the study covered these also; in particular, this report contains a substantial amount of information on attitudes to national morning newspapers.

The study of readers involved two sample surveys. The first was a general, random-sample survey of the adult population throughout Great Britain. It was felt, however, that within the general population there are small groups who have particular interest in and knowledge of the performance of the regional and local press and that it was important to get indications of the opinions and attitudes of these groups. A general sample survey of the public on the scale envisaged would produce only small numbers of members of these groups—too small for separate analysis. Because of this a second survey was undertaken —a survey among some sorts of people in influential positions in their communities who might be thought to have special knowledge of a special interest in the regional and local press's treatment of local affairs.

Parts 1 and 2 of this volume cover these surveys.

Part 3 is the report of a postal survey of editors and journalists which investigated their backgrounds and careers and included questions on their attitudes to the jobs they did and on their opinions on various issues concerning the newspaper industry.

PART 1:
THE ATTITUDES
OF
THE GENERAL PUBLIC

INTRODUCTION

Sampling and Fieldwork

The survey was spread over 149 parliamentary constituencies in Great Britain south of the Caledonian Canal. These were selected randomly with probability proportional to 1971 Census population after stratification by region, by an indicator of population density and by car ownership. Within each selected constituency, one ward was selected and within each selected ward two polling districts. Selection of wards and polling districts was random with probability proportional to electorate.

Within each selected polling district, 11 addresses were randomly selected from the electoral registers with probability proportional to the number of electors listed at addresses. In fieldwork, interviewers listed all persons aged 16 or over currently resident at selected addresses and selected one for interview by a random grid technique.

In general, selection of addresses with probability proportional to number of electors and selection of one person for interview at each selected address balance out. Exceptions occur in cases of death, changes in occupancy or household composition, and in cases where the household contains young people, or people who for some other reason are not listed in the electoral registers. Allowance was made for these exceptions by weighting at the data processing stage. This weighting made the sample representative of the population of Great Britain south of the Caledonian Canal aged 16 or over and living in private households.

The sampling method described above yielded an issued sample of 3,278 addresses. This was reduced by addresses found to be empty or demolished or to be institutions to 3,138 addresses. A total of 2,401 interviews was achieved, a response rate of 77%.

The second appendix to this part of the report includes a comparison of the breakdown of the achieved sample by region and demographic characteristics. There is no notable discrepancy between the survey figures and official population figures.

Fieldwork took place between 24 September 1975 and 9 January 1976.

A fuller account of the sampling and weighting methods and of the fieldwork are included in the second appendix to this part of the report.

The Questionnaire

A copy of the questionnaire used is included as an appendix to this part of the report. It is in three sections.

(*a*) *Main Questionnaire*

The questions in this part of the questionnaire were asked of all respondents. They cover readership, television viewing and radio listening habits, questions on the respondent's news interests and the sources from which he seeks that news, questions on a number of general topics and background data on the respondent and his or her circumstances.

(*b*) *Provincial Newspaper Sheet*

These questions were asked for each regional or local daily newspaper of which the respondent said he saw one or more issue in an average week and of each regional or local weekly newspaper of which the respondent said he saw one or more issue in an average month. They cover the sorts of news and features the respondent read in the newspaper, his awareness of its ownership, his views on its political sympathies and on the attention it pays to various groups in the community and a range of questions on his attitudes to it.

(*c*) *National Newspaper Sheet*

This was an abbreviated version of the provincial newspaper sheet. The questions were limited to awareness of ownership, views on political sympathies and a range of questions on attitudes.

It was asked of national morning newspapers of which the respondent said he saw one or more issue in an average week. In order to keep down the length of the interview and to avoid undue repetition, in those cases where the respondent read two or more national morning newspapers, he was questioned about only one. The one to be asked about was selected by random grid technique. In total figures for national newspapers, this imbalance has been corrected by weighting at the data processing stage.

Notes and Definitions

The ownership and circulation size of newspapers are frequently used as breakdown categories in this report. Ownership and circulation data were taken from the 1975 edition of the *Newspaper Press Directory*. This was also used as a guide to the frequency of appearance of newspapers where this was unclear.

In practice, circulation size is used as a breakdown category only for provincial evening newspapers. For a very large number of local weekly titles, circulation figures are available only for the editorial or advertising group of which they form a part. It was felt that breaking down results by circulation only for those weeklies for which circulation data were available might give an unrepresentative and misleading picture.

The main categorisation of newspapers used in this report is:
  national morning newspapers;
  regional morning newspapers;
  provincial evening newspapers;
  local weekly newspapers.

The London *Evening News* and *Evening Standard* have been omitted from most analyses. They are different in character from the evening newspapers published outside London. Also, we have reservations about how accurately the survey measured their readership (see pages 18–19). Where they have been included, reference is made to "evening newspapers" rather than "provincial evening newspapers".

Where figures are shown for "national morning newspapers", these include the *Morning Star*. Because of the very small number who read it, however, figures for the *Morning Star* are not shown where national morning newspapers are broken by title.

Local newspapers published four or five times a week in the middle of the day have been classed as provincial evenings. Local newspapers published two or three times a week in the middle of the day have been classed as local weeklies. Weekly freesheets have been omitted from the analyses. They are different in character from local weeklies, but the numbers reading them were too small for separate analysis.

The most serious classification problem is that of the Glasgow published *Daily Record*. The *Daily Record* is the largest morning newspaper published outside London and in 1974 accounted for just under a third of all sales of such newspapers. In format and style, it is much closer to the popular national morning newspapers than to any other morning newspaper published outside London. Although separately edited, it shares a substantial part of its feature content with the commonly owned *Daily Mirror*, which does not circulate widely in Scotland.

There is no completely satisfactory way of classifying the *Daily Record*. It is in some ways misleading to treat it as part of the national morning press. It is also in some ways misleading to treat it as part of the regional morning press. The sample of *Daily Record* readers interviewed in this survey is, however, rather small for meaningful separate analysis. The solution adopted has been to link it with the *Daily Mirror* in most analyses and treat the *Daily Mirror/Daily Record* as a national morning newspaper. In the discussion of readership patterns and the separate discussion of Scotland, however, some alternative analyses are shown treating the *Daily Record* as a regional morning.

The *Scottish Daily Express*, now printed in Manchester, is also rather more than simply a regional edition of the *Daily Express*, although it has not been analysed alternatively in the same way as the *Daily Record*.

Regions used are Registrar General's standard regions or combinations of these. Socio-economic group data for households and people in work are based on a collapsed version of the Registrar General's socio-economic groups.

Where data are analysed by breakdown categories such as age or socio-economic group of the respondent or newspaper circulation, cases in which this was not established or was not recorded by the interviewer are omitted. Sample sizes shown in breakdown categories may, therefore, add to less than the total sample.

For convenience of layout, some tables in this report are set out with percentage breakdowns running vertically and some with percentage breakdowns running horizontally. The placing of percentage signs in the tables indicates the direction in which percentages should be read.

Where percentages are shown in this report, they are shown to the nearest whole percentage unit. The cumulative effect of this rounding means that percentage figures do not always total exactly to 100% or whatever other overall total is shown for them.

Figures for sample size shown in this report are based on the sample before weighting. They show the actual number of interviews carried out which form the base for the data. All percentage figures shown, however, are calculated from the data after weighting.

The symbol * is used in tables in this report to stand for quantities less than 0·5%.

CONCLUSIONS

Two in three adults read national morning newspapers regularly. Two in five read local weeklies, one in three reads an evening and one in ten a regional morning.

These different types of newspaper do not appear all to be in direct competition. Those which do appear to be treated as alternatives by readers are:

national mornings *or* regional mornings
regional mornings *or* evenings
evenings *or* local weeklies

The numbers who watch television news regularly are as large as the numbers who read a morning newspaper regularly. The two are not alternatives. People who watch television news regularly are, if anything, more likely than average to be regular newspaper readers.

The reason why some sorts of newspaper appear to be in competition while others do not becomes clearer when one looks at the sorts of news in which people are interested, at the sources they think are useful in keeping up to date with their interests and at what they actually read in the regional and local press.

Different people are interested in different sorts of news and news interests vary considerably between different groups in the community. A very major news interest, however, and one which is uniformly high among almost all groups is an interest in local and regional news.

The main sources seen as useful for keeping up to date with general and political news, news about business and union affairs and news about some forms of sport are television and the national newspapers, particularly television. For some sorts of news about leisure interests, magazines are the prime source. By far the main source of regional and local news, however, is seen to be the regional and local press.

This is confirmed by what people say they read in regional and local newspapers. In fact, the item the largest numbers of people say they usually look at in regional mornings and provincial evenings is the list of television and radio programmes. Beyond this, the items most commonly read in regional mornings balance between general and political news on one hand and local news and comment on the other. In provincial evenings, the emphasis shifts to local news and comment. In local weeklies, the items most widely read can all be described as local news and comment. These differences probably explain the reasons why some of these sorts of newspaper appear to be treated as alternatives while others are not.

Individual national morning newspapers have distinct readership profiles. Each is addressing a somewhat different section of the public. The survey results suggest that, generally, this is not the case for the regional and local press. Regional and local newspapers are, by and large, read by broad cross-sections of the public in the areas in which they circulate.

This difference may help explain some of the differences between people's views on national mornings and their views on the regional and local press. Regional and local newspapers are less likely than the national mornings to be seen as supporting any one political party. They are also less likely to be seen as partial in their reporting of disputes between employers and unions. For the provincial evenings, however, this is not because they were more likely to be seen as impartial, but because they are thought more likely not to print much about it at all.

The regional and local newspapers were less likely than the national mornings to be seen as ready to criticise anyone if they deserve it. They were not widely thought to pay too much or too little attention to the views of particular groups in reporting on controversial local issues. It was, on the other hand, widely thought that they should pay more attention to what people regarded as the main problems of the areas in which they lived.

These results suggest that the regional and local press is not generally seen as particularly partial in its news coverage or comment, but that it may be seen as less ready to take definite positions on issues of controversy than the national press.

Perhaps because of this, the comments on the news made by provincial evenings and local weeklies were thought interesting by fewer than said this of the comments made in the national mornings.

With regard to most of these points, the regional mornings stood between the national morning press on the one hand and the provincial evenings and local weeklies on the other.

The provincial evenings were thought to tend more towards sensationalism than the rest of the regional and local press. They were also more widely seen as likely to get their facts wrong, as carrying too much advertising and, although this was a minority view, to be more afraid of offending their advertisers.

There were some differences between views on the larger and smaller provincial evenings. Views on the larger ones tended to be closer to views on the popular mornings. Views on the smaller ones tended to be closer to views on the local weeklies.

There were some differences between views on the provincial evenings owned by groups with national newspaper interests and provincial evenings with other ownership. These were, however, fairly minor differences and may be a function of differences in circulation size. Most readers of regional and local newspapers did not, in fact, know who owned the newspapers they read and were unaware of whether they had group links with other newspapers.

In the regional and local press, readers' letters are among the items most widely read. One of the questions asked of people in the survey was whether they had ever themselves written to newspapers. 11% said that they had done so at some time, 2% that they had done so in the past two years. Most of those who had written to newspapers had last written to regional or local newspapers. Letters addressed to these appear to have a very much better chance of being published than letters addressed to national newspapers.

Two other subjects covered by the survey which were unrelated to its main purpose were which national mornings people would like to keep if some had to close and how aware people are of the Press Council and its functions.

Readers of national morning newspapers tended, naturally enough, to wish to keep the morning newspapers they themselves read. Beyond this, the newspapers they wanted to keep tended to be those a little further towards the quality end of the quality-popular dimension than the ones they themselves read.

Just under one in six people claimed to know what the Press Council does and were able to give a broadly accurate description of its work.

MAIN FINDINGS
1. Newspaper Reading, Television Watching and Radio Listening

SUMMARY

The survey shows 83% of adults regularly reading some daily newspaper. 66% say they regularly read a national morning, 9% that they regularly read a regional morning and 34% that they regularly read an evening. If the *Daily Record* is treated as a regional morning rather than linked with the *Daily Mirror*, regular readership of national mornings falls to 63% and that of regional mornings rises to 13%.

43% of respondents claimed to read a local weekly newspaper regularly. In all, 70% claimed to read some local or regional newspaper regularly, whether morning, evening or weekly.

These figures overlap. Many people read several of these types of newspaper regularly. Some types of newspaper, however, seem to be treated to some extent as alternatives to others. The combinations to which this applies are:

a national morning *or* a regional morning;

a regional morning *or* an evening;

an evening *or* a local weekly.

The survey results suggest that the national morning press is *not* currently in competition for readers with the provincial evening or weekly press and that the regional morning press is *not* in competition for readers with the local weekly press.

Outside the South East, the proportion of people who read *some* regional or local newspaper regularly does not vary much by region. There are, however, quite large regional variations in the *types* of regional or local newspapers people read regularly. The regional morning press, for example, is very much stronger in Scotland than elsewhere.

Men, and people in skilled manual jobs, are a little more likely than average to read national morning newspapers regularly. Apart from this, national morning newspaper readers are, broadly, a cross-section of the population. There are very large differences, however, in the readership profiles of the different national mornings. The different national mornings have, to a large extent, to cater for different groups within the community.

As with national mornings, the readers of the regional and local press form, broadly, a cross-section of the adult population. People who are not in work and, a linked group, older people, are less likely than average to read evening newspapers. Men, and possibly older people, are a little more likely than average to read regional mornings. The differences are not, however, very great.

The scale of the survey was not large enough to allow for disaggregation to particular regional and local newspapers. The trend of the figures, however, strongly suggests that, in general, individual regional and local newspapers have much less distinct readership profiles than the national mornings. Regional and local newspapers are, largely, read by a broad cross-section of the communities within which they circulate, without heavy weighting towards particular groups within these communities.

On average, people spend very considerably more time watching television and a good deal more time listening to the radio than they spend reading newspapers. The numbers who say they watch television news six or seven days a week are as high as the numbers saying they read a national or regional morning newspaper regularly.

Television and radio news do *not*, however, appear to be alternatives to newspapers. Regular television news watchers are, if anything, more likely than average to read newspapers regularly. Regular listening to radio news appears to have little to do with whether people read newspapers regularly or not.

MAIN FINDINGS

Readership Definitions

This survey is essentially concerned with how people use newspapers and what they think of them. As background, however, it is necessary to start with a discussion of the numbers of people who read newspapers of different sorts and how this relates to their television viewing and radio listening habits.

A word of caution is needed at the outset. It is well established that, in measuring newspaper readership by survey methods, quite large differences in levels of claimed readership can be produced by quite small variations of the questions asked. The most commonly used questioning technique, developed for the *National Readership Surveys*, involves prompting respondents with a booklet showing reproductions of the mastheads of all publications covered in the survey.

The present survey is principally concerned with the regional and local press. The very large number of titles involved makes the use of reproductions of mastheads impracticable. Because of this difference in the method of asking the questions, the readership figures presented in this report should not be treated as comparable with those from the *National Readership Surveys*. In general, one would expect that using masthead booklets would tend to produce rather higher figures.

Also, "readership" can be defined in several different ways. Probably the most common definition used is "average issue readership", the number who claim to have read or looked at any issue of the publication during a period matching its publication frequency (ie read or looked at any issue of a particular weekly newspaper during the past week etc). For purposes of this survey, however, it has seemed more appropriate to talk in terms of regular readers and occasional readers. We have defined regular readers as those who claimed to read or look at five or more issues of a particular daily in an average week or three or more issues of a weekly in an average month and occasional readers as those who claimed to read or look at one or more issues over these periods.

"Regular readership" figures will tend to be lower than "average issue readership" figures. A comparison of the results obtained for "regular readership" in this survey with the corresponding figures from the *National Readership Survey* is given in the second appendix to this part of the report.

Newspaper Readership

Those interviewed were asked which daily newspaper they read or looked at at all nowadays and, for such each title mentioned, how many issues they read or looked at in an average week. 83% claimed regular readership (five or six issues a week) of some daily newspaper.

Broken by type of newspaper, claimed regular and occasional readership of daily newspapers was:

TABLE 1.001
DAILY NEWSPAPER READERSHIP BY TYPE OF NEWSPAPER

	Read regularly (5-6 issues per week)	Read occasionally (1-4 issues per week)	Read regularly or occasionally
Sample: All respondents	2,401 %	2,401 %	2,401 %
A morning newspaper	72	14	86
A national morning	66	16	82
A regional morning	9	3	12
An evening newspaper	34	13	47

It will be immediately apparent that there is overlap between readership of the different types of newspaper.

These figures treat the *Daily Mirror* and *Daily Record* as if they were one, national newspaper. If the *Daily Record* is treated as a regional morning, the overall national figures change only slightly. For regular readership, they become:

TABLE 1.002
DAILY NEWSPAPER READERSHIP BY TYPE (*DAILY RECORD* TREATED AS REGIONAL MORNING)

	Read regularly (5-6 issues per week)
Sample: All respondents	2,401 %
A morning newspaper	72
A national morning (excluding *Daily Record*)	63
A regional morning (including *Daily Record*)	12
An evening newspaper	34

Respondents were also asked which local weekly newspapers they read or looked at at all nowadays and, for each title they mentioned, how many they read or looked at in an average month. 43% claimed regular readership (3-4 issues a month) of some local weekly newspaper. A further 6% claimed to read one or two issues a month of such a newspaper giving a total regular or occasional readership of 49%.

In all, 70% claimed regular readership of some local or regional newspaper, whether regional morning, evening or local weekly. If the *Daily Record* is treated as a regional morning, the figure becomes 71%.

It was uncommon for people to claim to read more than one newspaper of any particular type regularly. 13% of all those interviewed claimed regular readership (five or six issues a week) of two or more national mornings, and 6% claimed regular readership (three or four issues a month) of two or more local weeklies. The numbers claiming regular readership of two or more regional mornings or two or more evenings were negligible.

The overlap in claimed regular readership between the four types of newspaper was:

TABLE 1.003

OVERLAP OF READERSHIP BETWEEN TYPES OF NEWSPAPER

	Total Sample	Regular Readers of:			
		National Mornings	Regional Mornings	Evenings	Local Weeklies
Sample	2,401	1,624	212	813	1,062
	%	%	%	%	%
(who are also) *Regular readers of:*					
National mornings	66	—	39	64	73
Regional mornings	9	6	—	5	11
Evenings	34	33	20	—	23
Local weeklies	43	47	52	30	—

Readership of the four types of newspaper might have been independent. Those who read newspapers of one type might have been no more or less likely than anyone else to read newspapers of the other types. Had this been so, the columns of this table would match. The proportion of readers of evenings who also read weeklies, for example, would be the same as the proportion of the population in general who do so. This is clearly not the case. The degree to which it is not the case can be shown more clearly by reworking the figures.

In the table below, the readership of each particular type of newspaper among regular readers of other types of newspaper is expressed as a ratio of the readership of that type of newspaper among people in general. (*Example:* 30% of people who read evenings also read local weeklies. 43% of people in general read weeklies, giving a ratio of $\frac{30}{43} = 0.7$.)

TABLE 1.004

DUPLICATION RATIOS OF REGULAR READERSHIP OF TYPES OF NEWSPAPER

	National Mornings	Regional Mornings	Evenings	Local Weeklies
National mornings	—	0.6	1.0	1.1
Regional mornings	0.6	—	0.6	1.2
Evenings	1.0	0.6	—	0.7
Local weeklies	1.1	1.2	0.7	—

This pattern is virtually unaffected if the *Daily Record* is classified as a regional morning rather than linked to the *Daily Mirror* as a national. On that basis, the overlap in claimed regular readership becomes:

TABLE 1.005
OVERLAP OF READERSHIP BETWEEN TYPES OF NEWSPAPER (*DAILY RECORD* TREATED AS A REGIONAL MORNING)

	Total Sample	Regular Readers of:			
		National Mornings (*excluding* Daily Record)	Regional Mornings (*including* Daily Record)	Evenings	Local Weeklies
Sample	2,401	1,553	283	813	1,062
	%	%	%	%	%
(who are also) *Regular readers of:*					
National mornings	63	—	28	62	68
Regional mornings	12	5	—	8	16
Evenings	34	33	21	—	23
Local weeklies	43	47	55	30	—

The resulting duplication ratios do not differ notably from those shown above. They are:

TABLE 1.006
DUPLICATION RATIOS OF REGULAR READERSHIP OF TYPES OF NEWSPAPER (*DAILY RECORD* TREATED AS A REGIONAL MORNING)

	National Mornings (*excluding* Daily Record)	Regional Mornings (*including* Daily Record)	Evenings	Local Weeklies
National mornings	—	0·4	1·0	1·1
Regional mornings	0·4	—	0·6	1·3
Evenings	1·0	0·6	—	0·7
Local weeklies	1·1	1·3	0·7	—

For three combinations of types of newspaper, the overlap of regular readership is substantially below what one would have expected had their readership been independent. These are:
- national mornings and regional mornings
- regional mornings and evenings
- evenings and local weeklies

The comparison of regular readership of national mornings and of evenings among those who do and do not read regional mornings regularly is:

TABLE 1.007
READERSHIP OF OTHER DAILIES BY READERSHIP OF REGIONAL MORNINGS

	Regional Morning (*excluding* Daily Record)		Regional Morning (*including* Daily Record)	
	Read regularly	Not read regularly	Read regularly	Not read regularly
Sample	212	2,189	283	2,118
	%	%	%	%
National Morning				
Read regularly	39	69	28	68
Not read regularly	61	31	72	32
Evening				
Read regularly	20	35	21	35
Not read regularly	80	65	79	65

Where regional mornings circulate, it would appear that to a large extent people choose between them and national mornings. This is not the whole story however. There is more chance of the regional morning being treated as complementary to the national morning than there is of two national mornings being treated as complementary. Two in five regular readers of regional mornings also read a national morning regularly. Only one in five people who read national mornings regularly read two or more.

Regular readers of regional mornings are also substantially less likely than others to read evening newspapers regularly. Since the majority of regional mornings are linked with evening papers, it seems reasonable to conclude that this is a result of some people choosing between the two rather than a result of evening newspapers being less widely available in the areas where regional mornings circulate.

The comparison of regular readership of local weeklies among those who do and do not read evening newspapers is:

TABLE 1.008
READERSHIP OF LOCAL WEEKLIES BY READERSHIP OF EVENINGS

	Evening Newspaper	
	Read regularly	Not read regularly
Sample	813	1,588
	%	%
Local weekly		
Read regularly	30	50
Not read regularly	70	50

A very considerable majority of the population live within the circulation area of some evening newspaper and virtually all live in the circulation area of a local weekly. That those who read evenings are less likely than others to read weeklies is not, therefore, a simple area effect. It is not the case that those who read evenings do not have the opportunity to read weeklies or vice versa. It may be, however, that weeklies are stronger outside those towns with whose affairs evening newspapers particularly concern themselves.

In summary, therefore, there appears to be some degree of choosing between regional mornings, in areas where they exist, and national mornings and some degree of choosing between regional mornings and evenings. Evenings and local weeklies also appear to be, in some degree, alternatives. Whether or not a person reads a national morning, on the other hand, does not appear to have anything to do with whether he reads an evening newspaper or a local weekly newspaper and readership of regional mornings appears unrelated to readership of local weeklies.

Regional Differences in Newspaper Reading

So far we have discussed readership of newspapers of different types throughout Great Britain. There are, in fact, very substantial differences between regions. Claimed regular readership of national mornings was highest in the two areas where they are printed—the South East and the North West.

Readership of regional mornings in these areas was negligible. Claimed regular readership of regional mornings was well above average in Scotland. Claimed regular readership of some morning newspaper, whether regional or national, varied within much closer limits—between 67% and 78% in the six regions into which we split the country, suggesting a fairly uniform level of demand for morning newspapers, as such, irrespective of whether they are regional or national.

TABLE 1.009
READERSHIP OF DAILY NEWSPAPERS BY REGION

	Sample	A Morning Newspaper	A National Morning Newspaper	A Regional Morning Newspaper
		Regular Readers of:		
London and the South East	743	% 77	77	—
North West	325	% 69	68	1
East and West Midlands/East Anglia	456	% 67	64	9
South West and Wales	305	% 70	62	13
North/Yorkshire and Humberside	367	% 68	58	15
Scotland (*Daily Record* treated as a national)	205	% 78	54	36
Scotland (*Daily Record* treated as a regional)	205	% 78	23	65

Claimed readership of the three types of non-national newspaper varied by region as follows:

TABLE 1.010
READERSHIP OF REGIONAL AND LOCAL NEWSPAPERS BY REGION

	Sample	A Regional Morning, Evening or Local Newspaper	A Regional Morning Newspaper	An Evening Newspaper	A Local Weekly Newspaper
London and the South East	743	% 63	—	18	52
North West	325	% 75	1	41	53
East and West Midlands/East Anglia	456	% 73	9	50	30
South West and Wales	305	% 72	13	30	45
North/Yorkshire and Humberside	367	% 71	15	43	26
Scotland (*Daily Record* treated as a national)	205	% 76	36	26	52
Scotland (*Daily Record* treated as a regional)	205	% 82	65	26	52

It is necessary to make a reservation about the figure for evening newspapers in London and the South East. It is highly possible that the form of question used is responsible for the low claimed readership figure. In the question about readership of regional morning and evening newspapers, respondents were asked specifically about newspapers which were sold only in their part of the country. Allowing for the differences of method and of the definition of readership, figures for evenings outside London and the South East accord tolerably well with the *National Readership Survey* figures. In London and the South East, the figures in this survey are substantially lower than those in the *National Readership Survey*. The explanation appears to be that some people in London are under the impression that the London evenings circulate nationally.

Outside the South East, the level of claimed regular readership of some local or regional newspaper was fairly stable between regions. It varies only between 71% and 82% (82% in Scotland if the *Daily Record* is treated as a regional morning). There were very large variations, however, in the types of local or regional newspaper which were read. This can be taken to suggest a fairly uniform level of demand for local or regional newspapers—the actual types of papers read depending on particular local circumstances.

The People who Read Different Types of Newspaper

We have shown above that the types of local or regional newspaper people read vary with the part of the country they live in. Is there much variation in levels of readership between different groups within the community?

(*a*) *Sex and Age*

Claimed regular readership of national mornings and of local or regional newspapers varied by sex and age as follows:

TABLE 1.011
NEWSPAPER READERSHIP BY SEX AND AGE

	Sample	Regular Readers of:			
		A National Morning	A Regional Morning	An Evening	A Local Weekly
Total	2,401	% 66	9	34	43
Sex Men	1,137	% 71	12	34	41
Women	1,262	% 62	7	34	45
Age 16–24	361	% 66	7	33	44
25–44	819	% 67	8	33	41
45–64	772	% 68	11	38	45
65 or over	431	% 64	11	26	43

Note:—Subsample bases total less than 2,401 due to cases where demographic data were not recorded.

Women are less likely than men to claim regular readership of morning newspapers, but there was no significant difference between the sexes in claimed regular readership of evenings and local weeklies. Old people are less likely than average to read evening newspapers. Apart from this, differences in levels of readership between sex and age groups are minor.

(*b*) *Employment and Status*

Respondents were asked whether they were in work (full-time or part-time). Those who were in work were asked for details of the jobs they did and these were subsequently coded to Registrar General's socio-economic groups.

Claimed regular readership of different types of newspaper varied by employment and by condensed socio-economic group as follows:

TABLE 1.012
NEWSPAPER READERSHIP BY OCCUPATION

	Sample	\multicolumn{4}{c}{Regular Readers of:}			
	Sample	A National Morning	A Regional Morning	An Evening	A Local Weekly
Total	2,401	% 66	9	34	43
In work	1,438	% 69	9	37	43
Not in work	963	% 63	10	29	43
Socio-economic group of employment[1]					
Professional/Employer/Manager	222	% 69	11	36	41
Junior non-manual	463	% 65	10	36	45
Skilled manual	412	% 76	7	39	41
Semi-skilled/unskilled manual	324	% 67	7	38	44

[1]*Note:*—Breakdown excludes 17 in the armed forces or giving insufficient detail of their jobs for coding.

Those who work, particularly skilled manual workers, are slightly more likely than average to claim regular readership of a national morning. Those who work are also more likely than average to be regular readers of evenings. Apart from this the differences are minor.

The socio-economic group figures shown above refer only to people in employment. It is common to classify households by the occupation or former career occupation of the household head. Looking at people's newspaper readership in terms of the condensed socio-economic group of the households in which they live gives:

TABLE 1.013
NEWSPAPER READERSHIP BY SOCIO-ECONOMIC GROUP OF HOUSEHOLD

	Sample	\multicolumn{4}{c}{Regular Readers of:}			
	Sample	A National Morning	A Regional Morning	An Evening	A Local Weekly
Total	2,401	% 66	9	34	43
Socio-economic group of household[1]					
Professional/Employer/Manager	480	% 68	12	33	42
Junior non-manual	477	% 64	11	32	45
Skilled manual	868	% 71	7	37	46
Semi-skilled/unskilled manual	410	% 62	9	33	40

[1]*Note:*—Breakdown excludes those in the armed forces, those giving insufficient information on job of head of household and those in households where head never had career occupation.

This analysis does not add substantially to the pattern already described.

(c) *Political Attitudes and Trade Union Membership*

Respondents were asked whether they usually thought of themselves as Conservative, Labour, Liberal or what. Those who identified themselves with a party were asked about the strength of their identification with that party. Answers were:

TABLE 1.014
IDENTIFICATION WITH POLITICAL PARTIES

	All respondents
Sample ...	2,401
	%
Conservative ...	36
Labour ...	33
Liberal ...	11
Nationalist ...	2
Other Party ...	1
None of these/not answered ...	17

14% identified themselves as very strongly Conservative and 10% as very strongly Labour.

In considering these figures, it must be borne in mind that answers to this question will vary over time. The answers given above refer to the time fieldwork was carried out, the last quarter of 1975.

25% of respondents said they were trade union members.

If we look at readers of particular types of newspaper, this time in profile, their political affiliations and trade union membership were:

TABLE 1.015
PARTY IDENTIFICATION AND UNION MEMBERSHIP BY NEWSPAPER READERSHIP

	Total Sample	Regular Readers of:			
		A National Morning	A Regional Morning	An Evening	A Local Weekly
Sample ...	2,401	1,624	212	813	1,062
	%	%	%	%	%
Conservative ...	36	36	41	37	37
Labour ...	33	35	23	37	31
Liberal ...	11	10	7	9	11
Nationalist ...	2	2	8	3	3
Other party/no party/not answered ...	18	17	21	14	17
Very strong Conservative ...	14	14	14	13	14
Very strong Labour ...	10	12	9	11	9
Trade union member ...	25	28	24	29	23

Regional mornings, strong in Scotland, have a substantial number of nationalist readers. Apart from this, readers of papers of different types match closely in political affiliation and trade union membership to the population as a whole.

The People who Read Different Newspapers

The numbers claiming regular readership of the individual national morning newspapers were:

TABLE 1.016
REGULAR READERS OF INDIVIDUAL NATIONAL MORNINGS

	Total
Sample	2,401
Regular readers of:	%
Daily Mirror/Record	26
The Sun	19
Daily Express	15
Daily Mail	10
The Daily Telegraph	7
The Times	2
The Guardian	2
Financial Times	1
Morning Star	*

We have shown above that those who read a national morning newspaper regularly are a little more likely than average to be men and a little more likely than average to be working in skilled manual jobs. By and large, however, they form a fair cross-section of the population.

This picture changes completely, however, if we look at the regular readers of particular national morning newspapers. There are quite large differences in the profiles of readers of different newspapers.

Compare, for example, the regular readers of the larger national dailies in terms of their sex and age, in terms of the jobs they do and in terms of their political views:

TABLE 1.017
READERSHIP PROFILES OF THE LARGER NATIONAL MORNINGS

	Regular Readers of:				
	The Daily Telegraph	Daily Express	Daily Mail	Daily Mirror/Record	The Sun
Sample	176	363	240	646	490
	%	%	%	%	%
Sex: Male	55	48	48	51	56
Female	45	52	52	49	44
Age: 16–24	8	11	9	16	22
25–44	38	26	27	37	39
45–64	38	38	40	36	28
65+	16	25	22	11	11
N/S	*	*	2	*	*
Working status:					
In work	65	61	57	66	70
Not in work	35	39	43	34	30
SEG of employment:					
Professional/Employer/ Manager	23	10	12	6	4
Junior non-manual	28	21	21	16	14
Skilled manual	10	16	14	23	31

TABLE 1.017—continued

	Regular Readers of:				
	The Daily Telegraph	Daily Express	Daily Mail	Daily Mirror/ Record	The Sun
SEG of employment (continued):					
Semi/unskilled manual ...	4	12	9	20	20
Forces/unclassifiable ...	—	1	1	1	*
Political view:					
Conservative	68	54	54	20	23
Labour	8	20	19	51	48
Liberal	11	7	14	8	12
Nationalist	—	2	*	4	1
Other/none/not stated ...	13	17	12	17	17

There is a choice of national morning newspapers and different sorts of people choose different newspapers. The nature and attitudes of the newspaper may determine the choice. Turning this round, however, it also means that, to a large extent, the newspaper has particular groups within the community to cater for.

The readers of evening newspapers and of local weekly newspapers are also, as we have shown above, broadly a cross-section of the population. In the particular areas in which they live, they have only a very limited choice, if any choice at all, of evening or weekly newspaper. This means that, by and large, local newspapers have to cater for potential readers in their circulation areas as a whole rather than particular groups within the communities they cover.

This is a crucial difference between the national and the provincial press and goes some way to explain the differences between them.

The Time People Spend Reading Newspapers

Those questioned about particular newspapers they read were asked how long, on average, they spent looking at particular issues of them. London evenings are very different in style and content from most provincial evenings. Excluding them, the split of stated reading time by type of newspaper was:

TABLE 1.018
TIME SPENT READING NEWSPAPERS

	Regular or Occasional Readers of:			
	National Mornings	Regional Mornings	Provincial Evenings	Local Weeklies
Sample	1,982	273	1,096	1,369
	%	%	%	%
Average time spent per issue:				
Less than 15 minutes	16	15	16	13
15 but under 30 minutes ...	22	26	22	18
30 minutes but under 1 hour ...	34	35	35	35
1 hour but under 2 hours ...	21	19	22	23
2 hours or more	7	5	5	11

Answers vary little by type of newspaper. On average, people spend more time on local weeklies than on newspapers of other types, but the difference is not great. Those who spend two hours or more looking at one issue of a newspaper are a very small minority. The considerable majority spend less than one hour doing so.

National newspapers vary considerably in size and content and one would expect that the amount of time their readers spend on them would also vary. Stated average amounts of time spent reading particular national mornings were:

TABLE 1.019
TIME SPENT READING INDIVIDUAL NATIONAL MORNINGS

	Regular or Occasional Readers of:					
	The Times/ Financial Times/The Guardian	The Daily Telegraph	Daily Mail	Daily Express	Daily Mirror/ Record	The Sun
Sample: All asked about these newspapers	133 %	183 %	233 %	354 %	591 %	472 %
Average time spent per issue:						
Less than 15 minutes	5	16	12	15	14	26
15 but under 30 minutes	24	21	22	21	23	23
30 minutes but under 1 hour	30	32	40	39	35	28
1 hour but under 2 hours	32	24	19	18	20	18
2 hours or more	9	8	6	7	8	4

People who read *The Times*, the *Financial Times* or *The Guardian* claim, on average, to spend more time on them than those who read other national mornings. People who read *The Sun* claim, on average, to spend less. Even among readers of *The Times*, the *Financial Times* or *The Guardian*, however, only two in five claim to spend an hour or more on average looking at a particular issue.

Television Viewing and Radio Listening Time

We have discussed above the amounts of time people spend reading newspapers. The amounts of time they spend watching television and listening to the radio are generally considerably greater. Those interviewed reported the amounts of time they spent watching television and listening to the radio on an average weekday as:

TABLE 1.020
TIME SPENT WATCHING TV AND LISTENING TO THE RADIO

	TV Viewing	Radio Listening
Sample: All respondents	2,401	2,401
Average weekday time:	%	%
None	3	16
Under 1 hour	7	29
1 but under 3 hours	44	31
3 but under 5 hours	32	11
5 hours or more	14	13

Only just over one in four of those reading a national morning or a provincial evening spend an hour or more reading one issue. Nine out of ten people spend an hour or more on an average weekday watching television. Just under half claim to spend three hours a day or more doing so. The amount of time spent watching television varies between different groups in the community. Those aged 65 and over are particularly likely to say they spend a lot of time watching television. Those in professional and managerial jobs are much less likely than others to so do. Among all groups, however, stated television viewing time is, on average, considerably greater than the time people say they spend reading newspapers.

People in general spend less time listening to the radio than they spend watching television. Time spent listening to the radio is also, however, generally greater than time spent reading newspapers.

Television and Radio News

Respondents were asked how often they watched BBC or ITN news on television and how often they listened to news bulletins on radio. They answered:

TABLE 1.021

FREQUENCY OF EXPOSURE TO TV AND RADIO NEWS

	TV News	Radio News
Sample: All respondents	2,401	2,401
	%	%
Never	5	29
Less than once a week	1	3
1–3 days a week	9	7
4–5 days a week	13	16
6–7 days a week	71	44
Not stated	*	*

The number saying they watched television news six or seven days a week was virtually identical with the number saying they read a national morning newspaper regularly. The number saying they listened to radio news six or seven days a week was also very substantial.

Regular exposure to television and radio news varied quite strongly with age and with occupation. Older people were more likely than the young to say they watched television news and that they listened to radio news six or seven days a week. Also, women and people in non-manual jobs were more likely than average to say they listened to radio news six or seven days a week. This did not, however, hold for television news. The comparisons were:

TABLE 1.022
FREQUENT EXPOSURE TO TV AND RADIO NEWS BY SOCIAL GROUP

	Sample	Watch TV news 6–7 days per week	Listen to radio news 6–7 days per week
All respondents	2,401	% 71	44
Sex: Men	1,137	% 70	40
Women	1,262	% 72	48
Age: 16–24	361	% 54	35
25–44	819	% 67	42
45–64	772	% 78	44
65+	431	% 79	53
Working status:			
In work	1,438	% 69	42
Not in work	963	% 75	48
SEG of employment:			
Professional/Employer/Manager	222	% 65	50
Junior non-manual	463	% 70	51
Skilled manual	412	% 68	30
Semi-skilled/unskilled manual...	324	% 71	38

The question arises whether television and radio news are followed in addition to or as alternatives to the reading of newspapers. The survey findings do not suggest that television and radio news are seen as alternatives to newspapers. If anything, regular watching of television news is more common among regular newspaper readers than among others. Regular listening to radio news and regular newspaper reading appear wholly unrelated. The comparisons are:

TABLE 1.023
FREQUENT EXPOSURE TO TV AND RADIO NEWS BY READERSHIP OF DAILY NEWSPAPERS

	Sample	Watch TV news 6–7 days per week	Listen to radio news 6–7 days per week
Total	2,401	% 71	44
Regular reader of a national morning:			
Yes	1,624	% 74	44
No	777	% 67	44
Regular reader of a regional morning:			
Yes	212	% 75	46
No	2,189	% 71	44
Regular reader of an evening:			
Yes	813	% 74	44
No	1,588	% 70	44

2. News Interests and Sources

SUMMARY

Respondents were asked how interested they were in each of a list of eleven types of news. The numbers saying they were very interested in these various types of news were:

TABLE 1.024
STRONG INTEREST IN DIFFERENT TYPES OF NEWS

	Total
Sample: All respondents	2,401
	%
General and Political News:	
news about what the Government is doing in Britain	49
news about what is happening in other countries	27
news about political parties	20
Trade Union and Business News:	
news about trade union affairs	16
news about business and industry	20
News on Sport and Leisure Interests:	
news about football	22
news about horse racing	7
news about fashions	14
news about people in the entertainment business	14
Local and Regional News:	
news about what is going on in this part of the country	58
news about what the local council is doing	39

Out of the list of eleven types of news, the one in which the largest number said they were very interested was news about what was going on in their own part of the country. The other category of local or regional news, news about what the local council is doing, came third after news about what the Government is doing.

There were quite large differences between different groups in the community in their levels of interest in some of the various different sorts of news.

Men, older people and those in professional or managerial jobs were more likely than average to say they were very interested in general and political news. People in work were more likely than average to be very interested in business and union news. Men, especially men in manual employment, were particularly likely to express interest in news about football and horse racing and young women were particularly likely to be interested in news about fashions and about people in the entertainment business.

Compared with the other categories of news, the level of interest in local and regional news was very uniform. It was somewhat lower than average among the young, but varied little between other groups in the community.

There was a link between reading a morning newspaper and interest in general and political news and in business and union news. There was also a link between readership of national morning newspapers and of evening newspapers and strong interest in news about horse racing and football.

Interest in general and political news and in trade union and business news was not particularly related to whether people read evening newspapers regularly or not and neither interest in these categories of news nor interest in news about football and horse racing varied much between those who read local weeklies and those who did not.

Regular readers of evenings and local weeklies and, particularly, readers of regional mornings, however, were more likely than average to say they were very interested in what was going on in their part of the country.

Asked what sources they found useful and most useful in keeping up to date with general and political news, news about trade unions and news about football, those interested in these sorts of news most commonly mentioned television, followed by national morning newspapers. Television and national mornings were mentioned with almost equal frequency as useful sources of news about business and industry. The sources most widely mentioned as useful for news about horse racing were national mornings, followed by television. For all these types of news, except news about football, the evening and weekly press were mentioned as useful sources by fewer than one in five of those who were interested in the subjects.

For regional and local news, however, the situation was quite different. The local evening and weekly press were the news sources most frequently mentioned as useful. The only other sources mentioned with any frequency were television and local radio.

Respondents were asked what they considered the main problem of their district and asked how they had come to know of it. The most frequent answers were that they had come to know of it through personal experience or personal contact. Two in five of those who were able to define a local problem, however, mentioned local newspapers as one of the sources from which they had got information about it, far more than mentioned any of the other information media.

MAIN FINDINGS

Interest in Different Types of News

Respondents were asked a series of questions about their interest in different sorts of news and about the sources from which they got news on subjects which interested them. The questions covered eleven types of news which can be broadly categorised under four heads:

General and Political News	— news about what the Government is doing in Britain
	— news about what is happening in other countries
	— news about political parties
Trade Union and Business News	— news about trade union affairs
	— news about business and industry
News on Sport and Leisure Interests	— news about football
	— news about horse racing
	— news about fashions
	— news about people in the entertainment business
Local and Regional News	— news about what is going on in this part of the country
	— news about what the local council is doing.

The list was designed to exemplify the position with regard to different sorts of news. It is, of course, not exhaustive. In particular, the list of types of news on sport and leisure interests could clearly be extended almost indefinitely.

(a) *General and Political News*

Overall, the levels of interest expressed in the three categories of news under this head were:

TABLE 1.025

INTEREST IN GENERAL AND POLITICAL NEWS

	News about what the Government is doing in Britain	News about what is happening in other countries	News about political parties
Sample: All respondents	2,401	2,401	2,401
	%	%	%
Very interested	49	27	20
Fairly interested	38	60	40
Not at all interested	13	13	39

Most respondents showed some interest, although women, younger people and those in manual jobs expressed less strong interest than others. Among all groups the level of interest in news about what the Government is doing in Britain was markedly higher than the level of interest in news about other countries or about political parties.

TABLE 1.026
INTEREST IN GENERAL AND POLITICAL NEWS BY SOCIAL GROUP

	Sample	News about what the Government is doing in Britain		News about what is happening in other countries		News about political parties	
		Very interested	Very or fairly interested	Very interested	Very or fairly interested	Very interested	Very or fairly interested
Total	2,401	% 49	87	27	87	20	60
Sex:							
Men	1,137	% 56	89	31	88	26	66
Women	1,262	% 42	85	23	85	16	57
Age:							
16–24	361	% 25	75	13	82	12	44
25–44	819	% 48	90	23	89	15	61
45–64	772	% 57	88	32	90	25	66
65 or over	431	% 53	85	33	84	28	63
Working Status:							
In work	1,438	% 49	88	27	87	19	61
Not in work	963	% 48	85	27	85	22	60
Socio-Economic Group of Employment:							
Professional/ Employer/ Manager	222	% 66	93	36	94	28	77
Junior non-manual	463	% 50	88	29	91	22	66
Skilled manual	412	% 45	86	23	84	16	59
Semi/unskilled manual	324	% 41	85	22	81	15	49

The numbers who said they were very or fairly interested in general and political news varied with newspaper reading as follows:

TABLE 1.027
INTEREST IN GENERAL AND POLITICAL NEWS BY NEWSPAPER READERSHIP

	Sample	What the Government is doing in Britain		What is happening in other countries		Political parties	
		Very interested	Very or fairly interested	Very interested	Very or fairly interested	Very interested	Very or fairly interested
Regular readers of:							
A national morning							
Yes	1,624	% 52	89	29	88	23	63
No	777	% 42	83	23	84	16	57
A regional morning							
Yes	212	% 58	92	30	93	31	74
No	2,189	% 48	86	27	86	19	59
An evening							
Yes	813	% 49	88	27	87	20	59
No	1,588	% 48	86	27	86	21	62
A local weekly							
Yes	1,062	% 51	89	26	88	23	66
No	1,339	% 47	85	28	86	19	57

People who read a morning newspaper regularly, whether national or regional, are more likely than average to express strong interest in news about what the Government is doing in Britain and in news about political parties. There does not, however, appear to be any relationship between strong interest in general and political news and regular readership of evening or local weekly newspapers.

Those who said they were very interested or fairly interested in each category of news were asked to pick from a list of news sources all those which they found useful in keeping up to date and well informed on news of that category and to pick also the one source they found most useful. Because there are large areas of the country where they do not circulate, regional mornings were not included in the list of news sources.

News sources seen as useful for keeping up to date on general and political news were:

TABLE 1.028
USEFUL SOURCES FOR KEEPING UP TO DATE WITH GENERAL AND POLITICAL NEWS

	What the Government is doing in Britain		What is happening in other countries		Political parties	
	All sources	Most useful source	All sources	Most useful source	All sources	Most useful source
Sample: All very or fairly interested in that sort of news	2,075	2,075	2,067	2,067	1,467	1,467
	%	%	%	%	%	%
Television	76	53	84	58	74	52
National mornings	57	29	57	24	54	30
National Sundays	23	4	29	5	22	5
National radio	24	7	31	8	21	6
Local evenings	10	2	9	2	7	1
Local weeklies	1	*	2	*	1	*
Local radio	3	1	5	1	2	1
Magazines	1	*	5	1	2	1
None of these/Don't know	2	2	2	2	2	2

Answers for the three categories of news are very similar. The source which was mentioned as useful by far the most frequently was television. For each of the three categories of general and political news, more than half of those with any interest said television was their one most useful source.

National morning newspapers were mentioned as useful sources by just over half those interested in these categories of news with between 24% and 30% saying national mornings were their one most useful source.

National Sundays and radio were quite widely mentioned as useful sources, but very seldom as people's single most useful source.

No more than one in ten of those with any interest in general and political news saw local evenings as a useful source of such news. There was hardly any mention of local weeklies as a useful source.

(b) Trade Union and Business News

The levels of interest expressed in news about trade union affairs and news about business and industry were:

TABLE 1.029

INTEREST IN TRADE UNION AND BUSINESS NEWS

	News about trade union affairs	News about business and industry
Sample: All respondents	2,401	2,401
	%	%
Very interested	16	20
Fairly interested	33	44
Not at all interested	50	36

Interest in these categories of news was, naturally enough, higher among those in employment than among others. Among those in employment, it also varied with the type of work done and with union membership.

TABLE 1.030

INTEREST IN TRADE UNION AND BUSINESS NEWS BY OCCUPATION

	Sample	News about trade unions affairs		News about business and industry	
		Very interested	Very or fairly interested	Very interested	Very or fairly interested
Total	2,401	% 16	50	20	65
Working Status					
In work	1,438	% 19	56	23	71
Not in work	963	% 13	40	15	53
Socio-Economic Group of Employment					
Professional/Employer/ Manager	222	% 20	63	45	91
Junior non-manual	463	% 17	44	18	71
Skilled manual	412	% 23	62	23	71
Semi/unskilled manual	324	% 17	48	14	71
Trade union members	612	% 30	69	24	69

Those sections of the population among whom fewer than average numbers are in work—women, those aged under 25 and those aged 65 or over were below average in their level of interest in business and union news.

Interest in business and union news varied with readership of different types of newspaper as follows:

TABLE 1.031
INTEREST IN TRADE UNION AND BUSINESS NEWS BY NEWSPAPER READERSHIP

		Sample	News about trade unions affairs		News about business and industry	
			Very interested	Very or fairly interested	Very interested	Very or fairly interested
Regular readers of:			%			
A national morning	Yes	1,624	19	53	21	67
	No	777	11	43	16	55
A regional morning	Yes	212	19	60	24	74
	No	2,189	16	48	19	62
An evening	Yes	813	18	50	21	65
	No	1,588	15	49	19	63
A local weekly	Yes	1,062	15	50	20	64
	No	1,339	17	49	19	62

As with general and political news, the level of interest in business and union news was rather greater among those who read morning newspapers, whether national or regional, regularly than it was among those who did not. People's interest in business and union news appeared, however, to have little to do with whether they read evening or local weekly newspapers or not.

Those who were very interested or fairly interested in business and union news gave the sources they found useful and most useful for keeping up to date and well informed on it as:

TABLE 1.032
USEFUL SOURCES FOR KEEPING UP TO DATE WITH TRADE UNION AND BUSINESS NEWS

	For keeping up to date on news about:			
	Trade union affairs		Business and industry	
	All sources	Most useful source	All sources	Most useful source
Sample: All very or fairly interested in that sort of news	1,168	1,168	1,535	1,535
	%	%	%	%
Television	65	44	53	34
National mornings	52	31	55	36
National Sundays	18	4	22	10
National radio	20	7	14	5
Local evenings	10	3	12	6
Local weeklies	1	*	4	2
Local radio	3	1	3	1
Magazines	3	2	3	1
None of them/Don't know	6	7	5	5

As with general and political news, the sources most widely seen as useful are television and national morning newspapers. For business and union news, however, television has not the predominance over national mornings that was evident for general and political news. The numbers mentioning television and national newspapers as their most important single source of news about business and industry were virtually equal.

National Sundays and radio were quite frequently mentioned, but mainly as subsidiary sources.

Only 10% of those interested in trade union affairs and 12% of those interested in business and industry mentioned evening newspapers as a useful source of news on these topics. The numbers mentioning local weeklies as a source were very small indeed.

(c) *News about Sport and Leisure Interests*

The levels of interest expressed in the four categories of news under this head were:

TABLE 1.033
INTEREST IN NEWS ABOUT SPORT AND LEISURE INTERESTS

	News about football	News about horse racing	News about fashions	News about people in the entertainment business
Sample: all respondents	2,401	2,401	2,401	2,401
	%	%	%	%
Very interested	22	7	14	17
Fairly interested	26	10	33	49
Not at all interested	52	83	53	34

Men were a good deal more likely than women to express strong interest in news about football and horse racing. 38% of men said they were very interested in news about football and 11% that they were very interested in news about horse racing. The corresponding figures for women were 8% and 4%. Interest in news about football was highest among skilled manual workers and interest in news about horse racing was generally higher among manual workers than others.

Interest in news about the two sports varied with newspaper readership as follows:

TABLE 1.034
INTEREST IN NEWS ABOUT SPORT BY NEWSPAPER READERSHIP

		Sample	News about football		News about horse racing	
			Very interested	Very or fairly interested	Very interested	Very or fairly interested
Regular readers of:			%			
A national morning	Yes	1,624	26	53	9	20
	No	777	14	38	4	12
A regional morning	Yes	212	23	56	6	20
	No	2,189	22	47	7	16
An evening	Yes	813	27	51	10	21
	No	1,588	20	46	5	15
A local weekly	Yes	1,062	24	48	7	17
	No	1,339	21	47	7	17

People who read a national morning regularly are more likely to say they are interested in news about football and horse racing than those who do not. The same applies, although less markedly, to those who read an evening newspaper regularly.

There does not appear to be any connection between strong interest in news about football or horse racing and readership of regional mornings or local weeklies.

Among those with any interest in news about the two sports, the news sources seen as useful and most useful were:

TABLE 1.035
USEFUL SOURCES FOR KEEPING UP TO DATE WITH NEWS ABOUT SPORT

	Football		Horse racing	
	All sources	Most useful source	All sources	Most useful source
Sample: All very or fairly interested in that sort of news	1,167	1,167	413	413
	%	%	%	%
Television	61	36	46	29
National mornings	54	30	67	55
National Sundays	32	15	12	2
National radio	10	2	8	2
Local evenings	20	8	14	6
Local weeklies	7	2	2	1
Local radio	4	1	8	–
Magazines	1	*	2	1
None of these/Don't know	4	5	3	4

Again, the two main news sources mentioned were television and national morning newspapers, with national mornings as decidedly the most useful source of news about horse racing. The other most commonly mentioned sources, particularly for news about football, were national Sundays and local evenings.

Unlike all the other categories of news so far discussed, interest in news about fashions and about people in the entertainment business was stronger among women than men and stronger among those aged under 25 than among others. The comparison was:

TABLE 1.036
INTEREST IN NEWS ABOUT LEISURE INTERESTS BY SOCIAL GROUP

	Sample	News about fashions		News about people in the entertainment business	
		Very interested	Very or fairly interested	Very interested	Very or fairly interested
		%			
Total	2,401	14	47	17	66
Sex: Men	1,137	3	19	12	57
Women	1,262	24	71	22	74
Age: 16–24	361	25	60	26	76
25–44	819	14	52	14	66
45–64	772	13	45	17	67
65+	431	6	29	14	55

Interest in news about fashions and about people in the entertainment business showed no very great relationship to the types of newspapers which people read. The comparison was:

TABLE 1.037

INTEREST IN NEWS ABOUT LEISURE INTERESTS BY NEWSPAPER READERSHIP

		Sample	News about fashions		News about people in the entertainment business	
			Very interested	Very or fairly interested	Very interested	Very or fairly interested
Regular readers of:						
A national morning	Yes	1,624	% 14	45	18	68
	No	777	% 15	50	15	63
A regional morning	Yes	212	% 12	37	12	59
	No	2,189	% 14	48	18	67
An evening	Yes	813	% 16	48	20	70
	No	1,588	% 13	46	16	65
A local weekly	Yes	1,062	% 15	49	17	69
	No	1,339	% 14	46	17	64

Useful sources of news mentioned by those with some interest in news about fashions and news about people in the entertainment business were:

TABLE 1.038

USEFUL SOURCES FOR KEEPING UP TO DATE WITH NEWS ABOUT LEISURE INTERESTS

	Fashions		People in the entertainment business	
	All sources	Most useful source	All sources	Most useful source
Sample: All very or fairly interested in that sort of news	1,121	1,121	1,616	1,616
	%	%	%	%
Television	37	20	62	43
Magazines	49	40	22	15
National mornings	35	18	38	19
National Sundays	22	9	23	9
Local evenings	7	3	8	3
Local weeklies	4	1	3	1
National radio	2	*	11	4
Local radio	*	—	3	1
None of these/Don't know	6	9	3	5

On fashions, magazines were the predominant news source. Television and national mornings were also important and national Sundays were a common subsidiary source.

On people in the entertainment business, television was the predominant news source. National mornings and magazines were also important and national Sundays were a common subsidiary source.

Local evenings and weeklies were of very minor importance as sources of news either on fashions or on people in the entertainment business.

(*d*) *Local and Regional News*

Overall the levels of interest expressed in the two categories of news under this head were:

TABLE 1.039
INTEREST IN LOCAL AND REGIONAL NEWS

	News about what is going on in this part of the country	News about what the local council is doing
Sample: All respondents	2,401	2,401
	%	%
Very interested	58	39
Fairly interested	36	40
Not at all interested	6	21

It will be noted that, compared with the other categories of news discussed above, interest in local and regional news is very high. Almost everyone expressed some interest in news about what was going on in their part of the country. Almost three in five expressed strong interest. This was substantially more than expressed strong interest in any of the other categories of news covered. There was substantially less interest in news about what the local council is doing, but if the eleven categories of news covered are ordered by the numbers expressing strong interest in them, local council news comes third. The overall comparison is:

TABLE 1.040
RANK ORDERING OF INTEREST IN DIFFERENT TYPES OF NEWS

	Very interested	Rank order	Not at all interested	Rank order
		highest to lowest		lowest to highest
Sample: All respondents	2,401		2,401	
	%		%	
Local and regional news				
News about what is going on in this part of the country	58	1	6	1
News about what the local council is doing	39	3	21	4
General and political news				
News about what the Government is doing in Britain	49	2	13	2=
News about what is happening in other countries	27	4	13	2=
News about political parties	20	6	39	7
Trade union and business news				
News about business and industry	20	7	36	6
News about trade union affairs	16	9	50	8
News about sport and leisure interests				
News about football	22	5	52	9
News about people in the entertainment business	17	8	34	5
News about fashions	14	10	53	10
News about horse racing	7	11	83	11

We have seen earlier that levels of interest in the other sorts of news discussed varied with sex and, in several cases, with age and the sort of jobs people do. There was much less variation in the level of interest in local and regional news. Young people showed rather less interest than older people. Apart from this, the picture was very uniform.

TABLE 1.041
INTEREST IN LOCAL AND REGIONAL NEWS BY SOCIAL GROUP

	Sample	News about what is going on in this part of the country		News about what the local council is doing	
		Very interested	Very or fairly interested	Very interested	Very or fairly interested
Total	2,401	% 58	94	39	79
Sex: Men	1,137	% 56	94	38	76
Women	1,262	% 59	95	40	81
Age: 16–24	361	% 45	93	23	65
25–44	819	% 55	95	35	80
45–64	772	% 64	96	46	84
65 or over	431	% 59	92	46	78
Working Status					
In work	1,438	% 57	95	36	79
Not in work	963	% 59	94	43	79
SEG of Employment					
Professional/Employer/Manager	222	% 57	97	32	76
Junior non-manual	463	% 57	94	38	81
Skilled manual	412	% 58	95	36	77
Semi/unskilled	324	% 55	93	38	79

There was some variation by region. Those in London and the South East and those in the North West expressed slightly less interest than average. Those in Scotland expressed slightly more:

TABLE 1.042
INTEREST IN LOCAL AND REGIONAL NEWS BY REGION

	Sample	News about what is going on in this part of the country		News about what the local council is doing	
		Very interested	Very or fairly interested	Very interested	Very or fairly interested
London and the South East	743	% 52	94	36	81
North West	325	% 52	93	35	74
East and West Midlands/East Anglia	456	% 55	94	39	78
South West and Wales	305	% 65	96	42	79
North/Yorkshire and Humberside	367	% 66	95	40	76
Scotland	205	% 67	94	50	86

The relationship between the newspapers people read and their interest in local and regional news was:

TABLE 1.043
INTEREST IN LOCAL AND REGIONAL NEWS BY NEWSPAPER READERSHIP

			Sample	What is going on in this part of the country		News about what the local council is doing	
				Very interested	Very or fairly interested	Very interested	Very or fairly interested
Regular readers of:							
A national morning	Yes	...	1,624	% 59	95	41	80
	No	...	777	% 56	93	36	77
A regional morning	Yes	...	212	% 76	99	49	89
	No	...	2,189	% 56	94	38	78
An evening	Yes	...	813	% 63	97	41	81
	No	...	1,588	% 55	93	38	78
A local weekly	Yes	...	1,062	% 63	97	43	84
	No	...	1,339	% 54	92	36	75

There is a clear relationship between reading regional and local newspapers, particularly regional mornings, and strong interest in what is going on in one's own part of the country.

The sources people said they found useful and most useful in keeping up to date on local and regional news were:

TABLE 1.044
USEFUL SOURCES FOR KEEPING UP TO DATE WITH LOCAL AND REGIONAL NEWS

	For keeping up to date on news about:			
	What is going on in this part of the country		What the local council is doing	
	All sources	Most useful source	All sources	Most useful source
Sample: All very/fairly interested in that sort of news	2,270	2,270	1,893	1,893
	%	%	%	%
Local evening newspapers ...	41	31	38	32
Local weekly newspapers	38	29	47	41
Television	31	17	10	5
Local radio	16	8	8	5
National radio	4	1	1	*
National morning newspapers ...	10	5	3	2
National Sunday newspapers ...	2	1	1	*
Magazines	1	*	*	*
None of these/Don't know ...	7	7	14	14

In contrast to the situation with all the other types of news covered, the local press, evening or weekly, was more commonly mentioned than any other medium as the most useful source of news. Because of their limited circulation regional mornings were not included in the list of media covered in this question.

The only other source widely seen as useful in keeping up to date on news about what is going on in this part of the country is television. The national press appears to have a very minor role with regard to news of this sort. It is less important than local radio.

Summary of News Sources

We have talked so far about the association of different media with different types of news only in the context of people who show some interest in these types of news. As a summary, it may be helpful to present all mentions of television, the national morning press and the local press as useful on the base of all those who were interviewed. This gives a broad overall indication of the types of news for which the different media are seen as more and less useful sources.

TABLE 1.045
TYPES OF NEWS FOR WHICH DIFFERENT MEDIA ARE SEEN AS USEFUL SOURCES

	Local Weeklies	Rank Order	Local Evenings	Rank Order	National Mornings	Rank Order	TV	Rank Order
Sample: All respondents	2,401 %		2,401 %		2,401 %		2,401 %	
A useful source of:								
General and political news:								
news about what is happening in other countries	2	4=	8	5	50	1=	72	1
news about what the Government is doing in Britain	1	8=	9	3=	50	1=	66	2
news about political parties	1	8=	4	8	33	4	45	3
Business and union news:								
news about trade union affairs	1	8=	5	7	26	5=	35	5
news about business and industry	2	4=	2	10	35	3	34	6
News on sport and leisure interests:								
news about football	3	3	9	3=	26	5=	29	8
news about horse racing	*	11	2	10=	11	9	8	10=
news about fashions	2	4=	3	9	16	8	17	9
news about people in the entertainment business	2	4=	6	6	25	7	41	4
Local and regional news:								
news about what is going on in this part of the country	36	2	38	1	9	10	30	7
news about what the local council is doing	37	1	30	2	2	11	8	10=

This table suggests that television is the predominant source of general and political news and is seen as a very important source of most other sorts of news except very local news. The national morning press, again, is seen as a useful source for a wide variety of types of news, but not for local or regional news.

Evening newspapers and local weekly newspapers are seen as the prime sources of local and regional news. Evening newspapers are also seen, to some extent, as a source of general and political news and of some sorts of news about sport and leisure interests. These are, however, very much subsidiary functions. Local weekly newspapers are not seen as a significant source of anything other than local news.

Sources of News on District Problems

Local newspapers are seen largely as a source of local news. To what extent are they seen as sources of information on the problems of the areas in which they circulate rather than simply a source of information on local events? A series of questions was put to respondents with the object of getting a broad measurement of this.

Respondents were asked, without any prompting, what they thought were the most important issues and problems facing their district nowadays. Those who mentioned several were asked to nominate one as the most important. They were then asked to say how they had come to know of that issue or problem, choosing as many sources of information as they wished from a prompt list, which included "local newspapers" as a category.

Further questions on the adequacy of local press coverage of the problems people mentioned are discussed in Section 4 of this part of the report.

Most people were able, without prompting, to say what they thought were the main issues or problems facing their districts. Four out of five mentioned some problem.

One in ten said their district had no problems at all and one in ten could not say what the problems were. The incidence of the view that the area had no problems did not vary greatly by region or by political view and can be taken as broadly equivalent to a "don't know" answer.

Some of the problems mentioned were highly area-specific and some of the answers were highly individual, reflecting the special interests of individual respondents.

A broad grouping of the problems people mentioned gives:

TABLE 1.046
MAIN PROBLEMS OF RESPONDENTS' DISTRICTS

	All problems of district	One main problem
Sample: All respondents	2,401	2,401
	%	%
Economic		
Unemployment/redundancies/threatened closures	18	14
Cost of living		
High rates/rate increases	11	7 ⎫
High rents/rent increases	2	1 ⎪ 11
High fares	2	1 ⎪
Cost of living/no money about	5	2 ⎭
Environmental problems		
Juvenile deliquency/vandalism	8	6 ⎫
Dirt/pollution	5	3 ⎬ 10
Noise	2	1 ⎭
Housing		
Shortage of housing	11	7 ⎫ 10
Poor quality of housing stock	6	3 ⎭
Social facilities		
Lack of/poor leisure and recreation facilities	10	6 ⎫ 8
Lack of/poor shops	3	2 ⎭
Transport		
Lack of/poor public transport	6	3 ⎫
Poor roads/no road building	7	4 ⎬ 7
Other public transport problems	1	* ⎭
Social services		
Lack of/poor schools	6	4 ⎫
Lack of/poor medical facilities	2	1 ⎬ 7
Lack of/poor personal social services	3	2 ⎭
Planning threat		
Threat of new road/airport/other physical development	6	4
Other specific problems	14	9
No problems in district	10	10
Vague answer/Don't know	10	11

The problems mentioned varied somewhat by region. People in Scotland and the North of England were particularly likely to mention environmental problems. People in Scotland were the most likely to mention housing. People in London and the South East were less likely than average to mention unemployment and threatened closures and more likely than average to mention housing. The comparison was:

TABLE 1.047

MAIN PROBLEMS OF RESPONDENTS' DISTRICTS BY REGION

	Region					
	North/ Yorks/ Humberside	N. West	Midlands/ E. Anglia	S. West & Wales	London & South East	Scotland
Sample	367	325	456	305	743	205
	%	%	%	%	%	%
Single Main Problem of District						
Economic	16	18	15	20	7	15
Cost of living	11	8	11	9	12	9
Environmental problems	12	13	9	5	7	11
Housing	7	5	7	8	14	16
Social facilities	5	6	8	7	9	8
Transport	8	6	7	5	8	2
Social services	3	6	8	8	6	6
Planning threat	2	8	2	6	5	3
Other specific problems	8	8	9	9	10	9
No problems/Vague answer/Don't know	28	21	23	23	20	20

The district problems perceived by people of different political views were broadly similar. There were differences of degree, but of degree only. Labour party supporters were more likely than Conservatives to mention housing, environmental problems or problems of social or public facilities as the single main problems of the districts in which they lived. Conservative Party supporters were more likely than Labour Party supporters to mention the cost of living, especially increased rates.

The comparison was:

TABLE 1.048

MAIN PROBLEMS OF RESPONDENTS' DISTRICT BY RESPONDENTS' POLITICAL VIEWS

	Conservative	Liberal	Labour	Very strong Conservative	Very strong Labour
Sample	860	255	806	321	240
	%	%	%	%	%
Single main problem of district:					
Economic	14	16	13	11	15
Cost of living	13	11	8	12	10
Environmental problems	6	9	11	8	10
Housing	8	12	13	10	14
Social facilities	6	7	9	6	7
Transport	8	6	6	6	5
Social services	7	6	6	9	6
Planning threat	5	6	3	4	3
Other specific problems	10	12	7	10	8
No problems	22	14	23	24	20

When those who were able to name one main problem of the district in which they lived were asked how they had come to know of it, they answered:

TABLE 1.049

SOURCES OF INFORMATION ON MAIN PROBLEM OF DISTRICT

	Total
Sample: All mentioning one main problem of the district	1,889
	%
Learned about it from:	
personal experience	76
what people say	58
local newspapers	39
television	11
national newspapers	9
local radio	6
national radio	3
magazines	1

Most people see personal experience and personal contact with other people as their main sources of information about the main problems of their districts. Two out of five, however, mentioned the local press as an information source, far more than mentioned any other news medium.

The degree to which the local press was seen as a source of knowledge varied, however, with what people saw as the main problem. More than half of those who saw the main problem of their district as one of planning threat or as an economic problem of unemployment or threatened closures mentioned the local press as an information source.

Of those who saw the main problem of their district as one of poor transport facilities or lack of social or recreational facilities, however, only one in five mentioned the local press as an information source.

Mention of the local press as an information source varied with the main perceived problem as follows:

TABLE 1.050

MENTION OF LOCAL NEWSPAPERS AS A SOURCE OF INFORMATION ON MAIN DISTRICT PROBLEM BY NATURE OF MAIN PROBLEM

Main perceived problem	Sample	Local newspapers mentioned as a way in which people found out about problem
Planning threat	98	% 70
Economic	343	% 55
Cost of living	259	% 40
Environmental	198	% 37
Housing	220	% 33
Social services	153	% 32
Social facilities	183	% 21
Transport	157	% 19

The local press's treatment of these problems will be discussed in Section 4 of this part of the report.

3. What People Read in Regional and Local Newspapers

SUMMARY

Those who read regional and local newspapers were asked which of a list of seventeen types of item or feature they usually looked at in them.

The items most widely mentioned as usually looked at were:

TABLE 1.051

MAIN ITEMS READ IN REGIONAL AND LOCAL NEWSPAPERS

Rank order	Regional Mornings
1	List of TV and radio programmes
2	Comment on local issues
3	News about what the Government is doing in Britain
4 =	{ News about what is happening in other countries / News about what the local council is doing

Rank order	Provincial Evenings
1	List of TV and radio programmes
2	News about what the local council is doing
3	Comment on local issues
4	Readers' letters
5	News about what the Government is doing in Britain

Rank order	Local Weeklies
1	Comment on local issues
2	News about what the local council is doing
3	Readers' letters
4 =	{ Reports of local court cases / Advertisements of items for sale or wanted

For regional mornings, both national and local news items were commonly mentioned. For provincial evenings, national news was less commonly mentioned. National news does not feature among the items commonly read in local weeklies at all. The prominence of readers' letters in the lists of items commonly read in provincial evenings and local weeklies should be noted.

There were large differences between men and women and between people of different age groups in the items and features they read. The findings discussed earlier suggest that a main function of regional and local newspapers is to supply regional and local news. This is not, however, a single, uniform commodity. The regional and local press are supplying a variety of different sorts of local news to a variety of different groups in the community.

MAIN FINDINGS

The Types of News and Feature which Appear in Regional and Local Newspapers

In the previous section, we discussed in rather broad terms the sorts of news that interest different sorts of people and the sources which they say are useful in keeping up to date on these sorts of news. In this section, the discussion becomes rather more specific. Here we will discuss the types of news item and feature people say they read in particular regional and local newspapers.

Those who said they read one or more issues of a regional morning or provincial evening in an average week and those who said they read one or more issues of a local weekly in an average month were asked a series of questions about the particular regional and local newspapers they said they read. Some of these questions related to the types of news item and feature which appear in the newspapers and the types of item and feature which they read.

Seventeen types of item or feature were covered. Aggregated by type of newspaper, the numbers who said these items always or sometimes appeared in the newspapers they read were:

TABLE 1.052

AWARENESS OF CONTENT OF REGIONAL AND LOCAL NEWSPAPERS

	Appears always or sometimes in		
	Regional Morning Newspapers	Provincial Evening Newspapers	Local Weekly Newspapers
Sample: All newspapers read regularly or occasionally	273	1,096	1,369
	%	%	%
General and political news			
News about what the Government is doing in Britain	94	96	50
New about what is happening in other countries	95	91	32
Local news			
News about what the local council is doing ...	91	98	97
News about local sport	95	99	98
Reports of local court cases	94	98	96
Pictures and reports of weddings and funerals	86	97	97
News about local business and industry ...	92	98	95
News about local trade union affairs	93	93	80
Comment			
Comment about local issues	94	98	97
Readers' letters	96	96	94
Classified advertising/announcements			
List of TV and radio programmes	100	99	66
Announcements of births, deaths and marriages	97	98	95
Advertising of items for sale or wanted ...	95	100	98
Advertising of jobs	99	100	97
Features			
Women's page	76	77	67
Gardening page or column	78	82	72
Articles about cars or motoring	96	96	86

Apart from the special interest features, most of the items covered are thought to appear in virtually all newspapers. Predictable exceptions are that local weekly newspapers are frequently said not to carry general and political news or a list of television and radio programmes. A much less predictable exception is that only four out of five of those questioned about local weekly newspapers said that news about local trade union affairs ever appears there. This was a markedly lower figure than those for the other categories of local news covered.

It did not appear to be the case that lower perceived level of coverage of news about local trade union affairs was a feature of any particular newspaper group or type of owner. The level of awareness of trade union news in local weekly newspapers did not differ significantly between those answering on weeklies owned by groups with national newspaper interests and those answering on weeklies with other ownership. The figure for weeklies owned by the largest single group, the Westminster Press, was virtually the same as the figure for local weeklies as a whole.

Items Read in Regional and Local Newspapers

What people think appears in newspapers and what they read in newspapers are, of course, two different things. The numbers of those questioned about particular newspapers who claimed to read the various types of item or feature with any frequency were:

TABLE 1.053
ITEMS READ IN REGIONAL AND LOCAL NEWSPAPERS

	Always make a point of looking at it in:			Always make a point of looking/usually look at it in:		
	Regional Morning Newspaper	Provincial Evening Newspaper	Local Weekly Newspaper	Regional Morning Newspaper	Provincial Evening Newspaper	Local Weekly Newspaper
Sample	273	1,096	1,369	273	1,096	1,369
	%	%	%	%	%	%
General and political news						
News about what the Government is doing in Britain	30	22	12	63	51	23
News about what is happening in other countries	30	21	8	62	49	14
Local news						
News about what the local council is doing	27	33	39	62	62	69
News about local sport	27	28	26	45	46	43
Reports of local court cases	20	23	29	44	43	54
Pictures and reports of weddings and funerals	20	23	32	26	40	53
News about local business and industry	21	22	26	50	46	52
News about local trade union affairs	13	14	13	27	29	27
Comment						
Comment about local issues	29	31	39	66	61	72
Readers' letters	27	34	39	50	54	61
Classified advertising/announcements						
List of TV and radio programmes	40	47	15	70	67	25
Announcements of births, deaths and marriages	29	30	34	45	40	46
Advertising of items for sale or wanted	19	27	29	44	49	54
Advertising of jobs	16	23	27	40	40	43
Features						
Women's page	12	19	16	20	30	26
Gardening page or column	12	14	14	25	25	24
Articles about cars or motoring	13	13	12	30	27	24

Ranking the five types of item most widely mentioned as always or usually read in the three types of newspaper gives:

TABLE 1.054
RANKING OF ITEMS READ IN REGIONAL AND LOCAL NEWSPAPERS

Rank order	Regional Mornings	%
1	List of TV and radio programmes	70
2	Comment on local issues	66
3	News about what the Government is doing in Britain	63
4 =	{ News about what is happening in other countries	62
	{ News about what the local council is doing	62

Rank order	Provincial Evenings	%
1	List of TV and radio programmes	67
2	News about what the local council is doing	62
3	Comment on local issues	61
4	Readers' letters	54
5	News about what the Government is doing in Britain	49

Rank order	Local Weeklies	%
1	Comment on local issues	72
2	News about what the local council is doing	69
3	Readers' letters	61
4 =	{ Reports of local court cases	54
	{ Advertisements of items for sale or wanted	54

The five items most widely read in local weeklies are all specifically local in character. All five of these items are rather more widely read in local weeklies than in either provincial evenings or regional mornings. Pictures and reports of weddings and funerals were also more widely read in local weeklies than in either of the other two types of newspaper.

In regional morning and provincial evening newspapers, the item that the largest number of people always make a point of looking at is the list of television and radio programmes. Two in five always make a point of looking at them. Two in three usually look at them.

After the list of TV and radio programmes, there are four categories of news which are usually read in regional mornings by roughly equal numbers of people—the two categories of general and political news, comment on local issues and news about what the local council is doing.

The numbers who say they usually look at comment on local issues and news about what the local council is doing in provincial evenings are very close to the equivalent figures for regional mornings. The numbers who say they usually look at general and political news in provincial evenings are substantially lower.

Differences between Groups in the Community

This is the overall picture. There are, however, quite large differences between different groups in the community in their readership of different items on the list. Let us look first at the reading habits of men and women. The numbers reading regional mornings are too small for further sub-analysis. Ranking the five types of item men and women most frequently say they always or usually look at in provincial evenings and local weeklies gives:

TABLE 1.055

RANKING OF ITEMS READ IN LOCAL NEWSPAPERS BY SEX

Rank order	Provincial Evenings			
	Men (Sample: 545)	%	Women (Sample: 549)	%
1	List of TV and radio programmes	69	List of TV and radio programmes	68
2	News about what the local council is doing	65	Comment on local issues / Pictures and reports of weddings and funerals...	60 / 60
3	News about local sport	64		
4	Comment on local issues	63	Announcements of births, deaths and marriages	59
5	News about what the Government is doing in Britain	59	News about what the local council is doing	59

Rank order	Local Weeklies			
	Men (Sample: 639)	%	Women (Sample: 730)	%
1	News about what the local council is doing	72	Comment on local issues	75
2	Comment on local issues	70	Pictures and reports of weddings and funerals	71
3	News about local business and industry	60	News about what the local council is doing / Readers' letters	68 / 68
4	Advertisements of items for sale and wanted	56		
5	Readers' letters	53	Announcements of births, deaths and marriages	60

Women were much more likely than men to read announcements of births, deaths and marriages, pictures and reports of weddings and funerals, readers' letters and, predictably enough, the women's page. Men were much more likely than women to read news about local sport, news about local business, industry and trade union affairs, articles about cars and motoring and, in provincial evenings, general and political news.

There were also substantial differences by age in the items people usually read in local newspapers. The comparison between different age groups of the items on the list most frequently mentioned as always or usually looked at in provincial evening and local weekly newspapers was:

TABLE 1.056
RANKING OF ITEMS READ IN LOCAL NEWSPAPERS BY AGE

Rank order	Provincial Evenings			
	16–24 (Sample: 175)	%	25–44 (Sample: 387)	%
1	List of TV and radio programmes	69	List of TV and radio programmes	66
2	News about local sport	52	Comment on local issues	60
3	Advertising of jobs	49	News about what the local council is doing	56
4=	Comment on local issues	44	Advertising of items for sale or wanted	51
	News about what the local council is doing	44	News about what the Government is doing in Britain	51

Rank order				
	45–64 (Sample: 364)	%	65 and over (Sample: 162)	%
1	News about what the local council is doing	72	News about what the local council is doing	69
2	List of TV and radio programmes	71	List of TV and radio programmes	68
3	Comment on local issues	70	Readers' letters	66
4	Readers' letters	66	Comment on local issues	60
5	News about what the Government is doing in Britain	56	News about what the Government is doing in Britain	58

Rank order	Local Weeklies			
	16–24 (Sample: 216)	%	25–44 (Sample: 469)	%
1	Advertising of jobs	53	Comment on local issues	73
2	Advertising of items for sale or wanted	53	News about what the local council is doing	68
3=	Comment on local issues	49	Readers' letters	57
	Pictures and reports of weddings and funerals	49	Advertising of items for sale or wanted	57
4	News about local sport	48	News about local business and industry	50

Rank order				
	45–64 (Sample: 456)	%	65 and over (Sample: 218)	%
1	Comment on local issues	80	News about what the local council is doing	79
2	News about what the local council is doing	77	Comment on local issues	75
3	Readers' letters	70	Readers' letters	70
4	Reports of local court cases	61	Pictures and reports of weddings and funerals	63
5	News about local business and industry	59	Reports of local court cases	61
			Announcements of births, deaths and marriages	61

The largest differences are between those under 25 and older people. In general the very young mentioned fewer of the seventeen items as ones they usually read than older people did. The only items they mentioned more frequently than people in general were news about local sport, articles about cars and motoring, the list of TV and radio programmes and advertising for jobs.

People over 65 were considerably more likely than average to say they looked at announcements of births, deaths and marriages and pictures and reports of weddings and funerals both in provincial evenings and in local weeklies.

There are comparable, although rather smaller, differences between the items read by those who work and those who do not and between people who do different sorts of job.

In Section 2 we showed that people expressed more interest in news about what is going on in their own parts of the country than in any other sort of news and that this interest was widespread among most sections of the community. We also showed that the regional and local press is seen as the main source of such news. What we have shown above is that news about what is going on in one part of the country is not one category of news. It splits into a wide variety of sub-categories, many of which are of varying degrees of interest to different sorts of people. Provincial evenings and local weeklies are seen primarily as sources of regional and local news but, even as such, they are providing different sorts of regional and local news for a variety of different interest groups.

Differences by Circulation and by Ownership

Compared to the differences between the sorts of item different groups in the population read in provincial evening and local weekly newspapers, any differences between what is read in provincial evenings of different size or between what is read in provincial evenings or local weeklies of different ownership are relatively minor.

There were some items which were more frequently mentioned as usually read in small-circulation evenings than in large-circulation evenings. The items for which this difference was appreciable were all items of specifically local interest and all items which, generally, were more frequently read in local weeklies than in provincial evenings. They were:

TABLE 1.057
ITEMS READ IN PROVINCIAL EVENINGS BY CIRCULATION

	Circulation			
	Up to 40,000	40,000–100,000	100,000–200,000	Over 200,000
Sample	168 %	299 %	376 %	277 %
Always make a point of looking at/usually look at				
pictures and reports of weddings and funerals	51	50	38	21
announcements of births, deaths and marriages	52	42	39	26
comment on local issues	69	66	61	48
reports of local court cases	49	46	43	34
news about what the local council is doing	67	68	58	53
advertising of items for sale or wanted ...	56	53	48	42

The only items more commonly mentioned as usually read in the large-circulation evenings by any appreciable margin were the list of television and radio programmes and the two categories of general and political news.

One can conclude that the smaller-circulation provincial evenings are closer than the large ones to local weeklies, either in their character or in the way their readers use them.

There were only very small differences between what people said they usually read in provincial evenings and local weeklies owned by groups with national newspaper interests and what people said they usually read in local newspapers of different ownerhip. These differences did not appear to follow any consistent or meaningful pattern.

4. Attitudes to Newspapers

SUMMARY

General Attitudes to Newspapers

Regular and occasional readers of national and regional morning newspapers, of provincial evenings and of local weeklies were asked to say how true or otherwise each of a list of seventeen statements was of each of the particular newspapers they read.

People were questioned only about those newspapers they read regularly or occasionally. The comparisons below are, therefore, comparisons of the views of readers of different newspapers or types of newspapers on the newspapers they read, rather than a comparison of the views of the general public on all newspapers.

One group of statements, which can be broadly described as referring to depth of news coverage was:

— The comments it makes on the news are usually interesting.
— It helps me understand how what is happening in the country will affect me.
— Its standard of reporting is first class.

All the national mornings were favourably rated by their readers on all three of these points, but with quite large differences between titles. The quality national mornings tended to be more favourably rated than the popular national mornings, with the *Daily Express* and the *Daily Mail* coming in between.

Views on the standard of reporting of the regional mornings among their readers were very similar to views on the *Daily Express* and *Daily Mail* among their readers. Views on how interesting their comments are and on the degree to which they help people understand how they will be affected by what is happening in the country were similar to those on the popular mornings.

Provincial evenings were seen less favourably by their readers than regional mornings on all these points, with the small provincial evenings viewed less favourably than the larger ones.

Local weeklies were rated less favourably by their readers on all these points than provincial evenings.

Another group of statements refers to the contents of newspapers. They were:
— It always has the latest national news.
— It has too little news in it.
— It has too much advertising in it.

Considerable majorities of readers said of all the national mornings that they always had the latest national news. Only minorities thought they had too little news in them or too much advertising. Again, however, answers varied with title, the answers on the quality nationals being more favourable than those on the popular nationals.

Regional mornings were less likely than the popular national mornings to be seen as having too little news in them, but were also less likely to be seen as always having the latest national news. Answers on the amount of advertising they contained were similar to those on the popular nationals.

Compared with the regional mornings and all the national mornings except *The Sun*, provincial evenings and local weeklies were more widely seen as having too little news in them. Provincial evenings were also less likely than morning newspapers, whether national or regional, to be seen as having the latest national news. Both provincial evenings and local weeklies were described much more widely than national mornings as having too much advertising in them. This applied particularly to provincial evenings and, among these, particularly to the larger ones. 50% of readers of provincial evenings said it was very or fairly true that they contained too much advertising.

A further group of statements refers to criticisms which are sometimes made of the popular press. They were:
— It exaggerates the sensational aspects of the news.
— It sometimes goes too far in invading people's grief.
— It prints too many silly or trivial stories.
— It always concentrates on the bad news.
— It often gets its facts wrong.

Here again, answers on the national morning newspapers varied by title according to the usual quality-intermediate-popular classification.

Answers on the provincial press all fell within the range of answers on different national morning newspapers. Regional mornings and local weeklies were seen as about as likely to exaggerate sensational aspects of the news or to invade private grief as *The Daily Telegraph*, one of the quality national mornings, and for getting facts wrong, answers on the regional mornings were virtually the same as those on *The Daily Telegraph*. Local weeklies were thought somewhat more likely to get their facts wrong and both regional mornings and local weeklies were seen as printing too many silly or trivial stories about as frequently as the *Daily Express*.

The provincial evenings were not seen as any more likely to print silly or trivial stories than the rest of the regional and local press. They were, however, seen as more likely than the rest of the regional and local press to exaggerate sensational aspects of the news and to invade private grief, although not to the same degree as the popular national mornings. Also, the provincial evenings were more widely seen as often getting their facts wrong than the rest of the provincial press. On this point, answers on the provincial evenings were similar to those on the popular national mornings.

On the statement "Reading it is always enjoyable" there was little difference between answers on the intermediate and popular national mornings and answers on the regional and local press. Somewhat over two in five readers said it was very true that they always found reading their newspapers enjoyable. People were more likely, however, to say that they would miss regional mornings and provincial evenings a lot if they stopped being published than they were to say this of the intermediate or popular mornings or of local weeklies.

Few people thought any newspapers were afraid of offending their advertisers. Answers on this point for regional mornings and local weeklies were similar to those on national mornings. Provincial evenings were somewhat more widely seen as afraid of offending their advertisers, but still by only a minority of their readers.

The national mornings—particularly the *Daily Mirror*—were all widely seen as willing to criticise anyone if they deserve it. Fewer readers said this was very true of regional mornings, the provincial evenings or the local weeklies.

Political and Industrial Sympathies

The majority of the readers of *The Daily Telegraph*, the *Daily Mail* and the *Daily Express* saw them as supporting the Conservative Party. The majority of the readers of the *Daily Mirror* saw it as supporting the Labour Party. *The Sun* was less associated with party partisanship. 57% of its readers saw it as not supporting any one party.

Regional mornings were less strongly associated with party partisanship than most of the national mornings. 60% of readers of regional mornings said they supported no one party. The provincial evenings and local weeklies were seen as partisan even less frequently. Three in four readers of provincial evenings and four in five readers of local weeklies said they supported no one political party. Among the minority who said the regional and provincial papers they read supported one party, two in three said they supported the Conservative Party. Among provincial evenings, perceived party support varied little with the size of the newspaper or its ownership.

Asked about the space given to the employers' case and the unions' case when the two disagree, considerable majorities of readers said of both national and regional mornings that they report both sides of things fully. National mornings were, however, twice as likely as regional mornings to be seen as partial in their coverage of such disputes.

Fewer people thought provincial evenings reported both sides of things fully in employer-union disputes than thought this of regional mornings. This was not because they thought provincial evenings were more likely to be partial in their reporting. It was because they thought provincial evenings were more likely than regional mornings not to print much about it at all. This applied even more strongly to local weeklies. Two in five readers of local weeklies said that when employers and unions disagree, local weekly papers do not print much about it at all.

The larger provincial evenings were more likely than the smaller to be seen as reporting both sides of industrial disputes fully. There was no great difference by ownership in views on the reporting of industrial disputes by provincial evenings.

Local Groups and Issues

Considerable majorities of readers of regional and local newspapers could not mention any particular groups to whose views the papers they read paid too much or too little attention when reporting on controversial local issues. Readers of provincial evenings were, however, rather more ready to say that they pay too little attention to the views of some people than were readers of regional mornings or local weeklies. The groups whose views were most commonly mentioned as disregarded by provincial evenings were young people and people in the lower income groups. These were also the groups whose views were most commonly mentioned as disregarded in regional mornings and local weeklies.

Respondents were asked to say what was the most important issue or problem facing their district and readers of regional and local newspapers who identified a main problem were asked how much attention they thought their newspapers gave to it. Most said of regional mornings, provincial evenings and local weeklies that they gave at least some attention to the problem. Most also said, however, that they should give more.

MAIN FINDINGS

The Questions Asked

A main purpose of the study was to examine people's attitudes to the regional and local press and to set these in the context of their attitudes to the national morning press. This part of the report discusses a series of questions designed to do this.

It was thought important that the examination should be carried out on the basis of attitudes to specific newspapers rather than on the basis of generalised attitudes to categories of newspaper. It was also thought important that it should be carried out on the basis of informed attitudes—that people should not be asked about newspapers they had rarely, if ever, seen. Accordingly, the questions were asked of each regional or local daily newspaper of which respondents said they usually saw one or more issues a week and of each local weekly newspaper of which they said they saw one or more issues a month. The London evening newspapers have, it was felt, a rather special character. They are substantially different from most provincial evening newspapers. Since the sample of readers of London evening newspapers which would be obtained in this study would have been rather small for separate analysis, they were not covered in this section of the questionnaire.

To provide a basis for comparison, respondents were also asked most of the questions about national morning newspapers of which they read one or more issues in an average week. In order that the questionnaire should not become unduly repetitive, when people said they read several national morning newspapers, one only of these was selected for coverage by a random procedure.

It is important to stress that the views discussed in this section are the views of people who usually see one or more issues per week, or four weeklies per month, of the newspapers they are talking about. It seems fair to assume that reading a particular newspaper usually implies that it has some use or interest for the reader. It is very possible that more hostile views on some particular newspapers might have been expressed by people who do not read them but feel themselves qualified to judge them.

This section of the report is divided into three sub-sections:

Sub-Section 1 *General Attitudes to Newspapers* compares the national, regional and local press on a number of points, mainly related to editorial approach and treatment of news.

Sub-Section 2 *Political and Industrial Sympathies* examines how people perceive the national, regional and local press's treatment of political parties and of industrial disputes.

Sub-Section 3 *Local Groups and Issues* examines how people perceive the regional and local press's treatment of local groups and local issues.

Sub-Section 1   General Attitudes to Newspapers

Those questioned about individual newspapers were taken through a list of seventeen statements and asked to say how true each statement was of each newspaper about which they were asked. They answered by choosing one of a list of four answers shown them on a card:

Very true
Fairly true
Not very true
Not at all true

In the discussion below, it will be useful to summarise answers on particular statements as mean scores. This can be done by assigning a "score" to each of the possible answers, summing the scores of the answers given and averaging them on a base of all those giving an answer. The scoring system used below is:

Very true	+3
Fairly true	+1
Not very true	−1
Not at all true	−3
Don't know	0

There is thus a possible spread of mean scores from +3 (everyone answering said the statement was "very true") to −3 (everyone answering said the statement was "not at all true").

On the basis of the answers given, the statements can be classified into three groups.

For eleven of the seventeen statements, mean scores for particular national morning newspapers fell into an order which closely matched the conventional quality-popular classification of national mornings:

Quality	*The Times*
	Financial Times
	The Guardian
	The Daily Telegraph
Intermediate	*Daily Mail*
	Daily Express
Popular	*Daily Mirror/Record*
	The Sun

This group of eleven statements can be split on the basis of the relationship between answers on national newspapers and answers on provincial evenings and local weeklies. This gives the three groups:

Group A Mean scores for national morning newspapers on this group of six statements follow the quality-popular classification and the mean scores for provincial evenings and local weeklies fall outside the range of scores for national mornings.

Group B Mean scores for national morning newspapers on this group of five statements again follow the quality-popular classification but mean scores for provincial evenings and local weeklies fall within the range of scores for national mornings.

Group C For this group of six statements mean scores for national mornings do not follow the quality-popular classification in any clear-cut way. Answers on these will need individual discussion.

Group A Statements

The six statements for which mean scores for national mornings followed the quality-popular dimension and which distinguished between all national dailies on the one hand and provincial evenings and local weeklies on the other referred to two themes—depth of news coverage and content.

(i) *Depth of Coverage*

The three statements referring to depth of news coverage were:

— The comments it makes on the news are usually interesting.
— It helps me understand how what is happening in the country will affect me.
— Its standard of reporting is first class.

Answers given on these three statements for the three different types of regional and local newspaper were:

TABLE 1.058
OPINIONS ON DEPTH OF NEWS COVERAGE IN THE REGIONAL AND LOCAL PRESS

	Regional Mornings	Provincial Evenings	Local Weeklies
Sample: All newspapers read regularly or occasionally	273	1,096	1,369
	%	%	%
The comments it makes on the news are usually interesting			
Very true	35	28	23
Fairly true	57	59	57
Not very true	5	8	13
Not at all true	*	2	4
Don't know	3	3	3
Mean score	+1·6	+1·3	+1·0
It helps me to understand how what is happening in the country will affect me			
Very true	21	16	8
Fairly true	56	50	25
Not very true	12	22	26
Not at all true	6	11	39
Don't know	4	2	2
Mean score	+0·9	+0·5	−1·0
Its standard of reporting is first class			
Very true	38	24	18
Fairly true	44	49	52
Not very true	12	15	20
Not at all true	2	6	5
Don't know	5	6	6
Mean score	+1·5	+0·9	+0·7

Summarised, the comparison of answers on the regional and local press with answers on the national daily press is:

TABLE 1.059
OPINIONS ON DEPTH OF NEWS COVERAGE IN NATIONAL AND LOCAL NEWSPAPERS

	Sample	Comments usually interesting		Helps me understand how what is happening will affect me		First class standard of reporting	
		Very true	Mean score	Very true	Mean score	Very true	Mean score
The Times/F.T./ The Guardian	133	59%	+2·1	53%	+1·9	65%	+2·3
The D. Telegraph	183	51%	+2·0	46%	+1·7	48%	+1·8
D. Mail	233	47%	+1·8	36%	+1·3	37%	+1·6
D. Express	354	44%	+1·7	27%	+1·1	38%	+1·5
D. Mirror/Record	591	39%	+1·6	32%	+1·3	33%	+1·3
The Sun	472	35%	+1·6	29%	+1·0	31%	+1·1
Reg. mornings	273	35%	+1·6	21%	+0·9	38%	+1·5
Prov. evenings	1,096	28%	+1·3	16%	+0·5	24%	+0·9
Local weeklies	1,369	23%	+1·0	8%	−1·0	18%	+0·7

It is generally thought fairly true that provincial evenings and, to a slightly lesser extent, local weeklies usually make interesting comment on the news. Provincial mornings are, however, somewhat more favourably judged for their comment—about as favourably as the popular national mornings. Opinions of the comment on news in intermediate and quality national mornings are even more favourable.

Local weeklies are definitely not seen as helping people to understand how what is going on in the country will affect them. The provincial evenings are more commonly seen as helpful in this respect, although not as much as regional mornings.

Regional mornings are, however, somewhat less favourably rated in this respect than most national mornings.

Fewer than one in five thought it very true that the standard of reporting in their local weekly newspapers was first class. One in four thought this of provincial evening newspapers. More than one in three of those questioned about regional mornings thought it very true that their standard of reporting was first class. Views on the standard of reporting in regional mornings were similar to those on reporting in the intermediate national mornings. They were more favourable than views on the reporting in the popular national mornings.

Views on provincial evenings varied with their size. Large-circulation evenings tended to be more favourably viewed than small-circulation evenings on all three points discussed in this section. The largest-circulation evenings were almost as favourable rated as regional mornings for the interest of their comment and for helping people understand how they will be affected by what is happening in the country.

Views on provincial evenings, split by circulation were:

TABLE 1.060
OPINIONS ON DEPTH OF NEWS COVERAGE IN PROVINCIAL EVENINGS BY CIRCULATION

Circulation	Sample	Comments usually interesting		Helps me understand how what is happening will affect me		First class standard of reporting	
		Very true	Mean score	Very true	Mean score	Very true	Mean score
Up to 40,000 ...	168	22%	+1·1	14%	+0·1	16%	+0·5
Over 40,000–100,000	299	29%	+1·4	15%	+0·4	22%	+0·8
Over 100,000–200,000	376	29%	+1·4	18%	+0·5	25%	+1·1
Over 200,000 ...	227	34%	+1·5	18%	+0·8	30%	+1·1

Note: Excludes 26 respondents answering on provincial evenings whose circulation was not established.

There was no notable difference between evenings owned by groups with national newspaper interests and other evening newspapers in ratings for the interest of their comments and for whether they help people understand how they will be affected by what is going on. The evenings owned by national groups were, however, less favourably rated for the standard of their reporting. The comparison was:

TABLE 1.061
OPINIONS ON REPORTING STANDARD OF PROVINCIAL EVENINGS BY OWNERSHIP

		First class standard of reporting	
Ownership	Sample	Very true	Mean score
Owned by a group which controls national newspapers	492	20%	+0.7
Others	604	27%	+1.1

The ownership of local weekly newspapers did not appear to have any relation to how they were rated on the three points discussed in this section.

(ii) *Content*

The three statements referring to content which produced broadly similar patterns of answers were:
— It always has the latest national news.
— It has too little news in it.
— It has too much advertising in it.

In summary, answers on these three statements for national morning newspapers and for the three types of regional and local newspapers were:

TABLE 1.062
OPINIONS ON CONTENT OF NATIONAL AND LOCAL NEWSPAPERS

	Sample	It always has the latest national news		It has too little news in it		It has too much advertising in it	
		Very true	Mean score	Very/ fairly true	Mean score	Very/ fairly true	Mean score
The Times/ Financial Times/The Guardian ...	133	71%	+2.3	7%	−2.2	6%	−1.9
The Daily Telegraph ...	183	76%	+2.5	3%	−2.2	14%	−1.4
Daily Mail ...	233	69%	+2.3	13%	−1.7	21%	−1.3
Daily Express ...	354	69%	+2.3	16%	−1.5	25%	−0.9
Daily Mirror/ Record ...	591	60%	+2.1	29%	−0.9	29%	−0.7
The Sun ...	472	56%	+1.8	35%	−0.7	28%	−0.8
Regional mornings ...	273	47%	+1.4	22%	−1.1	28%	−0.7
Provincial evenings ...	1,096	35%	+1.0	38%	−0.5	50%	+0.2
Local weeklies ...	1,369	6%	−1.5	37%	−0.5	39%	−0.3

As one might expect, regional and local newspapers are seen as less likely to have the latest national news than the national mornings. Regional mornings and provincial evenings are, however, quite favourably rated on this point. Almost half those questioned on them thought it very true that they always had the latest national news. Just over one in three thought this of provincial evenings.

It might have happened that respondents treated the two statements "It has too little news in it" and "It has too much advertising in it" as equivalent. In fact, they did not. The pattern of answers which emerges is quite a complex one.

For all the newspapers and types of newspaper covered, the balance of opinion is against the view that they have too little news in them. People were, however, more likely to say this of provincial evenings and local weeklies than of any of the rest. No distinction appears on this point between provincial evenings and local weeklies.

When they were asked about the statement "It has too much advertising in it", however, there was a quite clear distinction between answers on provincial evenings and local weeklies. Half those questioned said this was true of provincial evenings. Less than two in five said it was true of local weeklies. It was more common, however, for people to say this of provincial evenings and local weeklies than it was for them to say it of any other sorts of newspapers.

Regional mornings were rated quite favourably for their news content. Less than one in four thought they had too little news in them. Views on local mornings were, in this respect, more favourable than views on popular national mornings. On the point of advertising content, however, answers on provincial mornings were very similar to those on the popular national mornings. They were more likely to be seen as having too much advertising in them than the quality or intermediate national mornings.

An analysis by circulation shows that the largest provincial evenings are more likely than the rest to be seen as having too much advertising in them and the smallest are more likely than the rest to be seen as carrying too little news. The comparison was:

TABLE 1.063

OPINIONS ON NEWS AND ADVERTISING CONTENT OF PROVINCIAL EVENINGS BY CIRCULATION

Circulation	Sample	It has too much advertising in it		It has too little news in it	
		Very/quite true	Mean score	Very/quite true	Mean score
Up to 40,000	168	50%	+0·2	47%	−0·1
40,000 but under 100,000	299	47%	0	36%	−0·5
100,000 but under 200,000	376	48%	0	37%	−0·5
200,000 or over	227	59%	+0·6	38%	−0·5

There was no notable difference between provincial evenings or between local weeklies owned by different groups in answers on any of the three statements discussed above.

Group B Statements

This group of five statements all relate to criticisms which have been made of the approach to news or to the coverage of news by the press. All the criticisms were generally seen by respondents as more applicable to the popular national morning press than to the quality national morning press, with the regional and local press falling somewhere between the two.

The five statements were:
— It exaggerates the sensational aspects of the news.
— It sometimes goes too far in invading people's grief.
— It prints too many silly or trivial stories.
— It always concentrates on the bad news.
— It often gets its facts wrong.

Summarised answers on these statements for the national morning newspapers and for the three categories of regional and local newspaper were:

TABLE 1.064
OPINIONS ON APPROACH TO NEWS OF NATIONAL AND LOCAL NEWSPAPERS

Very or fairly true		Exaggerates sensational aspects	Invades private grief	Silly or trivial stories	Concentrates on the bad news	Gets its facts wrong
The Times/F.T./The Guardian	%	5	7	3	9	3
The Daily Telegraph	%	21	21	2	15	15
Daily Mail	%	46	27	18	23	16
Daily Express	%	48	39	22	29	25
Daily Mirror/Record	%	63	45	43	38	31
The Sun	%	62	46	45	35	33
Regional mornings	%	20	16	20	21	15
Local weeklies	%	19	16	21	17	23
Provincial evenings	%	36	24	26	32	33
Mean score						
The Times/F.T./The Guardian		−2·1	−2·0	−2·4	−1·6	−2·0
The Daily Telegraph		−1·2	−1·3	−2·1	−1·3	−1·1
Daily Mail		−0·2	−0·7	−1·4	−0·8	−1·1
Daily Express		0	−0·3	−1·1	−0·7	−0·7
Daily Mirror/Record		+0·6	+0·1	−0·3	−0·3	−0·3
The Sun		+0·7	0	−0·1	−0·4	−0·4
Regional mornings		−1·1	−1·2	−1·2	−1·0	−1·1
Local weeklies		−1·3	−1·3	−1·1	−1·2	−0·8
Provincial evenings		−0·5	−1·0	−0·9	−0·6	−0·4

Note: Bases as in Table 1.062

The only majority criticism was that the popular national mornings exaggerate the sensational aspects of the news. Between 40% and 50% of those answering thought that the intermediate national mornings also exaggerate the sensational aspects of the news and between 40% and 50% of those answering thought the popular national mornings sometimes go too far in invading people's grief and print too many silly or trivial stories.

The level of criticism of the regional mornings was approximately equivalent to the level of criticism of *The Daily Telegraph* for sensationalism, invading private grief and getting its facts wrong and approximately equivalent to the level of criticism of the *Daily Mail* for printing silly or trivial stories and concentrating on the bad news.

Answers on local weeklies were very similar to those on regional mornings with the exception that local weeklies were thought more likely to get their facts wrong.

Provincial evenings were more widely criticised on all five points than either regional mornings or local weeklies. Even so, the level of criticism on most points was in general considerably lower than the level of criticism of the popular national mornings. The only exception to this was on the newspapers' tendencies to get their facts wrong. On this point, answers on provincial evenings were very similar to those on the popular national mornings. Both these types of newspaper were more heavily criticised for getting their facts wrong than any other newspapers.

There were some differences between answers on provincial evenings of different size, but these differences did not form a clear or consistent pattern. The smallest evenings were less likely than average to be seen as sometimes invading private grief. They were, on the other hand, more likely than average to be seen as often getting their facts wrong. The large evenings were more likely than the small ones to be seen as always concentrating on the bad news. The comparison between answers on newspapers of different sizes was:

TABLE 1.065
OPINIONS ON APPROACH TO NEWS OF PROVINCIAL EVENINGS BY CIRCULATION

Very or fairly true	Exaggerates sensational aspects	Invades private grief	Silly or trivial stories	Concentrates on the bad news	Gets its facts wrong
Circulation	%				
Up to 40,000	34	16	28	24	41
40,000–100,000	39	24	29	29	33
100,000–200,000	35	25	22	33	30
Over 200,000	40	28	31	39	35
Mean score					
Circulation					
Up to 40,000	−0.7	−1.3	−0.8	−0.9	0
40,000–100,000	−0.3	−0.8	−0.9	−0.6	−0.4
100,000–200,000	−0.5	−1.0	−1.0	−0.6	−0.5
Over 200,000	−0.3	−0.8	−0.7	−0.4	−0.4

Note: Bases as in Table 1.063

There are no notable differences by ownership either for provincial evening or for local weekly newspapers.

Group C Statements

On these six statements, answers on national mornings did not follow the conventional quality-intermediate-popular classification as closely as answers on the statements discussed above. The six statements can be conveniently divided into three groups as follows:

(i) *interest in ordinary people's problems*
— It takes an interest in ordinary people's problems.

(ii) *attachment to newspapers*
— Reading it is always enjoyable.
— I would miss it a lot if it stopped being published.

(iii) *objectivity and willingness to criticise*
— It gives fair coverage to all points of view.
— It is afraid of offending its advertisers.
— It is prepared to criticise *anybody* if they deserve it.

(i) *Interest in Ordinary People's Problems*

The quality national mornings were seen as less likely than other newspapers to take an interest in ordinary people's problems. The *Daily Mirror* was more widely seen as taking an interest in ordinary people's problems than any other newspaper. Apart from this, there were no very notable differences. The comparison was:

TABLE 1.066
OPINIONS ON INTEREST IN ORDINARY PEOPLE'S PROBLEMS OF NATIONAL AND LOCAL NEWSPAPERS

	It takes an interest in ordinary people's problems		
	Sample	Very true	Mean score
The Times/Financial Times/The Guardian	133	7%	−0.2
The Daily Telegraph	183	9%	+0.4
Daily Mail	233	32%	+1.2
Daily Express	354	29%	+1.1
Daily Mirror/Record	591	41%	+1.5
The Sun	472	30%	+1.2
Regional mornings	273	27%	+1.2
Provincial evenings	1,096	33%	+1.4
Local weeklies	1,369	25%	+1.4

There were no notable differences in answers on this statement between provincial evenings of different size or between provincial evenings or local weeklies of different ownership.

(ii) *Attachment to Newspapers*

The two statements under this head, "Reading it is always enjoyable" and

"I would miss it a lot if it stopped being published" might have been taken by respondents as equivalent. In fact, they were not. The pattern of answers on the two statements is similar, but there are important differences. How much people enjoy newspapers and how much they would miss them if they stopped being published are not quite the same thing. Summarised answers on the two statements and the differences between these answers are:

TABLE 1.067
ATTACHMENT TO NATIONAL AND LOCAL NEWSPAPERS

	Very true			Very or fairly true		
	Always enjoyable	Would miss it a lot	Difference	Always enjoyable	Would miss it a lot	Difference
The Times/F.T./The Guardian	44%	48%	+4%	83%	78%	−5%
The Daily Telegraph	55%	57%	+2%	93%	73%	−20%
Daily Mail	42%	37%	−5%	92%	59%	−33%
Daily Express	48%	42%	−6%	90%	61%	−29%
Daily Mirror/Record	45%	44%	−1%	87%	64%	−23%
The Sun	43%	38%	−5%	87%	56%	−31%
Regional mornings	43%	54%	+11%	90%	76%	−14%
Provincial evenings	42%	47%	+5%	86%	72%	−14%
Local weeklies	41%	41%	—	86%	68%	−18%

	Mean score		
	Always enjoyable	Would miss it a lot	Difference
The Times/FT/The Guardian	+1.5	+1.4	−0.1
The Daily Telegraph	+1.9	+1.4	−0.5
Daily Mail	+1.7	+0.6	−1.1
Daily Express	+1.8	+0.8	−1.0
Daily Mirror/Record	+1.7	+0.9	−0.8
The Sun	+1.6	+0.4	−1.2
Regional mornings	+1.7	+1.5	−0.2
Provincial evenings	+1.5	+1.1	−0.4
Local weeklies	+1.5	+0.9	−0.6

Note: Bases as on Table 1.066

Almost everyone says it is very or fairly true that they enjoy the newspapers they read. Rather fewer agree that they would miss them a lot if they stopped being published.

The stated level of enjoyment does not vary greatly. It is somewhat lower for *The Times*, the *Financial Times* and *The Guardian* and for provincial evenings and local weeklies than it is for most other newspapers. The newspapers fewest readers say they would miss a lot, however, are the intermediate and popular national dailies.

More people think it very true that they would miss the quality national mornings, the regional mornings and the provincial evenings a lot than say it is very true that reading them is always enjoyable. The reverse is the case for the intermediate and popular national mornings. For local weeklies, the numbers with strongly favourable views on the two statements are the same. A similar pattern emerges if one looks at the numbers who say the statements are very or fairly true and at the mean scores.

Two explanations seem possible. One is that the quality national mornings and the regional and local press are seen by their readers as offering something they want other than enjoyment—perhaps a particular sort of news or a distinctive interpretation of news. The other is that readers of these newspapers might find it more difficult to find an acceptable alternative if they ceased publication—perhaps because of style and content for the quality national mornings, perhaps because there are no other newspapers with the same geographical coverage in the case of the regional and local press.

There was no notable difference either by ownership or by size in people's stated level of enjoyment of provincial evening or local weekly newspapers. Nor was there any difference by ownership in the degree to which people said they would miss local weeklies. On this point, however, there was some difference between provincial evening newspapers, both by ownership and circulation. Those talking about the provincial evenings owned by groups which also control national morning newspapers and those talking about the smaller-circulation provincial evenings were somewhat less likely than average to say they would miss them a lot if they stopped being published. The comparison was:

TABLE 1.068

ATTACHMENT TO PROVINCIAL EVENINGS BY CIRCULATION AND OWNERSHIP

	Sample	Would miss it a lot if it stopped being published	
		Very true	Very or fairly true
Ownership:			
Owned by a group which controls national newspapers	492	45%	67%
Others	604	49%	74%
Circulation:			
Up to 40,000	168	42%	67%
40,000–100,000	299	40%	69%
100,000–200,000	376	50%	77%
Over 200,000	227	52%	74%

(iii) *Objectivity and Willingness to Criticise*

Of all the seventeen statements used, the statement "It gives fair coverage to all points of view" produced the smallest differences between different newspapers and different types of newspaper. In summary the comparison of answers on this statement was:

TABLE 1.069

OPINIONS ON FAIRNESS OF COVERAGE OF POINTS OF VIEW OF NATIONAL AND LOCAL NEWSPAPERS

	Sample	Very true	Mean score
It gives fair coverage to all points of view			
The Times/Financial Times/The Guardian	133	32%	+1·3
The Daily Telegraph	183	32%	+1·2
Daily Mail	233	41%	+1·5
Daily Express	354	32%	+1·3
Daily Mirror/Record	591	32%	+1·1
The Sun	472	32%	+1·2
Regional mornings	273	35%	+1·5
Provincial evenings	1,096	35%	+1·3
Local weeklies	1,369	29%	+1·3

Among the national mornings, the one most widely thought to give fair coverage to all points of view was the *Daily Mail*; it is not clear why this should be so.

There were no notable differences by ownership between provincial evenings or local weeklies in answers on this statement. Nor was there any notable difference between provincial evenings by size of circulation.

On all newspapers, the balance of opinion was that they are not afraid of offending their advertisers. There were, however, more people who refused an answer on this statement than there were on any of the other statements. An appreciable minority were unwilling to make a judgement one way or the other.

In summary, answers and numbers refusing an answer were:

TABLE 1.070

OPINIONS ON FEAR OF ADVERTISERS AMONG NATIONAL AND LOCAL NEWSPAPERS

	Sample	Very or fairly true	Mean score	Question not answered
It is afraid of offending its advertisers				
The Times/Financial Times/The Guardian	133	13%	−1·5	11%
The Daily Telegraph	183	11%	−1·4	25%
Daily Mail	233	24%	−0·8	21%
Daily Express	354	15%	−1·1	25%
Daily Mirror/Record	591	16%	−1·2	21%
The Sun	472	17%	−1·0	24%
Regional mornings	273	16%	−1·1	28%
Provincial evenings	1,096	25%	−0·6	25%
Local weeklies	1,369	19%	−1·0	23%

The newspapers least widely seen as afraid of offending their advertisers were the quality national mornings. The newspapers most widely so seen among readers were the provincial evenings, which, as we have seen above, were also the only group of newspapers for which the balance of opinion was that they have too much advertising in them.

Among the national mornings the one most likely to be seen as afraid of offending its advertisers was the *Daily Mail*. There was no notable difference between answers given by people talking about provincial evenings or local weekly newspapers of different ownership or between answers given by people talking about local weekly newspapers of different size.

For all newspapers, most people said it was very or fairly true that they are willing to criticise anyone if they deserve it. Among the national morning newspapers, willingness to criticise anyone was associated rather less with *The Daily Telegraph* than with any other newspaper. Only just over one in three of those questioned about it said it was very true that it was willing to criticise anyone if they deserve it.

For the other newspapers the numbers saying this ranged from 43% to 52%.

Regional mornings, provincial evenings and, particularly, local weeklies were less associated with criticism of anyone who deserves it than any of the national mornings.

Summarised answers on this question were:

TABLE 1.071
OPINIONS ON READINESS OF NATIONAL AND LOCAL NEWSPAPERS TO CRITICISE THOSE WHO DESERVE IT

	Sample	Very true	Mean score
It is prepared to criticise anyone if they deserve it			
The Times/Financial Times/The Guardian	133	43%	+1·8
The Daily Telegraph	183	37%	+1·3
Daily Mail	233	49%	+1·7
Daily Express	354	44%	+1·7
Daily Mirror/Record	591	52%	+1·8
The Sun	472	45%	+1·7
Regional mornings	273	32%	+1·3
Provincial evenings	1,096	29%	+1·1
Local weeklies	1,369	25%	+0·8

This time there was a difference between provincial evenings of different ownership. Those owned by groups with national newspaper interests were less associated with willingness to criticise than those owned by others. There was also some difference between provincial evenings by circulation size. The largest were somewhat more widely seen as ready to criticise than the rest. The comparison of answers for provincial evening newspapers of different ownership and size was:

TABLE 1.072
OPINIONS ON READINESS OF PROVINCIAL EVENINGS TO CRITICISE THOSE WHO DESERVE IT BY OWNERSHIP AND CIRCULATION

	Sample	Very True	Mean Score
It is prepared to criticise anybody if they deserve it:			
Evening Newspaper Ownership:			
All groups with national newspaper interests	492	24%	+0·8
All other	604	34%	+1·3
Evening Newspaper Circulation:			
Up to 40,000	168	27%	+0·9
40,000–100,000	299	28%	+0·9
100,000–200,000	376	27%	+1·0
Over 200,000	227	35%	+1·4

There was no notable difference between answers on weekly newspapers of different ownership.

Sub-Section 2 Political and Industrial Sympathies
Political Parties

Those questioned about particular newspapers were asked whether they would say that the newspaper generally supported any one political party. If they said it did, they were asked which party it generally supported.

Aggregated by type of newspaper, answers on party support were:

TABLE 1.073
OPINIONS ON PARTIES SUPPORTED BY DIFFERENT TYPES OF NEWSPAPER

	National Morning Newspapers	Regional Morning Newspapers	Provincial Evening Newspapers	Local Weekly Newspapers
Sample	1,976	273	1,096	1,369
	%	%	%	%
Supports one party–	58	37	22	17
namely: Conservative	31	25	16	11
Labour	25	9	5	5
Liberal	1	2	1	*
Other	*	2	*	*
Does not support any one party	39	60	75	81
Don't know	3	3	3	2

Most of those questioned about national mornings saw them as supporting particular political parties. Substantial majorities of those reading regional and local newspapers saw them as not supporting any one political party. This varied with type of newspaper. Three in five of those asked about regional mornings said they did not support any one political party. Four in five of those questioned about local weeklies said this of them.

Where provincial newspapers were seen as supporting a political party, it was generally the Conservative Party. More than two-thirds of identifications of provincial newspapers with parties were identifications with the Conservative Party.

The situation with regard to national morning newspapers only becomes clear when they are split by title. This gives:

TABLE 1.074
OPINIONS ON PARTIES SUPPORTED BY PARTICULAR NATIONAL NEWSPAPERS

	The Times/ Financial Times/ The Guardian	The Daily Telegraph	Daily Mail	Daily Express	Daily Mirror/ Record	The Sun
Sample	133	183	233	354	591	472
	%	%	%	%	%	%
Supports one party–	49	81	63	66	65	37
namely: Conservative	35	80	58	62	5	9
Labour	5	1	5	3	59	23
Liberal	7	—	1	1	*	1
Other	1	—	—	—	*	*
Does not support any one party	50	16	35	33	33	57
Don't know	1	3	2	1	2	6

The newspaper most widely identified with a political party was *The Daily Telegraph*; that least widely identified with a political party was, by a large margin, *The Sun*. The number identifying *The Sun* with one particular political party was the same as that for regional mornings—still substantially higher than the numbers so identifying provincial evenings or local weeklies.

There was something approaching a balance in perception of party support among those questioned about national mornings. 31% thought the paper they read supported the Conservative Party, 25% that it supported the Labour Party. This overall result represents something approaching a balance in readership, however, rather than a balance in number of titles. The mass-circulation *Daily Mirror* was predominantly identified with the Labour Party. When it was identified with any particular party, the next largest circulation paper, *The Sun*, was generally identified with the Labour Party. *The Times*, *Financial Times*, *The Daily Telegraph*, *Daily Express* and *Daily Mail* were, when identified with a party, predominantly identified with the Conservative Party.

The readership of individual local papers is too small for separate analysis. Broken by ownership and circulation, however, perceived political identification varied little.

For provincial evening newspapers, the comparison was:

TABLE 1.075
OPINIONS ON PARTIES SUPPORTED BY PROVINCIAL EVENINGS BY OWNERSHIP AND CIRCULATION

		OWNERSHIP		CIRCULATION			
	All Provincial Evenings	All Owning Nationals	All Others	Up to 40,000	40,000–100,000	100,000–200,000	Over 200,000
Sample	1,096	492	604	168	299	376	227
	%	%	%	%	%	%	%
Supports one party—	22	21	23	23	21	20	24
namely: Conservative	16	15	16	18	13	15	16
Labour	5	5	6	5	7	5	6
Liberal	1	1	1	*	2	—	1
Other	*	—	*	—	—	—	*
Does not support any one party	75	77	74	76	77	76	74
Don't know	3	2	3	1	2	4	3

The picture is remarkably uniform. Even if one takes the figures for individual owners, where sample sizes are such that sampling error is high, no significant differences emerge. For the four largest evening newspaper groups, the comparison is:

TABLE 1.076
OPINIONS ON PARTIES SUPPORTED BY PROVINCIAL EVENINGS BY MAIN OWNERS

	Sample	Supports no one political party	Supports Conservative Party
Evening newspapers owned by:			
Westminster Press	103	75	19
Thomson	188	76	15
Associated Newspapers	182	79	14
United Newspapers	103	72	19

These figures refer, of course, to answers on a number of different newspapers aggregated together. It could be that there are individual provincial evening newspapers which are generally seen by their readers as committed to the views of one political party to the same extent as national morning newspapers. From the overall figures, however, it is clear that, if such provincial evenings exist at all, they are extremely few in number.

Broken by ownership, perceived political identification of local weekly newspapers was:

TABLE 1.077

OPINIONS ON PARTIES SUPPORTED BY LOCAL WEEKLIES BY OWNERSHIP

	All Local Weeklies	OWNERSHIP	
		All Owning Nationals	All Others
Sample	1,369	318	1,051
	%	%	%
Supports one party–	17	17	16
namely: Conservative	11	12	11
Labour	5	4	5
Liberal	*	1	*
Other	*	—	*
Does not support any one party	81	82	81
Don't know	2	2	2

There was no notable difference in perception of political support between weeklies belonging to groups with national newspaper interests and those with other ownership. There was only one newspaper group, the Westminster Press, about whose weeklies sufficient respondents were questioned for a reliable separate analysis to be made. 83% of readers of Westminster Press weeklies said they supported no one political party and 12% that they supported the Conservative Party, figures not significantly different from those for weeklies in general.

As with provincial evenings, there may be local weeklies which are perceived as identified with one political party as widely as most national mornings are. If such newspapers do exist, however, they are very few.

It can, of course, be argued that the perception of political identification in newspapers depends on the political identification of the respondent. We have shown already in Section 1, however, that for all practical purposes readers of provincial evenings and of local weeklies are, in their political views, a cross-section of the population. Perception of the political views of evening and weekly neswpapers, analysed by the political views of respondents, are:

TABLE 1.078

OPINIONS ON PARTIES SUPPORTED BY EVENINGS AND WEEKLIES BY POLITICAL VIEWS OF RESPONDENT

	PROVINCIAL EVENINGS Political view of respondent				LOCAL WEEKLIES Political view of respondent			
	Conservative	Liberal	Labour	No party	Conservative	Liberal	Labour	No party
Sample	389	113	404	153	504	174	420	216
	%	%	%	%	%	%	%	%
Supports one party–	22	24	22	17	15	18	17	15
namely: Conservative	13	19	17	12	9	13	12	12
Labour	7	4	6	4	6	3	6	4
Liberal	1	1	*	1	1	1	—	—
Other	—	—	*	—	1	—	*	—
Does not support any one party	77	71	75	76	83	80	79	81
Don't know	1	5	3	7	2	2	4	4

Only very small differences emerge. It seems fair to conclude that people's perceptions of the political views of the regional and local newspapers they read are largely independent of their own political views.

We can find differences in perception of the political views of regional and local newspapers only if we look at the small minorities of those questioned who describe themselves as very strongly Conservative or very strongly Labour. Here the comparison is:

TABLE 1.079

OPINIONS ON PARTIES SUPPORTED BY EVENINGS AND WEEKLIES AMONG VERY STRONG SUPPORTERS OF THE MAIN PARTIES

	PROVINCIAL EVENINGS Political view of respondent		LOCAL WEEKLIES Political view of respondent	
	Very strong Conservative	Very strong Labour	Very strong Conservative	Very strong Labour
Sample	137	120	179	122
	%	%	%	%
Supports one party–	21	30	14	27
namely: Conservative	12	22	6	17
Labour	8	8	8	11
Liberal	—	—	—	—
Other	—	—	1	—
Does not support any one party	78	69	84	71
Don't know	1	1	2	2

Very strong Labour supporters are more likely than very strong Conservatives to see provincial evenings and local weeklies as supporting the Conservative Party. Even among the very strong Labour supporters, however, a very considerable majority saw their provincial evenings and local weeklies as supporting no one particular political party.

So far, we have discussed people's perceptions of how newspapers favour particular political parties. We turn now to their perceptions of unfair coverage of particular political parties by newspapers. Those respondents who said that newspapers about which they were questioned supported one particular party were asked whether they thought the newspaper gave fair coverage to the views of other parties. If they said no, they were asked to name the other parties to which it did not give fair coverage.

When the questionnaire was designed, we assumed that people would answer questions on fairness of coverage of other parties in terms of the party they themselves supported. The actual survey results suggest that people's perceptions of unfair coverage are often more widely spread than we had expected. It was very common for people to see particular newspapers as being unfair to two or more other parties and as being unfair to parties which they themselves did not support. This suggests the possibility that the form of question used may have been too restricted. If it is possible for people to take the view that a newspaper is unfair in its coverage of several political parties, it may also be possible that some people could take the view that a newspaper does not support any one political party, keeps a balance between perhaps two or more, but is still unfair in its coverage of one. The form of the questions used did not allow for this answer. The figures on perception of unfair coverage quoted below should, therefore, be treated as minimum estimates.

Aggregated by type of newspaper, views on the fairness of the coverage newspapers gave to parties which they did not support were:

TABLE 1.080

OPINIONS ON UNFAIRNESS OF COVERAGE OF POLITICAL PARTIES BY TYPE OF NEWSPAPER

	National Morning Newspapers	Regional Morning Newspapers	Provincial Evening Newspapers	Local Weekly Newspapers
Sample	1,976	273	1,096	1,369
	%	%	%	%
Does not support any one party	39	60	75	81
Supports one party but gives fair coverage to the views of other parties	36	26	13	11
Supports one party and does not give fair coverage to the views of other parties—	25	11	9	6
namely: Conservative	11	3	2	2
Labour	10	6	5	3
Liberal	13	7	4	3
Other	1	3	1	2
Don't know	1	3	3	2

One in four of those questioned on national morning newspapers said there were political parties to whose views the paper on which they were answering did not give fair coverage. Only one in ten said this of regional mornings or provincial evenings. Only just over one in twenty said it of local weeklies.

TABLE 1.081

OPINIONS ON UNFAIRNESS OF COVERAGE OF POLITICAL PARTIES BY INDIVIDUAL NATIONAL MORNINGS

	The Times/ Financial Times/The Guardian	The Daily Telegraph	Daily Mail	Daily Express	Daily Mirror/ Record	The Sun
Split by title, answers on national mornings were:						
Sample	133	183	233	345	591	472
	%	%	%	%	%	%
Does not support any one party	50	16	35	33	33	57
Supports one party but gives fair coverage to the views of other parties	37	52	40	43	36	19
Supports one party and does not give fair coverage to the views of other parties—	12	29	23	23	29	18
namely: Conservative	1	1	1	2	24	11
Labour	9	25	20	17	1	3
Liberal	6	14	13	14	16	9
Other	—	2	1	4	*	1
Don't know	1	3	2	1	2	6

The newspapers most associated with unfair coverage were *The Daily Telegraph*, the *Daily Mail*, the *Daily Express* and the *Daily Mirror*. The *Daily Telegraph*, the *Daily Mail* and the *Daily Express* were quite commonly seen as not giving fair coverage to Labour Party views; the *Daily Mirror* was quite commonly seen as not giving fair coverage to Conservative Party views. All four papers were quite commonly seen as not giving fair coverage to the views of the Liberal Party. Thus overall, mention of unfair coverage of Liberal Party views was at least as common as mention of unfair coverage of the views of the two main parties.

The level of unfairness of coverage perceived in regional mornings is equivalent to that perceived in the least unfair of the national mornings.

In the discussion above of the parties which people perceive provincial evening and local weekly newspapers as supporting, we found no notable difference between provincial evenings of different ownership or circulation size or between local weeklies of different ownership. The same applies to people's perceptions of these newspapers' unfairness in coverage of political parties.

There was, likewise, no very great difference in the frequency with which people of different political views saw provincial evenings and local weeklies as giving unfair coverage to political parties. The comparison of the answers of supporters of different parties was:

TABLE 1.082
OPINIONS ON UNFAIRNESS OF COVERAGE OF POLITICAL PARTIES BY LOCAL NEWSPAPERS BY POLITICAL VIEWS OF RESPONDENT

	PROVINCIAL EVENINGS Political views of respondent				LOCAL WEEKLIES Political views of respondent			
	Conservative	Liberal	Labour	No party	Conservative	Liberal	Labour	No party
Sample	389	113	404	153	504	174	420	216
	%	%	%	%	%	%	%	%
Does not support any one party	77	71	75	76	83	79	80	81
Supports one party but gives fair coverage to the views of others	12	14	13	14	12	10	10	10
Supports one party and does not give fair coverage to the views of others–	10	10	9	3	5	11	10	9
namely: Conservative	5	1	2	1	2	1	1	2
Labour	3	8	8	2	1	5	6	3
Liberal	5	6	5	1	2	5	5	2
Other	1	—	*	—	*	3	2	1
Don't know	1	5	3	7	*	—	1	*

Some differences emerge if we look at the views of those minorities who express very strong support for the Conservative or Labour Parties. Even among these, however, only small minorities claimed to perceive unfairness in newspaper coverage.

TABLE 1.083
OPINIONS ON UNFAIRNESS OF COVERAGE OF POLITICAL PARTIES BY LOCAL NEWSPAPERS AMONG VERY STRONG SUPPORTERS OF THE MAIN PARTIES

	PROVINCIAL EVENINGS Political views of respondent		LOCAL WEEKLIES Political views of respondent	
	Very strong Conservative	Very strong Labour	Very strong Conservative	Very strong Labour
Sample	137	120	179	122
	%	%	%	%
Does not support any one party	78	69	84	71
Supports one party but gives fair coverage to the views of others	11	15	11	16
Supports one party and does not give fair coverage to the views of others	10	15	5	12
namely: Conservative	6	2	3	*
Labour	2	13	1	8
Liberal	7	5	2	7
Other	2	—	—	3
Don't know	1	1	*	1

Unions and Management

Those questioned about particular newspapers were also asked about the fullness of their coverage of employers' and unions' cases when the two disagreed and on the trend of the newspapers' comment on such disagreement.

Aggregated by type of newspaper, answers on fullness of coverage were:

TABLE 1.084

OPINIONS ON FULLNESS OF COVERAGE OF INDUSTRIAL DISPUTES BY TYPE OF NEWSPAPER

	National Morning Newspapers	Regional Morning Newspapers	Provincial Evening Newspapers	Local Weekly Newspapers
Sample	1,976	273	1,096	1,369
	%	%	%	%
When employers and unions disagree:				
Reports both sides of things fully...	58	68	55	44
Gives more space to the employers' case	12	8	8	4
Gives more space to the unions' case	17	7	8	3
Does not print much at all ...	6	10	20	42
Don't know	7	7	10	7

Considerable majorities thought both national and regional morning newspapers usually reported both sides of industrial disputes fully. National mornings were, however, twice as likely as regional mornings to be seen as partial in their coverage. 29% of those questioned about national mornings said they usually gave more space to one side as compared to only 15% of those questioned about regional mornings.

Provincial evenings were less likely than regional mornings to be seen as reporting both sides of things fully. Only 55% of those answering on provincial evenings said this of them as compared to 68% of those answering on regional mornings. This was not, however, because provincial evenings were more likely to be seen as partial in their coverage. It was because they were more widely seen as unlikely to print much about the matter at all.

This difference between regional mornings and provincial evenings is carried further with local weeklies. Two out of five of those answering on provincial weeklies said that when employers and unions disagree, local weekly newspapers do not print much about it at all, as many as said they report both sides of the disagreement fully. The numbers who thought local weeklies were partial in their coverage, giving more space to one side or the other, were very small.

There was not a great deal of difference between individual national mornings in the numbers who thought they would report both sides of industrial disagreements fully. Among the minorities who thought national mornings would be partial in their coverage *The Sun* and, especially, the *Daily Mirror* were on balance thought likely to give more space to the unions' case. Other national morning newspapers were generally thought likely to give more space to the employers' case.

For provincial evening newspapers, answers varied with ownership and circulation as follows:

TABLE 1.085

OPINIONS ON FULLNESS OF COVERAGE OF INDUSTRIAL DISPUTES IN PROVINCIAL EVENINGS BY OWNERSHIP AND CIRCULATION

	OWNERSHIP			CIRCULATION			
	All provincial evenings	All groups owning nationals	All others	Up to 40,000	40,000–100,000	100,000–200,000	Over 200,000
Sample	1,096	492	604	168	299	376	227
	%	%	%	%	%	%	%
When employers and unions disagree:							
Reports both sides of things fully	55	51	57	49	47	57	63
Gives more space to the employers' case	8	8	9	8	6	9	11
Gives more space to the unions' case	8	9	7	12	7	9	6
Does not print much about it at all	20	22	18	19	29	17	10
Don't know	10	10	10	11	10	8	11

The larger provincial evenings tended to be somewhat more widely seen as reporting both sides fully. There was no great overall difference between the ways in which provincial evenings owned by groups with national newspaper interests and other provincial evenings were seen as dealing with news of disagreements between employers and unions. There were, however, some differences between perceptions of the four largest groups. The Westminster Press evenings were less likely to be mentioned as giving more space to the unions' case than others. The Thomson evenings were less likely than others to be seen as reporting both sides of things fully. The comparison between individual groups is, however, based on small sample sizes and these figures should be treated with caution.

TABLE 1.086

OPINIONS ON FULLNESS OF COVERAGE OF INDUSTRIAL DISPUTES IN PROVINCIAL EVENINGS BY MAIN OWNERS

	Evening Newspapers owned by:			
	WP	Thomson	AN	UN
Sample	103	188	182	103
	%	%	%	%
When employers and unions disagree:				
Reports both sides of things fully	54	46	54	62
Gives more space to the employers' case	7	12	5	8
Gives more space to the unions' case	2	12	10	13
Does not print much about it at all	25	21	22	11
Don't know	12	9	9	7

There was no significant difference by ownership in perceptions of weekly newspapers' treatment of news about disputes between employers and unions.

One might expect some differences in the pattern of answers to this question between people of different political views and for people with union affiliations. There were differences, but not very large ones. Trade unionists, Labour Party supporters and especially those who described themselves as strongly Labour were more likely than average to see evening newspapers as giving more space to the employers' case. Conservative Party supporters were more likely than Labour Party supporters to see both provincial evenings and local weeklies as not printing much about disputes between employers and unions at all. The comparisions were:

TABLE 1.087

OPINIONS ON FULLNESS OF COVERAGE OF INDUSTRIAL DISPUTES IN LOCAL NEWSPAPERS BY POLITICAL VIEWS OF RESPONDENTS AND BY UNION MEMBERSHIP

	Political party support					Trade union members
	Cons.	Lib.	Lab.	Very strong Cons.	Very strong Lab.	
Sample	389	113	404	137	120	338
	%	%	%	%	%	%
Provincial evenings:						
Reports both side of things fully	55	56	55	54	54	59
Gives more space to the employers' case	4	7	14	2	23	13
Gives more space to the unions' case	9	9	8	5	9	9
Does not print much about it at all	24	17	16	30	12	16
Don't know	8	12	7	8	2	3

	Political party support					Trade union members
	Cons.	Lib.	Lab.	Very strong Cons.	Very strong Lab.	
Sample	504	174	420	179	122	328
	%	%	%	%	%	%
Local Weeklies:						
Reports both sides of things fully	41	47	48	38	46	48
Gives more space to the employers' case	2	6	6	1	10	6
Gives more space to the unions' case	4	2	2	6	2	3
Does not print much about it at all	45	38	39	47	37	39
Don't know	8	8	6	8	5	4

Despite the differences noted above, the general trend of comment by supporters of different parties was similar. Between 54% and 56% of the supporters and even of the strong supporters of the main political parties who were questioned about provincial evenings said they reported both sides of things fully. Even among strong Labour Party supporters, only 10% said that the local weeklies about which they were questioned gave more space to the employers' case.

Those who said the newspapers they read reported both sides of industrial disputes fully or said they gave more space to the case of either unions or employers were asked a further question about the trend of editorial comment in these newspapers. Those who said the newspapers they read printed little about industrial disputes were not asked this question. Since there were large differences between types of newspaper in the numbers of readers who thought they printed little about industrial disputes and hence in the numbers who were asked the question about editorial comment, the answers to this question are somewhat difficult to interpret. In general, they follow the pattern of the answers on coverage described about. The numbers saying that, in their editorial comment, regional and local newspapers tend to favour either employers or unions when the two disagree were very small, much smaller than the numbers saying this of the national mornings.

Sub-Section 3 Local Groups and Issues

The two previous sub-sections have discussed the answers to questions which were put to all respondents questioned about particular newspapers, whether national, regional or local. The questions discussed in this sub-section were intended to cover the perceived local biases and sympathies of the regional and local press and were put only to those questioned about particular local and regional newspapers.

Treatment of Local Groups

In one series of questions, respondents answering on particular regional or local newspapers were shown a card listing ten social or special interest groups. They were asked to say whether, when reporting on controversial local issues, the newspaper often paid too much or too little attention to any of the views of these sorts of people. The list on the card was intended to be fairly comprehensive of the sorts of people and groups to whose opinions too much or too little attention might be thought to be paid. As a safeguard, however, respondents were asked whether they could think of any other groups or sorts of people, apart from those listed, to whose views the newspapers about which they were questioned often paid too much or too little attention. In fact, hardly any respondents mentioned any such people.

The numbers who said that too much or too little attention was paid to the opinions of the various listed social or special interest groups in reporting controversial local issues in regional or local newspapers were:

TABLE 1.088
ATTENTION PAID TO THE VIEWS OF COMMUNITY GROUPS IN THE REGIONAL AND LOCAL PRESS

	Pays too much attention			Pays too little attention		
	Regional Mornings	Provincial Evenings	Local Weeklies	Regional Mornings	Provincial Evenings	Local Weeklies
Sample	273	1,096	1,369	273	1,096	1,369
	%	%	%	%	%	%
To the views of:						
Young people	3	4	3	12	17	14
People in the lower income groups	1	2	1	10	16	10
Religious people	1	2	2	5	10	6
The police	2	2	2	5	9	7
Local businessmen	6	5	—	5	8	5
Local councillors	5	12	5	3	6	5
Officials of the local council	4	11	9	2	6	4
Local trade union leaders	3	6	2	3	4	6
Big commercial companies	6	9	3	2	4	5
People in the higher income groups	2	7	4	1	4	4
None of these	78	64	72	71	57	68

Three points are immediately apparent. Firstly, even when prompted by a list, only a minority of people questioned about regional or local newspapers will say that they pay too much or too little attention to the views of any particular groups in their reporting of controversial local issues. Secondly, people are slightly more ready to mention groups to which the newspapers pay too little attention than to mention groups to which they pay too much. Thirdly, people are more likely to see provincial evenings as paying too much attention to the views of some groups and too little attention to the views of others than they are so to see either regional mornings or local weeklies. Even for provincial evenings, however, only just over two in five mentioned any group to whose views the newspaper gives too little attention and only just one in three mentioned any group to whose views it gives too much.

People's opinions on the groups to whose views the regional and local press pays too much or too little attention were quite diverse. No one group was mentioned as having too much or too little attention paid to its views by more than one in six of the respondents talking about any of the three main types of regional or local newspaper.

The groups to whose views too little attention was most commonly said to be paid were young people (by 17% for provincial evenings, 14% for local weeklies and 12% for regional mornings) and people in the lower income groups (by 16% for provincial evenings, 10% for local weeklies and 10% for regional mornings). There was also some mention of provincial evenings paying too little attention to the views of religious people (10%) and the police (9%).

The groups to whose views provincial evenings were most commonly said to pay too much attention were local councillors (12%), officials of the local council (11%) and big commercial companies (9%). The only group at all commonly mentioned as one to whose views local weeklies pay too much attention was officials of the local council (9%). There was not any one group to whose views regional mornings were said to pay too much attention by any substantial number of those questioned about them.

There was very little difference by circulation size in views expressed on the partiality of provincial evenings. If we compare the largest (those with a circulation over 200,000) with the smallest (those with a circulation not exceeding 40,000) we find the largest somewhat more associated with paying too much attention to the views of big commercial companies (13% to 5%) and with paying too little attention to the views of religious people (14% to 7%). Apart from this, differences by circulation are trivial.

Differences by type of ownership are also, in general, not very large. Local weeklies owned by groups with national newspaper interests were somewhat more likely than local weeklies owned by others to be seen as paying too much attention to the views of people in the higher income groups and a little more likely than local weeklies owned by others to be seen as paying too little attention to people in the lower income groups. A similar, though smaller difference, was evident between views on the treatment of different income groups by provincial evenings with different types of ownership.

The local weeklies owned by groups with national newspaper interests were also slightly more likely than those owned by others to be seen as paying too much attention to the views of big commercial companies and as paying too little attention to the views of young people. There were only trivial differences by ownership in answers on the other types of people listed. In detail, the comparison for the types of people mentioned above was:

TABLE 1.089
ATTENTION PAID TO THE VIEWS OF COMMUNITY GROUPS IN LOCAL NEWSPAPERS BY OWNERSHIP

	Provincial evening pays too much attention		*Provincial evening pays too little attention*	
	Owned by groups owning national newspapers	Others	Owned by groups owning national newspapers	Others
Sample	492	604	492	604
	%	%	%	%
To the views of:				
Young people	4	5	18	16
People in the lower income groups	2	2	19	14
Big commercial companies	10	8	3	4
People in the higher income groups	10	5	3	4

TABLE 1.089—*continued*

	Local weekly pays too much attention		Local weekly pays too little attention	
	Owned by groups owning national newspapers	Others	Owned by groups owning national newspapers	Others
Sample	318	1,051	318	1,051
	%	%	%	%
To the views of:				
Young people	3	3	21	12
People in the lower income groups ...	1	1	19	8
Big commercial companies	10	3	8	4
People in the higher income groups	11	3	4	4

Some of the groups mentioned on the list are groups quite frequently mentioned in party political argument. It may be interesting, therefore, to look at the differences between the answers of those of differing political views.

Very strong Labour Party supporters were more likely than very strong Conservative Party supporters to mention groups to whose views too little attention was paid, both in provincial evenings and in local weeklies. In particular they were rather more likely than very strong Conservatives to say that too little attention was paid to the views of the young and to the views in the lower income groups.

Very strong Conservatives were rather more likely than very strong Labour supporters to think too little attention was paid to the views of local businessmen in provincial evenings, although not in local weeklies.

Very strong Labour Party supporters were more likely than very strong Conservatives to think that provincial evenings paid too much attention to the views of big commercial companies and that local weeklies paid too much attention to the views of people in the higher income groups. They were also slightly more likely to say that too much attention is paid to the views of local businessmen in both sorts of newspapers.

These differences also appeared, although less markedly, between the views of the general run of supporters of the two main political parties. They should not, however, be exaggerated. The numbers involved were in no case very large and even among very strong Conservatives appreciable numbers said provincial evening newspapers paid too little attention to the views of the young and those in the lower income groups.

The comparison between the answers of people of different political views for the groups mentioned above is shown in the next table.

TABLE 1.090

ATTENTION PAID TO THE VIEWS OF COMMUNITY GROUPS IN LOCAL NEWSPAPERS BY POLITICAL VIEWS OF RESPONDENTS

	Provincial Evening Pays too much attention to					Provincial Evening Pays too little attention to				
	Cons.	Lib.	Lab.	Very strong Cons.	Very strong Lab.	Cons.	Lib.	Lab.	Very strong Cons.	Very strong Lab.
Sample	389	113	404	137	120	389	113	404	137	120
	%	%	%	%	%	%	%	%	%	%
The views of:										
Young people	5	5	4	5	6	4	21	18	12	24
People in the lower income groups	3	—	1	5	1	12	19	21	11	22
People in the higher income groups	5	7	9	5	11	5	3	3	6	6
Big commercial companies	6	11	12	3	17	5	2	2	4	1
Local businessmen	2	4	9	2	9	13	10	6	11	4
None of the ten groups	65	63	62	67	61	57	55	56	58	48

	Local Weekly Pays too much attention to					Local Weekly Pays too little attention to				
	Cons.	Lib.	Lab.	Very strong Cons.	Very strong Lab.	Cons.	Lib.	Lab.	Very strong Cons.	Very strong Lab.
Sample	504	174	420	179	122	504	174	420	179	122
	%	%	%	%	%	%	%	%	%	%
The views of:										
Young people	4	2	3	4	—	9	18	16	9	18
People in the lower income groups	1	1	*	2	—	7	13	13	6	18
People in the higher income groups	2	11	6	1	9	5	4	4	4	4
Big commercial companies	3	10	6	4	9	5	4	5	6	13
Local businessmen	2	9	6	2	7	6	7	6	7	6
None of the ten groups	75	65	72	76	74	73	66	61	74	53

Local Issues

In Section 2 we discussed the answers to questions on what people felt was the most important issue or problem facing their district and how they had come to know of it. Those who were questioned on particular regional or local newspapers who had mentioned a main problem were asked how much attention the newspaper they were talking about paid to that problem. Those who said it paid no attention at all or only paid some attention were asked whether they thought the newspaper should give more attention to the problem.

Split by type of regional or local newspaper, answers were:

TABLE 1.091
ATTENTION GIVEN TO MAIN DISTRICT PROBLEM BY REGIONAL AND LOCAL NEWSPAPERS

	Regional Morning Newspapers	Provincial Evening Newspapers	Local Weekly Newspapers
Sample: All mentioning a main problem	232	833	1,074
	%	%	%
Newspaper gives problem:			
A lot of attention	22	21	28
Some attention	56	51	49
No attention at all	23	27	23
Newspaper should give more attention to problem	56	60	55

Answers were very similar for all three types of newspaper. In each case, less than three in ten thought the newspaper gave a lot of attention to the main problem of the district and in each case the majority of respondents thought it should give more. The answers suggest that the regional and local press's treatment of what people regard as the most important problems of their district is quite widely seen as inadequate.

The smallest provincial evenings were more widely seen than the rest as giving a lot of attention to what people regarded as the main problem of their districts and it was less frequently said of them that they should give more attention to it. The comparison between provincial evenings of different circulation size was:

TABLE 1.092
ATTENTION GIVEN TO MAIN DISTRICT PROBLEM IN PROVINCIAL EVENINGS BY CIRCULATION

	Circulation size			
	Up to 40,000	40,000–100,000	100,000–200,000	Over 200,000
Sample: All mentioning a main problem	135	226	271	181
	%	%	%	%
Newspaper gives problem:				
A lot of attention	31	18	20	18
Some attention	44	63	49	48
No attention at all	25	19	31	34
Newspaper should give more attention to problem	52	65	61	60

For provincial evening newspapers, there was little difference between answers on newspapers of different types of ownership. 21% of those answering on provincial evenings owned by groups with national newspaper interests thought they gave a lot of attention to the main problem of the area and 62% thought they should give it more. The corresponding figures for provincial evenings of other ownership were 21% and 59%.

There was somewhat more difference by ownership between local weeklies. 62% of those talking about local weeklies owned by groups with national newspaper interests said they should give more attention to the main problem of the district as compared to 53% of those talking about local weeklies with other ownership.

For both provincial evening and local weekly newspapers, Labour Party supporters were somewhat more likely than supporters of other political parties to say that the newspaper should pay more attention to what they regarded as the main problem of the district. 63% of Labour Party supporters talking about provincial evenings and 60% of Labour Party supporters talking about local weeklies said this.

5. Ownership and Choice

SUMMARY

Only a minority of readers of the regional and local press are aware of the ownership of the newspapers they read. Asked to say who owned the newspaper they read, only one in three readers of provincial evenings and rather fewer of the readers of local weeklies could give a name and a substantial minority of the names given were wrong ones.

It might be thought that, even though they did not know names, people who read provincial or local newspapers which are owned by large groups might be aware that they are so owned. This does not apear to be the case. Of those reading Thomson provincial evenings, for example, only 2% said that the paper they read was owned by a group owning twenty or more other newspapers.

A series of questions was asked on what benefits people thought there were or would be in having a choice of two or more evening newspapers in their area. Only one in three of those in areas where two or more evening newspapers are available thought there was any benefit to them in having a choice. In areas where there is currently no choice, only one in six thought they would benefit in any way from having a choice.

MAIN FINDINGS

The Concept of Monopoly

There are two aspects of the organisation of the regional and local press which have sometimes been criticised on the grounds that they tend to monopoly. One is the concentration of ownership in a fairly small number of large groups, several of which also have interests in national newspapers and in other media. The other is that, in most areas, there is only one regional or local newspaper of any particular type (morning, evening or weekly) so that the public has no choice. It is not clear whether the public are aware of the concentration of ownership of regional and local newspapers in large groups and it is not clear how they feel about the fact that they do or do not have a choice of regional or local newspapers. A series of questions was put to respondents to seek an indication of the situation with regard to these points.

Ownership

In the discussion of people's answers to questions about particular provincial evening and local weekly newspapers above, answers have sometimes been broken down by the ownership of the newspaper which people read. This breakdown was based on the actual ownership of the newspapers concerned. Do the reading public know what this is?

Respondents were asked, for each newspaper about which they were questioned, to say who owned it. Answers for the following nine large groups were subsequently coded as correct or incorrect:

Westminster Press (Pearson Longman)
Thomson Organisation
Beaverbrook[1]
Associated Newspapers
News International
Reed
United Newspapers (UN)
Birmingham Post and Mail (BPM)
Scottish and Universal Newspapers (SUITS)

The first six control national newspapers or are members of groups which control national newspapers.

Answers giving a parent company or a main group subsidiary as the owner or naming a leading figure in the group were accepted as correct (eg Pearson Longman for Westminster Press, Harmsworth for Associated Newspapers, Murdoch for News International etc).

TABLE 1.093
AWARENESS OF OWNERSHIP OF PROVINCIAL EVENING NEWSPAPERS BY OWNERSHIP

	Total	Owned by group owning national newspapers	Owned by other main group (UN, BPM, SUITS)	Other
Sample	1,096	492	191	413
	%	%	%	%
Gave name of owner	32	29	31	36
Gave correct name of owner ...	—	23	19	—
Gave incorrect name of owner ...	—	6	12	—

[1] Since the time of fieldwork, the Beaverbrook provincial newspaper interests have been sold.

One in three respondents thought they knew who owned the provincial evening about which they were questioned, claimed awareness of ownership being slightly lower for the newspapers owned by the large groups than for others. An appreciable number of those answering on evenings owned by the groups with national newspaper interests, however, and a larger number of those reading evenings owned by other large groups in fact gave wrong answers. Only one in five was able to name the owner correctly.

For the four groups for which samples are large enough for separate analysis, the level of correct identification of ownership was:

TABLE 1.094

AWARENESS OF OWNERSHIP OF PROVINCIAL EVENINGS BY MAIN OWNER GROUPS

	Sample	Ownership correctly identified
Thomson	188	% 27
Westminster Press	103	% 19
Associated Newspapers	182	% 14
United Newspapers	103	% 11

Awareness of the ownership of local weekly newspapers was somewhat lower than awareness of the ownership of provincial evenings. For local weeklies, answers were:

TABLE 1.095

AWARENESS OF OWNERSHIP OF LOCAL WEEKLIES BY OWNERSHIP

	Total	Owned by group owning national newspapers	Owned by other main group (UN, BPM, SUITS)	Other
Sample	1,369	315	122	929
	%	%	%	%
Gave name of owner	28	24	24	30
Gave correct name of owner	—	14	10	—
Gave incorrect name of owner	—	9	14	—

Only one in seven of those questioned about a local weekly owned by a group with national newspaper interests was able to identify correctly who owned it.

People may, of course, be aware that a newspaper belongs to a large group without knowing the name of that group. As a check on this, whether they knew the name of the company which owned the newspaper about which they were questioned or not, people were asked whether it owned other newspapers and, if so, how many. Answers on provincial evenings were:

TABLE 1.096
AWARENESS OF GROUP CONNECTIONS OF PROVINCIAL EVENING NEWSPAPERS BY OWNERSHIP

	Total	Owned by a group owning national newspapers	Owned by other main group (UN, BPM, SUITS)	Other
Sample	1,096	492	191	413
	%	%	%	%
Owns no other newspapers	9	9	6	9
Don't know	51	50	51	53
Does own other newspapers	40	41	43	38
Owns: 1 to 4	26	26	32	23
5 to 9	3	3	1	5
10 to 15	*	*	1	*
16 to 19	—	—	—	—
20 or more	1	2	*	—
Don't know how many	9	10	8	8

Only just over two in five of respondents answering on evening newspapers owned by the main groups were ready to say that the company owning the evening newspaper about which they were questioned owned any other newspapers. Most of those who did think the company owned other newspapers thought it might own between one and four other newspapers. The numbers who had any accurate idea of the scale of the main groups were very small.

Answers on the four groups for which sample sizes are adequate for separate analysis were:

TABLE 1.097
AWARENESS OF GROUP CONNECTIONS OF PROVINCIAL EVENING NEWSPAPERS BY MAIN GROUPS

	Provincial Evenings owned by:			
	Thomson	AN	UN	WP
Sample	188	182	103	103
	%	%	%	%
Owns no other newspapers	7	10	4	11
Don't know	45	58	67	51
Does own other newspapers	49	32	29	38
Owns: 1 to 4	28	26	19	20
5 to 9	3	2	1	2
10 to 15	*	—	—	1
16 to 19	—	—	—	—
20 or more	2	1	—	2
Don't know how many	14	4	10	14

It would seem fair to assume that quite a number of those who said the company which owned the newspaper about which they were talking owned others, but that they did not know how many, were in fact aware that the group was a large one. Even if all of them were aware of this, however, the numbers of those answering on provincial evenings owned by the largest groups who know that these newspapers are members of large groups would still seem strikingly low.

As with awareness of the name of the owner, awareness of the size of the groups to which they belonged was lower for local weekly newspapers than for provincial evenings. Answers on local weekly newspapers were:

TABLE 1.098
AWARENESS OF GROUP CONNECTIONS OF LOCAL WEEKLY NEWSPAPERS BY OWNERSHIP

	Total	Owned by a group owning national newspapers	Owned by other main group (UN, BPM, SUITS)	Other
Sample	1,369	315	122	929
	%	%	%	%
Owns no other newspapers	10	7	45	11
Don't know	59	61	68	58
Does own other newspapers	31	33	29	31
Owns: 1 to 4	19	21	15	19
5 to 9	4	2	2	5
10 to 15	1	1	—	1
16 to 19	—	—	—	—
20 or more	*	1	—	*
Don't know how many	7	8	12	6

Choice in Local Newspapers

The questions discussed below were designed to give some indication of people's reactions to the idea of choice in local newspapers. Respondents were asked whether there was more than one evening newspaper sold in their area, so that they could make a choice. Those who said there was were asked whether they thought they benefited at all from having more than one evening newspaper in their area. Those who said there was not were asked whether they thought they would benefit in any way if there were.

Most people in London and the South East, where at least one of the London evenings circulates in most of the main population centres, said they had a choice of evening newspapers. In the rest of the country, only 29% said they had. A few people said there was no evening newspaper and a few were not sure. Answers on availability of evenings newspapers were:

TABLE 1.099
NUMBERS OF EVENING NEWSPAPERS CIRCULATING BY AREA

	London and South East	Rest of the country
Sample	743	1,658
	%	%
Two evenings sold in area	72	29
One evening sold in area	19	64
No evenings sold in area	2	3
Don't know	7	4

Of those who said they had a choice between two evening newspapers, 35% said they thought the choice was of some benefit to them. There was no difference between London and the South East and the rest of the country in the number of those with a choice who said it was a benefit.

In the areas where there were not two evening newspapers circulating, only 17% thought they would benefit in any way if there were. This is half as many as the number of those who had a choice who thought they did benefit. It is possible to interpret this to mean that many people only realise the benefits of choice when they have it. More probably it merely means that many people accept the *status quo*, whatever that may be.

One argument sometimes made in criticism of lack of choice in local newspapers is that it limits people to receiving one political view in editorial comment. It may, therefore, be interesting to look at the views on the benefits of choice of those of different political views. This gives:

TABLE 1.100
ATTITUDES TO CHOICE IN EVENING NEWSPAPERS BY POLITICAL VIEW

	Those who have two or more evenings to choose between		Those who do not have two or more evenings to choose between	
	Sample	Think choice a benefit	Sample	Think choice would be a benefit
Political view				
Conservative	385	35%	394	14%
Liberal	120	36%	107	21%
Labour	348	36%	425	20%
Very strong Conservative	134	32%	152	12%
Very strong Labour	104	28%	128	28%

Among those who do not have a choice, twice as many of those who describe themselves as very strongly Labour as of those who describe themselves as very strongly Conservative think they would benefit from having one. Among those who do have a choice, people's own political attitudes appear to have nothing to do with whether they think the choice a benefit or not.

One gloss on this might be that the sort of choice in local newspapers which very strong Labour supporters might want is not the sort of choice they would be likely to get, given the existing organisation of the press. Another might be that the answers among those who do not currently have a choice of evenings simply reflect the attitudes of strong supporters of different parties to the *status quo*.

The answers people gave when asked what benefits they got or thought they might get from choice were, in the main, very vague. There were, however, some differences between the answers of those who said they had a choice and the answers of those who said they did not. The comparison was:

TABLE 1.101

PERCEIVED BENEFITS OF CHOICE BY WHETHER CHOICE AVAILABLE AND BY REGION

	Already have a choice and think they benefit from it			Do not have a choice and think they would benefit from it
		Area		
	Total	London and South East	Rest of country	Total
Sample	391	196	195	198
Stated benefit:	%	%	%	%
Gives/would give a variety of points of view	50	58	41	51
Leads/would lead to fairer comment	11	9	13	24
Covers/would cover news from different parts of the area	24	12	32	10
Gives/would give coverage of both local and national news	4	7	—	2
Gives/would give a choice of features/cartoons	8	8	8	4
Represents/would represent views of different social/political groups	3	3	4	2
You still have one paper left if there is a strike	1	1	—	—
Other/vague answers	6	8	3	12
Don't know	3	5	2	4

The main point mentioned by all groups is that a choice of evening newspapers in an area gives or would give a variety of points of view. Another point quite frequently mentioned is that having two evening newspapers leads or would lead through competition to a fairer standard of comment. This view was held less widely among those who did not have a choice than among those who did.

The only other point mentioned by any substantial group of respondents was that the different newspapers do or would cover news from different parts of the area. This answer was common among those outside London and the South East who already had a choice. It means simply that some respondents live between the core circulation areas of two evenings and have some interest in the local news from both sides of them.

6. Letters to the Editor

SUMMARY

11% of respondents claimed to have written a letter to a newspaper some time. 2% claimed to have done so in the past two years.

Letter writers were more likely than average to be men and in professional or managerial jobs. Their political views were not, however, radically different from those of people in general.

Most of those who had written to newspapers had last written to a provincial or local newspaper. Chances of having the letter published were much better if it was addressed to a provincial or local paper. Two-thirds of those last writing to a provincial or local paper said their letters had been published as compared to only 30% of those last writing to a national newspaper.

MAIN FINDINGS

We have seen in Section 3 that readers' letters are among the most widely read items in local newspapers, especially for women. Who write these letters?

Among the sample we interviewed, 11% claimed to have written a letter for publication to the editor of a newspaper at some time. 2% claimed to have done so within the past year.

Among those who claimed ever to have done so, last stated time of writing was:

TABLE 1.102
TIME SINCE LAST LETTER SENT TO THE NEWSPAPERS

	Total
Sample: All ever writing letters to an editor for publication	230
Last wrote:	%
Less than 1 year ago	17
1 but under 2 years ago	11
2 but under 5 years ago	24
5 years ago or more	47

That the figure for those writing in the past year is higher than the figure for those last writing between one and two years ago and that these two figures combined are higher than the figure for those last writing between two and five years ago suggest that a limited number of people write letters to newspapers frequently and that a much larger number of people do so occasionally. Another possibility is that those who last wrote some time ago had forgotten about it, but this seems unlikely.

Below we compare the characteristics of those who said they had written to the newspapers in the past two years (a group which will include all the frequent correspondents) with all those who have ever written to a newspaper and with the sample we interviewed as a whole. In considering the figures given below, it should be borne in mind that the numbers who had written to newspapers in the past two years were very small and that the figures for that group are, therefore, liable to quite large sampling error. The comparison is:

TABLE 1.103
PROFILE OF THOSE WHO WRITE LETTERS TO THE NEWSPAPERS

	All writing in past 2 years	All ever writing	Total sample
Sample	70	230	2,401
	%	%	%
Sex:			
Men	57	54	47
Women	43	46	53
Age:			
16–24	17	9	14
25–44	42	34	33
45–64	22	39	34
65 and over	18	18	18
Working Status:			
In work	66	65	60
Not in work	34	35	40
Socio-Economic Group of Employment:			
Prof/Emp/Man	25	17	9
Junior non-manual	13	24	19
Skilled manual	22	15	16
Semi/unskilled manual	6	9	14
Forces/unclassifiable	—	1	2
Political View:			
Conservative	39	44	36
Liberal	17	15	11
Labour	25	25	33
Nationalist	2	1	3
Other party/No party/Not stated	17	15	17
Very strongly Conservative	16	20	14
Very strongly Labour	13	11	10

The letter writers are not a cross-section of the population. Most strikingly, they are much more likely than average to be employers or to be in professional or managerial jobs. They are also more likely to be men than women. They are not, however, notably older than people in general and, their political views do not appear to be radically different from those of people in general. The writers are possibly more likely than average to be Liberal and a little less likely than average to be Labour. The difference is not, however, a very large one.

The sorts of newspaper to which people said they had last written were:

TABLE 1.104
TYPE OF NEWSPAPER LAST WRITTEN TO

	Total
Sample: All ever writing to newspapers	230
	%
Last wrote to:	
National morning	29 ⎫
National Sunday	5 ⎬ 35
London evening	1 ⎭
Regional morning	6 ⎫
Provincial evening	30 ⎪
Local weekly	22 ⎬ 63
Regional Sunday	5 ⎭
Can't recall/Not stated	1

A very considerable majority of those writing to newspapers had last written to the regional or local press rather than the national press.

54% of those who had written to newspapers claimed that the last letter they had written was published. There was a very marked difference in the letter's chances of publication, however, by the sort of newspaper to which it had been addressed. A comparison of the addressees of the published and unpublished letters gives:

TABLE 1.105
TYPE OF NEWSPAPER LAST WRITTEN TO BY WHETHER LETTER WAS PUBLISHED

	Last letter was:	
	Published	Not Published
Sample: All ever writing to a newspaper	131	99
	%	%
Last wrote to:		
National morning	16 ⎫	43 ⎫
National Sunday	5 ⎬ 21	6 ⎬ 52
London evening	— ⎭	2 ⎭
Regional morning	9 ⎫	1 ⎫
Provincial evening	36 ⎪	25 ⎪
Local weekly	30 ⎬ 77	13 ⎬ 48
Regional Sunday	3 ⎭	8 ⎭
Can't recall/Not stated	1	1

Three-quarters of the published letters had been directed at the regional or local press.

Chances of publication of last letters written, depending on the type of newspaper to which they were addressed, were:

TABLE 1.106
CHANCES OF PUBLICATION OF LETTERS BY TYPE OF NEWSPAPER WRITTEN TO

	National/ London Evening	Regional or Local Newspaper
Sample: All last writing to that sort of newspaper	82	146
	%	%
Letter was:		
Published	30	66
Not published	70	34

7. Other Topics of Enquiry

SUMMARY

This section covers two points unrelated to the main aims of the enquiry.

National Mornings People would want to Keep

Readers of national morning newspapers were asked which three national mornings they would want to keep, if some had to close. They tended to mention the newspapers they themselves read and other newspapers slightly further up the quality-popular scale from these. Thus *The Sun* and *Daily Mirror* readers might mention the *Daily Mail* or *Daily Express*, *Daily Mail* and *Daily Express* readers *The Daily Telegraph* and so on. Few mentioned newspapers closer to the popular end of the scale than those they read among the three they would most wish to continue. Thus *The Sun* was mentioned by fewer people than read it, while *The Times* was mentioned by far more than look at it even occasionally.

The Press Council

Just under half those interviewed claimed to have heard of the Press Council. Only one in four of those interviewed, however, claimed to know what it does. Some of these, in fact, had mistaken ideas about what it does. Just under one in six of those interviewed claimed to know what the Press Council does and were able to give a broadly accurate description of its work.

MAIN FINDINGS

National Mornings People would want to Keep

The survey was principally concerned with the regional and local press, but one group of questions was put which referred to national morning newspapers only. These questions were on the national morning newspapers people would want to see continue if some had to cease publication.

Respondents were shown a list of the national morning newspapers. It was pointed out to them that some of these newspapers are in financial difficulties and that it has even been suggested that some may have to close. They were asked which newspaper they would most want to keep in that event, which second most and which third most. The question was, in fact, asked of all respondents. It seems reasonable, however, to limit the report of answers to those who said they looked at or read at least one issue of some national morning in an average week. The answers of those who do not read national mornings appear rather irrelevant.

The answers given by those who said they looked at or read at least one issue of some national morning in an average week were:

TABLE 1.107
NATIONAL MORNINGS PEOPLE WOULD WANT TO KEEP

	Regular or occasional readers of national mornings			
	Most	Second most	Third most	All mentions
Sample	1,982	1,982	1,982	1,982
	%	%	%	%
Would want to keep:				
Daily Mirror/Record	29	18	9	55
Daily Express	17	18	17	52
The Sun	17	16	8	41
The Daily Telegraph	11	9	10	29
Daily Mail	10	12	14	35
The Times	7	7	8	22
The Guardian	5	6	5	17
Financial Times	1	3	3	7
Morning Star	*	1	1	2
Don't know/Don't care	3	11	26	—

It is immediately evident that the answers given do not exactly reflect readership levels.

Claimed regular and occasional readership of national morning newspapers among those interviewed were:

TABLE 1.108
CLAIMED READERSHIP OF NATIONAL MORNINGS

	Read regularly (5–6 issues in an average week)	Read regularly or occasionally (1+ issues in an average week)
Sample: All respondents	2,401	2,401
	%	%
Daily Mirror/Record	26	37
The Sun	19	30
Daily Express	15	22
Daily Mail	10	14
The Daily Telegraph	7	12
The Times	2	4
The Guardian	2	4
Financial Times	1	2
Morning Star	*	1
None of these	34	18

The differences between these figures and those on the newspapers people would want to keep can be brought out more clearly be relating them. This can be done by expressing the numbers who say they would want to keep each newspaper as a ratio of the number of people who in fact read it.

Before doing this, it is important to stress one point. Broadly speaking, people want to keep the newspapers they read rather than those they do not and the newspapers with a lot of readers are those which a lot of people say they want to keep. Whatever may appear below once the effects of size of readership have been eliminated from the comparison, it is still the case, for example, that substantially more readers of national mornings say they would most like to keep the *Daily Mirror* or *Daily Record* than say this of any other newspaper.

In the table below, coverage is limited to those who said they read at least one issue of a national morning in an average week. The answers of those who do not seem of rather less importance. For each newspaper, the number who say they would like to keep it most and the number who mention it among the three they would most like to keep are expressed as ratios of the number who say they read that newspaper regularly and the number who say they read it regularly or occasionally. This gives:

TABLE 1.109
RATIOS OF WISH TO KEEP NEWSPAPERS TO NEWSPAPER READERSHIP

	Most want to keep to Regular or occasional readers	Most want to keep to Regular readers	In the three to keep to Regular or occasional readers	In the three to keep to Regular readers
The Times	1·3	2·6	4·4	8·8
The Guardian	1·1	2·5	3·3	7·8
Financial Times	0·3	0·7	2·2	5·7
The Daily Telegraph	0·8	1·2	2·0	3·2
Daily Mail	0·6	0·8	2·1	3·0
Daily Express	0·6	0·9	1·9	2·8
Daily Mirror/Record	0·6	0·9	1·2	1·7
The Sun	0·5	0·7	1·1	1·7

Note: Morning Star omitted because of small sample base.

The four sets of ratios in the table all put the national mornings into something very close to the conventional quality-intermediate-popular ordering. In all four sets of figures the ratio of the number of people who want to keep *The Times* to the number of people who read it is very high and the ratio of the number of people who want to keep *The Sun* to the number who read it is low. There are, however, some interesting exceptions.

In the ratios calculated from the three newspapers readers of national mornings would most like to keep, the *Financial Times* fits between *The Guardian* and *The Daily Telegraph*. In terms of the *one* newspaper people would most like to keep, however, the ratios for the *Financial Times* are similar to those for *The Sun*. In particular, the ratio of those who would most like to keep it to those who read one issue or more of it a week is the lowest for any of the eight newspapers.

The explanation for this is that the *Financial Times* is more commonly read in conjunction with another national morning than is the case for any of the other newspapers, presumably because of its special character and content. *Financial Times* readers are quite happy to put it *among* the newspapers they would most like to keep. Those of them who read it in conjunction with another newspaper are, however, less ready to say it is the *one* newspaper they would most like to keep.

A second point for comment is that the relationship between the intermediate mornings (the *Daily Express* and *Daily Mail*) and the popular mornings (the *Daily Mirror* and *The Sun*) differs markedly, depending on whether one considers the ratios based on the one newspaper people would most want to keep or the ratios for the three newspapers they would most want to keep. On the one newspaper people would most want to keep, the ratios for the *Daily Mail*, the *Daily Express* and the *Daily Mirror* are virtually identical, with that for *The Sun* only slightly lower. There is a very clear gap between the intermediate and popular national mornings, however, in the ratios for the three newspapers people would most want to keep.

The key to this appears to be the number of newspapers people read. Few read three with any regularity. The popular national mornings are mentioned among the three newspapers people would most like to keep by only marginally more people than read them regularly or occasionally. The intermediate national mornings are mentioned among the three newspapers people would most like to keep by twice as many people as read them. People who read the popular mornings do not differ greatly from people who read the intermediate mornings in their desire to keep the newspapers they read. Among those who do *not* read the popular mornings, however, few say they would like to keep them. The intermediate mornings, on the other hand, are frequently described as worth keeping by non-readers.

This brings us to the case of *The Times*. The ratios shown for *The Times* are remarkable. The ratio of the number of people who count it among the three newspapers they would most like to keep to the number of people who read or look at even one issue of it in an average week is 4·4. In other words, more than three-quarters of those who say it is among the three national mornings they would most want to keep are people who seldom if ever read it.

The situation with regard to *The Guardian* is comparable, if not quite so striking.

In summary, then, the main factor influencing people's views on the national morning newspapers they would like to keep if some had to cease publication is the newspapers they themselves read. They want to see the newspapers they read survive. Beyond this, their stated concern is largely for the newspapers somewhat further towards the quality end of the quality-popular continuum than the newspapers they in fact read. Answers suggest that the process is continuous but accelerates towards the quality end of the spectrum. At the extremes, few people who never read *The Sun* are much concerned with its continued existence if some national morning has to close. Quite a number of those who never read *The Times*, however, appear concerned with *its* continued existence. Whether their concern would lead them to any such action as buying it is a separate question not covered by the survey.

The Press Council

A further topic which was covered by the survey but is not particularly related to the regional and local press was awareness of the existence and functions of the Press Council.

People were asked whether they had heard of the Press Council. Those who said they had or said they were uncertain whether they had or not were asked whether they knew what it did. Claimed awareness of the Press Council and of its functions was:

TABLE 1.110
CLAIMED AWARENESS OF THE PRESS COUNCIL AND ITS FUNCTIONS

Claimed awareness	Total	Those who claim to:	
		Know what it does	Do not know what it does
Heard of Press Council	46%	21%	25%
Uncertain	2%	*	2%
Have not heard of Press Council	52%	—	52%
Total	100%	21%	79%

Sample: All respondents: 2,401.

More than half the respondents said they had not heard of the Press Council. 46% said they had. More than half of these 46%, however, said they did not know what the Press Council does. Only one in five respondents, 21%, claimed to know what the Press Council does.

That people claim to know the function of the Press Council does not necessarily mean that they actually do know. The accounts given by people of the Press Council's functions were:

TABLE 1.111
OPINIONS ON FUNCTION OF PRESS COUNCIL

	Total
Sample: All claiming to know what the Press Council does	504
	%
Listens to/rules on complaints by the public against the press	7
Listens to/rules on complaints against the press (no mention of the public)	14
Regulates/is a watchdog on the press (no detail given of how)	46
Other comments about fairness of coverage/treatment in newspapers	10
Defends journalists/newspapers when they are criticised	3
A guard against libel/checks news stories for libel	4
A trade union for journalists/arbitrator for the newspaper unions	4
An association of newspaper proprietors	1
A press agency/pools news	1
Other/vague answers	14

The first four categories above can be taken as broadly correct. Coders were instructed not to code more than one category out of the four. They can, therefore, be added together. This gives a total of 77% of those who claimed to know what the Press Council does who were able to give a broadly accurate description of its functions. When people are asked to answer questions of this sort in their own words, there is always some element of incoherence in the answers given. The figure of 77% can, therefore, be taken as a minimum estimate.

Applying this figure to the 21% of all respondents who claimed to know what the Press Council does gives a figure of 16% of the general public, just under one in six, who claim to know what the Press Council does and are able to show that they actually do know.

The group who claimed to have heard of the Press Council and to know what it does was not a cross-section of the population. Claimed awareness of the Press Council's functions was below average among women, among the very young and among the old. It was very much above average among employers and those in professional or managerial jobs. The comparison was:

TABLE 1.112
PROFILE OF PEOPLE CLAIMING TO KNOW WHAT THE PRESS COUNCIL DOES

		Sample	Claim to have heard of the Press Council and to know what it does
	Total	2,401	21%
Sex	Men	1,137	31%
	Women	1,262	12%
Age	16–24	361	9%
	25–44	819	25%
	45–64	772	25%
	65 and over	431	15%
Working status	In work	1,438	15%
	Not in work	963	25%
Socio-Economic Group of Employment	Prof/Emp/Manager	222	47%
	Junior non-manual	463	25%
	Skilled manual	412	23%
	Semi-skilled/unskilled manual	324	13%

APPENDICES

Appendix 1: Scotland and the *Sunday Post*

INTRODUCTION

The pattern of newspaper readership in Scotland is markedly different from that in any of the other parts of Great Britain. It may be useful to summarise the results of the survey of the general public with regard to Scotland, pointing out the differences between behaviour and attitudes there and in the rest of Great Britain. This section also summarises the results of the survey with regard to the *Sunday Post*, a Scottish newspaper very different in character from the rest of the Sunday press.

A preliminary comment on sample sizes is necessary. The sample for the survey of the general public was divided between the various parts of Great Britain on a population basis. Of the total of 2,401 interviews, 205 (9%) were carried out in Scotland. In total, this sub-sample is adequate for meaningful separate analysis. The possibilities of further sub-analysis of the Scottish sample, looking at particular groups of people within Scotland are, however, very limited. Thus many breakdowns which are meaningful on the basis of Great Britain as a whole would not produce reliable data on the basis of Scotland alone.

MAIN FINDINGS

Readership

(a) Morning Newspapers

Throughout Great Britain as a whole, 72% of respondents said they read five or six issues a week of some particular morning newspaper. The number saying this was somewhat higher in Scotland (78% of respondents) than in England and Wales (71% of respondents).

There was a very marked difference between Scotland and the rest of Great Britain in the types of morning newspaper which people said they read regularly and in the particular morning newspapers they said they read.

The comparison of levels of readership of individual national mornings and of the *Daily Record* in Scotland and the rest of Great Britain was:

READERSHIP OF INDIVIDUAL NATIONAL MORNINGS BY REGION

	Great Britain	England and Wales	Scotland
Sample	2,401	2,196	205
	%	%	%
Read 5–6 issues a week of:			
Daily Mirror/Record	26	25	38
The Sun	19	21	4
Daily Express	15	14	19
Daily Mail	10	11	2
The Daily Telegraph	7	8	1
The Times	2	2	1
The Guardian	2	2	—
Financial Times	1	1	*
Morning Star	*	*	2

The *Daily Record* was more widely read in Scotland than its counterpart, the *Daily Mirror* in England and Wales. *The Sun*, the *Daily Mail* and the quality national mornings were all read less in Scotland than in England and Wales.

The higher readership of the *Daily Express* and the lower readership of the *Daily Mail* may be accounted for by the greater Scottish identity of the *Scottish Daily Express*. The existence of the *Daily Record* as a separate, Scottish title may likewise account for the lower Scottish readership of its competitor *The Sun*.

Even if the *Daily Record* is treated as being, in effect, part of the national morning press, the regional morning press is very much stronger in Scotland than in the rest of the country and the national morning press much weaker.

If the *Daily Record* is seen as part of the regional morning press, the regional morning press is very much stronger in Scotland than the national morning press.

READERSHIP OF TYPES OF MORNING NEWSPAPER BY REGION

	Great Britain	England and Wales	Scotland
Sample	2,401	2,196	205
	%	%	%
Read 5–6 issues a week of:			
a national morning (including *Daily Record*)	66	68	54
a regional morning (excluding *Daily Record*)	9	6	36
a national morning (excluding *Daily Record*)	63	68	23
a regional morning (including *Daily Record*)	12	6	65

(b) *Evenings and Weeklies*

Claimed regular readership of evening newspapers was somewhat lower among those interviewed in Scotland than among those interviewed in England and Wales and claimed regular readership of local weeklies somewhat higher. The comparison was:

READERSHIP OF EVENING AND WEEKLY NEWSPAPERS BY REGION

	Great Britain	England and Wales	Scotland
Sample	2,401	2,196	205
	%	%	%
Read 5–6 issues of an evening in an average week	34	35	26
Read 3–4 issues of a local weekly in an average month	43	42	52

(c) *Sunday Newspapers*

We have noted above the differences between Scotland and the rest of Great Britain in the morning newspapers people read. There are even more striking differences for Sunday newspapers:

READERSHIP OF SUNDAY NEWSPAPERS BY REGION

	Great Britain	England and Wales	Scotland
Sample	2,401	2,196	205
	%	%	%
Read 3-4 issues in an average month of:			
News of the World	24	25	13
Sunday Mirror	24	26	3
Sunday People	22	23	12
Sunday Express	20	21	11
The Sunday Times	10	10	10
The Observer	5	5	6
Sunday Telegraph	4	4	1
Sunday Post	10	3	66
Sunday Mail	4	*	39

The Sunday newspaper field in Scotland is dominated by the *Sunday Post* and the *Sunday Mail*, both published in Glasgow. Of the national Sundays, only *The Sunday Times* and *The Observer* have a claimed regular readership in Scotland comparable to their claimed regular readership in England and Wales.

It will be noted that, in England and Wales, 3% of respondents claimed to read the *Sunday Post*. Given the larger population of England and Wales, these readers outside Scotland accounted for 30% of all those claiming to read the *Sunday Post* regularly.

In fact, *Sunday Post* readership in England and Wales was largely confined to northern areas. Two-thirds of the *Sunday Post* readers outside Scotland were in the North or North West of England. 11% of respondents in these two regions claimed to read it regularly.

Television Viewing and Radio Listening

Respondents in Scotland were slightly more likely than those in England and Wales to say that, on an average weekday, they spent a lot of time watching television and to say that they watched television news regularly. The comparison was:

TIME SPENT WATCHING TELEVISION BY REGION

	Great Britain	England and Wales	Scotland
Sample	2,401	2,196	205
	%	%	%
Average weekday time watching television:			
None	3	3	2
Under 1 hour	7	7	5
1 but under 3 hours	44	44	38
3 but under 5 hours	32	32	34
5 hours or more	14	13	21
Watch TV news 6-7 days a week	71	71	77

There was no notable difference between Scotland and the rest of Great Britain in radio listening habits.

News Interests and Sources

Respondents in Scotland were more likely than those in England and Wales to express strong interest in regional and local news—both news about what is going on in their part of the country and news about what the local council is doing. Apart from this, the news interests of people in Scotland were broadly similar to those of people in the rest of Great Britain. The comparison was:

INTEREST IN DIFFERENT TYPES OF NEWS BY REGION

	Very interested		
	Great Britain	England and Wales	Scotland
Sample	2,401	2,196	205
	%	%	%
Local and Regional News:			
news about what is going on in this part of the country	58	57	67
news about what the local council is doing	39	38	50
General and Political News:			
news about what is happening in other countries	27	26	33
news about what the Government is doing in Britain	49	48	51
news about political parties	20	20	25
Business and Union News:			
news about trade union affairs	16	16	22
news about business and industry	20	19	22
News on Sport and Leisure Interests:			
news about football	22	22	22
news about horse racing	7	7	10
news about fashions	14	14	15
news about people in the entertainment business	17	18	11

Asked to choose from a pre-arranged list the sources which they found most useful in keeping up to date with news on these topics, some Scottish respondents appear to have been confused by the expression "national morning newspapers". The figures suggest that different respondents treated newspapers like the *Daily Record* and *The Scotsman* in different ways. Because of this it is not possible to interpret the answers given on national morning newspapers. With regard to other media, local evening newspapers (less read in Scotland) were much less commonly mentioned as the most useful source of regional and local news than was the case in England and Wales. Television also was less commonly mentioned in Scotland than in England and Wales as the single most useful source of news about what is going on in the respondent's own part of the country. It was, however, rather more commonly mentioned in Scotland as the one most useful source of news about other countries, news about trade union affairs, news about fashions and news about people in the entertainment business.

What People Read in Newspapers

Taken through a list of seventeen items and asked which they usually look at or always make a point of looking at in their local evening newspapers, readers in Scotland gave answers broadly similar to the answers given by readers in England and Wales. There were only two differences large enough to be meaningful. Evening newspaper readers in Scotland were substantially more likely than those in England and Wales to say they usually looked at pictures and reports of weddings and funerals and at reports of local court cases. The comparison was:

ITEMS LOOKED AT IN LOCAL EVENINGS BY REGION

	England and Wales	Scotland	Difference
Sample: All reading 1+ issues of a local evening in an average week	1,025	71	
	%	%	
Usually/always look at:			
pictures and reports of weddings and funerals	38	57	+19%
reports of local court cases	42	58	+16%

There were more differences between Scotland and the rest of Great Britain in what people said they looked at in local weekly newspapers. Weekly newspaper readers in Scotland tended to mention more out of the 17 items as ones which they usually looked at. There was only one item, the gardening page or column, for which the number of usual readers was lower in Scotland than in England and Wales. The five items showing the largest differences were:

ITEMS LOOKED AT IN LOCAL WEEKLIES BY REGION

	England and Wales	Scotland	Difference
Sample: All reading 1+ issues of a local weekly in an average month	1,217	152	
	%	%	
Usually/always look at:			
pictures and reports of weddings and funerals	49	76	+27%
readers' letters	57	84	+27%
women's page	23	48	+25%
reports of local court cases	51	74	+23%
advertising of jobs	41	59	+18%

The very large differences by country in the numbers claiming they usually look at readers' letters and at reports of weddings and funerals in their local weekly newspapers were sufficient to produce a difference in the order of items most frequently read. The items most widely mentioned as usually read in local weeklies in Scotland and in the rest of Great Britain were:

RANKING OF ITEMS LOOKED AT IN LOCAL WEEKLIES BY REGION

Rank order	Local Weeklies			
	England and Wales (Sample 1,217)		Scotland (Sample 152)	
1	comment on local issues ...	71%	comment on local issues ...	86%
2	news about what the local council is doing ...	70%	readers' letters	84%
3	readers' letters	57%	pictures and reports of weddings and funerals...	76%
4	advertisements of items for sale and wanted ...	54%	reports of local court cases	74%
5	reports of local court cases	51%	news about what the local council is doing ...	71%
	news about local business and industry	51%		

The questions about items read were also put to readers of the *Sunday Post*. Their answers were different from the overall pattern of answers on regional mornings, provincial evenings or local weeklies. The items most frequently mentioned as usually looked at among *Sunday Post* readers (including its readers in England) were:

RANKING OF ITEMS LOOKED AT IN THE *SUNDAY POST*

Sample: Regular or occasional readers	Sunday Post 203	
Rank order	Always/usually look at:	
1	readers' letters	75%
2	news about what the Government is doing in Britain...	63%
3	list of TV and radio programmes	61%
4	news about other countries	61%
5	comment on local issues	49%

The most notable feature of these answers is the very prominent position occupied by readers' letters. We have seen earlier that those who read local weeklies in Scotland are more likely than their English counterparts to claim that they usually look at the readers' letters in them. We now see that readers' letters are, by some margin, the most widely read feature in the dominant Sunday newspaper in Scotland. Scots are, however, no more likely than English or Welsh people to write to the press. 11% of those interviewed in Scotland said that they had written to the newspapers at some time or other, the same figure as that for Great Britain as a whole.

Attitudes to Newspapers

Readers of local and regional newspapers were taken through a list of 17 statements and asked to say how true each was of each of the local or regional newspapers they read. For evening newspapers, there were few notable differences in the answers given between Scotland and the rest of Great Britain. Scottish evening newspaper readers were more likely than those in the rest of Great Britain to say it was not true that their newspapers often got their facts wrong. They were also less likely to say it was very true that their evening newspaper had too much advertising and slightly less likely to say it was true that they had too little news in them.

There were also few differences between Scotland and the rest of Great Britain in the answers given on weekly newspapers. Weekly newspaper readers in Scotland were less likely than those in England and Wales to think their newspapers had too much advertising in them. They were marginally more likely than those in England and Wales to say it was very true that they would miss their local weekly newspaper a lot if it stopped being published. Apart from this, the differences by country were trivial.

One would expect that, since it is a Sunday newspaper, answers on the *Sunday Post* would be somewhat different from answers on the other newspapers covered. In general, answers on the *Sunday Post* are closer to answers on regional mornings than to answers on any of the other types of newspaper covered. On two statements, however, answers on the *Sunday Post* are more favourable than the answers on any other newspaper or type of newspaper for which answers have been analysed. These statements are "it takes an interest in ordinary people's problems" and "reading it is always enjoyable". On these two statements, answers on the *Sunday Post* compared with answers on other main newspapers and types of newspaper as follows:

ATTITUDES TO THE *SUNDAY POST* AND OTHER NEWSPAPERS

	Sample	"It takes an interest in ordinary people's problems"		"Reading it is always enjoyable"	
		Very true	Mean score	Very true	Mean score
Sunday Post	203	53%	+2.0	69%	+2.3
Daily Mirror/Record	591	41%	+1.5	45%	+1.7
The Sun	472	30%	+1.2	43%	+1.6
Daily Mail	233	32%	+1.2	42%	+1.7
Daily Express	354	29%	+1.1	48%	+1.8
Regional mornings	273	27%	+1.2	43%	+1.7
Provincial evenings	1,096	33%	+1.4	42%	+1.5
Local weeklies	1,369	35%	+1.4	41%	+1.5

Political and Industrial Sympathies

Asked whether the newspapers they read supported any one political party, which party if any they supported and whether they gave fair coverage to other parties, evening newspaper readers in Scotland gave answers virtually identical to those of evening newspaper readers in the rest of Great Britain.

Scottish readers of local weekly newspapers were marginally more likely than those in England and Wales to say their newspaper did not support any one political party. With this exception, answers on the political positions of Scottish weeklies were similar to those on weeklies in the rest of Great Britain. Neither evenings nor weeklies were at all widely seen in Scotland as supporting the SNP or as giving unfair coverage to the views of the SNP.

The *Sunday Post* was rather more closely identified with party support than were evenings or local weeklies. The numbers saying it supported one party were similar to the numbers saying this of regional mornings. Only 60% of *Sunday Post* readers said it supported no one party. 33% said it supported the Conservatives.

12% of *Sunday Post* readers said it did not give fair coverage to the views of the Labour Party, 9% that it did not give fair coverage to the views of the Liberal Party and 5% that it did not give fair coverage to the views of the SNP.

More of the evening newspaper readers in Scotland than of those in England and Wales were ready to say that when employers and unions disagree, the local evening newspaper reports both sides of things fully. This was partly because a substantial number in England and Wales had no opinions on the point. The comparison was:

OPINION ON FULLNESS OF COVERAGE OF INDUSTRIAL DISPUTES IN LOCAL EVENING NEWSPAPERS BY REGION

	England and Wales	Scotland
Sample: All reading 1 + issues of a local evening in an average week	1,025	71
	%	%
Evening newspaper:		
Reports both sides of things fully	53	69
Gives more space to the employers' case	8	9
Gives more space to the unions' case	8	4
Does not print much about it at all	20	16

There was no notable difference between the views of weekly newspaper readers in Scotland and in the rest of Great Britain on this point.

Readers of both evening and weekly newspapers in Scotland were less likely than those in the rest of Great Britain to pick out any particular groups in the community as ones to whose views their newspapers paid too much or too little attention in reporting on controversial local issues.

Appendix 2: Sampling and Fieldwork

SAMPLING

It was decided that the survey should cover persons aged 16 and over living in private households in Great Britain south of the Caledonian Canal.

Northern Ireland was excluded because, while it seems likely that the position of the local press there is substantially different from that in the rest of the country, the sub-sample interviewed there with interviews spread in proportion to population, would be too small for separate analysis. Scotland north of the Caledonian Canal was also excluded because of the very high cost of fieldwork there relative to the rest of the country.

The sampling method was as follows:

(1) Selection of parliamentary constituencies

The parliamentary constituencies in Great Britain south of the Caledonian Canal were split between the Registrar General's ten standard regions. Parliamentary constituencies in the South East were further split between those in the GLC area and the rest.

Within each of the eleven regions, constituencies were then split into three groups:
— constituencies within metropolitan counties or, in Scotland, in the Clydeside conurbation.
— borough constituencies outside the metropolitan counties.
— county constituencies.

This grouping was intended as an indicator of urban or rural character.

Within each of the three groups within each region, constituencies were then ordered by the proportion of their households which had cars at the time of the 1971 census. The level of car ownership in an area relates closely to its social composition and the ordering by level of car ownership was carried out as an indicator of social composition.

Having ordered the constituencies in this way, the 1971 census population of each was then recorded and constituency populations were cumulated within region.

It was decided that a total of 149 constituencies should be selected. This total was allocated between regions in proportion to population. Within each region, the appropriate number of constituencies was then selected by the random starting number and fixed interval method from the cumulated population lists.

This yielded a sample of parliamentary constituencies in Great Britain south of the Caledonian Canal selected randomly with probability proportional to population after stratification by region, by an indicator of urban/rural character and by an indicator of social composition.

(2) Selection of polling districts

For each of the 149 parliamentary constituencies, wards were listed, with their electorates, from the OPCS publication *New Districts for Old*. Ward electorates were then cumulated within constituency and one ward was eslected by random number from the cumulated list for each constituency.

For each selected ward, polling districts were listed, with their electorates from *New Districts for Old*. Polling district electorates were then cumulated and two polling districts were selected by the random starting number and fixed interval method from the cumulated list for each ward.

(3) Selection of addresses

Within each selected polling district, the names of eleven electors were selected from the electoral registers, using the random starting number and fixed interval method. The addresses listed for these electors constituted the sample of addresses for the survey.

Where the selected address was clearly an institution, it was deleted and replaced by selecting a further elector by random number and taking the address listed for him or her.

It is important to note that this method does not give all addresses an equal chance of selection. The probability of an address being selected is in proportion to the number of electors listed at it in the electoral registers.

(4) Selection of respondents

On establishing that an address was a private address and not an institution the interviewer's first task was to make a systematic list on her Respondent Selection Sheet of all the people aged 16 or over who were presently resident there. This was done in strict alphabetical order. Where more than one household lived at an address, those in all the households were included in the list.

Interviewers then selected one of the listed people as potential respondent using a random number grid based on the total number of people listed and the last digit of the address serial number.

No substitution was permitted. If the potential respondent selected was away during the fieldwork period or sick and incapable of being interviewed, no interview was carried out at that address.

It will be noted that only one interview was sought at each address, irrespective of the number of people aged 16 or over who were resident there. This goes some way to correct the imbalance created by selecting addresses with probability proportional to the number of electors listed under them in the electoral registers. The imbalance was fully corrected at the data processing stage by weighting each record of interview by a factor consisting of:

$$\frac{\text{number of persons aged 16+ at address}}{\text{number of persons listed for address in the electoral register}}$$

For 1,760 of the 2,401 interviews (73%) the number of persons aged 16 or over resident at the address and the number of persons listed for the address were the same so that the weighting factor applied was 1.

FIELDWORK

Fieldwork was carried out between 24 September 1975 and 9 January 1976. A total of 109 interviewers was used on the project. All of these were trained interviewers and all were personally briefed on the project before starting work. Personal recall checks were made by a supervisor at 164 (5%) of the issued addresses. Postal checks were carried out for 1,231 productive addresses (51%) of the productive addresses covered.

The response rate achieved in fieldwork was as follows:
RESPONSE SUMMARY

Issued addresses			3,278
Less:			
empty	84		
demolished	19		
institutions	16		
business premises only	4		
untraceable	17	140	
Total possible interviews		3,138	100%
Less:			
personal refusal by selected person	195	6%	
total refusal of information	187	6%	
no contact with anyone	75	2%	
proxy refusal	55	2%	
no contact with selected person	53	2%	
broken appointment	49	2%	
away/in hospital	39	1%	
senile/incapacitated	35	1%	
ill at home	22	1%	
speaks inadequate English	11	*	
known to interviewer	1	*	
Total non-response		7,252	23%
Interviews obtained		2,416	77%
Less rejected at editing stage		15	*
Interviews used in analysis		2,401	77%

THE STRUCTURE OF THE ACHIEVED SAMPLE

The comparison of the achieved sample after weighting with population data from other sources was:

COMPARISON OF SURVEY SAMPLE TO DATA FROM OTHER SOURCES—DEMOGRAPHIC CHARACTERISTICS

	Survey Sample	1971 Census
	%	%
Standard Region:		
North	6	6
North West	13	12
Yorkshire and Humberside	9	9
West Midlands	9	9
East Midlands	6	6
East Anglia	3	3
South West	6	7
South East	31	32
Wales	6	5
Scotland	11	10
		(Persons aged 16 and over)
Sex: Men	47	48
Women	53	52
Age: 16–24	14	17
25–44	33	32
45–64	34	32
65+	18	18

COMPARISON OF SURVEY SAMPLE TO DATA FROM OTHER SOURCES—DEMOGRAPHIC CHARACTERISTICS—continued

	Survey Sample	General Household Survey (Persons aged 16 and over)
	%	%
Working Status:		
Working	60	62
Not working	40	38
	(All in work)	(All in work)
Socio-Economic Group of Employment:		
Professional/Employer/Manager	16	13
Junior non-manual	32	31
Skilled manual	28	29
Semi-skilled/unskilled manual	23	27

As noted in the Introduction, the definitions of readership used in this report are different from those used in the *National Readership Survey*. For national mornings, the comparison of NRS "average issue" readership with "regular readership" (5–6 issues a week) and "occasional readership" (1+ issue a week) as defined for this report is:

COMPARISON OF SURVEY READERSHIP RESULTS WITH *NATIONAL READERSHIP SURVEY* RESULTS

	This survey (persons aged 16 and over)		National Readership Survey (persons aged 16 and over)
	Regular readers	Regular occasional readers	Average issue readers
	%	%	%
Daily Mirror/Record	26	37	35
The Sun	19	30	28
Daily Express	15	22	19
Daily Mail	10	14	12
The Daily Telegraph	7	12	9
The Times	2	4	3
The Guardian	2	4	3
Financial Times	1	2	2

There is a close correspondence in the relative readership of different newspapers between the data from the two sources.

Appendix 3: The Questionnaire

P.395   *September* 1975

Survey of Attitudes to the Press
Respondent Selection Sheet

ONE RESPONDENT SELECTION SHEET MUST BE COMPLETED FOR EACH ADDRESS ISSUED.

Listed Address.. Area Code ....

.... Address Serial No. ....
                                                                                                                                       ↑
                                                                                                                                       last
                                                                                                                                       digit

1. **Address Summary**

                                                                                                     Ring One Code Only

    Traceable, residential and occupied ...   .   1 ⟶ 2
    No trace of address   2
    Address vacant/derelict   3
    Premises demolished   4
    Business/industrial premises only   5
    Address an institution   6
    No contact with anyone at address after .... calls   7
    Complete refusal of information   8

2. List all persons aged 16+ who live at the ADDRESS in alphabetical order (going first on surnames, then christian names), in the grid below.

Persons aged 16+ *at Address*	Person No.
	1
	2
	3
	4
	5
	6
	7
	8
	9
	10

Total no. of persons aged 16+ at address ....

If there is only one person aged 16+, seek to interview that person, recording the result on the back of this sheet. If there are two or more, use the grid on the back of this sheet to select the person to be interviewed.

3. Use the column on the grid headed with the last digit of the address serial number. Go down the column until you come to the line for the total number of persons aged 16+ at the address. The number printed where the row and column meet is the person number of the person you must interview. NO SUBSTITUTES MAY BE TAKEN.

No. of persons aged 16+	Last Digit of Address No.									
	1	2	3	4	5	6	7	8	9	0
One	1	1	1	1	1	1	1	1	1	1
Two	2	1	2	1	2	1	2	1	2	1
Three	3	2	1	3	1	2	1	3	2	2
Four	1	2	4	2	3	4	3	2	1	3
Five	4	5	3	1	5	3	2	1	4	2
Six	3	4	5	6	1	2	4	3	5	1
Seven	6	3	7	2	7	5	1	4	6	5
Eight	5	1	6	1	4	3	7	2	8	4
Nine	9	4	8	6	2	1	5	6	3	7
Ten or more	2	4	1	3	6	5	10	7	9	8

Person No. Selected	Full Name

4. **Final Result**

Ring One Code Only

Interview obtained ... ... 1 (attach questionnaire)

No interview obtained because:
—selected person not contacted (e.g. never in) ... 2
—selected person personally refused interview ... 3
—selected person broke appointment and could not be recontacted 4
—selected person ill (at home) during survey period... 5
—selected person away/in hospital during survey period 6
—selected person senile/incapacitated 7
—refusal, on behalf of selected person, by someone else in household 8
—other reason for no interview (WRITE IN) 9

Name of Interviewer .... Interviewer No. ....
(BLOCK CAPS)

Date of Interview ..../............./...............

Attach this Sheet to the front of the Questionnaire relating to this Address.

Survey of Attitudes to the Press

P.395 September 1975

We are carrying out a survey for the Royal Commission on the Press on the newspapers people read and what they think of them.

Time interview started (WRITE IN).. Record No. (1–4)
Card 10 (5/6)

Area Code .... (7–9)

Address No. .... (10–11)

No. of electors listed at address .... (12–13)
(FROM SAMPLE ISSUE SHEET)

Total No. of adults (16+) living at address .... (14–15)
(FROM RESPONDENT SELECTION SHEET)

PART 1

EXPOSURE TO MEDIA

1. (a) SHOW CARD A This is a list of the national morning newspapers. Which of these, if any, do you ever read or look at nowadays? What others?
PROBE TO "NONE"

(b) ASK OF EACH MENTIONED AT (a) How many issues of .... do you read or look at in an average week?

	1 (a) Read/ look at at all	1 (b) Issues in an average week		Col./ Code	Skip to
		Less than one	1 2 3 4 5 6		
The Times	A	0	1 2 3 4 5 6	(16)	
Financial Times	A	0	1 2 3 4 5 6	(17)	
The Guardian	A	0	1 2 3 4 5 6	(18)	
Daily Telegraph	A	0	1 2 3 4 5 6	(19)	
Daily Express	A	0	1 2 3 4 5 6	(20)	
Daily Mail	A	0	1 2 3 4 5 6	(21)	
Daily Mirror (Daily Record: Scotland) ...	A	0	1 2 3 4 5 6	(22)	
The Sun	A	0	1 2 3 4 5 6	(23)	
Morning Star	A	0	1 2 3 4 5 6	(24)	
Reads/Looks at none of these	0				
				(25)	

Total No. of national morning newspapers read/looked at weekly or more often (TOTAL CODED 1–6 at Q. 1 (b)) .... (26).

Part 1—*continued*

		Card 10	Col./ Code	Skip to

2. (a) SHOW CARD B This is a list of all the *Sunday* newspapers published in Great Britain. Some are regional and for these the place where they are published is shown in brackets. Which of these, if any, do you ever read or look at nowadays? What others? PROBE TO "NONE".

(b) ASK OF EACH MENTIONED AT (a) How many issues of .... do you read or look at in an average month?

	2 (a) Read/ look at at all	2 (b) Issues in an average month Less than one					
Sunday Times	A	0	1	2	3	4	(27)
Observer	A	0	1	2	3	4	(28)
Sunday Express	A	0	1	2	3	4	(29)
Sunday Mirror	A	0	1	2	3	4	(30)
The People	A	0	1	2	3	4	(31)
Sunday Telegraph	A	0	1	2	3	4	(32)
News of the World	A	0	1	2	3	4	(33)
Sunday Mercury (Birmingham)	A	0	1	2	3	4	(34)
Sunday Sun (Newcastle) ...	A	0	1	2	3	4	(35)
The Independent (Plymouth)	A	0	1	2	3	4	(36)
Sunday Post (Glasgow) ...	A	0	1	2	3	4	(37)
Sunday Mail (Glasgow) ...	A	0	1	2	3	4	(38)
Reads/looks at none of these	0						(39)

3. (a) Is there any local or regional *daily* newspaper which you ever read or look at nowadays (it does not matter whether it is published in the morning or the evening)? IF YES Which? What others? PROBE TO "NONE". ... ... (40)

    Yes 1   Q. 4
    No 2   Q. 4

(b) IF YES TO (a) Which? What others? PROBE TO "NONE"

(c) ASK OF EACH MENTIONED AT (b)
How many issues of .... do you read or look at in an average week?

3 (b) (WRITE IN EXACT TITLE(S))	3 (c) Issues in an average week Less than one							
....	0	1	2	3	4	5	6	(41–47)
....	0	1	2	3	4	5	6	(48–54)
....	0	1	2	3	4	5	6	(55–61)
....	0	1	2	3	4	5	6	(62–68)

Part 1—*continued*

Card 10

	Col./Code	Skip to
4. (a) Is there any local or regional *weekly* newspaper which you ever read or look at nowadays (this includes any weekly newspaper which may be delivered free of charge to your household)?	(69)	
Yes	1	
No	2	Q. 5

(b) IF YES TO (a). Which? PROBE FOR EXACT TITLE. CHECK COPY FOR EXACT TITLE IF POSSIBLE. What others? (PROBE TO "NONE")

(c) ASK OF EACH MENTIONED AT (b) How many issues of .... do you read or look at in an average month?

4 (b) WRITE IN EXACT TITLE(S)	4 (c) Issues in an average month					
	Less than one	1	2	3	4	
....	0	1	2	3	4	(70–76) P395 (78–80) Card 20 (5/6)
....	0	1	2	3	4	(7–13)
....	0	1	2	3	4	(14–20)
....	0	1	2	3	4	(21–27)
....	0	1	2	3	4	(28–34)

	Col./Code	Skip to
5. (a) Do you watch television at all nowadays?	(35)	
Yes	A	
No	0	Q. 6
IF YES TO 5 (a), ASK 5 (b) and 5 (c)		
(b) On an average *weekday*, about how many hours do you spend watching television?		
Less than 1 hour a day	1	
1 but under 3 hours a day	2	
3 but under 5 hours a day	3	
5 hours a day or more	4	
(c) Do you ever watch the BBC or ITN news on television? IF YES: On average about how many days a week do you watch the news on television?	(36)	
Never watch	0	
Less than once a week	1	
1–3 days a week	2	
4–5 days a week	3	
6–7 days a week	4	

Part 1—*continued*

Card 20	Col./Code	Skip to

(37)

6. (a) Do you listen to the radio at all nowadays?
   Yes ... ...   A   Q. 7
   No   0

   IF YES TO 6 (a) ASK 6 (b) and 6 (c)

   (b) On an average *weekday*, about how many hours do you spend listening to the radio?
   Less than 1 hour a day   1
   1 hour but under 3 hours a day   2
   3 hours but under 5 hours a day   3
   5 hours or more a day   4

   (c) Do you ever listen to news bulletins on radio? IF YES: On average about how many days a week do you listen to the news on radio?   (38)
   Never listen   0   Q. 7
   Less than once a week   1
   1–3 days a week   2
   4–5 days a week   3
   6–7 days a week   4

   (d) IF EVER LISTENS AT (c) On *weekdays*, at what time of day do you usually listen to news bulletins? Do you usually listen to them ....   (39)

   READ OUT: .... before 9.30 am   1
   .... between 9.30 am and 5.30 pm   2
   .... or after 5.30 pm   3
   None of these—Respondent does not listen on weekdays ...   0

Card 20

PART 2

News Sources

7. SHOW CARD C. I am going to mention a number of different sorts of news, I would like you to tell me, for each, how interested you are in keeping up to date and well informed about news of that sort.

	Very interested	Fairly interested	Not at all interested	
—news about what is happening in other countries	1	2	3	(40)
—news about what the government is doing in Britain	1	2	3	(41)
—news about political parties	1	2	3	(42)
—news about trade union affairs ...	1	2	3	(43)
—news about business and industry ...	1	2	3	(44)
—news about what is going on in this part of the country	1	2	3	(45)
—news about what the local council is doing	1	2	3	(46)
—news about horse racing	1	2	3	(47)
—news about football	1	2	3	(48)
—news about fashions	1	2	3	(49)
—news about people in the entertainment business	1	2	3	(50)

Part 2—*continued*

Card 20

ASK Q. 8 (a) SEPARATELY FOR EACH TYPE OF NEWS IN WHICH RESPONDENT IS VERY OR FAIRLY INTERESTED (Q. 7). START BY TICKING IN LEFT HAND MARGIN TYPES OF NEWS TO BE ASKED ABOUT.

8. (a) SHOW CARD D Which, if any, of these do *you yourself* find useful in keeping up to date and well informed on .... (TYPE OF NEWS)? Any others? PROBE TO "NO". (MORE THAN ONE CODE MAY BE RINGED).

ASK Q. 8 (a) ABOUT: (TICK)

(b) IF TWO OR MORE SOURCES MENTIONED AT (a) Which *one* of these do *you yourself* find *most* useful in keeping up to date and well informed about .... (TYPE OF NEWS)?

		National morning news-papers	National Sunday news-papers	Local evening news-papers	Local weekly news-papers	Maga-zines	TV	National radio stations	Local radio stations	None of these	
News about what is happening in other countries	(a)	1	2	3	4	5	6	7	8	0	(51)
	(b)	1	2	3	4	5	6	7	8	0	(52)
News about what the government is doing in Britain	(a)	1	2	3	4	5	6	7	8	0	(53)
	(b)	1	2	3	4	5	6	7	8	0	(54)
News about political parties	(a)	1	2	3	4	5	6	7	8	0	(55)
	(b)	1	2	3	4	5	6	7	8	0	(56)
News about trade union affairs	(a)	1	2	3	4	5	6	7	8	0	(57)
	(b)	1	2	3	4	5	6	7	8	0	(58)
News about business and industry	(a)	1	2	3	4	5	6	7	8	0	(59)
	(b)	1	2	3	4	5	6	7	8	0	(60)
News about what is going on in this part of the country	(a)	1	2	3	4	5	6	7	8	0	(61)
	(b)	1	2	3	4	5	6	7	8	0	(62)
News about what the local council is doing	(a)	1	2	3	4	5	6	7	8	0	(63)
	(b)	1	2	3	4	5	6	7	8	0	(64)
News about horse racing	(a)	1	2	3	4	5	6	7	8	0	(65)
	(b)	1	2	3	4	5	6	7	8	0	(66)
News about football	(a)	1	2	3	4	5	6	7	8	0	(67)
	(b)	1	2	3	4	5	6	7	8	0	(68)
News about fashions	(a)	1	2	3	4	5	6	7	8	0	(69)
	(b)	1	2	3	4	5	6	7	8	0	(70)
News about people in the entertainment business	(a)	1	2	3	4	5	6	7	8	0	(71)
	(b)	1	2	3	4	5	6	7	8	0	(72)

P395 (78–80)

Part 2—*continued*

Record No. (1–4)
Card 30   (5/6)

9. (a) What do you think are the important issues and problems facing this district nowadays? PROBE FULLY. RECORD ANSWERS FULLY. IF NO PROBLEMS AT ALL MENTIONED SKIP TO PART 3.

(7–11)

0U0

....

(b) IF TWO OR MORE ISSUES OR PROBLEMS MENTIONED AT (a) Of the issues and problems you have mentioned, which *one* do you yourself see as *most* important?

(12–16)

0U0

....

	Card 30	Col./ Code	Skip to
9. (c) ASK OF SINGLE PROBLEM MENTIONED AT 9 (a) OR PROBLEM NAMED AS MOST IMPORTANT AT 9 (b) How have you come to know of .... (PROBLEM)? Was it in any of these ways? SHOW CARD E Any others?			
PROBE TO "NO"		(17)	
From personal experience		1	
From what people I meet say		2	
From local newspapers		3	
From local radio		4	
From television		5	
From national newspapers		6	
From national radio		7	
From magazines		8	

PART 3

ATTITUDES TO PARTICULAR NEWSPAPERS

THERE ARE TWO TYPES OF NEWSPAPER SHEET.

ONE (YELLOW) IS FOR LOCAL OR REGIONAL MORNING, EVENING, WEEKLY AND SUNDAY NEWSPAPERS.

THE OTHER (BLUE) IS FOR NATIONAL DAILY NEWSPAPERS (THOSE LISTED ON CARD A).

COMPLETE ONE LOCAL OR REGIONAL NEWSPAPER SHEET FOR:

—EACH LOCAL OR REGIONAL DAILY OF WHICH AT LEAST ONE ISSUE IS READ/LOOKED AT ONCE OR MORE IN AN AVERAGE WEEK (CODES 1-6 AT Q. 3 (b))

—EACH LOCAL OR REGIONAL WEEKLY OF WHICH AT LEAST ONE ISSUE IS READ/LOOKED AT IN AN AVERAGE MONTH (CODES 1-6 AT Q. 4 (b))

—EACH REGIONAL SUNDAY OF WHICH AT LEAST ONE ISSUE IS READ/LOOKED AT IN AN AVERAGE MONTH (CODES 1-6 AT Q. 2 (b) FOR PAPERS WITH A TOWN LISTED)

COMPLETE A NATIONAL NEWSPAPER SHEET ONLY IF RESPONDENT READS/LOOKS AT AT LEAST ONE ISSUE OF A NATIONAL MORNING IN AN AVERAGE WEEK (CODES 1-6 AT Q. 1 (b)). IF HE READS/LOOKS AT MORE THAN ONE TITLE, USE GRID BELOW TO SELECT ONE TO ASK ABOUT AND RING NUMBER CHOSEN IN GRID.

No. of Nationals Read/Looked at	Last Digit of Address No.									
	1	2	3	4	5	6	7	8	9	0
One	1	1	1	1	1	1	1	1	1	1
Two	2	1	2	1	2	1	2	1	2	1
Three	3	2	1	3	1	2	1	3	2	2
Four	1	2	4	2	3	4	3	2	1	3
Five	4	5	3	1	5	3	2	1	4	2
Six	3	4	5	6	1	2	4	3	5	1
Seven	6	3	7	2	7	5	1	4	6	5
Eight	5	1	6	1	4	3	7	2	8	4
Nine	9	4	8	6	2	1	5	6	3	7

NUMBERS REFER TO THE ORDER IN WHICH THE NATIONALS READ ARE PRINTED ON THE QUESTIONNAIRE AT Q. 1.

PART 4

GENERAL

		Card 30	Col./ Code	Skip to

10. (a)	ASK ALL
	Have you ever written a letter for publication to the editor of a newspaper? ... ...
	             Yes ... ...
	             No ... ...
	IF YES TO (a) ASK (b)–(e)
			(18)
			A
			0
				Q. 11

(b)	When did you last do so? Less than 1 year ago ... ... 1 but under 2 years ago ... ... 2 but under 5 years ago ... ... Longer ago		1 2 3 4	
(c)	To which newspaper did you *last* write? PROBE FOR EXACT TITLE		(19–24)	
(d)	What was that letter about? PROBE FULLY. RECORD ANSWERS FULLY........................		(25–27)	

(e)	Was that letter published?
	      Yes ... ...
	      No ... ...
			(28)
			1
			2	

11. (a)	ASK ALL Is there more than one evening newspaper sold in this area so that you can make a choice? Yes, more than one sold ... ... No, only one sold ... ... No evening newspaper sold at all		(29) 1 2 3	Q. 11b Q. 11c Q. 12

(b)	IF YES AT (a) Do you think you benefit at all from having more than one evening newspaper in this area? IF YES How? PROBE FULLY. RECORD ANSWERS FULLY
	      Yes ... ...
	      No ... ...
	....
	....
			(30)
			1
			2
			(31)
				Q. 12

(c)	NOW SKIP TO Q. 12
	IF NO AT (a) Do you think you would benefit in any way if there were more than one evening newspaper in this area? IF YES How? PROBE FULLY. RECORD ANSWERS FULLY
	      Yes ... ...
	      No ... ...
	....
	....
			(32)
			1
			2
			(33)
				Q. 12

Part 4—*continued*

		Card 30	Col./Code	Skip to

ASK ALL
12. SHOW CARD A This is a list of all the national daily newspapers. You may have heard that some of them are in financial difficulties. It has even been suggested that some may have to close. If that happened, which *one* would you yourself most want to keep? And which after that? And which after that?

	Want to keep:		
	Most (34)	2nd most (35)	3rd most (36)
The Times	1	1	1
Financial Times	2	2	2
The Guardian	3	3	3
Daily Telegraph	4	4	4
Daily Express	5	5	5
Daily Mail	6	6	6
Daily Mirror (*Daily Record* Scotland)	7	7	7
The Sun	8	8	8
Morning Star	9	9	9
Don't know/Don't care	0	0	0

13. (a) Have you heard of the Press Council? (37)
    Yes ... 1
    No ... 2   Q. 14
    Uncertain ... 3

   IF YES OR UNCERTAIN ASK (b)

   (b) Do you know what it does? (38)
    Yes ... 1
    No ... 2

   (c) IF YES TO (b) What does it do? PROBE FULLY. RECORD ANSWERS FULLY

   ....
   ....
   ....
   ....   (39–40)
   ....

PART 5

CLASSIFICATION DATA

Card 30

	Col./Code	Skip to

14. (a) Were you born in this county/(region SCOT)? — (41)
- Born in county/region ... 1 — Q. 14c
- Not born in county/region ... A — Q. 14b

(b) IF NOT BORN IN COUNTY/REGION How long have you lived in this county/(region Scot.)?
- 10 years or more ... 2
- 5 but under 10 years ... 3 — Now ask
- 2 but under 5 years ... 4
- Under 2 years ... 5 — Q. 14d

(c) Were you born in this district, that is within about five miles of this address? — (42)
- Born in district ... 1 — Q. 15
- Not born in district ... A — Q. 14d

(d) ASK IF NOT BORN IN DISTRICT ("No" to 14 (a) or 14 (c)) How long have you lived in this district?
- 10 years or more ... 2
- 5 but under 10 years ... 3
- 2 but under 5 years ... 4
- Under 2 years ... 5

ASK ALL

15. (a) Are you a member of any of these types of organisation? SHOW CARD K. IF YES Which? Any others? PROBE TO "NONE"
FOR EACH ORGANISATION INFORMANT IS MEMBER OF ASK (b) AND (c)

(b) Have you attended any meetings of .... in the last 12 months? (RECORD IN GRID BELOW)

(c) Are you an official or committee member of ....?
(RECORD IN GRID BELOW)

	(a) Membership		(b) Attended a meeting		(c) Official or Committee member		
	Yes	No	Yes	No/D.K.	Yes	No	
Trade Union ...	A	2	4	5	7	B	(43)
Professional Association	A	2	4	5	7	B	(44)
Business group or club ... (e.g. Rotary, Chamber of Commerce)	A	2	4	5	7	B	(45)
Political Party ...	A	2	4	5	7	B	(46)
Parents' Association ...	A	2	4	5	7	B	(47)
Tenants' or Ratepayers' Association ...	A	2	4	5	7	B	(48)
Any other community or pressure group ...	A	2	4	5	7	B	(49)
Any public body or committee ...	A	2	4	5	7	B	(50)

Part 5—*continued*

	Col./ Code	Skip to

Card 30

16. (a) Are you a member of any of these types of organisation? SHOW CARD L. PROBE: "Any others" until "No" RECORD IN COLUMN (a) OF GRID BELOW.

    (b) Do you help to organise or run any of these? (NOT DEPENDENT ON MEMBERSHIP.) RECORD ANSWERS IN COLUMN (b) OF GRID BELOW.

	(a) *Member*		(b) *Run*	
	Yes	No	Yes	No
			(51)	
Sports club	A	B	1	C
A club for hobbies or other leisure activities	A	B	2	C
Youth club, scouts or guides	A	B	3	C
Charitable organisation	A	B	4	C
Voluntary welfare organisation	A	B	5	C
Military Training Group	A	B	6	C
Church club or group	A	B	7	C
Social club of any kind	A	B	8	C
Any other type of club or organisation (specify)	A	B	9	C
None of these	A		0	

17. (a) Generally speaking, do you usually think of yourself as Conservative, Labour, Liberal, (*Wales/Scotland only*: Nationalist) or what?
    RING ONE CODE ONLY (52)

    Conservative ... 1
    Labour ... 2
    Liberal ... 3
    Nationalist ... 4
    Other (specify) ... 5
    None of these/Don't know ... Y
    UNLESS NONE OR DON'T KNOW AT (a)

    (b) How strongly .... (Party) do you generally feel— (53)
    READ OUT ... very strongly ... 1
    ... fairly strongly ... 2
    or ... not very strongly ... 3

(54)

Sex
Male ... 1
Female ... 2
Age last birthday (55–56)
(WRITE IN) ...

(57)
Household Status
Head of household ... 1
Housewife ... 2
Both head of household and housewife ... 3
Other ... 4

No. in household aged:
0–4 years ... (58)
5–15 years ... (59)
16–59 years ... (60)
60 or more years ... (61)
Total in household (62–63)
(incl. respondent)

			Col./ Code	Skip to
		Card 30		
Activity Status (64)	*Age completed full-time education*		(65)	
	14 or under		1	
Working full-time (31+ hours) 1	15		2	
	16		3	
Working part-time (10–30 hours) 2	17		4	
	18		5	
Seeking work 3	19		6	
Retired/sick 4	20		7	
Non-working housewife 5	21 or over		8	
Full-time student ... 6	Not yet completed full-time education		9	
Other (WRITE IN) 7				

OCCUPATION (PRESENT OR LAST MAIN PAID JOB) OF RESPONDENT
Name/title of job............
Description of activity ....

Skill/training/qualifications/experience required for job............

(66– 67)

Supervision/management responsibilities (incl. no. of people supervised) ....
Industry/business/profession (of employer) ....
No. of people employed at place of work............
Employment status:
  Employee ... ... A
  Self-employed ... ... B

OCCUPATION (PRESENT OR LAST MAIN PAID JOB) OF HEAD OF HOUSEHOLD IF OTHER THAN RESPONDENT
Name/title of job............
Description of activity ....

Skill/training/qualifications/experience required for job............

(68– 69)

Supervision/management responsibilities (incl. no. of people supervised) ....
Industry/business/profession (of employer)............
No. of people employed at place of work............
Employment status:
  Employee ... ... A
  Self-employed ... ... B

Time Interview completed............ (73)
(70–72)   Card Set ... 1
Duration of interview .... minutes   Used ... 2
(RING)
Name of Interviewer............
(74-76)
Interviewer No. ....

Date of Interview............   P395   (78–80)

P.395

Local or Regional Newspaper Sheet

COMPLETE ONE OF THESE SHEETS FOR:

—EACH LOCAL OR REGIONAL DAILY OF WHICH ONE OR MORE ISSUE IS READ OR LOOKED AT IN AN AVERAGE WEEK (Q. 3 (c))

—EACH LOCAL OR REGIONAL WEEKLY OF WHICH ONE OR MORE ISSUE IS READ OR LOOKED AT IN AN AVERAGE MONTH (Q. 4 (c))

—EACH LOCAL OR REGIONAL SUNDAY OF WHICH ONE OR MORE ISSUE IS READ OR LOOKED AT IN AN AVERAGE MONTH (Q. 2 (b))

Area Code .... Record No. (1–4)

Address No. .... Card 4 (5)

Local/Regional Newspaper Sheet No. .... (6)

Newspaper Title (Exact)...

0U0

.... (7–12)

....

1. (a) SHOW CARD F This is a list of features which often appear in local or regional newspapers. Are there any of these features which *never* appear in the .... ?

   (b) ASK SEPARATELY OF EACH FEATURE WHICH APPEARS. SHOW CARD G
   When you read the .... (PAPER), how often do you look at .... ?
   Which of the Statements on the card best describes what you do?

	1 (a)		1 (b)				
	Never appears	Don't know whether it appears	Never look at	Some- times look at	Usually look at	Always make a point of looking at	
Announcements of births, deaths and marriages...	0	1	3	4	5	6	(13)
Advertising of jobs ...	0	1	3	4	5	6	(14)
Advertising of items for sale or wanted ...	0	1	3	4	5	6	(15)
List of TV and radio pro- grammes	0	1	3	4	5	6	(16)
Women's page	0	1	3	4	5	6	(17)

Card 4

2. (a) SHOW CARD H This is another list of things which often appear in local or regional newspapers. Are there any of these which *never* appear in the .... (PAPER)?

(b) ASK SEPARATELY OF EACH FEATURE WHICH APPEARS When you read the .... (PAPER) how often do you look at ....? Which of the statements on the card best describes what you do?

SHOW CARD G AGAIN

	1 (a)		1 (b)				
	Never appears	*Don't know whether it appears*	*Never look at*	*Sometimes look at*	*Usually look at*	*Always make a point of looking at*	
News about what is happening in other countries	0	1	3	4	5	6	(18)
News about what the government is doing in Britain	0	1	3	4	5	6	(19)
News about what the local council is doing	0	1	3	4	5	6	(20)
News about local business and industry	0	1	3	4	5	6	(21)
News about local trade union affairs	0	1	3	4	5	6	(22)
News about local sport	0	1	3	4	5	6	(23)
Reports of local court cases	0	1	3	4	5	6	(24)
Pictures and reports of weddings and funerals	0	1	3	4	5	6	(25)
Comment about local issues	0	1	3	4	5	6	(26)
Gardening page or column	0	1	3	4	5	6	(27)
Articles about cars and motoring	0	1	3	4	5	6	(28)
Readers' letters	0	1	3	4	5	6	(29)

Card 4

3. (a) SHOW CARD I When it is reporting on controversial local issues, do you think .... (PAPER) often pays *too little attention* to the views of any of these sorts of people? Any others? PROBE TO "NO"

(b) Apart from the ones on the card, are there any other *sorts of people* or *groups* to whose views the .... (PAPER) often pays *too little* attention? Any others? PROBE TO "NO"

(c) SHOW CARD I When it is reporting on controversial local issues, do you think .... (PAPER) often pays *too much attention* to the views of any of these sorts of people? Any others? PROBE TO "NO"

(d) Apart from the ones on the card, are there any other *sorts of people* or *groups* to whose views the .... (PAPER) often pays *too much* attention? Any others? PROBE TO "NO"

	3 (a/b) Pays too little attention (30)	3 (c/d) Pays too much attention (31)	Col./ Code	Skip to
3 (a/c)				
Officials of the local council	1	1		
Local councillors	2	2		
Big commercial companies	3	3		
Local businessmen	4	4		
Local trade union leaders	5	5		
Religious people	6	6		
People in the higher income groups	7	7		
People in the lower income groups	8	8		
The police	9	9		
Young people	0	0		
None of these	X	X		
3 (b/d)				
Others (WRITE IN) ...			(32–	35)

4. (a) REFER BACK TO MAIN PROBLEM OF DISTRICT IDENTIFIED AT Q. 9 (a) or Q. 9 (b) OF MAIN QUESTIONNAIRE. You mentioned earlier that the main issues or problem facing this district nowadays is............... (PROBLEM). How much attention does .... (PAPER) give to this problem? Would you say it gives it a lot of attention, some attention or no attention at all? (36)

Lot of attention	1	Q. 5
Some attention	2	
No attention at all	3	

(b) IF SOME ATTENTION OR NO ATTENTION AT (a) Do you think the .... (PAPER) *should* give more attention to .... (PROBLEM)? (37)

Yes	1
No	2

Card 4

5. SHOW CARD J I am going to read out some comments people have made about newspapers. I would like you to tell me how true each of them is of the .... (PAPER).

IF LAST DIGIT OF ADDRESS NO. IS EVEN, READ LIST TOP TO BOTTOM.
IF IT IS ODD READ LIST BOTTOM TO TOP. RING ORDER READ.

Top to bottom	A
Bottom to top	B

	Very true	Fairly true	Not very true	Not true at all	Don't know	
It helps me to understand how what is happening in the country will affect me	1	2	3	4	9	(38)
It exaggerates the sensational aspects of the news	1	2	3	4	9	(39)
It takes an interest in ordinary people's problems	1	2	3	4	9	(40)
The comments it makes on the news are usually interesting	1	2	3	4	9	(41)
It always concentrates on the bad news	1	2	3	4	9	(42)
It is afraid of offending its advertisers	1	2	3	4	9	(43)
Reading it is always enjoyable ...	1	2	3	4	9	(44)
It often gets its facts wrong ...	1	2	3	4	9	(45)
It has too much advertising in it ...	1	2	3	4	9	(46)
I would miss it a lot if it stopped being published	1	2	3	4	9	(47)
It gives fair coverage to all points of view	1	2	3	4	9	(48)
It prints too many silly or trivial stories	1	2	3	4	9	(49)
Its standard of reporting is first class	1	2	3	4	9	(50)
It sometimes goes too far in invading people's grief	1	2	3	4	9	(51)
It always has the latest national news	1	2	3	4	9	(52)
It is prepared to criticse *anybody* if they deserve it	1	2	3	4	9	(53)
It has too little news in it	1	2	3	4	9	(54)

	Card 4	Col./ Code	Skip to

6. (a) Judging by what you have read in it, would you say the .... (PAPER) generally supports any one political party? IF YES Which? (55)

    No   0   Q. 7
    Yes—Conservative   1
           Labour   2
           Liberal   3
           Other (specify) ....

(b) IF YES TO (a) Do you think it *does* or *does not*, give fair coverage to the views of other political parties?

(c) IF DOES NOT AT (b) To which parties' views does it not give fair coverage? Any others? PROBE TO "NO" (56)

    Does give fair coverage to the other parties   0
    Does not give fair coverage:
      —to Conservatives   1
      —to Labour   2
      —to Liberal   3
      —to Other parties (specify) ....

ASK ALL

7. (a) When employers and unions disagree, does the .... (PAPER) usually: (57)

    READ OUT:—Report both sides of things fully   1
              or—Give more space to the employer's case ...   2
              or—Give more space to the union's case   3
              or—Not print much about it at all   4   Q. 8

(b) UNLESS "NOT PRINT MUCH" AT (a) When it makes comments on disagreements between employers and unions, does the .... (PAPER): (58)

    READ OUT:—Tend to favour the employers   1
              or—Tend to favour the unions   2
              or—Try to judge fairly between them   3
                 Never makes comments   4

		Card 4	Col./ Code	Skip to

8. (a) Do you know the name of the company which owns .... (PAPER)? (59)
   No 1
   IF YES What is it? .... (60–62)

(b) ASK ALL Do you know whether the company which owns .... (PAPER) owns any other newspapers? (63)
   Yes—owns others 1
   No—does not own others ... ... 2 } Q. 9
   Don't know 3

IF "YES" TO (b) ASK (c) AND (d)
(c) About how many other newspapers does it own? (64)
   1–4 1
   5–9 2
   10–15 3
   20 or more 4
   Don't know 9

(d) Does it own any other *local* or *regional* newspapers (whether daily, weekly or Sunday) which are sold *here*? (65)
   Yes 1
   No ... ... 2 } Q. 9
   Don't know 3

(e) IF YES TO (d) Which other local or regional newspapers which are sold *here* does it own? Any others? PROBE TO "NO". PROBE FOR EXACT TITLES (66)
   ....
   ....

9. On average, about how long in all do you yourself spend reading or looking at a particular issue of .... (PAPER)? (67)
   Less than 10 minutes 1
   10 minutes but under ¼ hour 2
   ¼ hour but under ½ hour 3
   ½ hour but under 1 hour 4
   1 hour but under 2 hours 5
   2 hours or more 6

   P395 (78–80)

P.395

NATIONAL MORNING NEWSPAPER SHEET

COMPLETE ONE OF THESE SHEETS IF RESPONDENT READS/LOOKS AT ONE OR MORE ISSUE OF ANY **NATIONAL MORNING** IN AN AVERAGE WEEK. IF HE READS/LOOKS AT ONE TITLE ONLY, ASK THE QUESTIONS ON THIS SHEET ABOUT THAT ONE. IF HE READS/LOOKS AT TWO OR MORE, USE THE GRID IN THE MAIN QUESTIONNAIRE TO DECIDE WHICH ONE TO ASK ABOUT.

Area Code ....   Record No. (1–4)
Address No.   ....   Card 40   (5/6)
Newspaper Title..(7–12)

                                                     0U0

....

Blank (13–37)

Card 40

1. SHOW CARD J I am going to read out some comments people have made about newspapers. I would like you to tell me how true each of them is of the .... (PAPER).

   IF LAST DIGIT OF ADDRESS NO. IS EVEN READ LIST TOP TO BOTTOM. IF IT IS ODD READ LIST BOTTOM TO TOP. RING ORDER READ.

Top to bottom	A
Bottom to top	B

	Very true	Quite true	Not very true	Not true at all	Don't know	
It helps me to understand how what is happening in the country will affect me	1	2	3	4	9	(38)
It exaggerates the sensational aspects of the news	1	2	3	4	9	(39)
It takes an interest in ordinary people's problems	1	2	3	4	9	(40)
The comments it makes on the news are usually interesting	1	2	3	4	9	(41)
It always concentrates on the bad news	1	2	3	4	9	(42)
It is afraid of offending its advertisers	1	2	3	4	9	(43)
Reading it is always enjoyable ...	1	2	3	4	9	(44)
It often gets its facts wrong ...	1	2	3	4	9	(45)
It has too much advertising in it ...	1	2	3	4	9	(46)
I would miss it a lot if it stopped being published	1	2	3	4	9	(47)
It gives fair coverage to all points of view	1	2	3	4	9	(48)
It prints too many silly or trivial stories	1	2	3	4	9	(49)
Its standard of reporting is first class	1	2	3	4	9	(50)
It sometimes goes too far in invading people's private grief	1	2	3	4	9	(51)
It always has the latest national news	1	2	3	4	9	(52)
It is prepared to criticise *anybody* if they deserve it	1	2	3	4	9	(53)
It has too little news in it	1	2	3	4	9	(54)

	Card 40	Col./ Code	Skip to

2. (a) Judging by what you have read in it, would you say the .... (PAPER) generally supports any one political party? IF YES Which? (55)

No	0 Q. 3
Yes—Conservative	1
Labour	2
Liberal	3
Other (specify)...............	4

(b) IF YES TO (a) Do you think it *does*, or *does not*, give fair coverage to the views of other political parties?

(c) IF DOES NOT AT (b) To which parties' views does it not give fair coverage? Any others? PROBE TO "NO" (56)

Does give fair coverage to other parties	0
Does not give fair coverage:	
—to Conservatives	1
—to Labour	2
—to Liberal	3
—to Other (specify)	

ASK ALL

3. (a) When employers and trade unions disagree, would you say the .... (PAPER): (57)

READ OUT:—Reports both sides of things fully	1
or—gives more space to the employer's case	2
or—gives more space to the union's case	3
or—does not print much about it at all	4 Q. 4

(b) UNLESS "NOT PRINT MUCH" AT (a) When it makes comments on disagreements between employers and unions, does the .... (PAPER): (58)

READ OUT:—Tend to favour the employers	1
or—tend to favour the unions	2
or—try to judge fairly between them	3
Never makes comments	4

	Card 40	Col./ Code	Skip to

4. (a) Do you know the name of the company which owns .... (PAPER)? (58)
   No   1
   IF YES What is it? ....   (59–62)

   ....

(b) ASK ALL Do you know whether the company which owns (63)
   .... (PAPER) owns any other newspapers?
   Yes—owns others   1
   No—does not own others   2   } Q. 5
   Don't know   3

   IF "YES" TO (b) ASK (c) AND (d)
(c) About how many other newspapers does it own? (64)
   1–4   1
   5–9   2
   10–15   3
   20 or more   4
   Don't know   9

(d) Does it own any other *local* or *regional* newspapers (whether (65)
   daily, weekly or Sunday) which are sold *here*?
   Yes   1
   No   2   } Q. 5
   Don't know   3

(e) IF YES TO (d) Which other local or regional newspapers (66)
   which are sold *here* does it own? Any others? PROBE TO
   "NO". PROBE FOR EXACT TITLES
   ....
   ....

5. On average, about how long in all do you spend reading or (67)
   looking at a particular issue of .... (PAPER)?
   Less than 10 minutes   1
   10 minutes but under ¼ hour   2
   ¼ hour but under ½ hour   3
   ½ hour but under 1 hour   4
   1 hour but under 2 hours   5
   2 hours or more   6

		P395	(78–80)

PART 2:

THE ATTITUDES OF PEOPLE IN INFLUENTIAL POSITIONS

INTRODUCTION

Purpose of Survey

At an early stage in the design of a survey to study attitudes to the provincial press it was recognised that there would be considerable value in interviewing, in addition to the general public, a special sample of respondents occupying positions of influence in the local community. By the nature of their position, it was thought likely that they would have a greater involvement in local affairs than most members of the general public and that this would be reflected in greater readership of the provincial press; members of the special sample would thus be perhaps better able to make comparisons between different types of provincial paper. Also, more importantly, their greater involvement in community affairs would probably result in their having a greater knowledge of many of the events and issues that are reported in regional and local newspapers. They were also likely, in many cases, to have participated in the events reported or have had their views quoted in the papers' discussion of local, or indeed national, issues. They would, in some sense, be not only "consumers", but also "producers" of news in a way that few members of the general public sample were likely to be.

CONCLUSIONS

As part of a programme of research for the Royal Commission on the Press, SCPR interviewed a special sample of 350 people considered to be in positions of local influence; as in the survey of the general public, the object of the study was to examine and evaluate the role of the regional and local press. The special sample consisted of council officials, councillors, managing directors, trade union secretaries, and head teachers. In addition to having an informed opinion and interest in many of the topics covered by the provincial press, these groups were selected with the expectation that many would have been involved in events or issues reported on or discussed in the local newspapers.

In profile, the special sample was very different from the general public sample. Predominantly male and somewhat older than the average of the general public, they were also better educated and tended to be in the professional and managerial and skilled occupations. Although on average not resident in the locality as long, they were considerably more involved in local community affairs than the general public. The special sample contained slightly fewer Conservative and Liberal supporters and slightly more Labour supporters than was found in the sample of the general public; this may reflect the situation in the specific limited number of areas chosen for inclusion in the study and may not represent the political allegiances of all people in the categories covered.

The special sample were great consumers of news, even in comparison with professional and managerial respondents among the general public. They were more likely to read a number of national and provincial newspapers, and also to listen to radio and TV news. However, they spent less time, on average, reading each paper and less time listening to television and radio, suggesting that they are more selective in what they choose to read. 82% read a national daily paper and 33% a regional morning paper on a regular basis; 60% regularly read an evening paper and 46% a local weekly paper, all considerably greater proportions than was the case for the general public. Respondents in the special sample were also less likely to view different types of paper, eg provincial mornings and evenings, as alternatives.

Part of the greater readership of provincial newspapers may be explained by the need of the special sample to be informed of what was happening in the community. Larger proportions thought specialist journals and television "very" or "fairly" important for keeping them "... up to date and well informed" in their official capacity, than viewed regional newspapers in this light; nonetheless 61% of provincial evening papers were classed in this way by their readers. Although national newspapers were very marginally more important in this respect, local newspapers in general were mentioned by many more respondents as a source of information on the important local issues and problems. Provincial morning papers also compared with national dailies in the extent to which they helped respondents "... understand how what is happening in the country will affect my interests in the area", although they might have been expected to perform better in what could be considered an important role of the provincial newspapers. Indeed only 45% of readers of evening papers thought they performed this task at least "fairly well".

In addition to the use they made of the provincial press as readers, four out of five respondents had had some contact with the local press, most of whom had at some time taken positive steps to contact a newspaper. Relations were said to be at least "fairly good" by three-quarters of all respondents. Furthermore, the majority of councillors, trade union secretaries and managing directors were largely satisfied with the way the provincial press presented their point of view. This was important for the councillors and trade union secretaries, a majority of whom thought that provincial evening papers had a strong influence on the views of their readers, on whom many relied to elect them to office.

Although seemingly using the provincial press more than the general public, both as consumers and producers of news, many fewer among the special sample would miss the regional papers they read "a lot" if they stopped being published. Indeed, two out of five readers of provincial morning and evening papers would not miss them, and a majority would not miss their local weekly. Although it is probably true that the special sample have available other sources of information for local news—through personal contacts and through their occupation—nonetheless, it would appear possible that the provincial press is not performing the role respondents in the special sample would like to see it perform or at least it is not performing the role as adequately as it might.

The special sample are more critical of standards in the provincial press than are the general public. In terms of a general rating of a paper's quality however, most appear to be seen to perform well: 69% of regional mornings are rated as excellent, very good or fairly good, as are 51% of weeklies and 49% of evenings; only 9%, 12% and 13% respectively are considered as being rather poor or very poor. There is not a great deal of difference between different types of respondent in their overall rating.

The slight tendency, evident in the general rating on quality, for weeklies and, particularly, local evenings, to be less highly thought of than provincial morning papers by their readers is reflected also in the evaluation of particular aspects of newspaper standards. Provincial mornings are considered to be close to the national dailies in the extent to which they "always [have] the latest national news" while evenings receive a lower rating. Only 41% believe the reporting in their evening paper is "first class", 4% fewer than readers of weekly papers and 26% fewer than of provincial mornings; 56% of readers said their evening paper "often gets its facts wrong"; only one-third of readers of other provincial papers felt this way; furthermore 46% felt their evening newspaper printed "... too many silly or trivial stories".

On a different aspect of editorial standards, the extent to which the paper is seen as sensationalising aspects of the news, going too far in invading people's grief, and as always concentrating on the bad news, evening newspapers again came off worst. In all three cases the regional mornings were evaluated as being only somewhat below the quality national dailies that respondents read, although the popular dailies were rated much lower in these respects. Local weeklies were criticised even less in these respects. Overall, 45% of provincial papers were judged to "exaggerate the sensational aspects of the news"; 26% sometimes went "... too far in invading people's grief" and 30% "always concentrate on the bad news".

Trade union secretaries are the group most consistently critical of particular standards in the provincial press, although councillors and council officials are also often fairly critical.

If we turn our attention to specific articles of recent publication in which respondents had "some particular interest, involvement or knowledge" we find as many very favourable as very unfavourable comments made concerning the article. Indeed, when each article was rated for fairness, accuracy and the amount of coverage, the great majority received a high rating, with surprisingly little difference between types of newspaper. Among the criticisms made, biased or selective reporting or editing, and the limited space available in papers were most often cited as reasons for any fault.

Although there were a majority who expressed satisfaction with the way the provincial press fulfilled its role of providing information on important local issues, nonetheless a substantial minority expressed some dissatisfaction. No one specific local topic stood out as being treated better or worse than others. When each respondent was asked to comment on how the newspapers he read dealt with more general topic areas, most were considered to be treated fairly well, if not very well. There was very little discernible difference between types of newspaper. There were some differences between the groups of respondents, each noticeably more critical of the way articles in his own field were reported. Apart from this partisan view, local trade union activities stand out as the topic the coverage of which was most often criticised; it is the topic considered least well dealt with, of the list of topic areas, by managing directors, trade union secretaries, council officials and head teachers. The main reason advanced for saying this topic was "least well" dealt with was an insufficient coverage given it by the provincial press (it may be speculated that there is an association between this finding and another result showing trade union secretaries to be the one group least likely to contact their local paper).

In slightly more than half the cases respondents had felt at some time like complaining about something in the local press, but complaints had been actually made in only 29% of the cases. Complaints were rarely made to weekly papers, more often to provincial morning and evening papers. The main reasons for complaint were either inaccuracies in reporting or else unfairness or bias. Complaints were most often directed to the editor, less often to journalists and rarely elsewhere; in a majority of cases no satisfactory outcome was obtained by respondents.

Unfairness or bias was an important cause of complaint against the provincial press and, as we saw earlier, was also quite commonly advanced as a reason for being critical of specific articles or reports in which respondents had been involved. However, the incidence of complaint was not high and, when questioned directly, in two-thirds of the cases, respondents said of the provincial papers they read that "it gives fair coverage to all points of view"; in a similar proportion of cases, the newspapers were said to be " . . . prepared to criticise anybody if it thinks they deserve it". In specific terms, in 56% of the cases the provincial newspapers were said not to give too much attention to any particular group and in 47% of the cases not to give too little attention to any particular group. Those who were most often said to receive "too much attention" were local businessmen, big commercial companies, councillors and council officials. Receiving "too little attention" were "people in the lower income group" and trade union leaders.

In party political terms, the extent of siding with any political party varied with the type of paper. Local evening and weekly papers were considered less likely to be partisan than were provincial mornings or national dailies. In all, more than half of the provincial papers read were said not to support any one political party. Those that did take sides were mainly seen as supporting the Conservative Party though not always to the exclusion of fair coverage to other parties. In the 18% of cases where the provincial newspapers were said not to give fair coverage to all political parties, they were overwhelmingly seen as being biased against the Labour Party.

Although "news of local trade union activities" was considered to be the one topic "least well" dealt with by the provincial press, there was not the same feeling about the reporting of local industrial disputes. The criticism here was more that local evening or weekly papers did not report much about industrial disputes at all. The local papers that were thought to report or comment on local industrial disputes were said to be fair in their coverage in more than half the cases. There was a feeling, however, that when a paper does not judge fairly between employers and unions, it is the union's case that suffers. On the other hand, fewer than one-quarter of provincial papers were said to hinder " . . . good industrial relations".

There was very little difference perceived between provincial newspapers when classified by the type of ownership of the newspaper, either as regards general quality or specific aspects of editorial standards. When directly questioned on the value of competition between papers of different ownership, more than half of those with more than one evening paper circulating in their area felt they did not benefit as a result. Among those who had no choice of evening paper even fewer felt they would benefit from competition in their area. Their knowledge of the ownership situation among their local newspapers, although greater than among the general public, was still not high. In 45% of cases, respondents could not name the owner of the local papers they read and in almost as many cases, they did not know whether those papers had companion papers in the area or they could not name them.

Size of circulation was not a major influence on the perceived quality of provincial papers. The news service of larger circulation papers, however, was rated more highly although these papers did receive criticism on some aspects of editorial standards, noticeably in the extent to which they invaded people's grief, and concentrated on the bad news.

Three further topics, important though peripheral to the main subject, were touched upon. One concerned the Press Council which was generally felt, by the large majority who broadly knew its function, to perform its functions at least fairly well. The most common criticism of the Council was that it did not have sufficient power or "teeth".

A second topic concerned the freedom of the press; just over half of respondents felt the freedom of the press to be in danger. Printing unions, costs and inflation, and "The Government" were most often mentioned as representing the biggest threats.

A final topic concerned the national daily papers respondents would most want to keep if some were to disappear. The general public tended to opt either for papers they read or for the quality papers. This pattern was repeated among the special sample; since they already concentrated their reading on the quality papers, this meant that they were in most cases willing to forgo the popular dailies.

MAIN FINDINGS
1. Survey Method

The Choice of "Influential" Groups

The decision to interview a special sample was based largely on the assumption that they would play a significant role in the community life upon which the provincial press reported. The choice of types of people to interview was based on a consideration of those aspects of local affairs that are of interest to provincial newspapers and are also areas in which a minority of people are in a position to influence or affect the lives of others. Three broad spheres of community life were selected as suitable to cover. These were:

(i) The economic spheres.

(ii) Welfare, health and education.

(iii) Housing, roads and other aspects of urban development and planning.

Recreation and sports was not included although it is extensively covered in local papers, because its management is somewhat fragmentary making it very difficult to identify any persons in a position of great influence in the local community.

(i) *Economic*

The economic sphere is one of major importance as it encompasses the livelihood of those living in the area. It includes industrial and commercial interests, employment and investment. A substantial part of local newspapers' news reporting and comment is likely to relate to this sphere, including the interpretation of the local implications of national and international economic trends and events. In addition, much of the advertising covered by local newspapers is placed by people who hold important positions in the economic sphere. These were considered to include:

> Large employers in the area (which may be local branches of national or international companies but will almost certainly include the local authority).
>
> Medium sized employers (which are probably more likely to be locally based companies).
>
> Organisations representing small business and commercial interests, such as Chamber of Commerce or Chamber of Trade.
>
> Local trade union organisations representing employees in workplaces of all sizes.

(ii) *Welfare, Health and Education*

This sphere is concerned with several aspects of family life and is the source of much of the "human interest" news featured in regional and local newspapers and would include:

> Local councillors from all main parties who are particularly concerned with these issues.
>
> Local authority senior personnel in the appropriate departments, eg Directors of Education, Environmental Health Officers.
>
> Head teachers.

(iii) *Housing, Roads and Other Aspects of Urban Development*

Housing shortages, problems of slum clearance or renewal of old housing stock, escalating house prices and rents, the provision of finance for house purchase, traffic management schemes, motorway plans, new shopping centres—these are all matters of great concern in local areas and the subject of news and controversy in regional newspapers. In this sphere in particular, local newspapers have the opportunity to exercise their surveillance function of keeping the public informed of the plans of the council or of business interests.

In these areas the people in important positions locally are likely to include:

> Local councillors.
>
> Local authority officials.
>
> Some local businessmen.

This categorisation of local affairs suggested the division of the sample into five distinct groups, each with a particular interest in one of these spheres of community life identified as being important to the provincial press, but often, also, with overlapping interests in other spheres. The five groups selected for interview were as follows (the numbers in brackets represent the target sample to be interviewed in each):

> (i) *Local Councillors*, at city, borough or district level, at metropolitan level, and also at county or regional level ... ... (50)
>
> (ii) *Local Council Officials*, again in appropriate departments, eg Chief Planning Officers, Housing Managers ... ... (50)
>
> (iii) *Managing Directors*, included chairmen of Chambers of Commerce or Chambers of Trade ... ... (100)
>
> (iv) *Trade Union Secretaries*, in most cases at district level but, in a few instances, at branch level ... ... (100)
>
> (v) *Head Teachers* ... ... (50)

Thus the total number of interviews was to be 350.

The Selection of Sampling Points

The main attention of the survey was focused on the regional press. For this reason a decision was made to select areas each of which contained a local evening newspaper publication centre; 12 areas in all were chosen to represent the various types of provincial evening newspaper ownership. With a target of 350 achieved interviews, this meant that interviews would be conducted with some 30 or so people in each area.

The restriction of interviewing to 12 areas, and the selection of publication centres with varying types of newspaper ownership, was made partly for reasons of cost, but also so as to enable any very unrepresentative newspapers or ownership to be discovered and taken into account. The result is that while respondents may be considered as being representative of "influentials" in their own locality, the survey does not purport to be a representative sample of all "influential" persons in the country, even within the spheres of community life selected.

The 12 areas selected for study are listed below. The evening newspaper published in each is printed in brackets.

Bradford	(*Telegraph and Argus*)
Cambridge	(*Cambridge Evening News*)
Cheltenham	(*Gloucestershire Echo*)
Darlington	(*Evening Despatch*)
Derby	(*Derby Evening Telegraph*)
Glasgow	(*Evening Times*)
Leeds	(*Evening Post*)
Liverpool	(*Liverpool Echo*)
Newcastle	(*Evening Chronicle*)
Reading	(*Evening Post*)
Worcester	(*Evening News*)
Wrexham	(*Evening Leader*)

Selection of Individual Names

There is, of course, no available sampling frame of people holding responsible positions in local affairs. However, for each of the five groups of people selected for interview there was a list, or sometimes a combination of lists, that records the names required in each of the 12 areas so that a representative sample of each group could be selected. The sampling frames used for each group of respondents were as follows:

Councillors

All councillors in the United Kingdom are listed, together with their home addresses, in *The Municipal Year Book*. To draw a sample of councillors, names were randomly selected from within the relevant authorities. If the named person was found to have resigned as a councillor, no substitute was taken.

Council Officials

Similarly all senior council officials are listed, by local authority, in *The Municipal Year Book*. A random sample of posts relevant to the three spheres of local affairs already referred to—economic, welfare, education, housing and roads—were selected. The persons to be interviewed were the present incumbents of each post.

Managing Directors

Business establishments were selected within each of the 12 survey areas from the Kompass business directory. Kompass, however, does not list subsidiaries and branches that are located at addresses other than that of the head office. The list of firms in Kompass was therefore supplemented by a list of local establishments of national or international firms, supplied by employment exchanges in each area. Firms were then stratified by the number of employees and equal numbers selected at random from large (250+ employees), medium (100–250 employees) and small establishments to obtain a cross-sectional, though not fully representative, sample of establishments. In all cases the most senior management person at each establishment was sought for interview.

Trade Union Secretaries

The 30 trade unions with the largest membership were contacted and asked to supply names and addresses of persons filling the role of secretary at district level or its equivalent. This position is a common one in a majority of large unions although called by a variety of names, perhaps the most common being "District Secretary" or "Divisional Secretary". Some unions, however, had no district or divisional structure or person holding a position equivalent to that of District or Divisional Secretary in other unions. In such cases, branch secretaries were selected to represent the union within each area. A list of secretaries was received from 28 trade unions. Four had no branches within any of the 12 areas selected for study. In each area, secretaries were randomly selected from unions having a district/branch organisation within that area.

Head Teachers

Schools were randomly selected from a list of all schools in the area taken from the *Education Committees Year Book*. The head teacher was approached for interview at each school.

Questionnaire Development

Before a questionnaire was designed, 25 semi-structured interviews were conducted, in three towns, using a guide of topics drawn up in consultation with the Commission. This exploratory stage was designed to ensure that no major areas of interest were overlooked, and to define more clearly some of the topic areas. Respondents were questioned in some depth about their attitude to the provincial press.

The interviews were studied in detail and on the basis of the exploratory study a questionnaire was drafted and agreed by the Commission. It was then piloted among 20 people occupying the various positions to be covered in the sample. Small amendments were made to the questionnaire in the light of the pilot interviews before the final questionnaire was agreed.

Fieldwork and Response

Fieldwork was carried out between October 1975 and February 1976. Interviewing was conducted in most cases either at the respondents' places of work or else their homes. The interview lasted $1-1\frac{1}{2}$ hours on average but was variable according to the number of provincial newspapers seen by each respondent.

It was expected that the sample would be difficult to contact in many cases and might produce a quite high rate of refusal. As a result a total of 526 names were selected to yield 350 interviews, allowing for a response rate of 67%. Not all names were issued to interviewers, however, some being held in reserve so that if the response rate should be higher than expected the sample would not be biased in favour of the more readily accessible respondents. In the event, the overall response was 87%, very much higher than expected. There was some variability by type of respondents, with managing directors proving the most difficult to cover. (A detailed breakdown of response is given in the Appendices.)

2. A Profile of the "Influential" Sample

SUMMARY

Members of the special sample were predominantly male, in profile older than members of the general public sample, consisting of many more members with professional and managerial occupations and many fewer with semi- or unskilled manual occupations. They were also better educated. Although fewer members of the special sample had been born or had lived more than ten years in the community, the special sample was much more involved in community life.

In political viewpoint, the special sample was not so very different from the general public (although 14% of the special sample refused to disclose their viewpoint). There were 4% fewer Conservative supporters and 3% more Labour supporters. There were many fewer Liberal supporters, however—3%, as opposed to 11% among the sample of the general public.

At a number of points throughout the report we shall be comparing the attitudes of the "influential" sample with those of the general public. Not surprisingly the special sample differs from the sample of the general public in a number of ways.

MAIN FINDINGS

Age

Compared with the general public few members of the special sample were under 25 years of age or 65 and over. There was little difference between groups of respondents in age profile; head teachers tended to be a little older and trade union secretaries a little younger than the average in the special sample.

TABLE 2.001
AGE OF RESPONDENTS IN THE "INFLUENTIAL" SAMPLE

	"Influential" Sample	General Public Sample
Base: All respondents	350	2,401
	%	%
Aged 16–34	8	33
35–44	22	14
45–54	35	18
55–64	31	16
65 or over	4	18

Sex

Only 24 (7%) respondents in the special sample were women. Half the women were head teachers, representing just less than a quarter (24%) of this group. The proportion of female respondents in the other groups was as follows:

Council officials	4%
Councillors	14%
Managing directors	0%
Trade union secretaries	3%

Socio-Economic Grouping

Not surprisingly the "influential" sample were mainly in the professional and managerial groups. Managing directors, council officials and head teachers would, in any case, be classed as such according to the Registrar General's *Classification of Occupations*.

Of the 100 trade union secretaries interviewed, 47 were full-time officials of their union, and would be classed as "Intermediate non-manual employees". The remaining 53 trade union secretaries were all in other full-time employment (apart from one who had retired) and their socio-economic grades are noted below. Similarly, all the councillors, apart from four non-working housewives, were either in, or else had retired from, other full-time employment.

TABLE 2.002

SOCIO-ECONOMIC GROUPING OF COUNCILLORS AND LAY TRADE UNION OFFICIALS

	Councillors	Lay Trade Union Officials	Total "Influential" Sample	General Public[1]
Base: All respondents	51	53	350	2,401
	%	%	%	%
Professional/managerial	41	28	67	20
Intermediate and junior non-manual	24	43	23	20
Skilled manual	25	34	9	35
Semi-skilled or unskilled manual	4	4	1	17
Non-working housewife	8	—	1	5

[1] The socio-economic grouping given for the general public sample is based on the occupation of the head of household.

Terminal Education Age

Given the preponderance of professional and managerial occupations and the position respondents held in the community it is not surprising to find that overall the "influential" sample finished their full-time education at a later age than the general public sample. There is some difference within the "influential" sample, however; more than half of trade union secretaries finished their education before the age of 16, as did 41% of councillors. 90% of head teachers, however, went on with their education to at least the age of 21.

TABLE 2.003

TERMINAL EDUCATION AGE

	"Influential" Sample	Councillors	Council Officials	Managing Directors	Trade Union Secs.	Head Teachers	General Public Sample
Base: All respondents	350	51	52	97	100	50	2,401
	%	%	%	%	%	%	%
15 years of age or under	26	41	2	15	54	2	65
16–17	24	27	33	30	22	2	21
18–20	10	10	21	15	2	6	5
21 years of age or over	39	22	44	38	22	90	5

Length of Association with the Local Area

Respondents in the "influential" sample were less likely to have been born in the county in which they now reside than were members of the general public sample; nonetheless almost three-quarters had lived in the county for 10 years or more.

TABLE 2.004

LENGTH OF ASSOCIATION WITH THE COUNTY

	"Influential" Sample	General Public Sample
Base: All respondents	350	2,401
	%	%
Born in county	40	66
Not born in county but lived here 10 years or more	33	26
Lived here 5 but less than 10 years	11	6
Lived here 2 but less than 5 years	7	4
Lived here under 2 years	4	3

Involvement in Community Affairs

Another measure of association with the local community was the extent of involvement with local clubs and organisations. The special sample were much more active in social and community affairs in their area than were members of the general public; 64% of respondents in the "influential" sample belong to at least one local club or organisation, compared with only 19% of the general public. They were also far more likely to belong to a political party (even when excluding councillors from the figures) and to belong to organisations such as tenants' or ratepayers' associations or local community groups. Those who were members were also more likely than those in the general public to participate fully in their activities by attending meetings and holding positions.

TABLE 2.005
MEMBERSHIP OF LOCAL ORGANISATIONS

	"Influential" Sample	General Public Sample
Base: All respondents	350	2,401
	%	%
Member of:		
Business group or club	23	2
Political party	40	5
Parents' association	22	6
Tenants' or ratepayers' association	8	6
Any other community or pressure group	9	2
Any public body or committee	41	2

Trade Union Membership

50% of the "influential" sample were trade union members; among those who were not trade union secretaries, the figure was 31%. In the sample of the general public 25% belonged to trade unions. However, we should remember that most of the "influential" sample were working full-time and, furthermore, were predominantly male. In fact male trade unionists represent more than half (53·6%) of the male working population, and more than 60% of male employees in employment[1]. Very few of the trade union members who were not in the trade union secretaries group had been officials in the past and only one was currently an official.

TABLE 2.006
TRADE UNION MEMBERSHIP AND ACTIVITY

	"Influential" Sample	Councillors	Council Officials	Managing Directors	Trade Union Secs.	Head Teachers
Base: All respondents	350	51	52	97	100	50
	%	%	%	%	%	%
Not trade union member	48	47	19	90	2	88
Trade union member	50	51	81	6	97	10
Attended meeting in last year	41	47	33	3	97	4
Not attended meeting in last year	9	4	48	3	—	6
Official or committee member	31	22	4	—	96	2

Tenure of Other Positions in the Community

A small number of respondents who were selected as members of groups other than the local councillors were also, or had been, local councillors. The

---

[1] Figures apply to 1974 and were obtained from the *Annual Abstract of Statistics* 1976 The figure for trade unionists, male and female, as a total of the working population was 45·9%.

proportion of each group who were currently councillors or had been in the past are as follows:

	Who are Councillors at present %	Who were Councillors in past %
Trade Union Secretaries	10	8
Managing Directors	2	3
Head Teachers	2	—

No council officials were, or had ever been, councillors.

In addition, a number of respondents had also held the position of magistrate. No council officials had ever held such a position, but among the other groups the percentages were as follows:

	Who are Magistrates at present %	Who were Magistrates in past %
Trade Union Secretaries	9	2
Managing Directors	4	—
Head Teachers	4	—
Councillors	10	2

Thus, although results are presented in this report in terms of membership of the groups within which respondents were selected, there is in fact some overlap between groups and some respondents have interests and concerns of a wide nature.

Political Viewpoint

As in the survey of the general public, respondents in the special sample were asked for their political views; 14% of respondents refused to answer the question, including more than half the council officials. Of those who replied to the question, 80% generally supported one of the two main political parties, although not always being fully committed to that view.

TABLE 2.007
POLITICAL VIEW OF RESPONDENTS

	"Influential" Sample	Councillors	Council Officials	Managing Directors	Trade Union Secs.	Head Teachers	General Public Sample
Base: All respondents	350	51	52	97	100	50	2,401
	%	%	%	%	%	%	%
Very strongly Conservative	11	25	6	23	1	—	14
Fairly/not very strongly Conservative	21	6	8	47	5	32	22
	32	31	13	70	6	32	36
Very strongly Labour	22	45	4	—	48	6	10
Fairly/not very strongly Labour	15	8	6	3	32	18	22
	36	53	10	3	80	24	33
Liberal	9	14	10	7	3	22	11
Nationalist	1	—	2	—	—	2	2
Communist	1	—	—	—	3	—	} 1
Other party	2	—	2	4	3	—	
Neutral/no party	3	2	12	2	2	—	17
No answer	14	—	52	13	—	20	—

3. Consumers of News

SUMMARY

The "influential" sample are great consumers of news, both compared with the general public as a whole and with the professional and managerial sector to which many of the special sample belonged. This greater consumption of news is reflected in both the national and provincial press where members of the special sample are more likely to read a paper regularly, and also to read a greater number of papers. Only 2% read no national daily, and 3% read no provincial paper; figures for the general public are 15% and 30% respectively. Furthermore almost three-quarters (73%) read more than one national daily title in a week, and 29% read more than one provincial paper regularly; figures for the general public were 31% and 15% respectively. Less time, however, is spent on average reading each edition suggesting perhaps a greater selectivity on the part of respondents in the special sample.

The greater consumption of news extends also to television and radio; although listening less to these media, the special sample nonetheless listens to as much television news and more radio news than was found to be the average for the general public (although here the special sample more closely resembles the pattern of the professional and managerial sector).

There is quite wide variation between the groups that make up the "influential" sample. Council officials and councillors stand out as readers of the provincial daily press but only just over one-third of councillors regularly read a provincial *weekly* paper. This was the only case, however, in which any of the groups making up the special sample read less than members of the general public.

INTRODUCTION

The decision to undertake a special study among selected groups of people was made on the basis that their opinions of the local press and its role would have an interest over and above that of the study of attitudes among the general public. The groups were chosen on the grounds that they were thought to be in a special position *vis-à-vis* the local press, in that they were probably "producers" of local news as well as being likely to be particularly keen "consumers" of local news compared with the population as a whole.

Much of the information collected as background to the attitudinal questions allows us to test the assumptions on which the study was based. We look first at what we have called the "consumption" of news by the "influential" sample—the extent to which they not only read newspapers but also magazines and journals and, further, the extent to which they listen to or watch news on radio and television. Later sections of the report investigate the relative importance of each news source for these groups and look more closely at the function of each type of news medium. Throughout, particular attention will be focused on the regional press as the main object of study.

MAIN FINDINGS
Newspaper Readership
The National Press

Two-thirds of the adult population regularly read a national newspaper (ie read five or more issues a week). The table below shows that the proportion of the special sample who regularly read a national newspaper is even higher even when allowance is made for the particular socio-economic and demographic characteristics of the "influential" sample—the preponderance of men, the dominance of the professional and managerial occupations, and their tendency to be older compared with the general public—they still appear to be particularly keen readers of the national press.

TABLE 2.008
REGULAR READERSHIP OF NATIONAL DAILY NEWSPAPERS

	Base	*Proportion Regularly Reading National Daily Newspapers*
"Influential" sample	350	82%
General public sample:		
All respondents	2,401	66%
Male respondents	1,137	71%
Respondents aged 35+	1,563	67%
Professional/managerial respondents	480	68%

Not only does a higher proportion of the special sample regularly read the national press, but they also, on average, read a greater number of different national newspapers during a week than do members of the general public.

TABLE 2.009
NUMBER OF NATIONAL NEWSPAPER TITLES READ OR LOOKED AT AT LEAST ONCE A WEEK OR MORE OFTEN

	"Influential" Sample	*General Public Sample*
Base: All respondents	350	2,401
	%	%
None	5	17
One	24	51
Two	34	21
Three	22	7
Four	10	2
Five or more	6	—

The difference between the mean number of titles read in a week by the "influential" sample, as opposed to the sample of the general public, is quite considerable—2·3 titles compared with 1·3 for the general public.

When we compare the proportion in both samples who read a national daily once a week or more with the proportion who read one regularly, ie five or more times a week, we can see that quite a lot of the difference in the mean number of titles read is a reflection of the number of papers read occasionally, ie less than five times, but at least once, a week. Only 2% of the special sample read no national daily papers at least once in an average week, but 18% do not read one regularly; a third of the general public do not read one regularly. Similarly almost three-quarters (71%) of the special sample read two or more different national daily papers in an average week yet many fewer (41%) read two or more regularly. However, this is still a considerably higher percentage than the 13% of the general public who regularly read two or more national dailies. The mean number of national dailies read regularly by members of the "influential" sample who read one at all on a regular basis was 1·7, compared with 1·4 for members of the general public who read any regularly.

TABLE 2.010

OCCASIONAL AND REGULAR READERSHIP OF NATIONAL DAILY NEWSPAPERS

	No. of papers read at least once a week		No. of papers read at least 5–6 times a week	
	"Influentials"	General Public	"Influentials"	General Public
Base: All respondents	350	2,401	350	2,401
	%	%	%	%
National dailies				
None read	2	18	18	34
One read	24	51	41	53
Two or more read	74	30	41	13

The higher level of readership of the national daily press is reflected also in readership of Sunday newspapers. Members of the "influential" sample read an average of 1·7 Sunday newspapers each on a regular basis (ie three or four issues in a month), compared with 1·3 for the general public sample. As we would expect there is also a qualitative difference between the two samples; 50% of titles read regularly by the "influential" sample were what might be described as quality Sunday papers (ie *The Sunday Times*, *The Observer* and *Sunday Telegraph*); 15% of titles read by the general public fit into this category.

The Regional and Local Press

A similar pattern emerges when we compare the readership of regional and local newspapers by the two samples; indeed the tendency for the "influential" groups to read more newspapers than the general public is even more marked. Some of this greater readership of regional daily papers may be due to an extent to the sampling method adopted for the selection of respondents in the "influential" sample. All were selected from towns that were publishing centres for regional evening papers, where circulation is commonly higher than in more peripheral districts. In addition, 5 of the 12 were centres of publication for regional morning papers. Although this may account in part for the difference in levels of readership between the two samples, it is not a large enough factor to detract from the general proposition that members of the "influential" sample are more likely to be readers of the provincial daily press. As with national dailies, the level of readership of the professional and managerial section of the general public is very little different from that of the full general public sample.

TABLE 2.011

READERSHIP OF THE PROVINCIAL AND LOCAL PRESS

	"Influential" Sample	General Public Sample	Professional/ Managerial in General Public Sample
Base: All respondents	350	2,401	480
	%	%	%
Regular Readership of Regional Mornings[1]:			
None read regularly	67	91	88
One or more read regularly	33	9	12
Two or more read regularly	3	*	*
Regular Readership of Regional Evenings:			
None read regularly	40	66	67
One or more read regularly	60	34	33
Two or more read regularly	2	*	*
Regular Readership of Local Weekly Papers:			
None read regularly	54	57	58
One or more read regularly	46	43	42
Two or more read regularly	9	6	6

[1]For morning and evening papers regular readership is defined as reading five or more issues and occasional readership one to four issues in an average week. For weekly papers regular readership is defined as reading three or more issues and occasional readership one to two issues in an average month.

Table 2.012 below shows the overlap in readership of different types of daily newspapers. Over two-thirds of the "influential" sample regularly read more than one type of daily newspaper; fewer than a third of the general public do so. There is little variation by age, social class, or sex within the general public. The difference that does exist between the two samples is largely accounted for by the larger proportion of the general public who only read national newspapers regularly, and by the numbers (one in six of the adult population) who read no daily papers regularly at all.

It would appear evident from what has been said so far that, measured in terms of the number of newspaper titles read, the members of the "influential" sample are significantly greater "consumers" of both the national and local daily press than either the general public or those similar to them in terms of age, sex and social class.

TABLE 2.012

OVERLAP OF REGULAR READERSHIP OF DAILY NEWSPAPERS

	"Influential" Sample	General Public Sample	Professional/ Managerial in General Public Sample
Base: All respondents	350	2,401	480
	%	%	%
National morning, regional morning and evening papers read regularly	15	1	1
Local morning and evening papers read regularly (no national daily)	5	1	2
National and local evening papers read regularly	34	21	20
National and local morning papers read regularly	9	3	4
National papers only read regularly	24	42	43
Local morning papers only read regularly	4	4	5
Local evening papers only read regularly	6	11	10
None of these read regularly	3	17	15

Among the general public, the analysis of the patterns of overlap between regular readership of national and regional newspapers suggested that certain types of newspaper were seen as alternatives to each other; it was relatively rare for people to read regularly:

— both a national and a regional morning newspaper

— both a regional morning and an evening newspaper

— both a regional evening and a local weekly newspaper.

On the other hand, it was quite likely that people would regularly read both a national morning and a provincial evening paper or a local weekly, or both a regional morning and a local weekly paper, suggesting that these types of newspaper are seen as complementary to each other.

This pattern was not replicated by the special sample. As the following table shows, those who regularly read a regional morning were almost as likely as those who did not to read a national daily paper regularly; those who read a regional morning were also as likely as those who did not to read a provincial evening newspaper. The pattern was similar to that shown by the general public only where provincial evenings and weeklies were concerned; whereas 60% of the total sample read a provincial evening paper, only 43% of readers of local weeklies did so.

The difference between the special sample and that of the general public is shown even more clearly in the second table below in which the overlap of readership between different types of newspaper is expressed as a ratio.

TABLE 2.013

OVERLAP IN CLAIMED REGULAR READERSHIP OF THE NATIONAL AND PROVINCIAL PRESS

	Total Sample	Regular Readers of:			
		National Mornings	Regional Mornings	Evenings	Local Weeklies
Base: All respondents	350	288	115	211	161
	%	%	%	%	%
Who are also regular readers of:					
National mornings	82	—	73	81	86
Regional mornings	33	29	—	33	32
Evenings	60	59	60	—	43
Local weeklies	46	44	44	33	—

TABLE 2.014

THE DUPLICATION OF REGULAR READERSHIP OF THE DIFFERENT TYPES OF NEWSPAPER

	National Mornings	Regional Mornings	Evenings	Local Weeklies
	(Figures in brackets are those for the general public)			
National mornings	—	0·9 (0·6)	1·0 (1·0)	1·0 (1·1)
Regional mornings	0·9 (0·6)	—	1·0 (0·6)	1·0 (1·2)
Provincial evenings	1·0 (1·0)	1·0 (0·6)	—	0·7 (0·7)
Local weeklies	1·0 (1·1)	1·0 (1·2)	0·7 (0·7)	—

The figures above represent the number of regular readers of one type of paper who are also regular readers of another expressed as a ratio of all regular readers of the first type of paper (eg 29% of those who regularly read a national morning also read a regional morning; 33% of the total sample regularly read a regional morning. The duplication ratio is thus $\frac{29}{33} = 0·9$).

It seems from these tables that provincial morning and evening newspapers are regarded by local influential people as fulfilling a different function from each other and from the national daily press and are not treated as alternatives to anything like the same extent as they are by the general public. This is further illustrated by the table below which shows not a great deal of difference in readership of national dailies or provincial evenings between those who do and those who do not read a regional morning newspaper. This is in marked contrast to the pattern shown by readers and non-readers of regional mornings among the general public.

TABLE 2.015

READERSHIP OF NATIONAL MORNINGS AND PROVINCIAL EVENINGS BY READERS AND NON-READERS OF REGIONAL MORNING NEWSPAPERS

	"Influential" Sample Regional Morning		General Public Sample Regional Morning	
	Read regularly	Not read regularly	Read regularly	Not read regularly
Base: All respondents	115	235	267	2,134
	%	%	%	%
National morning				
Read regularly	73	87	39	69
Not read regularly	27	13	61	31
Provincial evening				
Read regularly	60	60	20	35
Not read regularly	40	40	80	65

However, if we look at the overlap of readership of provincial evening and of local weekly papers, we can see quite a marked difference in readership of weeklies between those who read a provincial evening and those who do not. Indeed, this contrast is more marked than that seen among the general public suggesting that the "influential" sample see evening and weekly papers as alternatives, and not complementary, to a greater extent than do the general public.

TABLE 2.016

READERSHIP OF LOCAL WEEKLIES BY READERS AND NON-READERS OF PROVINCIAL EVENING NEWSPAPERS

	"Influential" Sample Provincial Evening		General Public Sample Provincial Evening	
	Read regularly	Not read regularly	Read regularly	Not read regularly
Base: All respondents	211	139	808	1,593
	%	%	%	%
Local Weekly				
Read regularly	33	65	30	50
Not read regularly	67	35	70	50

Time Spent Reading Newspapers

The "influential" sample show a very similar pattern to the general public in the average amount of time spent reading issues of national daily newspapers. There is, however, a marked difference between the two samples in the amount of time spent reading issues of the regional press. The table below suggests that the tendency for the special sample to read more regional newspapers than the general public is offset by their spending less time reading each issue.

TABLE 2.017

AVERAGE TIME SPENT READING EACH ISSUE OF NEWSPAPERS READ REGULARLY
(Comparative figures for the general public are printed in brackets)

	National Dailies		Regional Mornings		Regional Evenings		Local Weeklies	
Base: All papers read regularly by all respondents	333 (1,976)		168 (273)		278 (1,096)		215 (1,369)	
	%	%	%	%	%	%	%	%
Less than 10 minutes spent reading	5	(6)	8	(4)	12	(6)	13	(5)
10 minutes but under 15 minutes	13	(11)	17	(10)	21	(10)	17	(8)
15 minutes but under 30 minutes	22	(22)	31	(26)	33	(22)	25	(18)
30 minutes but under 1 hour	38	(34)	31	(35)	25	(34)	27	(35)
1 hour or more	22	(27)	13	(24)	9	(26)	17	(34)

Members of the "influential" sample thus tend to read more newspapers than do members of the general public, and to read them more regularly, but are likely to spend somewhat less time on average reading each individual regional (though not national) publication. They may, of course, spend more time in total reading the regional press, but it seems that they may be more selective than the general public in what they read in an issue. The differences in readership patterns between the two samples suggest that the regional press fulfils rather different needs for people of local influence from those it fulfils for the general public.

Use made of Radio and Television as News Sources

The figures for the amount of television viewing and radio listening also suggest a certain amount of selectivity by the special sample in comparison with the general public. Although seemingly watching far less television in an average week, and also listening for considerably shorter periods to the radio, they nonetheless watch television news bulletins almost as much as, and listen to radio news bulletins more than, the average member of the general public. This suggests a greater interest in news as such on the part of local influential people. In this respect, those members of the general public in professional and managerial occupations to which a majority of the special sample belong are somewhat similar. It therefore seems that it is in newspaper readership habits (especially those involving the regional press) that the "influential" sample differs most markedly from people with similar characteristics among the general public.

TABLE 2.018
HOURS SPENT WATCHING TV AND LISTENING TO RADIO ON AN AVERAGE WEEKDAY

	Television			Radio		
	"Influential" Sample	General Public Sample	Professional/ managerial in general public	"Influential" Sample	General Public Sample	Professional/ managerial in general public
Base: All respondents	350	2,401	480	350	2,401	480
	%	%	%	%	%	%
Don't watch/listen	1	3	3	7	16	11
Less than 1 hour a day	26	7	11	49	29	32
1 but under 3 hours a day	67	44	54	37	31	34
3 but under 5 hours a day	6	32	26	4	11	12
5 hours a day or more	1	14	6	2	13	10

TABLE 2.019
LISTENING TO NEWS BULLETINS ON RADIO AND TELEVISION

	Television			Radio		
	"Influential" Sample	General Public Sample	Professional/ managerial in general public	"Influential" Sample	General Public Sample	Professional/ managerial in general public
Base: All respondents	350	2,401	480	350	2,401	480
	%	%	%	%	%	%
Never watch/listen	1	5	4	12	29	22
Less than once a week	2	1	0	2	3	3
1–3 days a week	13	9	10	11	7	7
4–5 days a week	24	13	16	19	16	18
5–7 days a week	61	71	64	55	44	52

Listening to local radio was not the subject of any detailed enquiry and no comparable figures are available from the survey of the general public. One question was asked of the special sample and established that 44% never listened to local radio stations at all; of the 56% who did so, less than half thought them in any way important for keeping them "up to date and well informed"; national radio stations in contrast were thought of as important in this respect by over 60% of the "influential" sample.

News Consumption: A Comparison between Different "Influential" Groups

So far we have treated the "influential" sample as a homogenous group of people (as indeed we have treated the sample of the general public apart from appropriate reference to different age, sex and social class groups). However, it is not surprising to find some diversity among groups with such differing interests in news as councillors, council officials, managing directors, trade union secretaries and headmasters may reasonably be expected to have. In making these comparisons between groups it must be remembered that sample sizes are very small and require great caution in interpretation.

National Dailies

In terms of the number of national daily newspapers read or looked at in an average week, all five groups of respondents read more than was found to be the average among the general public. But whereas headmasters appear content in almost three out of four cases to read one or two different national daily papers in a week, many trade union secretaries and managing directors look at three or more—on average, twice as many as members of the general public read. The same pattern emerges when we look at the national Sunday press—a greater number of different newspapers read or looked at by managing directors and trade union secretaries, and fewer by headmasters and council officials.

TABLE 2.020

NUMBER OF DIFFERENT NATIONAL DAILY NEWSPAPERS READ OR LOOKED AT IN AN AVERAGE WEEK

	Managing Directors	Trade Union Secretaries	Councillors	Council Officials	Head Teachers	General Public
Base: All respondents	97	100	51	52	50	2,401
	%	%	%	%	%	%
None	2	2	8	10	6	3
One	10	27	25	24	42	51
Two	35	29	38	41	30	21
Three or more	53	42	27	27	20	10
Mean	2·6	2·6	2·1	2·3	1·8	1·3

If one looks at regular readership (five or more issues a week), however, managing directors and council officials emerge as readers of the widest range of national dailies on a regular basis, but they are correspondingly less likely to read other national dailies occasionally. Councillors and trade union secretaries, in contrast, read less than the average number of national dailies regularly but read a particularly large number occasionally. Head teachers appear to read fewer national dailies regularly than is average among the special sample, and are only average in the number they read occasionally.

TABLE 2.021
READERSHIP OF NATIONAL DAILIES

	Any regular	Mean No. of titles read regularly	Any occasional[1]	Mean No. of titles read occasionally
Base: Total in each group	%		%	
All respondents ... (350)	82	1·4	51	0·9
Managing directors ... (97)	93	1·8	54	0·8
Council officials ... (52)	87	1·5	37	0·4
Trade union secretaries ... (100)	78	1·3	64	1·3
Councillors... ... (51)	73	1·1	55	1·1
Head teachers ... (50)	76	1·0	44	0·7
General public ... (2,401)	66	0·8	15	0·6

[1]Occasional readership is defined as reading a paper on 1–4 days in an average week.

Provincial Newspapers

All the special groups were greater readers of the provincial morning and evening papers than were members of the public but only council officials were more likely to read a local weekly regularly.

TABLE 2.022
READERSHIP OF PROVINCIAL NEWSPAPERS

	Morning read		Evening read		Weekly read	
	Regularly	Only occasionally	Regularly	Only occasionally	Regularly	Only occasionally
Base: All in each group	%	%	%	%	%	%
Total "influential" sample ...	33	11	60	16	46	5
Council officials ... (52)	50	10	79	8	52	10
Councillors... ... (51)	42	12	75	14	37	6
Trade union secretaries ... (100)	29	11	61	19	47	4
Managing directors ... (97)	29	12	45	20	46	3
Head teachers ... (50)	20	8	54	12	46	6
General public ... (2,401)	9	2	36	13	43	6

Council officials and councillors were the most likely to read a provincial morning and/or a provincial evening (a third read both); but councillors were the least likely of all the groups to read a local weekly being, in fact, the only group less likely to read them than the general public. This suggests a greater involvement on the part of council officials with affairs at the small scale local level and perhaps a lesser interest by councillors in very local affairs.

The trade union secretaries, managing directors and head teachers were more likely than the general public to read a provincial morning or evening paper but similar in the extent to which they read a local weekly regularly. All three groups were considerably less likely than the councillors and council officials to read either a provincial morning or an evening newspaper; they were also less likely to read both types of paper. The managing directors, followed by the head teachers, showed a particularly high proportion who read neither.

All groups, except head teachers, were considerably more likely to read both national and provincial mornings than were members of the general public. Council officials and councillors who we have seen were the two groups most likely to read both a provincial morning and evening paper are also the groups most likely to read both types of morning paper. Head teachers again come very close to the general public in not reading both a national daily and provincial morning.

Despite being average readers of local weeklies in comparison with other influential groups, head teachers also came close to the general public in the numbers reading both local weeklies and provincial evenings, largely as a result of their low numbers who read evening papers. Councillors, on the other hand, also have few of their numbers reading evenings and weeklies, but due to only one-third of these numbers regularly reading a weekly, council officials, once again, are the group most likely to read both, and least likely to read neither.

Only 10 members of the sample read no provincial newspapers on a regular basis (5 managing directors, 3 trade union secretaries, 1 council official and 1 head teacher). This represents less than 3% of the "influential" sample compared with a figure of 30% of the general public who read no provincial paper regularly.

TABLE 2.023
OVERLAP IN REGULAR READERSHIP WITHIN THE PROVINCIAL PRESS

	Total "Influential" Sample	Council Officials	Councillors	Trade Union Secs.	Managing Directors	Head Teachers	General Public Sample
Base: All respondents	350	52	51	100	97	50	2,401
	%	%	%	%	%	%	%
Regular readers of:							
Regional morning & evening	20	38	35	13	15	6	2
Regional morning only	13	12	8	16	13	14	7
Regional evening only	41	40	39	48	30	48	32
Neither	27	10	18	23	41	32	59
National daily & provincial morning	24	38	29	21	26	6	4
National daily & no provincial morning	58	48	43	57	67	70	63
Provincial morning & no national daily	9	12	13	8	3	14	6
Neither	9	2	13	14	4	10	28
Provincial evening & local weekly	20	38	9	22	13	12	10
Provincial evening & no local weekly	40	40	57	39	32	42	24
Local weekly & no provincial evening	26	13	20	25	33	34	33
Neither	14	9	14	14	22	12	33

We have seen earlier when comparing the readership patterns of the "influential" sample with that of the general public that there is not always a positive relationship between the number of newspaper titles read and the time spent reading newspapers. It might be expected that the more titles read, of any one type of newspaper, then the less time is spent reading each edition. Council officials follow this pattern, reading more provincial morning and evening titles than other groups but spending less time than others in reading each edition, perhaps suggesting that they are selective in what they read. Head teachers, on the other hand, do not look at many regional daily newspapers in an average week compared with the other groups, nor do they spend as much time, on average, reading each edition. They are not as great "consumers" of the provincial or national daily press as the other special groups (although, as we have already seen, they read more titles, and at greater length, than do the sample of the general public or even others in professional and managerial occupations).

Managing directors similarly spent relatively little of their time reading the regional daily newspapers they see regularly compared with other groups of our "influential" sample. The national press would appear to be a more important medium for this group where the provision of daily news is concerned.

The two remaining groups, councillors and trade union secretaries, appear to be great readers of the regional daily press both in terms of the numbers who regularly read a regional morning or evening paper or indeed the many who read both and also in terms of the amount of time they spend reading each issue.

TABLE 2.024
TIME SPENT READING EACH ISSUE (ON AVERAGE) OF PROVINCIAL NEWSPAPERS

	Regional Morning Papers					Provincial Evening Papers				
	Trade Union Secs.	Councillors	Managing Dirs.	Council Officials	Head Teachers	Trade Union Secs.	Councillors	Managing Dirs.	Council Officials	Head Teachers
Base: All newspapers read regularly	42	29	45	36	16	86	45	65	48	34
	%	%	%	%	Nos	%	%	%	%	%
Less than 15 mins	10	14	40	36	(4)	24	13	46	40	47
15 mins but under 30 mins	26	31	29	33	(7)	22	49	31	42	32
30 mins or more	64	55	31	31	(5)	53	38	23	19	18

Readership of local weeklies was too low for reliable comparisons to be made between groups in time spent reading them.

Other Media

There were no major differences between the various groups in the extent to which they watched television news, neither do the groups vary much in the extent to which they listen to news bulletins broadcast on the radio although in this case all listen to bulletins on more days in an average week than do the general public.

To sum up:

We can now present a profile of each group of respondents summarising and comparing the readership habits of each. As we have said, all groups read a greater number of each type of newspaper than do members of the general public.

Councillors: Great readers of the regional daily press with more than a third reading both regional morning and evening papers regularly. 70% read national dailies on a regular basis, 12% less than the average for the "influential" sample, although many read one or more national dailies on an occasional basis. Only just over a third of councillors read a local weekly paper regularly, less than any other group. In all types of daily newspaper councillors spend longer reading each issue than the average member of the special sample.

Council Officials: Also great readers of the regional daily press, but also of the local weekly and national daily press—expressed, that is, in terms of the number of different titles read regularly in an average week. However, council officials spend a relatively short time reading each issue of all types of newspaper.

Managing Directors: Like council officials, managing directors do not spend long reading each issue of any paper. However, only with national daily papers can they be said to be heavy readers in terms of regularly reading a number of papers. They are not very big readers of the regional daily press, and are also only average readers of the local weekly press.

Trade Union Secretaries: Most read a national daily regularly but they are also frequent occasional readers of other national daily papers. They are about average in the extent to which they read provincial dailies and local weekly papers, although in all cases they tend to spend longer reading each issue than average.

Head Teachers: Not great readers of either the national daily or provincial daily press either in terms of the number of titles read or the time spent reading them. In all cases, however, they are greater "readers" than either the general public as a whole, or other professional and managerial people within the general public. In addition, they are equal to other groups in the "influential" sample in the extent to which they read the local weekly press.

4. The Role and Importance of the Regional Press

SUMMARY

In this chapter we evaluate the role and importance of the regional press in two ways; first, by comparing the views of the special sample on the regional press with their views on the national press; secondly, by comparing the views of the special sample with those of the sample of the general public with regard to the regional press.

In the provision of the latest national news, the provincial dailies are considered to be almost as good as the national dailies by the "influential" sample. Provincial evenings and, particularly, local weeklies were less good than the provincial mornings in this respect and indeed in about half the cases readers thought that these types of newspaper contained too little news.

Provincial morning papers are also similar to national dailies in the extent to which their readers rate them as important in helping them ". . . to understand how what is happening in the country will affect my interests in the area". However, this is an area—the interpretation of national news in the local context—in which the provincial press might be expected to perform better than the national press. The provincial evenings were again regarded as less good than the provincial mornings in fulfilling this role.

Readers of the provincial press appear less critical when questioned on the press's role of presenting news in the district. National dailies are seen as only marginally more important for keeping readers among the special sample "up to date and well informed" in their official capacity (a role 61% of readers thought was an important one performed by evening papers). Readers of the national daily and provincial evening press rate the importance of their papers in this respect on a par with the rating given by all respondents to national radio, although specialist journals and television are thought more highly of in keeping respondents up to date and well informed. Local weekly papers are not considered important in this respect. Local newspapers in general, however, appear to be a more important medium as a source of information about the main issues and problems in the district—issues and problems which were frequently national issues reflected within the local context. Moreover a majority of councillors and trade union secretaries felt provincial daily papers were important for presenting their viewpoint to the public and, in the case of evening papers, had a strong influence on the views of their readers.

Although they are greater consumers of the provincial press than are members of the general public, members of the special sample are less attached to the provincial newspapers they read: two in five readers in the special sample would not miss the provincial morning or evening papers they read if they stopped being published while a majority would not miss their weekly papers. Very many more members of the general public would miss their provincial papers and many more claim that reading the paper is ". . . always enjoyable". Indeed only a bare majority of readers among the special sample said of their provincial evenings that they always enjoyed reading them. National daily newspapers were more highly thought of than provincial papers and individual papers would be missed more.

A majority of councillors, trade union secretaries and managing directors were satisfied with the way the provincial press presented the point of view of their organisation, claiming in the main that they had always been reported fairly or, at least, had had no occasion to complain. Councillors and trade union secretaries were slightly more critical than managing directors, the main complaints being that the papers did not present their point of view or else were biased against their point of view.

RELATIVE IMPORTANCE OF DIFFERENT MEDIA TO RESPONDENTS IN THEIR OFFICIAL CAPACITY

We have seen that all groups in the "influential" sample tend to be great readers of newspapers compared with the general public and to be involved in affairs that are reported in local newspapers. We may expect some correlation between the level of readership of the provincial press and a measure of its importance compared with the importance of other media. The fact that some rarely or never read local newspapers is in itself a measure of their importance to them. Those respondents who did read local newspapers (apart from provincial mornings which not all had an opportunity to read), were asked to say how important each was in keeping them "up to date" and "well informed" in their official capacity as a councillor, managing director, etc. In addition all respondents were asked to rate the importance of each of a list of media, using the same criterion.

Among newspapers the national dailies are seen as being the most informative by their readers, although only very marginally more important than provincial evening papers. Looking at national daily papers as a whole, however, masks the very great difference in views on the importance of what is usually termed the quality press as opposed to the more popular papers. A majority (61%) of national dailies read once a week or more were from among the quality papers. Their readers among the "influential" sample considered them to be either "very important" or "fairly important" in keeping them up to date and well informed in 81% of cases, compared with 31% among the popular papers.

A majority of readers of the local weekly press did not view it as being particularly important as a source of information in their official position.

TABLE 2.025
THE IMPORTANCE OF NEWSPAPERS IN KEEPING THE "INFLUENTIAL" SAMPLE
"UP TO DATE AND WELL INFORMED"

	National Dailies	Provincial Evenings	Local Weeklies
Base: All newspapers read at least once a week (dailies) or once a month (weeklies)	806	279	245
	%	%	%
Very important	28	27	14
Fairly important	35	34	30
Not very important	26	29	30
Not at all important	9	9	26
Never/rarely read	(5)	(24)	(49)

If we compare the value placed by the full sample (and not just readers) on the different types of newspaper with that placed on other communication media, we gauge something of the relative importance. It would appear that national dailies compare with national radio in importance as news sources with provincial evenings slightly less important. Specialist journals are considered by the greatest number to be important for keeping up to date and well informed, while television is also viewed as more important than any of the types of newspaper.

Local radio was not available to approximately one-third of respondents so that, although among their listeners it was viewed as being more important than local weekly newspapers, overall it appears roughly on a level with weekly papers as the least important medium.

TABLE 2.026
RELATIVE IMPORTANCE OF MEDIA IN KEEPING THE "INFLUENTIAL" SAMPLE
"UP TO DATE AND WELL INFORMED"

		Very important	Fairly important	Not very important	Not at all important	Never or rarely look/listen
Base: All respondents						
National daily newspapers	%	28	35	26	9	2
Provincial evenings ...	%	21	26	21	7	24
Local weeklies	%	8	15	17	15	45
Magazines and periodicals	%	13	24	29	25	8
Specialist journals ...	%	55	27	11	5	2
Television	%	31	39	22	7	1
National radio	%	27	33	23	13	4
Local radio	%	11	16	16	13	44

Council officials are often specialists and this is reflected in the fact that they are particularly likely to rate specialist journals and magazines and periodicals as very important in keeping them up to date and well informed. They also emerged as being particularly likely to read the provincial morning and evening newspapers and their need for the sort of information provided in these newspapers is demonstrated by an above average proportion saying that provincial evenings are very important to them. Nonetheless, only 28% of evenings were rated as very important in this respect, representing the view of only a quarter of council officials. National newspapers, television and national radio were all marginally more likely to be rated as important by council officials.

Although half the council officials claimed that they regularly read a local weekly newspaper (a higher proportion than in other groups), only 12% said that they found it very important in keeping them up to date and well informed—a figure that is little higher than is found in most of the other groups who were less likely to read a local weekly. It therefore seems probable that council officials read a local weekly primarily for reasons other than to keep themselves up to date and well informed.

Councillors were also very likely to read the daily provincial press, especially evening newspapers, and for them this was the most important medium for keeping up to date and well informed. Specialist journals were rated as very important by a similar number, but nonetheless by a much smaller proportion than was the case in any other group. Local radio was also more likely to be rated as very important by this group than by any of the others, bringing it up to a level comparable to the national dailies, television and national radio. Local radio is rated as very important by councillors more than twice as often as local weekly newspapers.

Three-fifths of the *trade union secretaries* read a provincial evening newspaper but only about a third of these rated it as very important in keeping them up to date and well informed, compared with about half the councillors who read one; specialist journals and the national media (especially television) seem to be most important to this group.

We saw earlier that neither *head teachers* nor *managing directors* were great readers of the provincial evening press and it is not surprising therefore to find that neither rates evening newspapers as being very important in providing the news to keep them well informed. Both groups attach more importance than do any of the other groups to national newspapers. In addition, head teachers are particularly likely to find television and national radio useful.

Head teachers as a group were just as likely to be regular readers of a local weekly newspaper; but they are no more likely than most of the other groups to rate them as very important in keeping them up to date and well informed. However, they rate them as fairly important to a much greater degree than do other groups with the result that half of them rate local weeklies as very or fairly important compared with about a third of council officials, councillors and trade union secretaries and only 16% of managing directors.

TABLE 2.027
RELATIVE IMPORTANCE OF MEDIA IN KEEPING "INFLUENTIAL" GROUPS "UP TO DATE AND WELL INFORMED"
(Proportion of each group rating each medium as "very important")

	Total	Council Officials	Councillors	Trade Union Secretaries	Managing Directors	Head Teachers
Base: All respondents 350	%	%	%	%	%	%
National daily newspapers	28	28	25	23	34	32
Provincial evenings	21	42	35	18	8	14
Local weeklies	8	12	12	8	2	10
Magazines and periodicals	13	29	10	9	13	10
Specialist journals	55	81	33	59	53	48
Television	31	29	29	41	18	42
National radio	27	25	27	28	21	36
Local radio	11	15	25	15	2	4

In conclusion, the importance of the regional press as an information source varies considerably between the groups that make up the "influential" sample. Councillors and council officials, for example, value the provincial evening press more than other groups, head teachers slightly more the weekly press. On the whole, however, when it comes to keeping themselves up to date and well informed in their positions, the provincial press is seen as playing a secondary role to the national press and television and specialist journals. Weekly newspapers and magazines and periodicals are not of much importance as information sources. Local radio was not available to many of our sample, but those who were able to listen to it found it more useful as an information source than weekly newspapers were found to be by their readers.

Importance of the Provincial Press in Understanding the Problems of the Area

Respondents were asked to rate newspapers (but only those newspapers they read once a week or more often) according to how much they helped them "to understand how what is happening in the country will affect my interests in the area". Here we are narrowing down the role of the press to the specific task of helping people to understand how national events are reflected in the local area. This is often considered to be one of the important roles of the provincial daily press, in addition to reporting regional news.

Interpreting the implications of national news for the local area would probably be considered less important a role for weekly newspapers and it is not surprising that they are not seen as fulfilling this role. In two-thirds of the cases, the provincial morning newspapers were thought to perform this function at least fairly well, compared with 45% for the provincial evenings. However, provincial morning newspapers are seen as no more informative in this respect than the national press which one would think had far less cause, or space, to undertake the task of helping local influential people to understand the local repercussions of national news.

TABLE 2.028
"IT HELPS ME TO UNDERSTAND HOW WHAT IS HAPPENING IN THE COUNTRY WILL AFFECT MY INTERESTS IN THE AREA"

	Provincial Morning Papers	Provincial Evening Papers	Local Weekly Papers	National Daily Papers[1]
Base: All papers read at least once a week (dailies) or once a month (weeklies)	168 %	278 %	215 %	333 %
Very true	27	10	9	31
Fairly true	42	35	13	37
Not very true	21	35	34	21
Not true at all	10	18	42	11

[1] Figures for national newspapers in tables are based on one read by each respondent selected at random from all national newspapers read at least once in an average week.

The local press appears to be more important than other media as a source of information about the main issues and problems in the district, but respondents' jobs, their personal experience and the people they meet were considered even more important sources of information on these issues; this is not surprising since the issues considered most important by respondents were usually to do with their particular sphere of interest and influence. National radio, television and magazines were less frequently mentioned than local newspapers as sources of information about the districts' issues and problems, but nonetheless each was mentioned by between a fifth and a third in this context. This seems to be because, as we shall see later, the important district problems were often national issues reflected within the local context.

TABLE 2.029
HOW RESPONDENTS CAME TO KNOW OF THE ISSUES AND PROBLEMS THEY CONSIDERED TO BE IMPORTANT IN THEIR DISTRICTS

	"Influential" Sample	General Public Sample
Base: All respondents	350	2,401
	%	%
From personal experience	74	60
Their job	79	*
What people they meet say	61	46
Local newspapers	48	30
Local radio	16	5
Television	27	9
National newspapers	33	7
National radio	20	3
Magazines	11	1
Membership of Council/other committees	7	*
Other sources	6	—

The Provincial Press as a Source of News

Most members of the special sample thought it at least fairly true that the national daily newspapers they read "always have the latest national news" and the provincial mornings were rated as only marginally lower in this respect, supporting the conclusion drawn earlier that regional mornings are in some respects alternatives to national dailies. In about a fifth of the cases, both national dailies and provincial mornings were rated as having too little news in them but the majority did not think this.

In rather more cases the provincial evening papers read were thought not to carry the latest national news but nonetheless over half of the readers considered that proposition at least fairly true. Most readers of local weeklies did not see them as carrying the latest national news. Both provincial evenings and local weeklies were thought in just under half the cases to have too little news, at least to some extent.

TABLE 2.030
PERCEPTIONS OF NEWS COVERAGE BY TYPES OF NEWSPAPER

	Provincial Morning Newspapers	Provincial Evening Newspapers	Local Weekly Newspapers	National Daily Newspapers
Base: All papers read at least once a week (dailies) or once a month (weeklies)	168	278	215	333
"It always has the latest national news"	%	%	%	%
Very true	32	16	—	50
Fairly true	49	42	5	37
Not very true	13	31	32	8
Not at all true	5	9	60	4
"It has too little news in it"				
Very true	5	12	16	3
Fairly true	19	33	29	14
Not very true	45	38	40	34
Not at all true	30	15	14	47

Overall Attachment to the Provincial Press

So far we have presented a picture of local influential people as being great readers of the provincial press, but as not heavily dependent on it for keeping them informed in their positions generally, or on the important problems facing the district in particular. Nor is it seen as being any more useful than other sources in helping respondents to understand the effects of national events on their interests in the area.

If these were the only roles that respondents saw the provincial newspapers as fulfilling, we would expect to find them little concerned if they stopped being published. This is not altogether what was found. Although the special sample are less enthusiastic about the regional press than the general public are, over half the readers of the regional mornings and evenings say that it is at least fairly true that they would miss them if they stopped being published. Only where local weeklies are concerned do readers say this in less than 50% of the cases.

TABLE 2.031
"I WOULD MISS IT A LOT IF IT STOPPED BEING PUBLISHED"

			Very true	Fairly true	Not very true	Not at all true
Provincial morning newspapers	168	%	33 (35)	26 (52)	27 (9)	13 (0)
Provincial evening newspapers	278	%	28 (34)	26 (48)	21 (9)	23 (5)
Local weekly newspapers	215	%	14 (29)	28 (55)	26 (9)	31 (3)
National newspapers	333	%	42 (43)	24 (20)	18 (19)	15 (16)

Base: All papers read at least once a week (dailies) or once a month (weeklies).
Figures for the general public are printed in brackets opposite figures for the "influential" sample.

If many do not find the provincial press particularly informative and a large minority would not much miss the provincial papers they read if they stopped being published, nonetheless reading them still remains something that is fairly enjoyable for most. It is interesting to note that among the general public similar proportions say that reading provincial papers is not always enjoyable as say they would not miss them a lot if they stopped being published. Among the special sample, however, many more readers of morning and weekly papers say they would not miss them if they ceased publication than say they do not always enjoy reading them, suggesting perhaps that as great consumers of the provincial press they would be happy to turn to other papers for the information and enjoyment they obtain.

TABLE 2.032
"READING IT IS ALWAYS ENJOYABLE"

			Very true	Fairly true	Not very true	Not at all true
Provincial morning newspapers	168	%	20 (43)	53 (47)	25 (7)	2 (2)
Provincial evening newspapers	278	%	13 (41)	38 (44)	39 (10)	7 (4)
Local weekly newspapers	215	%	17 (41)	47 (45)	30 (10)	4 (2)
National newspapers	333	%	36 (46)	44 (43)	16 (9)	2 (2)

Base: All papers read at least once a week (dailies) or once a month (weeklies).
Figures for the general public are printed in brackets opposite figures for the "influential" sample.

Once again members of the "influential" sample are less keen than members of the general public, particularly in relation to provincial evening papers.

The professional and managerial sector within the general public sample would miss their local evening and local weekly papers somewhat less than the sample as a whole, although their views are closer to those of the general public than to the "influential" sample. They were only marginally less likely to enjoy the papers they read than the full general public sample.

We have looked so far at the role and importance of the provincial press only among their readers and have taken no account of those who only occasionally, if at all, glance at copies of particular provincial newspapers. The role and importance of the newspapers is obviously likely to be small to these respondents. However, reasons why they are not read more regularly indicate some of the perceived limitations of the provincial press.

Regional morning newspapers did not circulate in all the areas selected for study. Questioning as to the reasons for not regularly reading these papers was therefore limited to those sampling points whose area was covered by a regional morning paper. As a consequence the bases for the tables are very small, and the results should be treated with caution. The most common reason given was that respondents had limited time to read newspapers and, since the large majority of them regularly read national morning newspapers, presumably many chose the national in preference to the regional dailies from which to get their information. About a fifth said explicitly that other newspapers gave them the information they needed. A quarter said that the regional morning paper was too local or limited in its reporting and a similar proportion said that it was biased.

The sampling points for this study were chosen specifically on the basis that a provincial evening newspaper circulated widely throughout the area. The question asked of very occasional or non-readers as to why they did not regularly read a particular local evening paper therefore had relevance in all areas. The reasons given are not markedly different from those provided by non-readers of the regional *morning* press, but rather fewer gave lack of time as a reason. The local or limited nature of the reporting in provincial evening papers was the main reason for not reading one.

TABLE 2.033
REASONS GIVEN FOR NOT READING REGIONAL MORNING OR EVENING NEWSPAPERS MORE THAN ONCE A WEEK

	Regional Morning Newspapers	Provincial Evening Newspapers
Base: All respondents not reading papers more than once a week	52	84
	%	%
Limited time to read newspapers	44	27
Reporting in papers is too local or limited	25	45
Other papers give me the information I need	19	18
Reporting in paper is poor/inaccurate	4	7
Paper is biased	23	7
Paper is only a rehash of another paper	—	4
Paper is only bought for specific features	23	17
Other reasons	21	11

Percentages add up to more than 100% as respondents could offer more than one reason, and would be asked about more than one paper they did not read.

The Importance of the Provincial Press as a Means of Influencing the Public

The groups selected to form the special sample were in many cases people who made use of the provincial press to publicise their activities or to present an image of themselves, of their firm or of their party group etc. It was therefore important to see to what extent they considered the press was able to influence readers' views. In all groups, the national press was most likely to be considered to have a very or fairly strong influence, followed by provincial evening newspapers; the local weekly newspapers were a poor third in this respect. Councillors, managing directors and trade union secretaries are three groups who might be particularly concerned to present an image of themselves or their party group, company or union to the public and to see the provincial press as providing a medium through which to influence the public. Councillors, subject to direct election from the general public, might be expected to be particularly keen to ensure that their views are presented to the public. Councillors and trade unionists are in fact more likely than other groups to consider the provincial evenings and local weeklies to have a strong influence on their readers but managing directors think less of the media's influence than do any of the other groups.

TABLE 2.034

PERCEIVED INFLUENCE OF TYPES OF NEWSPAPER ON THEIR READERS

			Provincial Evening Newspapers			Local Weekly Newspapers			National Daily Newspapers		
			Strong influence	Weak influence	No influence	Strong influence	Weak influence	No influence	Strong influence	Weak influence	No influence
All respondents	350	%	46	46	7	23	50	20	80	18	2
Councillors	51	%	63	33	4	37	39	12	86	12	—
Trade Union Secretaries	100	%	55	38	5	38	48	30	85	14	—
Council Officials	52	%	42	56	2	23	56	17	69	27	2
Head Teachers	50	%	42	50	6	18	58	17	74	24	—
Managing Directors	7	%	32	53	12	13	49	26	80	18	—

Councillors, managing directors and trade union secretaries were also asked to say, for each provincial morning, evening and local weekly newspaper that they read at least occasionally, how important that newspaper was for presenting the viewpoint of their party group, company or union district to the public in the area.

The majority of councillors tended to see both provincial evenings and weeklies as very important in presenting the views of their party group to the public, especially the former; two-fifths of them also regarded the provincial mornings as very important in this respect.

Trade union secretaries and managing directors were considerably less likely than councillors to consider any of the three types of regional newspaper as particularly important in presenting their viewpoint to people in the area. A majority of managing directors thought that local weeklies were definitely unimportant for presenting the point of view of their company, further illustrating their poor opinion of these newspapers.

TABLE 2.035
THE IMPORTANCE OF THE PROVINCIAL PRESS FOR PRESENTING THE POINT OF VIEW OF RESPONDENTS' PARTY GROUP/COMPANY/TRADE UNION TO THE PUBLIC IN THE AREA

	Councillors	Trade Union Secretaries	Managing Directors
	(29) %	(42) %	(45) %
Regional morning newspaper			
Very important	41	29	29
Fairly important	28	31	20
Not very important	21	24	29
Not at all important	7	14	18
	(45) %	(86) %	(65) %
Provincial evening newspaper			
Very important	71	34	23
Fairly important	16	26	25
Not very important	9	30	17
Not at all important	2	9	18
	(24) %	(58) %	(55) %
Local weekly newspaper			
Very important	58	24	11
Fairly important	17	12	18
Not very important	17	21	13
Not at all important	4	20	45

Base: All read at least once a week (dailies) or once a month (weeklies).

Most respondents in all three groups were satisfied with the way in which the regional morning newspapers they read put over the viewpoint of their firm, union or party group, but they were "fairly" rather than "very" satisfied. Trade unionists were the least satisfied.

The level of satisfaction with the treatment given to them by the provincial evening newspapers was similar. A fairly large proportion of managing directors and of trade union secretaries did not consider the local weekly newspapers to be at all important in presenting the viewpoint of their organisation and many of these were unable to express any opinion about the satisfactoriness of the coverage; but again it seems that trade unionists were most dissatisfied. Councillors, on the other hand, seemed to have a good opinion of the way in which the local weeklies presented the viewpoint of their party group.

TABLE 2.036
PROVINCIAL PRESS PRESENTATION OF THE POINTS OF VIEW OF RESPONDENTS' COMPANY, UNION DISTRICT OR PARTY GROUP

Satisfaction with presentation by:	Councillors	Trade Union Secretaries	Managing Directors
	(29) %	(42) %	(45) %
Regional morning newspaper—			
Very satisfied	10	12	29
Fairly satisfied	55	40	47
Fairly dissatisfied	21	24	4
Very dissatisfied	7	17	9
Don't know	7	7	7

TABLE 2.036—continued

	Councillors	Trade Union Secretaries	Managing Directors
	(45) %	(86) %	(65) %
Provincial evening newspaper—			
Very satisfied	18	9	15
Fairly satisfied	44	52	43
Fairly dissatisfied	18	13	2
Very dissatisfied	18	17	8
Don't know	2	8	8
	(24) %	(58) %	(55) %
Local weekly newspaper—			
Very satisfied	38	17	11
Fairly satisfied	38	29	35
Fairly dissatisfied	8	12	9
Very dissatisfied	6	19	4
Don't know	15	22	33

Base: All papers read at least once a week (dailies) or once a month (weeklies).

When asked in what way they were satisfied or dissatisfied with a provincial paper's presentation of their organisation's point of view, the fairness of coverage appeared the most important criterion on which presentation was judged although the amount of coverage given was also mentioned frequently. On the whole, comments on the fairness of the coverage were in the greater number satisfactory comments, but there were more complaints than praise about the amount of coverage, especially from trade unionists and councillors. Councillors were the only group to complain about inaccurate reporting to any extent. Overall there were a greater number of causes for satisfaction mentioned than for dissatisfaction.

TABLE 2.037
CAUSES OF SATISFACTION OR DISSATISFACTION WITH PROVINCIAL PRESS PRESENTATION OF RESPONDENTS' POINTS OF VIEW

	Councillors	Trade Union Secretaries	Managing Directors
Base	98	186	165
	%	%	%
Causes of satisfaction			
We are reported fairly/unbiased	22	19	17
Paper always gives us good or extensive coverage	8	5	9
We are always reported accurately	9	6	8
We have never had occasion to complain	11	12	10
Other causes for satisfaction	9	7	10
Causes of dissatisfaction			
They don't present our point of view/give us good coverage	20	20	7
The paper is biased or one-sided against us	13	14	4
Reports are inaccurate/poor reporting	14	4	3
Other causes for dissatisfaction	5	8	8

Base: All daily papers read once a week or more, and weekly papers read once a month or more.
Percentages may add up to more than 100% as respondents could offer more than one comment.

The Provincial Press as a Medium for Advertising

Respondents in the special sample were also questioned on the specific role of the provincial press as an advertising medium since many of our respondents were likely to be buyers of advertising space. Clearly this will not be true in all cases and quite large numbers among each group of respondents were unable to express an opinion on the service newspapers gave to their advertisers. Among those who expressed an opinion, there was very little dissatisfaction and only minor variance between the different types of newspaper or between the different groups of respondents. There is a slight indication that, at least among the provincial daily papers, a slightly better service is given by the larger circulation papers, though the difference is very small.

TABLE 2.038
"IT GIVES A GOOD SERVICE TO ITS ADVERTISERS"

		Very true	Fairly true	Not very true	Not at all true	Don't know
Regional morning newspaper ... 168	%	30	40	2	1	26
Provincial evening newspaper ... 278	%	43	31	4	1	20
Local weekly newspaper ... 215	%	39	38	3	1	18
Regional or provincial daily:						
Circulation up to 40,000 ... 78	%	31	40	6	1	22
Circulation 40,000–100,000 ... 163	%	40	32	4	2	22
Circulation more than 100,000 200	%	40	36	2	1	22

Base: All papers read at least once a week (dailies) or once a month (weeklies).

5. Standards in the Regional Press

SUMMARY

It was expected of the "influential" sample that they would not only be very concerned with standards in the provincial press, but would also be in a better position than the public as a whole to judge standards as a result of being both large "consumers" and also, in part, "producers" of news. The majority of respondents (81%) said they had had "dealings" with the provincial press and most had taken positive steps to contact the newspaper rather than speaking only when approached and relations with the provincial press were said to be at least "fairly good" in three-quarters of the cases. Furthermore, 70% of all provincial papers read by the special sample had contained an article or report in which respondents had ". . . some particular interest, involvement or knowledge".

In a general rating of the quality of papers, 69% of the special sample rated provincial mornings they read as at least "fairly good"; 51% of weeklies and slightly fewer (49%) of provincial evenings were rated at least "fairly good". Opinions on specific aspects of standards tended to follow the same pattern; national daily papers in general were considered as somewhat higher in standard than the provincial press overall, although on specific aspects, such as the standard of reporting, the extent to which papers get their facts wrong or print too many silly stories, and the level of interest in the news, the provincial mornings were definitely seen as better than the popular dailies. The provincial mornings, however, were seen as having higher standards than were the weekly papers, which in turn were perceived in a better light in these respects than the provincial evenings. Criticism of the evening papers was often substantial; only 41% say of them that their "standard of reporting is first class", 56% say they "often get [their] facts wrong" and 53% that they have "too much advertising".

Overall the provincial press is criticised much more by the special sample than by the general public, although the latter also appear slightly more critical of the evening press than of other provincial papers, particularly in comparison with the provincial morning papers read.

The criticism of the evening press extends into the area of sensationalism, more than half of the special sample saying that the evening papers they read "exaggerate the sensational aspects of the news"; however, this criticism was made much more frequently of the popular national dailies (80% of readers); only just over one-third of readers of provincial mornings and weeklies say this of their papers while fewer still believe that they "always concentrate on the bad news" or ". . . invade people's grief".

We have seen already that local newspapers in general are rated as the most important of the media as a source of information about what respondents considered to be the district's main issues and problems and indeed, on further questioning, in more than half the cases, provincial newspapers were said to give the problem at least some attention; on the other hand, 42% expressed dissatisfaction with the provincial press's treatment of local issues. When specific pre-selected topics were discussed, however, most were considered to be fairly well, if not very well, treated with, in this case, little discernible difference between the three types of provincial newspaper. News of local trade union activities stood out as the topic least well dealt with by the provincial press, largely attributed to insufficient coverage.

Asked to comment on standards in recent articles of interest, just over a third of comments could be classed as being very favourable towards the article with a similar number classed as very unfavourable. However, rating each article on a five-point scale, the large majority of respondents rated them as at least "fairly accurate" and "reasonably fair" and the amount of coverage as "about right". There was very little difference between types of paper in the quality attributed to specific articles. Articles on the topic of local industry and employment attracted slightly less favourable comments and less favourable ratings, especially as regards accuracy, but on the whole there was little variation by subject matter.

In the minority of cases where articles were less than satisfactory the main reasons given were the paper's limited space, biased or selective writing or poor and inaccurate reporting. The last two reasons were also those most frequently advanced when relations with the provincial press were said to be bad and were the major causes of complaints made to the newspapers.

INTRODUCTION

The provincial press has been shown to fulfil a rather different role for the special sample of local influential people from that which it plays for the general public. In particular, members of the special sample tend to be closely concerned with and involved in some of the issues that are reported in provincial newspapers (especially the dailies) and some of them regard the provincial press as an important medium of communication about the issues with which they are concerned to the people in the area. These local influential people are therefore likely to be not only very concerned about the standard of reporting in the provincial press but also in a particularly good position to form an opinion about it. They were therefore asked in detail for their opinions of the local newspapers that they saw fairly regularly (at least once a week or more often for the dailies and at least once a month for the weeklies). They were asked for their opinions about each newspaper's standards in general and also about recent articles concerned with events or issues with which they were involved or of which they had special knowledge. A limited subset of the questions were also asked for comparative purposes about one of the national daily papers that they read.

STANDARDS IN GENERAL

Respondents were asked at the end of a discussion of each provincial paper they read to rate the general quality of each paper on a six-point scale from "excellent" to "very poor". Very few rated any of them as "excellent" but around three in ten rated the provincial mornings as "very good" and a further third as "fairly good". The ratings for the provincial evenings and local weekly papers were not as favourable, the majority rating them as either "fairly good" or "average". Differences in rating between the five groups of respondents were not marked but it is interesting to note that there is more diversity of views among council officials (who read a particularly large number of regional newspapers) and head teachers (who were particularly likely to read the local weekly).

TABLE 2.039
GENERAL RATING OF THE QUALITY OF PROVINCIAL NEWSPAPERS:
A COMPARISON OF NEWSPAPER TYPES

	Score	Regional Morning	Provincial Evening	Local Weekly
Base: All provincial papers read		168	278	215
		%	%	%
Excellent	5	8	3	4
Very good	4	29	13	17
Fairly good	3	32	33	30
Average	2	18	32	31
Fairly poor	1	8	10	10
Very poor	0	1	3	2
Mean		3·10	2·55	2·66

Base: All papers read at least once a week (dailies) or once a month (weeklies).

TABLE 2.040
GENERAL RATING OF THE QUALITY OF PROVINCIAL NEWSPAPERS:
A COMPARISON BETWEEN "INFLUENTIAL" GROUPS

	Councillors	Managing Directors	Trade Union Secretaries	Council Officials	Head Teachers
Base: All provincial papers read	98	165	186	125	87
	%	%	%	%	%
Excellent	7	3	4	5	1
Very good	22	18	16	14	24
Fairly good	31	30	31	31	26
Average	24	34	34	26	31
Fairly poor	6	7	9	16	18
Very poor	6	1	2	0	0
Mean	2·81	2·71	2·65	2·63	2·59

Base: All papers read at least once a week (dailies) or once a month (weeklies).

The proportions rating each type of newspaper as "excellent", "very good", or "fairly good" approximates closely to the proportion rating as "very" or "fairly true" the statement "Reading it is always enjoyable". (See Table 2.032.) This statement was also asked about national newspapers and these received a slightly higher level of appreciation. It therefore seems likely that they would also have done so on the general rating scale.

Interestingly, when discussing whether the general quality of the papers had improved or declined in recent years, very little difference is seen between the different types of provincial newspaper. In all cases a small majority view the papers they read as having "remained about the same" in quality and in each case the proportion thinking they have declined is balanced by a similar proportion thinking they have improved (about a fifth for each type). Councillors are the only group where an appreciable proportion (35%) of readers claim that the provincial papers they read have declined. This is due solely to councillors claiming that almost half (49%) of the evening newspapers they read regularly (and they were heavy readers of the provincial evening press) had deteriorated in quality. Their opinions on the regional mornings and local weeklies were much the same as those of the other groups.

TABLE 2.041
CHANGES IN THE QUALITY OF PROVINCIAL NEWSPAPERS IN RECENT YEARS

	Regional Mornings	*Provincial Evenings*	*Local Weeklies*
Base: All provincial papers read	168	278	215
Quality has:	%	%	%
Improved	21	23	21
Declined	24	22	19
Remained the same	52	51	55

Base: All papers read at least once a week (dailies) or once a month (weeklies).

Some of the specific opinion statements that were put to respondents referred to particular aspects of standards, presenting for endorsement or rejection propositions that are often made about provincial newspapers.

Opinions on specific aspects of standards tend to follow the same pattern as the general rating; regional mornings were praised more and received less criticism from the readers than either provincial evenings or local weeklies. The superiority of regional mornings is most marked on the positive statements, "Its standard of reporting is first class" and "The comments it makes on the news are usually interesting", but they are also much less likely than weeklies or evenings to be rated as "printing too many silly or trivial stories". The provincial evening newspapers are criticised more frequently than either mornings or weeklies on the grounds that "It often gets its facts wrong" and that "It has too much advertising in it".

Just as regional mornings are viewed as having a higher standard than other types of provincial newspaper, so national dailies are thought of as being better still—their standard of reporting is considered to be better, their comments on news more interesting, they are not seen as having too much advertising, as printing too many silly or trivial stories nor as often getting their facts wrong. With national dailies, however, a very considerable difference is seen between the quality and the popular dailies. For example, readers of the quality dailies endorse the statement "Its standard of reporting is first class" as "very" or "fairly true" in 97% of the cases, compared with only 47% for the popular national dailies. The popular dailies are seen as very much closer to provincial evenings and local weeklies and as surpassed by the regional mornings on several of these propositions and receive a higher level of endorsement than any other type of newspaper on the statement "It prints too many silly or trivial stories".

TABLE 2.042

SOME SPECIFIC OPINIONS OF STANDARDS IN THE PROVINCIAL PRESS
(Proportion saying that statement is "very" or "fairly true")

	Provincial newspapers				All National Dailies	Popular National Dailies
	All	Mornings	Evenings	Weeklies		
Base: All papers read	661 %	168 %	278 %	215 %	333 %	120 %
Its standard of reporting is first class	49	67	41	45	83	47
The comments it makes on the news are usually interesting	68	83	66	64	93	74
It often gets its facts wrong	42	33	56	31	16	31
It prints too many silly or trivial stories	40	22	46	39	19	51
It has too much advertising in it	43	32	53	40	10	23

Base: All papers read at least once a week (dailies) or once a month (weeklies).

The various "influential" groups do not differ from each other to any great extent in the ratings they give on these propositions to the provincial newspapers they read. Councillors and trade union secretaries stand out in the extent to which they think that provincial papers have "too much advertising". Both groups claimed in three out of five of the cases that the papers they read have too much advertising, as opposed to about a third for the other groups. Council officials are particularly likely to endorse the statement "It often gets its facts wrong":

	It often gets its facts wrong (Very or fairly true) (Base 661 papers read) %
Council officials	54
Trade union secretaries	45
Councillors	38
Managing directors	38
Head teachers	32

Base: All papers read at least once a week (dailies) or once a month (weeklies).

Overall, council officials and trade union secretaries appear most critical of standards in the provincial press in terms of these particular propositions, confirming their lower rating of its overall quality (Table 2.040). Head teachers, however, seem to be the least critical on these specific points even although their mean score on the rating for overall quality was lower than for other groups. This seems to reflect the diversity of opinion among head teachers within the group. The "influential" sample respondents were more critical than were members of the general public sample on all these statements except the one concerned with the amount of advertising in provincial newspapers where both samples had similar views. It is also notable that the opinions of the general public do not vary as much as those of the "influential" sample according to the type of provincial newspaper; the gap between the public and the special groups of local influential people is less marked where their opinions of regional morning newspapers are concerned than is the case with the provincial evenings and local weeklies. As we have already seen, the "influential" groups differentiate more strongly in their opinions between the three types of newspaper than do members of the public.

It is noticeable that, as in other respects, the attitudes of the professional and managerial sector to evening and weekly papers (the sample of morning paper readers is too small) lie in between those of the full general public sample and those of the "influential" sample. In all cases, however, they are closer in their ideas to the general public.

TABLE 2.043
GENERAL STANDARDS IN THE PROVINCIAL PRESS:
THE OPINIONS OF "INFLUENTIALS" AND THE GENERAL PUBLIC

	All Provincial Papers Read	Regional Mornings	Provincial Evenings	Local Weeklies
	%	%	%	%
Proportion saying "very true" or "fairly true" to statements				
"Its standard of reporting is first class"				
"Influential" sample	49	67	41	45
General public sample	72	81	73	69
Professional/management			69	60
"The comments it makes on the news are usually interesting"				
"Influential" sample	69	83	66	68
General public sample	84	93	87	80
Professional/management			82	77
"It prints too many silly or trivial stories"				
"Influential" sample	40	22	46	40
General public sample	23	19	26	22
Professional/management			34	26
"It often gets its facts wrong"				
"Influential" sample	42	33	56	31
General public sample	26	15	33	23
Professional/management			30	25
"It has too much advertising in it"				
"Influential" sample	43	32	53	40
General public sample	42	28	50	39
Professional/management			51	40

It is often said that newspapers exaggerate the sensational aspects of the news; some opinion statements were therefore included in order to discover what opinions the special sample had on this issue and how they saw the provincial press as performing in this respect compared with the national press.

From the table below it seems that overall almost half consider the provincial evening press the most worthy of criticism in this respect. Once again the regional mornings received ratings very similar to those for the national mornings.

One way the press has been said by some to sensationalise the news is by always concentrating their attentions on the bad news. Less than a third endorsed this accusation in relation to the provincial newspapers they read, but once again the provincial evenings received more adverse ratings than did the mornings or weeklies. Only a quarter said of the provincial papers they read that "It sometimes goes too far in invading people's grief"; the local weeklies were particularly unlikely to have this said about them.

TABLE 2.044
PERCEPTIONS OF SENSATIONALISM IN NEWSPAPERS OF DIFFERENT TYPES

	All Provincial Papers Read	Regional Mornings	Provincial Evenings	Local Weeklies	National Dailies	Popular Dailies
Base	661	168	278	215	333	120
Proportion saying "very true" or "fairly true" to statements	%	%	%	%	%	%
"It exaggerates the sensational aspects of the news"	45	36	56	36	33	80
"It always concentrates on the bad news"	30	26	39	19	20	43
"It sometimes goes too far in invading people's grief"	26	29	31	15	23	56

Base: All papers read at least once a week (dailies) or once a month (weeklies).

In comparing the provincial press with the national dailies, a distinction needs to be made once again between quality nationals and the more popular dailies. On every statement the popular press received more adverse endorsement than did any of the types of regional newspaper; for example, in 8 out of 10 of the cases, popular dailies were said by readers in the "influential" sample to "exaggerate the sensational aspects of the news"; in less than 1 out of 10, quality papers were said to do so.

The general public once more were less critical than the "influential" sample of the provincial press, though again there were differences between "influential" groups with councillors and trade union secretaries being rather more critical than other groups. Professional and managerial respondents differed little in opinion from the rest of the general public sample.

Trade union secretaries' criticisms are once again particularly concentrated on the provincial evening press, but councillors are more critical of the local weeklies they read.

TABLE 2.045
SPECIFIC ASPECTS OF EDITORIAL STANDARDS IN THE PROVINCIAL PRESS

	"Influential" Sample	Trade Union Secs.	Councillors	Council Officials	Managing Directors	Head Teachers	General Public Sample
Base	661	186	98	125	165	87	3,102
Proportion saying "very true" or "fairly true" to statements	%	%	%	%	%	%	%
"It exaggerates the sensational aspects of the news"	44	46	50	39	40	37	27
"It always concentrates on the bad news"	29	39	28	32	24	12	23
"It sometimes goes too far in invading people's grief"	25	30	27	20	26	19	20

Base: All papers read at least once a week (dailies) or once a month (weeklies).

STANDARDS IN THE TREATMENT OF SPECIFIC ISSUES

Thus far we have examined the general opinions of the special sample of local influential people about the standards achieved by the provincial press. But all the groups were chosen because of their involvement in local issues and events, and we turn now to examine their opinions of the way in which these are treated in the local press. We start by identifying what the different groups of influential people see as being the major problems in their area and their views on how well these are covered by different types of provincial newspaper. Their opinions about the way certain important broad subject areas of relevance to the different groups are then investigated and their evaluation of specific recent press reports of events in which they were involved or of which they had special knowledge is described. Finally, their opinions of their relations with the provincial press and their experience of ways with which complaints have been dealt are examined.

Treatment of Important Area Problems by the Provincial Press

When asked to nominate the one most important issue or problem of the district, respondents, in the main, selected problems which were germane to their official position. As a result, although the list of problems covers a very large range of subjects, we can amalgamate many of these into broader topic areas, each largely the concern on one or two groups of respondents. One problem, however, that of unemployment, was nominated as the major problem by many respondents in all groups. It is by far the most frequently mentioned problem overall.

TABLE 2.046
MOST IMPORTANT LOCAL ISSUE

	"Influential" Sample	Council Officials	Councillors	Managing Directors	Trade Union Secretaries	Head Teachers
Base: All respondents	350 %	52 %	51 %	97 %	100 %	50 %
Economic and industrial problems						
Unemployment/redundancies	35	23	8	41	57	16
Economic crisis/inflation	5	12	4	3	4	2
Industrial relations/dispute	2	—	2	5	1	—
Shortage of labour	3	—	2	8	—	2
Labour productivity	1	2	—	3	1	—
Local government finance						
Financing of local government	3	4	6	2	3	—
High rates/rate increases	5	10	8	3	5	—
Cuts back in local government—general	1	—	—	—	1	2
Housing						
Shortage of housing	6	6	27	3	2	—
Poor quality of existing housing stock	3	1	18	1	1	—
Education						
Education policies	4	—	2	2	2	19
Poor educational facilities	1	—	—	—	—	4
Cuts back in education	2	4	—	—	4	4
Miscellaneous						
Threat of new road or airport	6	10	6	4	2	12
Cuts back/lack of social services	2	2	4	—	2	2
Poor hospitals/medical services	1	—	4	—	2	—
Poor transport facilities	1	—	—	3	—	4
Vandalism	3	2	4	—	2	12
Area has no problems	2	2	—	3	2	4
Other problems	14	23	8	16	7	16

Although unemployment is not the exclusive concern of managing directors and trade union secretaries, nonetheless respondents from these two groups make up the large bulk (80%) of "influentials" nominating unemployment.

Similarly, more than half of respondents nominating an education problem as the most important are head teachers and local government matters, while not the exclusive preserve or exclusive interest of councillors and council officials, are nonetheless an area mentioned most often by these two groups.

We have seen earlier (Table 2.029) that, although non-media sources (eg job or personal contacts) were often more frequently mentioned, the provincial press is the most commonly used of the media as a source of information on problems in the local area; 48% of respondents mentioned local newspapers when asked how they came to know of the areas' most important problem and the proportions were higher where the three broad topic areas we have mentioned were concerned; in 61% of cases respondents came to know of the problem of unemployment and redundancies through local newspapers; in the field of education the figure was 53%, and of local government 76%.

On the whole, the provincial press appear to fulfil the role of supplying information on local issues fairly well; in more than half the cases provincial papers were said by their readers to give the local problem nominated as the most important at least some attention. However, in a substantial minority of cases (42%) dissatisfaction was expressed. No one topic stands out as receiving either very much more, or else very much less, attention than the average. There is also a remarkable similarity between the different types of newspaper in the degree to which they are considered to give attention to the important local problems. Only trade union secretaries show any marked divergence, again proving themselves to be more critical of the provincial press.

TABLE 2.047
ATTENTION GIVEN TO THE IMPORTANT PROBLEMS OF THE AREA BY THE PROVINCIAL PRESS

	All Provincial Papers	Regional Mornings	Provincial Evenings	Local Weeklies
Base	632	162	265	205
	%	%	%	%
Paper gives a lot of attention	36	40	45	31
Paper gives some attention and should not give more	15	} 14	13	24
Paper gives no attention and should not give more	2			
Paper gives some attention and should give more	37	} 44	42	42
Paper gives no attention and should give more	5			

Base: All papers read by respondents specifying the area as having an important issue or problem.

Provincial Press Treatment of Broad Subject Areas

Respondents were asked to say for each provincial newspaper read how well they thought the newspaper treated each of a list of topics and from those treated badly to select one that was treated "least well". The topics selected for discussion all covered areas of particular concern to at least some groups of respondents but also of interest to most, if not all, provincial newspapers.

Most topics were considered to be fairly well, if not very well, treated by the provincial press. Only one topic—news of local trade union activities—was considered to be treated less than well in any substantial number of cases; trade union secretaries were particularly critical in this respect and thought that the provincial press did not cover their affairs well. There was very little difference between the three types of provincial newspaper though on the whole topics in provincial evenings were rated a little more highly than those in mornings or weeklies, in contrast to other aspects on which evenings were criticised more than the other types of newspaper.

TABLE 2.048

PROVINCIAL PRESS TREATMENT OF PARTICULAR TOPICS: A COMPARISON OF NEWSPAPER TYPES

	All Provincial Papers Read	Regional Mornings	Provincial Evenings	Local Weeklies
Base	661	168	278	215
	%	%	%	%
Proportion of papers treating topic "very well" or "fairly well":				
News of local industrial disputes	77	80	81	74
Local town redevelopment proposals ...	84	86	87	86
Activities of the Conservative Party on the Council	76	74	81	76
Activities of the Labour Party on the Council	71	70	73	73
Local educational matters	77	74	79	81
News of local industry	83	89	85	82
News of local trade union activities ...	56	63	56	57

Base: All papers read at least once a week (dailies) or once a month (weeklies).

There is a tendency for all groups of respondents to be most critical of the way in which the provincial press treats their own particular interests. Thus head teachers are more critical than other responders of treatment of local educational matters; councillors of the treatment of the activities of the two main political parties on the local council, and so on. Council officials, whose interests are perhaps rather more diverse than those of other groups, were the only exception.

TABLE 2.049

PROVINCIAL PRESS TREATMENT OF PARTICULAR TOPICS: THE VIEWS OF DIFFERENT GROUPS

	All	Councillors	Council Officials	Trade Union Secretaries	Managing Directors	Head Teachers
Base	661	98	125	186	165	87
	%	%	%	%	%	%
Proportion of papers treating topic "very badly" or "fairly badly"						
News of local industrial disputes	17	9	14	26	19	5
Local town redevelopment proposals	11	11	10	14	7	7
Activities of the Conservative Party on the Council	12	15	14	10	9	8
Activities of the Labour Party on the Council	19	28	17	25	8	9
Local educational matters	16	14	10	21	10	24
News of local industry	13	9	10	15	12	7
News of local trade union activities	36	34	26	59	25	15

Base: All papers read at least once a week (dailies) or once a month (weeklies).

After asking respondents to say, for each provincial paper they read, how well the paper treated the topics, they were asked to nominate one, from those dealt with badly, as the one dealt with "least well" by each paper. If we look at the results broken down first of all by the five groups of respondents, we see something of the same pattern emerging as that already identified—more dissatisfaction with the treatment of topics in their own field of interest. Council officials again prove an exception. However, "News of local trade union activities" is selected as the least well treated topic by substantial proportions in each group.

TABLE 2.050

TOPIC TREATED LEAST WELL BY THE PROVINCIAL PRESS: THE VIEWS OF DIFFERENT GROUPS

	All	Councillors	Council Officials	Trade Union Secretaries	Managing Directors	Head Teachers
Base	661	98	125	186	165	87
	%	%	%	%	%	%
News of local industrial disputes	8	2	10	6	15	1
Local town redevelopment proposals	5	2	8	4	3	5
Activities of the Conservative Party on the Council	5	10	6	1	4	6
Activities of the Labour Party on the Council	7	21	7	4	4	3
Local educational matters	8	7	6	5	8	21
News of local industry	3	4	4	2	4	1
News of local trade union activities	29	20	18	55	16	22
No topic treated badly	36	33	42	23	48	44

Base: All papers read at least once a week (dailies) or once a month (weeklies).

The main criticism made of provincial newspapers about the treatment of the topic treated "least well" was that they had not given the amount of coverage which respondents thought the topic deserved. Insufficient coverage was, in fact, by far and away the criticism most often levelled; the only other criticism which any numbers mentioned was of an unfair or biased coverage by some papers. Together these two represented almost two-thirds of the reasons given for nominating one topic as worst dealt with by the provincial press.

There is a marked difference between reasons given for saying that industrial disputes are least well treated and those given when news of trade union activities or local industry is selected. In the latter two cases the most important factor is insufficient coverage being given to the topic though some also complain of bias and that the newspapers only cover disputes. However, on the reporting of industrial disputes, other factors are seen as equally important: some pointed to a bias in the treatment of the topic while others complained of a tendency for the provincial press to sensationalise stories on this topic by printing sensational articles or headlines, or blowing up trivial incidents. A small number also complained that the paper only reported industrial disputes while never reporting other features of industrial relations.

TABLE 2.051

REASONS GIVEN FOR BAD TREATMENT OF TOPICS

	All Topics	Local Industrial Disputes	Local Trade Union Activities	Activities of Labour or Conservative Party	Local Educational Matters
Base	545	69	252	65	76
	%	%	%	%	%
Inaccurate reporting	7	9	4	9	11
Insufficient coverage	42	20	52	26	30
Unfair, biased coverage	22	23	17	43	17
Sensational treatment of topic	8	23	2	8	13
Paper doesn't explain the issues/ poor reporting	8	7	6	2	16
Not enough public interest in topic	3	4	2	—	3
Paper only reports disputes, never constructive	6	6	12	2	4
Paper oversimplifies/too trivial	2	4	1	—	—
Other answers	1	1	2	3	1

Base: All reasons given for the provincial press treating one topic "least well".

Local educational matters appears to be a topic slightly different from others. The main complaint is still of insufficient coverage, but it is also one in which sensational treatment of the subject matter is a problem (as we have noted earlier). In addition, it is a topic on which readers said that reporting was poor or the issues were not fully explained.

Involvement with the Provincial Press

We have mentioned that one of the criteria for choice of the types of people to form the "influential" sample was that they should not only be potentially interested in local news, but also that they should hold an important position in a sphere normally of interest to the provincial press. Education, local industry and local government are all subjects of news value to the provincial press. In addition to having a particular interest in subjects often dealt with by the provincial press it was therefore expected that many of the members of the special groups selected would have actually participated in the events reported upon by local newspapers, or at least would have had their opinions canvassed on many of the issues discussed in their columns. Indeed we shall see later that 70% of all provincial papers read by the special sample had contained a recent article or report in which respondents had ". . . some particular interest, involvement or knowledge". The descriptions they gave of the subject of the article or report indicated that we would be justified in calling the special sample "producers" of news in that they were involved in important ways in the events that local newspapers had reported or commented on.

Since a regional morning newspaper was not published in all the areas covered in this study, respondents were asked about their usual means of contact with the local evening and weekly newspapers only. The majority of respondents had some contact with these newspapers, though 81% said they had dealings with the evening papers compared with 54% who had dealings with the weeklies. 5% claimed no weekly paper circulated in their area.

Most of those who had dealings with the local press said that they took positive steps to contact the newspaper rather than speaking only when approached. Council officials were the most likely to have contact with both the local evenings and the local weeklies and to make positive approaches to the newspapers, suggesting a definite policy of using the local press as a communications medium on their part.

Head teachers, councillors and managing directors are very similar in the extent to which they have dealings with local evening newspapers, but head teachers were rather more likely than the other two groups to contact their local weekly newspaper, probably reflecting the more localised nature of many of their affairs.

The trade union secretaries were the least likely of all the groups to have any contact with the regional evening papers and were also more likely to talk to them only when approached. It turned out that some of the trade union secretaries did not contact the press themselves because it was someone else's job to do so. This had not been expected and therefore steps were not taken in the questionnaire to deal with this situation properly.

TABLE 2.052
APPROACHES MADE TO THE PROVINCIAL PRESS

	All Respondents	Council Officials	Head Teachers	Councillors	Managing Directors	Trade Union Secs.
Base: All respondents	350 %	52 %	50 %	51 %	97 %	100 %
Provincial evening newspapers						
Sometimes approaches paper	58	77	64	63	57	44
Speaks only when approached	19	10	20	22	18	25
Varies according to the paper	5	10	—	—	5	6
Never speaks to paper	18	2	10	12	16	23
Local weekly newspapers						
Sometimes approaches paper	32	52	40	26	29	24
Speaks only when approached	16	17	12	26	10	19
Varies according to the paper	3	6	—	2	2	3
Never speaks to paper	40	17	34	41	48	47
No weekly newspaper	5	4	8	2	5	4
Other answers	3	4	4	2	4	1

The reason for never speaking to the local evening paper or to the local weekly paper was often quite simply that they did not have anything to speak to them about; but there was also some feeling that the paper would not report topics or events of interest to respondents or that they would not report what was said accurately (a subject we shall discuss later in the report). A number of other derogatory comments were also made, particularly about local weekly papers—that they are "trivial", "not important" or "not very influential" as a result of which they are "not worth speaking to"; they are also said to be "out of date" or "a rehash of the daily paper".

TABLE 2.053
REASONS GIVEN FOR NEVER SPEAKING TO THE PROVINCIAL PRESS

	Provincial Evening Newspapers	Local Weekly Newspapers
Base: All who never speak to newspapers	51 %	140 %
Don't have anything to report	31	22
Paper would not report story	6	6
Paper would not report accurately	18	7
Someone else approaches paper (mainly trade union secretaries)	22	7
Don't want publicity	8	2
Derogatory comments eg trivial, unimportant paper	14	28
Paper out of date/rehash of daily papers	—	15
No weekly newspaper	—	8
Other reasons	16	9

It was thought that managing directors and council officials would in many cases not have direct contact with the press and they were asked whether this was the case. The table below shows that in many cases contacts with newspapers were handled by press personnel or public relations officers.

TABLE 2.054
RESPONSIBILITY FOR CONTACTS WITH THE PRESS

	Council Officials	Managing Directors
Base	52	89
	%	%
No one has special responsibility	25	24
Respondent has special responsibility	12	24
Press officer at establishment has responsibility ...	27	9
Public relations officer at establishment has responsibility	17	7
Press officer at head office has responsibility ...	—	12
Public relations officer at head office has responsibility	12	8
Personnel department has responsibility ...	—	6
Others	10	13

Base: All council officials and managing directors, excluding chairmen of Chambers of Commerce.

The method of approach to the local evening or local weekly papers varies between the groups of respondents. Managing directors and head teachers appear to deal far more with the editors than do either trade union secretaries or councillors, the latter two groups relying more heavily on contact with journalists. Council officials would appear to have considerable contact with both editors and journalists in addition to being more likely to issue press statements than other groups. There is very little difference between groups in methods of approach adopted to local weekly papers and so only summary results for the weekly press are presented in the following table.

TABLE 2.055
HOW APPROACHES ARE MADE TO THE PROVINCIAL PRESS

	Provincial Evening Newspapers					Local Weekly Newspapers
	Total	Council Officials	Managing Directors	Head Teachers	Councillors	Trade Union Secretaries	Total
Base	299	51	81	45	45	77	188
	%	%	%	%	%	%	%
Telephone or call to see editor	31	41	42	40	20	13	26
Editor telephones or calls	12	16	17	18	7	3	14
Telephone or call to see journalist	46	67	36	33	51	47	38
Journalist telephones or calls	42	37	36	38	42	53	44
Issues press statement ...	15	37	22	2	4	8	16
Writes a letter	4	4	2	9	2	5	5
Some other way	11	16	9	13	11	9	9

Base: All respondents who ever speak to provincial evening or local weekly newspapers.

One of the criteria for selection of the five groups that make up the "influential" sample, indeed one of the reasons for selecting a special sample at all, was that they were likely to be involved in events and issues reported in the provincial press and thus would be in a special position to evaluate the standard of reporting.

Each respondent was asked, for each provincial newspaper he read at least occasionally, whether or not an article or report had been published recently in which he had "some particular interest, involvement or knowledge". An affirmative answer was given in 70% of the cases.

Local weeklies were less likely than other types of newspaper to have contained such articles (63% compared with 77% for provincial morning and evening papers); managing directors and trade union secretaries were least likely to have been involved in a reported issue. These results reflect the fact that respondents were less likely to be in contact with local weekly papers than with the evenings (Table 2.052) and that managing directors and trade union secretaries were the two groups least likely to be in contact with provincial newspapers.

TABLE 2.056

PROVINCIAL PAPERS CONTAINING RECENT ARTICLES ON ISSUES IN WHICH RESPONDENTS WERE INVOLVED/PARTICULARLY INTERESTED

Read by:		Base	
	Councillors	98	84%
	Council officials	125	88%
	Managing directors	165	61%
	Trade union secretaries	186	65%
	Head teachers	87	75%

Base: All papers read at least once a week (dailies) or once a month (weeklies).

The articles covered a wide range of subjects but the majority could be grouped into three very broad topic areas that tie in with the interests of one or more groups of respondents; they were local industry and employment (mentioned in 16% of the cases), local government matters (32%) and education and schooling (15%). Housing and housing estate management, although not solely a local government concern, has been included for convenience under the general heading of "local government matters" and in fact was largely the concern of councillors and council officials.

One should not lose sight of the fact that here we are talking of those who felt the provincial press treated the topic of local education badly. More than three-quarters (77%) of all respondents felt the provincial newspapers they read dealt with this topic "very well" or at least "fairly well".

News about local trade union activities is the one topic that is quite frequently mentioned by members of all groups as being treated badly by the provincial press. Nevertheless there is far greater variation between the groups than between the different types of paper. There is a slight suggestion that provincial evenings are thought to treat the topic less well than other provincial papers but the difference is not very great. The proportions who said the papers they read dealt with this topic "badly" and those who chose it as the topic "least well" dealt with are as follows:

	"Badly"	"Least well"
Regional mornings	31%	29%
Provincial evenings	39%	34%
Local weeklies	32%	29%

Even less variation between newspaper types was perceived in the treatment of other topics.

TABLE 2.057

ARTICLES IN THE PROVINCIAL PRESS ON ISSUES IN WHICH RESPONDENTS WERE INVOLVED

	All	Councillors	Council Officials	Managing Directors	Trade Union Secretaries	Head Teachers
Base: all newspapers containing relevant recent articles	478	82	110	100	121	65
Local government matters	%	%	%	%	%	%
Meeting of the local council	4					
Housing/estate management	7					
Cuts back in local authority spending	2					
Local government finance	5					
Other local council matters	14					
Total in this category[1]	32	46	62	13	20	5
Local industry and employment						
Unemployment / redundancies	11					
Industrial disputes/strikes	5					
Total in this category[1]	16	1	3	23	35	2
Education/schooling	15	10	6	2	12	60
Health, hospitals	3					
Personal	3					
Chamber of Commerce meeting	*					
Common Market, referendum	*					
Other answers	34	32	25	54	26	29

Base: All articles appearing in the provincial press of particular interest to respondents.

[1] The numbers of each type of respondent involved in specific topics are too small to be analysed separately. Therefore, in this table, the totals in each category only are presented.

There was very little difference by type of provincial newspaper in the type of article mentioned but, as can be seen from the above table, the groups of respondents tended to mention articles in their particular spheres, indicating that they are indeed people who are closely involved in events covered by local newspapers.

Respondents were asked to express a general opinion of the way in which the article or report on the event/issue that they had been involved in had been written. The answers were recorded, tabulated and later coded into categories. If we group the answers according to whether they were generally very favourable comments made of the article, less favourable and unfavourable, we see that articles taken from provincial evenings receive slightly fewer very favourable comments and slightly more unfavourable comments. However, the difference is not nearly as marked as one might expect from the ratings of overall quality of each type of paper described earlier. Provincial mornings received more very favourable comments on their articles than did the local weeklies but also more unfavourable comments.

TABLE 2.058
RESPONDENTS' OPINIONS OF ARTICLES ON ISSUES/EVENTS IN WHICH THEY WERE INVOLVED

Article in:	All Provincial Papers	Regional Mornings	Provincial Evenings	Local Weeklies
Base	478	129	214	135
	%	%	%	%
Very favourable comments				
Reproduced press statement	5	4	8	3
Very accurately/correctly reported	21	23	17	23
Very fair/unbiased	6	10	5	4
Very good coverage/in great detail	2	2	2	2
Other favourable comments	7	9	6	7
TOTAL VERY FAVOURABLE COMMENTS	43	48	37	40
Less favourable comments				
Fairly accurate/not very accurate	9	9	10	8
Reasonably fair	7	5	7	10
Fairly good coverage	3	2	3	5
Other moderately favourable comments	9	9	10	10
TOTAL LESS FAVOURABLE COMMENTS	29	26	29	33
Very unfavourable comments				
Very inaccurate	11	11	10	12
Very biased/unfair	13	15	14	10
Poor coverage/article too short	8	10	8	7
Sensationalised/misleading	8	7	11	4
Disappointing/rehash of other reports	4	3	4	3
TOTAL VERY UNFAVOURABLE COMMENTS	46	46	48	36

Percentages add up to more than 100% as more than one comment could be made by each respondent.
Base: All articles of recent particular interest in the provincial press.

If we look briefly at the three main broad topic areas reported on we see that there is not a very great difference in comments made on each type of article. Local industry and employment as a topic receives slightly fewer very favourable and slightly more less favourable comments but otherwise the differences are not very great.

TABLE 2.059
COMMENTS MADE ON ARTICLES OF RECENT INTEREST BY TOPIC AREA

	All articles	Articles on local industry/ employment	Articles on local government	Articles on education
Base	478	77	154	73
	%	%	%	%
Very favourable comments ...	43	33	42	45
Less favourable comments... ...	29	40	25	30
Very unfavourable comments ...	46	50	51	48

Percentages add up to more than 100% as more than one comment could be made by each respondent.
Base: All articles of recent particular interest in the provincial press.

Following the separate assessment of each article, respondents were asked to rate it for accuracy, fairness and the amount of coverage. In the vast majority of cases, the articles were rated as at least "fairly" accurate and "reasonably" fair; there was rather more criticism of the amount of coverage given but nonetheless about two-thirds thought that the coverage was "about right". Articles on reports on local industry, in addition to attracting less very favourable comments in the open-ended question, also received slightly less favourable ratings on these scales, especially as regards accuracy.

TABLE 2.060
THE ACCURACY, FAIRNESS AND AMOUNT OF COVERAGE IN ARTICLES OF PARTICULAR INTEREST IN THE PROVINCIAL PRESS

	All articles	Articles on local industry/ employment	Articles on local government	Articles on education
Base	478	77	154	73
	%	%	%	%
Completely accurate	39	27	36	34
Fairly accurate	42	42	42	48
Fairly/very inaccurate	18	30	20	15
Completely fair	42	27	41	47
Reasonably fair	32	36	26	36
Rather/very unfair	25	36	32	17
Too much coverage	11	13	11	16
Too little coverage	21	27	25	13
Coverage just about right	66	58	63	69

Base: All articles of recent particular interest in the provincial press.

Not surprisingly, there is considerable overlap between articles considered accurate and also fair, and between articles considered inaccurate and also unfair. Considering articles on all topics the extent of overlap is as follows:

Completely/fairly accurate *and* completely/reasonably fair   73%

Completely/fairly accurate but not completely/reasonably fair   9%

Not completely/fairly accurate but completely/reasonably fair   2%

Not completely/fairly accurate *and* not completely/reasonably fair   15%

What is surprising, given the perceived difference in quality between provincial morning and evening papers is that in comparing articles or reports in each there is virtually no difference between the two in terms of accuracy (mornings 78% as accurate, evenings 80%), fairness (mornings 74%, evenings 71% completely or reasonably fair) or amount of coverage (both have 64% of articles where coverage is "just about right"). Local weekly papers which in general quality stood somewhere in between mornings and evenings, in fact appear slightly better in terms of the fairness, accuracy and amount of coverage given in their articles (the figures are: accurate 84%, fair 79%, just about right coverage 66%).

When an article or report was not rated as completely satisfactory, respondents were asked to say where they thought the fault lay and how it came about. In a fifth of the cases the fairly neutral comment was made that the newspaper "is limited by space/can't print everything", but in a similar proportion an attribution of biased or selective reporting was made; rather smaller proportions were put down to a poor standard of reporting, to lack of consultation by the newspaper and to attempts to sensationalise the story.

TABLE 2.061
REASONS FOR FAULTS IN RECENT ARTICLES APPEARING IN THE PROVINCIAL PRESS

	All
Base: Articles receiving less than completely satisfactory ratings	343
	%
Paper limited by space/cannot print everything	21
Biased/selective reporting	22
Biased/selective editing	6
Poor standard of reporting	16
Lack of consultation by paper	15
Sensationalising of story	13
Paper made story trivial	4
Paper not interested in subject	3
Paper's policy is biased/paper is prejudiced	2
Other answers	6

Percentages add up to more than 100% as more than one reason could be given.

As with the ratings themselves, there were only minor variations between types of newspaper in the reasons put forward as to why articles were less than completely satisfactory.

For the educational topics, the major complaint was of biased or selective reporting and editing (35%) but "poor reporting" was also of some importance (21%). We noted earlier that a tendency to sensationalise reports was cited as a reason for saying that the provincial press gave poor treatment of local education matters but when respondents were asked about specific articles rather than in general, sensationalism appeared to be no more frequently attributed to articles on education than to other topics.

In local government matters, one in five articles that were not completely satisfactory were said to have involved biased or selective reporting but in just as many cases the newspaper was excluded on the grounds that it "cannot print everything".

Articles on the broad subject of local industry and employment were said to be less than completely satisfactory in more than one in five (22%) of the cases as a result of a lack of consultation with our respondents by the newspapers. We have noted earlier how trade union secretaries, more than other groups, were not in direct contact with provincial newspapers and this may be a reason for the complaints of lack of consultation. By far the most frequent reason given, however (in 42% of the cases), was biased or selective reporting and, particularly in this field, unfair or biased editing.

Relations with the Provincial Press

We have seen some of the complaints made and shortcomings attributed to the provincial press, but have noted at the same time that the opinion of newspapers overall is quite high (if somewhat lower when it involves the reporting of respondents' own areas of interest). This overall impression that the provincial press is seen to be fairly good is reflected in the ratings that our respondents gave to their relations with the newspapers they read. Respondents claim to have "very good" relations in less than a third of the cases but in almost three-quarters of the cases relations are rated as being at least "fairly good"; there is not a great deal of variation between the groups of respondents; the there groups who claim that in more than 10% of cases they have non-existent relations with the local press are also those groups who were most likely to say that they "never spoke to the local newspaper".

TABLE 2.062
RESPONDENTS' OPINIONS OF PRESENT RELATIONS WITH THE PROVINCIAL PRESS

	Base	Relations are:				
		Very good	Fairly good	Not very good	Very bad	Non-existent
		%	%	%	%	%
All	661	31	43	10	2	13
Relations with company (Managing directors) or Chamber of Commerce	165	34	39	5	—	21
Relations with union district (TU secretaries)	186	24	45	12	3	13
Relations with school (Head teachers)	87	40	33	7	1	15
Relations with party group (Councillors)	98	30	47	15	3	3
Relations with Council (Council officials)	125	29	46	13	2	9

Base: All papers read once a week or more (dailies) or once a month or more (weeklies).

A majority of all groups of respondents except managing directors had at one time or another felt like complaining about something that had appeared in the provincial newspapers they read. There is, however, wide variation in the proportions who had, in fact, complained. Head teachers and trade union secretaries appear reluctant to make a complaint, in the majority of cases claiming either that a complaint would not do any good, would not receive any attention, or would serve only to make matters worse. When respondents felt like complaining they seem more likely actually to complain when a provincial daily is involved than when the complaint is against the local weekly paper.

TABLE 2.063

COMPLAINTS AGAINST THE PROVINCIAL PRESS

		Ever felt like complaining against paper			*Ever complained against paper*		
		No	Yes, once	Yes, more than once	No	Yes, once	Yes, more than once
All 661	%	46	9	44	23	9	20
Councillors 98	%	37	11	52	19	13	31
Council officials ... 125	%	38	6	56	24	6	32
Trade union secretaries ... 186	%	44	8	48	28	9	19
Head teachers 87	%	43	18	37	36	10	9
Managing directors ... 165	%	62	8	30	24	6	32

Base: All papers read at least once a week (dailies) or once a month (weeklies).

The main reasons for complaint were inaccurate reporting, unfairness and bias in the reporting. An important cause for dissatisfaction noticed earlier, that of insufficient coverage, was not often seen as a reason for complaining to the newspaper in question. When we compare the issues on which complaints were actually made with those respondents only *felt* like complaining about, it appears that respondents are more reluctant to complain about alleged unfairness, bias or sensationalising than they are about inaccuracies in a report.

Respondents had "non-existent relations" with the regional mornings they read in only 7% of cases and with the evenings in 8% of cases. However, almost a quarter (24%) had no relations with the local weekly press. The state of their relations with the different types of newspaper was uniformly good. In only 10% or so of cases for each type of newspaper did respondents who had any relations with the type of newspaper claim they did not have at least fairly good relations.

Respondents were asked further in what way they thought relations between themselves or their organisation and the local press was either good or not good. Where relations were good the main reason put forward was that the newspaper had always contacted respondents before a story had been printed or that there were good communications between themselves and the press. Otherwise the most important reason for good relations was that reporting had generally been good, fair and unbiased or, at least, had not been bad. Poor, biased, or inaccurate reporting appears as the major cause of poor relations.

Although respondents had good relations with the majority of provincial papers they read, this is not to say that they had never felt that they had reason to complain. In fact many had complained and many more had felt like complaining—and not only on one occasion—particularly to the provincial daily papers.

TABLE 2.064
HAD RESPONDENTS EVER FELT LIKE COMPLAINING ABOUT ANYTHING THAT APPEARED IN THE PAPERS THEY READ?

	Regional Morning Newspapers Read	Provincial Evening Newspapers Read	Local Weekly Newspapers Read
Base	168	278	215
	%	%	%
No, had not felt like complaining	39	35	66
Yes, had felt like complaining once only	12	9	8
Yes, had felt like complaining more than once	49	56	25

Base: All papers read at least once a week (dailies) or once a month (weeklies).

TABLE 2.065
REASONS FOR RESPONDENTS' COMPLAINTS TO NEWSPAPERS

	Issues on which respondents have complained	Issues on which respondents have "felt like complaining" but have not complained
Base	200	147
	%	%
Misquoting or inaccurate reporting of speech	10	4
Other inaccurate reporting	36	26
Lack of coverage	9	8
Unfair, biased reporting	24	27
Sensationalising of story	11	16
Paper's breach of trust	5	4
Other reasons	9	15

In just over half the cases where respondents had made a complaint, the outcome had not been satisfactory. Council officials and managing directors were most likely to say that complaints had been dealt with satisfactorily while in well over half the cases, both trade union secretaries and councillors said that their complaint had not had a satisfactory outcome.

TABLE 2.066
THE RESULT OF MOST RECENT COMPLAINTS MADE BY RESPONDENTS

	Number of papers to which complaints have been made	Satisfactory outcome	Unsatisfactory outcome
All respondents	208	97	111
Council officials	46	27	19
Managing directors	38	23	15
Head teachers	19	10	9
Trade union secretaries	52	20	32
Councillors	53	17	36

The complaints that were made were directed largely at the editor or at journalists. Less than 10% of complaints had been directed elsewhere, and only one respondent had complained to the Press Council. Respondents appear to have received the same degree of satisfaction whether they addressed their complaint to the editor or to a journalist.

TABLE 2.067
THE DIRECTION OF COMPLAINTS MADE AND THE OUTCOME OF COMPLAINTS

	Base		Satis-factory outcome	Unsatis-factory outcome	Don't know /Cannot remember
Complaints directed to:					
Editor	125	%	55	42	2
Journalist	65	%	48	49	3

The most frequently given reason for an unsatisfactory outcome was that the editor or journalist in question has failed to reply to the complaint, something that was said to have occurred in slightly less than one in ten (9%) of all complaints made. No one group of respondents appeared any more likely than other groups to suffer in this way, nor was their suffering attributed particularly to any one type of paper.

Respondents appeared more reluctant to make a complaint to a local weekly paper on occasions when they felt they had cause, yet when complaints were made a satisfactory outcome seemed more likely to come from a local weekly than from either type of regional daily paper. The proportion of complaints which had a satisfactory outcome was as follows:

Regional mornings	47%
Provincial evenings	44%
Local weeklies	70%

6. Does the Provincial Press Cover all Sections of the Community Fairly

SUMMARY

When questioned in general terms about the coverage given to different sections of the community, two-thirds of regional morning and local weekly papers and slightly less than two-thirds of provincial evening papers were said to give "fair coverage to all points of view". Furthermore two-thirds were said to be ". . . prepared to criticise anybody if it [the paper] thinks they deserve it".

Specifically, it could be said of less than a quarter that they were " . . . afraid of offending advertisers". In the sphere of politics, more than half of the provincial papers were seen as not supporting any one political party, although when they did so their support was thought to go mostly to the Conservative Party. However, in more than half the cases where papers were said to be partial towards one political party, this was not thought to be to the exclusion of fair coverage to the other parties. In the small number of cases where political bias was attributed (24% on regional morning papers, 20% on evenings and 11% for local weeklies), the Labour Party was said to be the one not given fair coverage.

The extent to which provincial papers were seen as taking sides in the political sphere varied between type of paper with evenings and weeklies seen as less partisan than provincial or national morning papers. Similarly, in the sphere of industrial relations, evenings and weeklies were seen as more likely than others not to report much about the subject at all. When reporting disagreements between employers and unions, or commenting on these disagreements, just over one-half of respondents felt that the provincial papers they read "report both sides of things fairly" and try to " . . . judge fairly between them". Those giving more space to one side or the other were fairly evenly divided between the two sides. However, when commenting on disagreements between employers and unions, there is a feeling (except among managing directors) that when papers do not judge fairly between the two sides it is to the detriment of the trade union side. Overall, less than one-quarter of provincial papers were thought to hinder ". . . good industrial relations".

When questioned on whether or not the papers they read gave too much or too little attention to a number of local bodies or groups, 56% of papers were said not to give too much attention to any local group and 47% were said not to give too little attention to any. Those to which any substantial number of papers gave too much attention were local councillors, local businessmen, big commercial companies and council officials; apart from special pleading for their area interests, respondents selected in any number only two groups as receiving too little attention from the provincial press—"people in the lower income group" and trade union leaders.

One important issue that was investigated was the extent to which the provincial press is seen to give fair coverage to the different people in the community, whatever their role, occupational or social position or political allegiance.

We have already noted in the discussion of articles or reports of particular interest appearing in each paper that, when asked to express an opinion on the way the article was written, articles were labelled unfair in some way in about one in five of the cases. When specifically asked to comment on the fairness of the article in question, in 25% of the cases they were rated as either rather unfair or very unfair, and in 75% of cases as reasonably or very fair. Similarly, when discussing provincial press treatment of a variety of selected topics, respondents were again asked an open-ended question and in roughly 20% of the cases newspapers were criticised for their treatment of various topics for introducing bias or unfairness into reporting.

Apart from standards of fairness in particular articles, or when discussing particular topics, we also sought in an earlier part of the interview to record respondents' overall impressions of the papers they read. They were asked firstly to judge whether or not "It gives fair coverage to all points of view". From what we have said already it is not surprising to find that in the majority of cases newspapers are considered to be fair in their coverage. In looking at particular articles we noted that the proportions considered to be either very fair or reasonably fair in each type of paper were as follows:

Regional mornings	74%
Provincial evenings	71%
Local weeklies	79%

A similar pattern is seen in the table below, although the differences between each type of newspaper are not great. It is interesting to note that national daily papers, although thought of as being of much higher quality, are not considered appreciably better in giving fair coverage to all points of view.

Two-thirds thought that provincial newspapers were "prepared to criticise anybody if they think they deserve it". Provincial newspapers as a whole were rated less highly than national newspapers in this respect but there was little difference between types of provincial newspaper. National dailies were rarely thought to mind offending advertisers; provincial mornings received a similar rating; it is perhaps significant that provincial evenings and local weeklies, which were most often thought to have too much advertising in them, were also seen as the most likely to be afraid of offending their advertisers.

TABLE 2.068
FAIRNESS OF COVERAGE BY TYPE OF NEWSPAPER

	All Provincial Papers	Regional Mornings	Provincial Evenings	Local Weeklies	National Dailies
Base	661	168	278	215	333
Proportion saying "very true" or "fairly true" to statements:	%	%	%	%	%
"It gives fair coverage to all points of view"	63	65	59	67	67
"It is prepared to criticise anybody if it thinks they deserve it"	67	70	68	64	81
"It is afraid of offending its advertisers"	21	10	27	20	10

Base: All papers read at least once a week (dailies) or once a month (weeklies).

If we compare the "influential" sample as a whole with the sample of the general public we can see a quite interesting distinction between, on the one hand, being thought to give fair coverage and, on the other hand, being thought to be "prepared to criticise anybody", or to offend advertisers. The general public once again appears less critical than members of the "influential" sample on the subject of fair coverage but have similar opinions on the other two statements.

TABLE 2.069
FAIRNESS OF COVERAGE IN THE PROVINCIAL PRESS: THE VIEWS OF DIFFERENT RESPONDENTS

	Councillors	Council Officials	Managing Directors	Trade Union Secretaries	Head Teachers	General Public Sample
Base	98	125	165	186	87	3,102
	%	%	%	%	%	%
Proportion saying "not very true" or "not at all true" to statements:						
"It gives fair coverage to all points of view"	35	35	28	35	21	13
"It is prepared to criticise anybody if it thinks they deserve it"	29	34	23	34	18	24
Proportion saying "very true" or "fairly true" to statement:						
"It is afraid of offending its advertisers"	29	6	10	39	14	23

Base: All papers read once a week or more (dailies) or once a month or more (weeklies).

In slightly more than one-third of the cases, provincial papers were said not to give fair coverage to all points of view. At a later stage of the interview we presented respondents with a list of types of local people and groups and asked them whether, in their view, the local newspapers they read paid the views of any of them too much attention when reporting on controversial issues; they were then asked whether the views of any of them were paid too little attention.

In addition to the pre-selected list of local people and groups, respondents were also given the opportunity of nominating others receiving too much or too little attention. Few availed themselves of the opportunity, however, and from those who did no major additional groups emerged as being particularly unfairly treated, the list being largely made up of a vast range of minority groups and interests.

In over half the cases, no "sorts of people" were thought to receive too much attention. Only four groups were picked on by any substantial number of respondents as receiving too much attention: local councillors, local businessmen, big commercial companies and officials of the local council. Needless to say, on the whole the different groups of respondents did not name the people most like themselves as receiving too much attention. There was quite wide diversity between the groups: local councillors particularly mentioned local businessmen as receiving too much attention, followed at some distance by "big commercial companies" and "people in higher income groups". Council officials did not mention any particular group very frequently but the group they were most likely to pick out (in 12% of the cases) was "local councillors". Trade union secretaries showed once again their tendency to be particularly critical of provincial newspapers by mentioning a number of sorts of people to an above average extent: that "local businessmen", "big commercial companies" and "people in the higher income groups" should be particularly mentioned by them is perhaps not surprising, but it is more unexpected that they should also pick out local councillors and council officials. Managing directors, on the other hand, do not, of course, think that "local businessmen" or "big commercial companies" get too much attention but are particularly prone to mention local councillors, council officials and local trade union leaders.

Head teachers were the least likely to mention any groups as receiving too much attention and the only group to stand out in their answers was local councillors.

TABLE 2.070
PEOPLE THE PROVINCIAL PRESS OFTEN PAYS TOO MUCH ATTENTION TO WHEN REPORTING ON CONTROVERSIAL LOCAL ISSUES

	All papers read by respondents	All papers read by:				
		Councillors	Council Officials	Trade Union Secretaries	Managing Directors	Head Teachers
Base ...	661	98	125	186	165	87
	%	%	%	%	%	%
Officials of the local council	11	8	4	15	15	5
Local councillors	17	8	15	20	24	16
Big commercial companies	10	12	6	21	4	3
Local businessmen	14	20	10	26	3	6
Local trade union leaders	6	2	6	1	12	8
Religious people	2	3	—	2	1	3
People in the higher income groups	6	10	3	11	3	1
People in the lower income groups	2	1	3	2	2	3
The police	2	5	1	3	2	—
Young people	4	5	4	2	6	1
None of these	56	51	65	48	59	62

Base: All papers read once a week or more (dailies) or once a month or more (weeklies).

Overall, more sorts of people are thought to receive too little attention from the provincial press than are thought to receive too much. It is not surprising to find that the groups respondents consider to receive too little attention are those most similar to the one they belong to. If we were to judge this to be a case of "special pleading", then the three groups who stand out as receiving too little attention are "young people", "people in the lower income groups" and "trade union leaders". In the latter case this would seem to confirm our earlier finding that respondents felt "local trade union activities" to be the topic most often "least well" dealt with by the provincial press.

TABLE 2.071
PEOPLE THE PROVINCIAL PRESS PAYS TOO LITTLE ATTENTION TO WHEN REPORTING ON CONTROVERSIAL LOCAL ISSUES

	All papers read by respondents	All papers read by:				
		Councillors	Council Officials	Trade Union Secretaries	Managing Directors	Head Teachers
Base ...	661	98	125	186	165	87
	%	%	%	%	%	%
Officials of the local council	12	10	24	12	5	9
Local councillors...	12	24	15	13	2	5
Big commercial companies	9	2	12	6	16	7
Local businessmen	11	6	11	8	19	10
Local trade union leaders	22	24	18	43	8	8
Religious people	12	8	19	12	10	13
People in the higher income groups ...	8	3	13	6	13	2
People in the lower income groups ...	19	20	18	28	9	15
The police	11	10	4	3	10	8
Young people	22	23	19	2	10	21
None of these	48	46	52	48	58	53

Base: All papers read once a week or more (dailies) or once a month or more (weeklies).

There is very little variation between types of newspaper in the numbers which gave either too much attention, or too little attention, to particular people. Slightly more regional mornings than other papers were said to give too little attention to "people in the lower income groups" and "young people". Local weeklies were more often thought to give too *much* attention to local councillors and religious people; in contrast fewer local weeklies were said to give too *little* attention to these two groups. Even the differences between types of newspaper, however, were not very great.

Respondents were also asked to say whether or not they felt each paper they read took "an interest in ordinary people's problems". The provincial press was considered to perform very well in this respect, much more so than the national dailies and particularly the quality dailies. The proportions who said it was either "very true" or "fairly true" that the paper they read took "an interest in ordinary people's problems" were as follows:

Regional mornings	80%
Provincial evenings	88%
Local weeklies	86%
National dailies	56%

Trade union secretaries were a little less convinced that the papers they read took an interest in ordinary people's problems than were other groups or were the general public.

PARTY POLITICAL BIAS

We have already touched on respondents' opinions of the quality of the provincial press reporting of local party politics. In an earlier question respondents were asked among a list of topics, to say how well they thought each local paper they read treated the activities of the Conservative Party and of the Labour Party on the Council. In three-quarters (76%) of the cases, the activities of the Conservative Party were thought to be treated either fairly well or very well; the proportion for the Labour Party was slightly less (71%). More than 10% of respondents, in each case, felt unable to judge either way, notably managing directors as a group. There was very little difference between types of newspaper, although slightly more between groups of respondents. Councillors were more critical of the treatment of the activities of both the Conservative Party and the Labour Party on the Council and were joined in the opinion by trade union secretaries as far as the Labour Party was concerned. Only councillors, however, selected the activities of either party as being the topic "least well treated" from the range of topics offered, to any marked extent (see Table 2.050).

The views of respondents on the way the provincial press reports the local political parties varies, as one would expect, according to respondents' declared political leanings: newspapers read by Conservative Party supporters in the sample were viewed as treating the activities of the Labour Party on the Council well to a greater extent than those of the Conservative Party. Among Labour supporters the situation is viewed as being the reverse.

TABLE 2.072
PROVINCIAL PRESS TREATMENT OF LOCAL COUNCIL ACTIVITIES: THE DIFFERENT VIEWS OF CONSERVATIVE AND LABOUR SUPPORTERS

	Base		Activities of the Conservative Party on Council			Activities of Labour Party on Council		
			Well	Badly	Don't know	Well	Badly	Don't know
Papers read by								
Conservative ...	204	%	66	16	7	74	10	16
Labour ...	277	%	85	10	5	67	28	4
Liberal ...	68	%	73	9	18	68	15	18
Other party ...	63	%	68	16	16	70	10	14

Base: All provincial papers read once a week or more (dailies) or once a month or more (weeklies).

There is also some correlation between the way respondents view the political bias of particular papers and the way they consider these papers report local council affairs. Provincial papers said generally to support the Conservative Party were said also to be more likely to report well the activities of the Conservative Party on the Council; and similarly for newspapers thought to support the Labour Party. More than half of all provincial newspapers, however, were not seen as supporting any one party and these were seen as reporting well the activities of each main party on the Council.

TABLE 2.073
PROVINCIAL PRESS TREATMENT OF THE ACTIVITIES OF THE CONSERVATIVE AND LABOUR PARTIES ON THE COUNCIL: A COMPARISON OF NEWSPAPER ALLEGIANCES

	Base		Activities of Conservative Party			Activities of Labour Party		
			Well	Badly	Don't know	Well	Badly	Don't know
Provincial papers supporting the Conservative Party	243	%	89	5	6	67	27	6
Provincial papers supporting the Labour Party	25	%	59	34	7	90	3	7
Provincial papers supporting the Liberal Party	29	%	67	30	3	53	43	1
Provincial papers supporting no political party	342	%	71	13	16	73	13	14

Base: All papers read at least once a week (dailies) or once a month (weeklies).

There were seen to be considerable differences between the types of newspaper in the extent to which they supported any one party. Regional morning newspapers and the national dailies read by respondents were more likely to be thought to support one political party than were either provincial evenings or local weeklies. Newspapers thought to support a particular party were usually believed to support the Conservative Party. A slightly greater proportion of national dailies read were thought to support the Labour Party, in the main a reflection of the number of respondents who read the *Daily Mirror*.

TABLE 2.074
PROVINCIAL PRESS SUPPORT FOR THE POLITICAL PARTIES

	Regional Morning Newspapers	Provincial Evening Newspapers	Local Weekly Newspapers	National Dailies
Base	168	278	215	333
	%	%	%	%
Paper supports *no* one political party	37	52	63	35
Paper supports one political party	61	46	35	65
Paper generally supports Conservative Party	51	37	25	48
Paper generally supports Labour Party	2	4	5	11
Paper generally supports Liberal Party	7	4	3	2
Paper generally supports other party	1	1	2	4
Paper supports party but gives fair coverage to views of other parties	35	26	23	41
Paper *does not* give fair coverage to views of other parties	24	20	11	24
Don't know	2	—	1	—

Base: All papers read at least once a week (dailies) or once a month (weeklies).

Although in quite high proportions of cases, provincial newspapers read were said generally to support one political party, this did not invariably lead to unfair coverage of other parties, thus supporting the view expressed by respondents earlier that 61% of all provincial papers read gave "fair coverage to all points of view". The provincial evening newspapers were least likely to be considered as giving fair coverage to views of parties other than the one supported.

Partisanship is seen to varying degrees by the different groups in the sample, even although in most cases they are commenting on the same newspapers. If we exclude local weeklies from consideration, where it is quite conceivable that different groups are talking about different papers, we nonetheless see quite marked differences between the way councillors and particularly, trade union secretaries view the political stance of newspapers and the way other groups view them. These two groups were also the two least likely to agree earlier that papers they read gave fair coverage to all points of view. Both these groups, of course, contain a high proportion of people strongly committed to the support of particular parties (25% of councillors were "strongly Conservative" and 45% "strongly Labour", 48% of trade union secretaries were "strongly Labour" and 1% "strongly Conservative").

TABLE 2.075
REGIONAL MORNING AND PROVINCIAL EVENING PRESS SUPPORT FOR THE POLITICAL PARTIES

	Managing Directors	Council Officials	Head Teachers	Councillors	Trade Union Secretaries
Paper read by	110	84	50	74	128
	%	%	%	%	%
Paper generally supports *no* one political party	56	54	52	39	34
Paper generally supports one political party	42	43	44	58	67
Paper generally supports Conservative Party	35	33	40	35	60
Paper generally supports Labour Party	5	2	2	7	5
Paper generally supports Liberal Party	—	7	2	14	7
Paper generally supports other party	1	—	—	3	2
Paper supports party but gives fair coverage to view of other parties	30	35	30	24	27
Paper supports party but does not give fair coverage to view of other parties	10	8	10	32	38
Don't know	2	—	4	1	2

Base: All provincial daily papers read once a week or more.

The papers that respondents view as not giving fair coverage to all political parties were overwhelmingly seen as unfair towards the Labour Party. The Liberal Party is also said by some members of each of our groups of respondents to be unfairly treated.

TABLE 2.076
PARTIES TO WHICH THE PROVINCIAL PRESS DOES NOT GIVE FAIR COVERAGE

Base: Cases where paper thought not to give fair coverage	136	
	%	
Does not give fair coverage to:		
Conservatives	11	
Labour	89	(Figures add up to more
Liberal	33	than 100% as more than
Communist	17	one answer could be given)
Other Parties	8	

Base: All papers read by respondents who do not give fair coverage to the views of all political parties.

BIAS ON INDUSTRIAL RELATIONS

Opinions on the way in which provincial newspapers treat business and trade union affairs and industrial relations was another specific subject that the study attempted to assess. We saw earlier that in 77% of the cases the provincial newspapers read were thought to treat "news of local industrial disputes" at least fairly well and in 56% of the cases "news of local trade union activities" was also considered to be treated well (see Table 2.048). However, trade union activities was the topic most often thought to be treated not very well by the provincial press and was also the one far and away most commonly selected from the list of seven topics presented to respondents as treated "least well". But the main complaint about the way in which trade union activities were treated was insufficient coverage; only 21% complained of bias. Bias was more often complained of by those who thought that news of local industrial disputes was the one topic least well dealt with. It was also quite commonly attributed to articles or reports of issues in which respondents had been personally involved that concerned local industrial relations. In both cases managing directors and trade union secretaries were the two groups most critical of press reporting in this field and most likely to suggest bias on the part of newspapers. When asked, however, to rate the article in terms of the fairness with which it dealt with the issue, a substantial majority of all groups of respondents viewed them as at least reasonably fair.

The fairness of the provincial press in its treatment of industrial disputes was given further attention a little later in the interview; respondents were asked to judge both the *reporting* of disagreements between employers and unions and also the *comments* the papers may make on such disagreements.

The majority view, already expressed, that the provincial press generally covers industrial disputes at least fairly well, is reflected again in that just over half of respondents believe the local papers they read "report both sides of things fully" and, when commenting on disagreements, "try to judge fairly between them [employers and unions]". Those seen to give more space to one side or the other are fairly evenly divided between the two sides.

Regional morning newspapers are seen as being very similar to the national dailies in the way they report disagreements between employers and unions though the national dailies thought to favour one or other side are more frequently seen as giving more space to the employer's side than as giving more space to the union's case.

Provincial evening newspapers show a similar pattern to the mornings but have a slightly higher proportion of readers saying the paper "does not report much about it at all". Local weeklies are seen as showing very little bias on this issue but in a third of the cases they are thought not to deal with the subject at all.

TABLE 2.077
PRESS REPORTING OF DISAGREEMENTS BETWEEN EMPLOYERS AND UNIONS:
A COMPARISON BETWEEN NEWSPAPER TYPES

	All Provincial Newspapers	Regional Morning Newspapers	Provincial Evening Newspapers	Local Weekly Newspapers	National Daily Newspapers
Base	661	168	278	215	333
	%	%	%	%	%
Reports both sides of things fully	54	58	53	50	60
Gives more space to the employer's case	15	19	18	8	23
Gives more space to the union's case	10	15	13	4	9
Does not report much about it at all	17	4	12	34	5
Don't know	4	4	4	4	3

Base: All provincial daily papers read once a week or more and weekly papers read once a month or more.

Trade union secretaries are a little less likely than other groups to consider that provincial daily papers report both sides fully but nonetheless almost half hold this view. Not surprisingly, those who disagree tend to believe that provincial newspapers favour the employer's rather than the union's side. Managing directors hold the opposite view.

TABLE 2.078
PROVINCIAL DAILY PRESS REPORTING OF DISAGREEMENTS BETWEEN EMPLOYERS AND UNIONS:
A COMPARISON BETWEEN TYPES OF RESPONDENT

	Managing Directors	Trade Union Secretaries	Councillors	Council Officials	Head Teachers
Base	110	128	74	84	50
	%	%	%	%	%
Reports both sides of things fully	54	51	51	60	68
Gives more space to the employer's case	3	38	27	8	8
Gives more space to the union's case	29	4	12	15	4
Does not print much about it at all	8	6	8	13	10
Don't know	6	2	1	4	10

Base: All provincial daily papers read once a week or more.

In addition to the group of trade union secretaries, a number of other respondents were trade union members. Trade union members are only a little more likely than non-members to perceive any bias on the part of the provincial press in its reporting of disagreements between unions and employers, but those who do perceive bias see it mainly as being against the unions. Trade union secretaries were more prone to perceive this bias than ordinary members.

TABLE 2.079

PROVINCIAL PRESS REPORTING OF DISAGREEMENTS BETWEEN EMPLOYERS AND UNIONS:
A COMPARISON BETWEEN TRADE UNION MEMBERS AND NON-MEMBERS

	Trade union non-members	Trade union members	Trade union members (excluding TU secs.)
Base	286	375	189
	%	%	%
Reports both sides of things fully ...	54	49	51
Gives more space to the employer's case	7	22	14
Gives more space to the union's case ...	16	5	8
Does not print much about it at all ...	17	20	23

Base: All provincial daily papers read once a week or more and weekly papers read once a month or more.

In just over half the cases, provincial papers that reported on disagreements between employers and trade unions were seen as trying to judge fairly between them. However, except among managing directors, a feeling exists that papers who do not try to judge fairly comment to the detriment of the trade union side. This view is again held most strongly by trade union members in general, and union secretaries in particular.

TABLE 2.080

PROVINCIAL PRESS COMMENTS ON DISAGREEMENTS BETWEEN EMPLOYERS AND UNIONS

	Base		Comments favour employers	Comments favour unions	Tries to judge fairly	Never comments	Don't know
Total	549	%	26	6	55	5	7
Managing Directors ...	127	%	7	13	67	9	4
Trade Union Secretaries	96	%	48	1	37	6	8
Councillors	83	%	27	7	45	7	13
Council Officials ...	92	%	16	8	66	1	9
Head Teachers ...	67	%	18	4	75	1	2
Trade Union non-members	240	%	14	9	65	6	6
Trade Union members	314	%	37	4	47	5	6
Trade Union members (excluding TU secs.)	158	%	25	6	61	2	6

Base: All provincial papers read which report on disagreements between employers and unions.

In their comments, as in their reporting, the national and regional mornings are seen as most likely to favour one side or the other, and local weeklies most likely to judge fairly between employers and unions.

TABLE 2.081
PRESS COMMENTS ON DISAGREEMENTS BETWEEN EMPLOYERS AND UNIONS: A COMPARISON BETWEEN TYPES OF NEWSPAPER

	Regional Mornings	Provincial Evenings	Local Weeklies	National Dailies
Base	155	234	133	307
	%	%	%	%
Tends to favour the employers	34	27	12	33
Tends to favour the unions	6	6	8	5
Tries to judge fairly between them	51	53	65	56
Never makes comments	4	5	8	—
Don't know	5	9	7	7

Base: All dailies read once a week or more and weeklies read once a month or more except those "not printing much" about employer-union disagreements.

One of the propositions put to respondents about the papers they read was that it "hinders good industrial relations". Overall respondents said in less than a quarter (23%) of the cases that it was "very" or "fairly true" that provincial papers hinder good industrial relations. Among those, however, who think that provincial newspapers favour one side or the other, around half think that the proposition is true.

TABLE 2.082
PROVINCIAL PRESS REPORTING OF INDUSTRIAL RELATIONS

	Base		"It hinders good industrial relations"	
			Very true or fairly true	Not very true or not at all true
Total sample	661	%	23	71
Paper reports both sides of things fully	354	%	13	83
Paper gives more space to employer's case	99	%	45	46
Paper gives more space to union's case	69	%	51	45
Paper does not print much about it at all	112	%	15	74
Paper's comments tend to favour the employers	131	%	49	49
Paper's comments tend to favour the unions	34	%	43	51
Paper tries to judge fairly between them	291	%	14	84
Paper never makes comments	29	%	21	79

7. Competition in the Provincial Press

SUMMARY

Attitudes to competition in the provincial press were measured in two forms; firstly by direct questioning of respondents, secondly by a comparison of answers to specific questions based on the ownership and size of circulation of the papers read.

To serve as a backcloth to the discussion of competition in the provincial press we asked respondents if they knew who owned their local paper, and how many other papers that company controlled. The results show that, although more knowledgeable than the general public, there still remained about 45% of cases where respondents were unable to say who owned the local papers they read, while in 40%, the respondents either did not know whether provincial papers they read owned companion papers in the locality or could not name them.

When directly questioned on the benefits or otherwise of competition, more than half of those who had more than one evening circulating in the local area felt they did not benefit as a result. Among those who did not have competing evenings, even fewer felt they might benefit.

Comparing the ratings of general quality given to papers of different ownership and size, we found very little difference. As regards specific aspects of editorial standards, there was also remarkably little difference by type of ownership. Differences between large circulation (100,000+ daily) and smaller circulation papers were more marked, the former being more likely to receive favourable ratings on items of news gathering and comment. This may, perhaps, result from a larger circulation enabling the provision of a better news service. In contrast, however, lesser circulation papers were less well thought of as regards the quality of the news—they were said to concentrate more on the bad news, and were seen as more likely to "invade people's grief".

If we compare standards in the weekly press based on ownership, we find, as with the provincial dailies, very little difference. In terms of circulation, larger circulation weeklies were valued more for news content and the standard of their reporting. Smaller papers are said to have too much advertising and to be more trivial and generally of a lower quality.

ATTITUDES TO COMPETITION IN THE PROVINCIAL PRESS

We have seen something of respondents' opinions of different types of provincial newspaper and have given some indication of the extent to which they are in competition with each other. In addition, for provincial evening newspapers, we collected further information by directly seeking opinions on the amount of competition within the field of the provincial press. Before doing so, however, we attempted to establish whether or not respondents knew the name of the company which owned the national daily and the provincial papers they read and whether it owned any other newspapers.

Respondents in the "influential" sample had a greater knowledge of the companies that owned newspapers than did members of the general public. Nonetheless, in 42% of the cases, our respondents said they did not know the name of the company owning the provincial papers they read.

TABLE 2.083

AWARENESS OF WHO OWNS THE PROVINCIAL PRESS

	"Influential" Sample	General Public Sample
Base	661	3,102
	%	%
Name of company not known	42	68
Name of company known, but no name given	3	—
Name of company known and name given	55	43

Awareness of ownership was highest among readers of provincial mornings, and lowest among readers of local weeklies and, perhaps surprisingly, of national dailies. The proportion of readers professing to know the name of the owners and able to provide a name was as follows:

Regional mornings	66%
Provincial evenings	57%
Local weeklies	43%
National dailies	40%

Among those papers owned by the major newspaper groups, a check was made on the accuracy of the answers. This check revealed that, by and large, when respondents claimed to know who owned the paper (as 54% did) then a large majority were able to give either the correct group name or, at least, the correct name of the subsidiary. Incorrect answers were given in only a little over 6% of cases.

While about half were unaware which company owned the provincial papers they read, most knew whether or not the company owned any other newspapers and whether it owned others sold in the area; indeed, three-quarters felt able to put a figure to the number of newspapers they thought the company owned. When asked which other local or regional newspapers selling in the area were owned by that company, the large majority who claimed to know the correct answer were found to do so.

TABLE 2.084

RESPONDENTS' KNOWLEDGE OF WHICH OTHER NEWSPAPERS CIRCULATING IN THE AREA ARE OWNED BY THE COMPANY OWNING PAPERS THEY READ

KNOWLEDGE OF WHETHER COMPANY OWNS OTHER PAPERS

(Base: 661 papers read)
%

Yes, owns others	67
No, does not own others	3
Don't know	29

IF OWNS OTHERS DOES IT OWN PROVINCIAL PAPERS SOLD IN RESPONDENT'S AREA

(Base: 444 papers read)
%

Yes, owns others locally	80
No, does not own others locally	11
Don't know	8

IF OWNS OTHERS LOCALLY

(Base: 378 papers read)
%

Correct answers given	85
Incorrect answers given	10
No answer given	4

Base: Answers given to question "Which other local or regional newspaper which are sold *here* does it own?"

Overall, it seems that in about 40% of cases respondents either did not know whether the papers they read had companion papers on sale in the area produced by the same group, or could not name them.

Most respondents (94%) claimed to know whether or not more than one evening newspaper was sold in their area, and 42% said that there was.

Among those who had more than one evening newspaper available in their area, over half considered that they did not benefit at all from the fact, and among those who did not have a choice of evening papers even fewer felt they would benefit if there were more than one paper.

TABLE 2.085

DO PEOPLE BENEFIT FROM A CHOICE OF PROVINCIAL NEWSPAPERS: THE VIEW OF THOSE WHO DO HAVE A CHOICE AND THE VIEW OF THOSE WHO DON'T

	Base	Yes, do benefit/ would benefit	No, do not benefit/ would not benefit
Respondents who do have choice of evening papers	146	43%	55%
Respondents who do *not* have choice of evening papers	204	35%	62%

The benefits that were said to occur from having a choice of newspapers were mainly of a general nature on the value of choice or of competition eg "competition is a good thing". Over a third, however, felt they got better coverage of local affairs as a result of having a choice of papers while others valued getting a different slant on the news. The perceived benefits, expressed by those who did not have a choice of evening papers at present, were rather different with a greater emphasis on improved standards. Some respondents did not think that their area could sustain more than one evening newspaper.

TABLE 2.086
BENEFITS FROM A CHOICE OF EVENING NEWSPAPERS

	Benefits from having choice of papers	Benefits that would accrue if there was choice of papers
Base	63	72
	%	%
Improved standard/quality	—	35
Better coverage of local affairs	38	21
Get different slant on news/point of view	17	19
General comment on the value of choice	33	10
General comment on value of competition	21	26
Area could not sustain two papers	—	7
Respondent doesn't/wouldn't read either	3	—
Other answers	2	6

Base: Those answering "do benefit/would benefit".

THE IMPORTANCE OF TYPES OF OWNERSHIP AND CIRCULATION SIZE ON STANDARDS IN THE PROVINCIAL PRESS

It is not easy in this study to isolate the relationship between attitudes to the provincial press, on the one hand, and either type of ownership or size (in terms of circulation) on the other, partly because of the small sample size but also for other reasons. Because of the disparity in size between dailies and weeklies, they are dealt with separately.

Provincial Dailies

The sample was clustered into 12 small areas of the country in which one, or at the most two, regional morning or provincial evening newspapers circulate. If we were to make comparisons between individual newspaper groups we would, in most cases, be covering only one newspaper published by each group—one that might quite possibly be unrepresentative of the group as a whole. Further, the number of readers of each group would be too small for the findings to be reliable. The only comparison we can hope to make—and in itself it is of some value—is the distinction between those owned by the large newspaper groups and those owned either by smaller groups or by individuals, families, etc. With the trend in newspaper ownership seemingly continuing in the direction of ownership by the large newspaper groups, it is important to see whether or not this may affect perceived editorial standards. We have looked elsewhere in the report at respondents' knowledge of ownership patterns in their local press and their attitudes towards competition in the provincial press. Here, however, we shall look again at the various features our respondents were asked to comment on, bearing in mind the type of ownership of the newspapers on which they were commenting.

As can be seen from the table below, only provincial evenings among daily papers have circulations lower than 40,000 and this must be borne in mind in interpreting the tables.

TABLE 2.087
CIRCULATION FIGURES FOR PROVINCIAL DAILY NEWSPAPERS READ BY RESPONDENTS

	Regional Morning Newspapers	Provincial Evening Newspapers
Base	168	278
	%	%
Less than 40,000	—	28
40,000–100,000	52	27
More than 100,000	48	43

Base: All provincial daily newspapers read once a week or more.

There is a strong association between the size of provincial dailies and type of ownership. The large circulation dailies (100,000+) and the very small ones (under 40,000) tend to be owned by the large newspaper groups. The sample is too small to analyse the results by size within ownership type, hence when we look at the relationship between either ownership or circulation and attitudes to press standards the effects of these two factors cannot be fully disentangled.

TABLE 2.088
THE RELATIONSHIP BETWEEN OWNERSHIP AND CIRCULATION IN THE PROVINCIAL DAILY PRESS

	Daily Circulation		
	Less than 40,000	40,000–100,000	More than 100,000
Base	78	163	200
Owned by large newspaper group	86%	57%	86%
Not owned by large newspaper group	14%	45%	14%

Base: All provincial daily newspapers read once a week or more.

As we can see below, the newspapers with circulations under 40,000 (ie the smaller evenings) receive a lower rating than the larger circulation daily provincial papers, but there is very little difference between those with circulations of 40,000–100,000 and those of over 100,000, or between newspapers owned by large groups and the remainder.

TABLE 2.089
GENERAL RATING OF THE QUALITY OF PROVINCIAL NEWSPAPERS: A COMPARISON OF TYPES OF OWNERSHIP AND OF CIRCULATION

Provincial Daily Papers		Owned by Large Group	Not Owned by Large Group	Circulation less than 40,000	Circulation 40,000–100,000	Circulation more than 100,000
Base		365	135	78	163	200
	Score	%	%	%	%	%
An excellent paper	(5)	5	3	1	7	4
A very good paper	(4)	18	17	9	20	24
A fairly good paper	(3)	32	28	24	38	31
An average paper	(2)	31	33	37	21	27
A fairly poor paper	(1)	11	10	19	7	8
A very poor paper	(0)	3	2	3	1	3
Mean		2·7	2·5	2·2	3·0	2·8

Base: All provincial daily newspapers read once a week or more.

If we look at the various aspects of editorial standards that contribute to the overall rating of a newspaper we see that there is remarkably little difference according to type of ownership. There is a slight tendency for papers owned by the large groups to be perceived as performing better in the way they relate what is happening in the country to the local area, but no overall pattern of difference emerges.

The difference between the larger circulation papers (which are in most cases owned by the large newspaper groups) and the smaller ones are rather more marked. If we look at the statements in groups 1 and 2 (in the table below) which concern themselves with news gathering and comment we can see that the larger circulation newspapers are more likely to receive favourable ratings than are the smaller ones. This would suggest that by virtue of their circulation size rather than ownership, provincial dailies are able to provide a better news service to their readers.

The larger circulation press, however, tend to be slightly less well thought of when the quality of the news service is concerned (items in group 3). They tend to concentrate on the bad news more and to invade private grief more. Again the differences are not great.

TABLE 2.090
A COMPARISON OF STANDARDS IN THE PROVINCIAL DAILY PRESS BY NEWSPAPER SIZE AND OWNERSHIP

	Owned by Large Group	Not Owned by Large Group	Circulation less than 100,000	Circulation more than 100,000
Base	365	135	241	200
Proportion Answering "Very True" or "Fairly True" to Statements	%	%	%	%
Group 1				
It helps me to understand how what is happening in the country will affect my interests in the area	56	42	51	58
Its standard of reporting is first-class	50	50	47	56
It always has the latest national news	63	64	63	72
Group 2				
The comments it makes on the news are usually interesting	71	70	69	76
Reading it is always enjoyable	58	64	58	61
It takes an interest in ordinary people's problems	85	89	82	89
Group 3				
It exaggerates the sensational aspects of the news	48	50	47	51
It sometimes goes too far in invading people's grief	32	25	24	38
It always concentrates on the bad news	37	27	33	37
It hinders good industrial relations	28	28	24	34
It often gets its facts wrong	41	42	58	61
Group 4				
It is afraid of offending its advertisers	22	26	17	26
It has too much advertising in it	45	45	42	49

Base: All provincial daily newspapers read once a week or more.

Local Weeklies

In the case of more than half the weekly papers, circulation figures were not available leaving too few papers whose circulation was known to analyse in very much detail. However, if we split this sample between those with a circulation of 20,000 an issue or more and those selling less than 20,000 we can see that the larger papers are valued more for their news content and their better standard of reporting. The small papers, on the other hand, are criticised for having too much advertising and printing too many silly or trivial stories, while in terms of general quality they are rated somewhat lower than the larger weekly papers.

Almost two-thirds of the local weekly papers read by the sample were not owned by any of the large newspaper groups. If we compare standards in these papers with the local weeklies that are owned by the major groups we see remarkably little difference. Slightly more weeklies owned by the major groups were said to have a first-class standard of reporting (52% as against 41%) and slightly fewer often get their facts wrong (29% as against 33%). On the other hand it was said more often of weeklies not owned by the large groups that comments they made on the news were interesting (68% as against 58% owned by large groups), and that they took an interest in ordinary people's problems (90% as against 82%). Otherwise, the differences were small.

8. Other topics of enquiry

SUMMARY

As in the survey of the general public, a few topics were included in the study that were not to do specifically with the provincial press; these were knowledge and experience of the workings of the Press Council, evaluation of national morning newspapers and opinions as to whether the freedom of the press is in danger.

More than four out of five respondents claimed to know what the Press Council did (compared to one in five of the general public), and virtually all of these were broadly correct in their description of its function. More than half who knew the functions of the Council felt those functions were performed at least fairly well, 21% thought they were performed poorly and a similar proportion did not know. The most common criticism was that the Council did not have sufficient power or "teeth".

Respondents were asked to evaluate the national morning newspapers and say which they would most want to keep. The quality dailies were the most favoured and, as with the general public, considerably more respondents wished them kept than actually read them and some were willing to forgo the popular dailies they did read.

Just over half the total of respondents felt the freedom of the press was in danger with the printing unions, costs and inflation, and "the Government" being most often selected as representing the biggest threat.

THE PRESS COUNCIL

Many more people in the "influential" sample had heard of the Press Council than was found to be the case among the general public; indeed only 3% had not heard of it. Furthermore, more than four out of five respondents in the "influential" sample claimed to know what the Press Council does compared with one in five of the general public.

TABLE 2.091
CLAIMED AWARENESS OF THE PRESS COUNCIL AND OF ITS FUNCTION

	"Influential" Sample	General Public Sample
Base: All respondents	350	2,401
	%	%
Heard of Press Council and knows what it does	82	21
Heard of Press Council and does not know what it does	15	25
Uncertain	*	2
Have not heard of Press Council	3	52

Slightly more than three-quarters (77%) of those among the general public who claimed to know what the Press Council does, were able to give a broadly accurate description of its functions; among the influential sample the figure was 97%. Thus 3% of respondents in the "influential" sample had never heard of the Press Council, 15% had heard of it but did not know what it did and a further 4% were not able to given an accurate description of its functions.

Council officials were particularly knowledgeable; only 8% did not know what the functions of the Press Council were. The proportions in the other groups were:

Councillors	20%	Trade Union Secretaries	23%
Managing Directors	24%	Head Teachers	26%

Respondents in the "influential" sample were asked to say how well they thought the Press Council performed its functions. The question was restricted to those who felt they knew what the Press Council did.

Many respondents did not feel able to voice an opinion. Of those who did, however, the majority thought the Press Council performed its functions at least "fairly well". No one group of respondents stood out as more critical than other groups, though trade union members and Labour voters tended to be slightly more critical than others.

TABLE 2.092
THE PERFORMANCE OF THE PRESS COUNCIL

Base	286
Press Council performs:	%
Very well	16
Fairly well	41
Rather poorly	17
Very poorly	4
Don't know	22

Base: All respondents claiming to know functions the Press Council fulfils.

Although more than half of those who claimed to know the function of the Press Council said they thought it performed its functions either very or fairly well, when asked to give reasons for their rating, many were rather critical. The reason most often given for saying the Council worked well was that its decisions had been fair and sensible; the most common criticism was that the Council did not have sufficient power or "teeth".

TABLE 2.093
OPINIONS OF THE FUNCTIONING OF THE PRESS COUNCIL

Base	286
	%
Positive assertion: Decisions have been fair/sensible/accurate	7
Qualified assertion: "As far as I know" decisions have been fair/sensible/accurate	17
Press Council has improved the standard of papers	7
Press Council usually finds in favour of public	1
Other generally favourable comments	11
Press Council does not have different powers	12
Has had little effect on standards of reporting	7
Council doesn't take sufficiently strong action	3
Has too limited terms of reference	1
Its decisions should be publicised more	3
Its functions should be better known	4
Council tends to be biased to/to whitewash papers	6
Press Council is not independent/too dependent on press industry	3
Other generally unfavourable comments	6
Don't know how well Press Council performs functions	14

Base: All respondents claiming to know functions the Press Council fulfils.

There was very little difference between groups of respondents in the comments on the Press Council; council officials and head teachers, neither of whom was particularly critical when asked how well the Council performed its functions, were particularly likely to say that the Press Council had insufficient power.

VALUATION OF NATIONAL MORNING NEWSPAPERS

As with the general public respondents in the "influential" sample were asked to nominate, in order of preference, the three national daily newspapers they would most want to keep, bearing in mind that some were currently in financial difficulties.

It was noted among the general public that, not surprisingly, people would want to keep the newspapers they read rather than those they do not. Since almost two-thirds of papers read by the "influential" sample on a regular basis were quality dailies, we would expect, and indeed find, that these are the newspapers most favoured if only three papers were to be kept. The difference between their views, and those of the general public, are presented in the table below:

TABLE 2.094

NATIONAL MORNINGS PEOPLE WOULD WANT TO KEEP

	"Influential" Sample				General Public Sample		Professional/ Managerial in General Public Sample	
	Most	2nd Most	3rd Most	Any Mention	Most	Any Mention	Most	Any Mention
	%	%	%	%	%	%	%	%
The Guardian	29	18	16	63	6	17	8	32
The Times	23	21	16	61	6	21	13	42
The Daily Telegraph	19	18	17	54	10	27	24	51
Financial Times	13	15	11	40	1	6	1	14
Daily Mirror	6	7	6	19	26	50	11	26
Daily Express	3	5	9	17	18	50	20	50
Daily Mail	2	5	9	15	9	33	9	30
Morning Star	1	3	1	6	*	2	—	2
The Sun	*	4	3	7	15	36	6	17
Don't know/ Don't care	2	2	8	6	7	19	5	12
	(Base: All respondents 350)				(Base: All respondents 2,401)		(Base: All professional/ managerial respondents 480)	

When we compare the proportion wanting to keep each paper with the proportion claiming regular and occasional readership of it, we can see an even closer distinction between quality and popular papers. The proportion wanting to keep each of the quality papers is considerably higher than the proportion who read them, while the proportion wanting to keep each of the popular papers is similar to or less than the proportion who read them.

Since few read as many as three titles in an average week, this would suggest that some respondents at least would be willing to forgo some of the popular papers they read in order to place one or more of the quality papers, which they do not read, among those papers to be kept.

TABLE 2.095
NATIONAL MORNINGS PEOPLE WOULD WANT TO KEEP BY EXTENT OF READERSHIP

	Among three would want to keep	Read regularly	Read regularly or occasionally
Base: All respondents	350	350	350
	%	%	%
The Guardian	63	20	35
The Times	61	23	38
The Daily Telegraph	54	23	39
Financial Times	40	23	37
Daily Mirror	19	14	21
Daily Express	17	15	24
Daily Mail	15	10	16
The Sun	7	8	16
Morning Star	6	3	5
Don't know/Don't care	2	N/A	N/A
None of these	N/A	2	2

There was little variation in the choices of different groups of respondents; the three papers most often included among those that should be kept are *The Guardian*, *The Times* and *The Daily Telegraph* as far as council officials, councillors and head teachers are concerned. Managing directors also most often selected *The Daily Telegraph* and *The Times* but the *Financial Times* received most "votes", at the expense of *The Guardian*. Among trade union secretaries, *The Daily Telegraph* was less and the *Daily Mirror* more frequently mentioned than in other groups as papers they wanted to keep. The only other group of respondents who in any number would want to keep the *Daily Mirror* were councillors.

The *Daily Express* and *Daily Mail* were listed among the three papers to be kept by between 13% and 20% in each group of respondents. Very few respondents, however, other than councillors and trade union secretaries, wished to keep the *Morning Star*.

PRESS FREEDOM

A third topic that does not particularly relate to the study of attitudes to the provincial press is that of press freedom. In this case the topic was not covered in the survey of the general public.

Respondents in the "influential" sample were asked to say whether they believed "that the freedom of the press is now in danger" and, if so, which groups represented any threat to that freedom. A number of factors, which a previous study had shown were often mentioned in this context, were presented on a card to respondents and they were asked to say which, if any, presented any threat to the freedom of the press.

Almost half (45%) did not believe that the freedom of the press was now in danger, while just over half the sample felt it was in danger.

Three items stand out from the list as being considered a threat to the freedom of the press—the printing unions, costs and inflation and "The Government". They were also the three most often selected as representing the biggest threat.

TABLE 2.096
THREATS TO THE FREEDOM OF THE PRESS

	Presenting any threat	Presenting biggest threat
Base: All respondents	350	350
	%	%
Freedom of press is in danger	52	
Freedom of press *not* in danger	45	
Don't know whether in danger	1	
No such thing as freedom of press	2	
Group presenting threat		
Printing unions	40	16
Costs/inflation	27	10
The Government	25	10
Political parties	19	4
Labour Party/Michael Foot	1	1
Proprietors/owners	18	4
The management	6	*
Journalists	12	1
Official Secrets Act/'D' Notices	10	1
Libel laws	6	1
Advertisers	9	1
Others	3	2

Given that the "Printing unions" and "The Government" are among those most often mentioned as posing a threat to press freedom, it is perhaps to be expected that the trade union members (41%) and Labour voters (32%) were less likely than others to see the freedom of the press as being in danger and also less likely to see the unions or the Government as presenting any threat.

There was also some variation between the five groups of respondents. Council officials and trade union secretaries stand out as less likely than others to see a threat to press freedom. They do not, however, differ from the sample as a whole in the factors they perceive as constituting a threat. Council officials, on the other hand, are less likely to view either proprietors and owners or "The management" as any threat; trade union secretaries are less likely to view the printing unions or journalists as threats. Managing directors were most likely to view the printing unions and journalists as a danger; head teachers were particularly concerned about "The Government" and political parties; councillors showed more than average concern about costs and inflation.

TABLE 2.097

THREATS TO THE FREEDOM OF THE PRESS: THE VIEW OF DIFFERENT GROUPS

	All Respondents	Councillors	Council Officials	Managing Directors	Trade Union Secs.	Head Teachers
Base	350	51	52	97	100	50
	%	%	%	%	%	%
Freedom of press *not* in danger	45	39	56	35	52	42
Don't know whether in danger	1	2	—	1	2	—
No such thing as freedom of the press	2	2	—	—	6	—
Group presenting any threat						
Printing unions	40	41	37	57	20	48
Costs/inflation	27	37	27	24	20	34
The Government	25	22	21	40	12	30
Political parties	19	14	15	29	10	30
Labour Party/Michael Foot	1	4	2	1	—	2
Proprietors/owners	18	22	10	14	22	20
The management	6	10	2	3	7	8
Journalists	12	10	15	17	4	16
Official Secrets Act/'D' Notices	10	12	8	10	12	6
Libel laws	6	12	4	5	9	—
Advertisers	9	8	10	4	14	10
Others	3	4	—	5	1	4

APPENDICES

Appendix 1: Response by Type of Respondent

	Trades Union Secretaries		Council Officials		Councillors		Head Teachers		Managing Directors/ Chamber Commerce		Total	
	No.		No.		No.		No.		No.		No.	
Target no. of interviews	100		50		50		50		100		350	
I. Addresses												
Addresses issued	138		75		74		74		165		526	
Never approached / not needed	32		21		16		19		23		111	
Addresses covered	106		54		58		55		142		415	
Out of scope:												
—not traced	—		—		2		—		3		5	
—dead	1		—		1		—		—		2	
—duplicate	1		—		—		—		1		2	
—firm dissolved	—		—		—		—		1		1	
—merged with another firm	—		—		—		—		1		1	
—no longer a councillor	—		—		2		—		—		2	
—"foreman" only	—		—		—		—		1		1	
Total out of scope	2		—		5		—		7		14	
		%		%		%		%		%		%
Total in scope	104	100	54	100	53	100	55	100	135	100	401	100
II. Individuals												
Interviews achieved	101[1]	97	52	96	51	96	50	91	98[1]	73	352	87·8
Non-response	3	3	2	4	2	4	5	9	37	27	49	12·2
—personal refusal	1	1	2	4	1	2	3	5	14	10	21	5·2
—proxy refusal	—	—	—	—	—	—	1	2	11	8	12	3·0
—busy until after deadline, but willing	—	—	—	—	—	—	—	—	5	4	5	1·2
—broken appointment	1	1	—	—	—	—	—	—	3	2	4	1·0
—away	—	—	—	—	1	2	—	—	3	2	4	1·0
—no contact	—	—	—	—	—	—	—	—	1	1	1	0·2
—ill	—	—	—	—	—	—	1	2	—	—	1	0·2
—in hospital	1	1	—	—	—	—	—	—	—	—	1	0·2

[1] One trade union secretary's questionnaire and one managing director's questionnaire were rejected at the editing stage as incomplete.

Appendix 2: Response by Town/Type of Respondent

(i) TRADE UNION SECRETARIES

	Wrexham	Cambridge	Reading	Cheltenham	Liverpool	Leeds	Bradford	Derby	Worcester	Glasgow	Newcastle	Darlington	Total	
	No.	No.	No.	No.	No.	No.	No.	No.	No.	No.	No.	No.	No.	%
Target no. of interviews	9	8	8	3	9	10	10	9	9	8	9	8	100	
I. Addresses														
Addresses issued	14	13	12	4	12	13	12	10	11	14	14	9	138	
Never approached/not needed	5	3	3	1	3	1	2	2	1	6	4	1	32	
Addresses covered	9	10	9	3	9	12	10	8	10	8	10	8	106	
Out of scope														
—duplicate	—	1	—	—	—	—	—	—	—	—	—	—	1	
—dead	—	—	—	—	—	—	—	—	—	—	1	—	1	
Total out of scope	—	1	—	—	—	—	—	—	—	—	1	—	2	
Total in scope	9	9	9	3	9	12	10	8	10	8	9	8	104	100
II. Individuals														
Interviews achieved	9	9	8	3	9	12	9	8	9	8	9	8	101	97
Non-response														
—personal refusal	—	—	1	—	—	—	1	—	1	—	—	—	3	3
—broken appointment	—	—	1	—	—	—	—	—	—	—	—	—	1	1
—in hospital	—	—	—	—	—	—	1	—	—	—	—	—	1	1

241

(ii) COUNCIL OFFICIALS

	Wrexham	Cambridge	Reading	Cheltenham	Liverpool	Leeds	Bradford	Derby	Worcester	Glasgow	Newcastle	Darlington	Total
	No.	No.	No.	No.	No.	No.	No.	No.	No.	No.	No.	No.	No.
Target no. of interviews	4	5	4	5	4	4	4	5	4	4	4	4	51
I. Addresses													
Addresses issued	6	7	6	8	6	6	6	6	6	6	6	6	75
Never approached/not needed	2	3	2	3	2	2	1	1	2	1	1	1	21
Addresses covered	4	4	4	5	4	4	5	5	4	5	5	5	54
Total out of scope	—	—	—	—	—	—	—	—	—	—	—	—	—
II. Individuals													
Interviews achieved	4	4	4	5	4	4	4	5	4	4	5	5	52 (96%)
Non-response	—	—	—	—	—	—	1	—	—	1	—	—	2 (4%)
—personal refusal	—	—	—	—	—	—	1	—	—	1	—	—	2 (4%)

(iii) COUNCILLORS

	Wrexham	Cambridge	Reading	Cheltenham	Liverpool	Leeds	Bradford	Derby	Worcester	Glasgow	Newcastle	Darlington	Total	
	No.	No.	No.	No.	No.	No.	No.	No.	No.	No.	No.	No.	No.	%
Target no. of interviews	3	3	5	7	4	3	4	3	4	5	4	5	50	
I. Addresses														
Addresses issued	6	5	6	9	6	6	5	6	6	6	6	7	74	
Never approached/not needed	3	2	1	2	—	—	—	2	2	1	2	1	16	
Addresses covered	3	3	5	7	6	6	5	4	4	5	4	6	58	
Out of scope														
—no trace	—	—	—	—	1	1	—	—	—	—	—	—	2	
—no longer a councillor	—	—	—	—	1	—	1	—	—	1	—	—	2	
—dead	—	—	—	—	—	—	—	—	—	—	—	—	1	
Total out of scope	—	—	—	—	2	1	1	—	—	1	—	—	5	
Total in scope	3	3	5	7	4	5	4	4	4	4	4	6	53	100
II. Individuals														
Interviews achieved	3	3	5	7	4	3	4	4	4	4	4	6	51	96
Non-response														
—personal refusal	—	—	—	—	—	2	—	—	—	—	—	—	2	4
—away	—	—	—	—	—	1	—	—	—	—	—	—	1	2
	—	—	—	—	—	1	—	—	—	—	—	—	1	2

(iv) HEAD TEACHERS

	Wrexham	Cambridge	Reading	Cheltenham	Liverpool	Leeds	Bradford	Derby	Worcester	Glasgow	Newcastle	Darlington	Total
	No.	*No.*	*No.*	*No.*	*No.*	*No.*	*No.*	*No.*	*No.*	*No.*	*No.*	*No.*	*No.*
Target no. of interviews	4	5	3	6	4	4	4	4	4	4	4	4	50
I. Addresses													
Addresses issued	6	6	6	9	6	6	5	6	6	4	5	9	74
Never approached/not needed	2	—	3	2	2	2	—	1	2	—	1	4	19
Addresses covered	4	6	3	7	4	4	5	5	4	4	4	5	55
Total out of scope	—	—	—	—	—	—	—	—	—	—	—	—	—
Total in scope	4	6	3	7	4	4	5	5	4	4	4	5	55
													% 100
II. Individuals													
Interviews achieved	4	5	3	6	4	4	3	5	4	3	4	5	50 91
Non-response													
—personal refusal	—	1	—	1	—	—	2	—	—	1	—	—	5 9
—proxy refusal	—	—	—	1	—	—	1	—	—	1	—	—	3 5
—ill	—	1	—	—	—	—	—	—	—	—	—	—	1 2
	—	—	—	—	—	—	1	—	—	—	—	—	1 2

(v) MANAGING DIRECTORS/CHAIRMEN OF CHAMBERS OF COMMERCE

	Wrexham	Cambridge	Reading	Cheltenham	Liverpool	Leeds	Bradford	Derby	Worcester	Glasgow	Newcastle	Darlington	Total	
	No.	No.	No.	No.	No.	No.	No.	No.	No.	No.	No.	No.	No.	%
Target no. of interviews	9	9	8	8	8	8	8	8	8	9	9	8	100	
I. Addresses														
Addresses issued	15	13	15	13	14	13	13	13	14	15	14	13	165	
Never approached/not needed	1	1	1	4	3	3	—	1	3	3	1	2	23	
Addresses covered	14	12	14	9	11	10	13	12	11	12	13	11	142	
Out of scope														
—"foreman" only	—	—	—	—	—	—	—	—	—	1	—	—	1	
—no trace	1	—	—	—	—	—	1	1	—	—	—	—	3	
—firm dissolved	—	—	—	—	—	—	—	—	—	1	—	—	1	
—merged with another firm	—	1	—	—	—	—	—	—	—	—	—	1	1	
—duplicate address	1	1	—	—	—	—	1	1	—	2	—	—	7	
Total out of scope	1	1	—	—	—	—	1	1	—	2	—	1	—	
Total in scope	13	11	14	9	11	10	12	11	11	10	13	10	135	100
II. Individuals														
Interviews achieved	10	7	8	8	8	5	7	10	9	8	9	9	98	73
Non-response														
—personal refusal	3	4	6	1	3	5	5	1	2	2	4	1	37	27
—proxy refusal	—	—	2	1	2	3	1	—	1	1	2	1	14	10
—busy until after deadline, but willing	2	3	1	—	1	1	—	—	—	1	2	—	11	8
—broken appointment	—	1	1	—	—	1	1	1	—	—	—	—	5	4
—away	1	—	2	—	—	—	2	—	—	—	—	—	3	2
—no contact	—	—	—	—	—	—	1	—	1	—	—	—	3	2
	—	—	—	—	—	—	—	—	—	—	—	—	1	1

Appendix 3: The Questionnaires

Press Study of Influentials

P396
October 1975

We are carrying out a survey for the Royal Commission on the Press on the newspapers people read and what they think of them.

	Col./Code	Skip to
TIME INTERVIEW STARTED (WRITE IN)		
RECORD No.	(1–4)	
CARD (10)	(5–6)	
AREA CODE	(7–8)	
SERIAL No.	(9–11)	
RESPONDENT IS:	(12)	
COUNCILLOR	1	
COUNCIL OFFICIAL	2	
TRADE UNION SECRETARY	3	
MANAGING DIRECTOR	4	
CHAIRMAN, CHAMBER OF COMMERCE	5	
HEADMASTER	6	

1. (a) SHOW CARD A This is a list of the national morning newspapers. Which of these, if any, do you ever read or look at nowadays? What others?
   PROBE TO "NONE"

   (b) ASK OF EACH MENTIONED AT (a) How many issues of .... do you read or look at in an average week?

	1 (a) Read/look at at all	1 (b) Issues in an average week		
		Less than one		
The Times	A	0	1 2 3 4 5 6	(13)
Financial Times	A	0	1 2 3 4 5 6	(14)
The Guardian	A	0	1 2 3 4 5 6	(15)
Daily Telegraph	A	0	1 2 3 4 5 6	(16)
Daily Express	A	0	1 2 3 4 5 6	(17)
Daily Mail	A	0	1 2 3 4 5 6	(18)
Daily Mirror	A	0	1 2 3 4 5 6	(19)
The Sun	A	0	1 2 3 4 5 6	(20)
Morning Star	A	0	1 2 3 4 5 6	(21)
Reads/Looks at none of these	0			(22)

Total No. of national morning newspapers read/looked at weekly or more often: (23)
(TOTAL CODED 1–6 AT Q. 1 (b)) ... .

		Card (10)	Col./ Code	Skip to

2. (a) SHOW CARD B This is a list of all the *Sunday* newspapers published in Great Britain. Some are regional and for these the place where they are published is shown in brackets. Which of these, if any, do you ever read or look at nowadays? What others?
PROBE TO "NONE"
   (b) ASK OF EACH MENTIONED AT (a) How many issues of .... do you read or look at in an average month?

	2 (a) Read/ look at at all	2 (b) Issues in an avarage month		
		Less than one	1 2 3 4	
Sunday Times	A	0	1 2 3 4	(24)
Observer	A	0	1 2 3 4	(25)
Sunday Express	A	0	1 2 3 4	(26)
Sunday Mirror	A	0	1 2 3 4	(27)
The People	A	0	1 2 3 4	(28)
Sunday Telegraph	A	0	1 2 3 4	(29)
News of the World	A	0	1 2 3 4	(30)
Sunday Mercury (Birmingham)	A	0	1 2 3 4	(31)
Sunday Sun (Newcastle) ...	A	0	1 2 3 4	(32)
The Independent (Plymouth)...	A	0	1 2 3 4	(33)
Sunday Post (Glasgow) ...	A	0	1 2 3 4	(34)
Sunday Mail (Glasgow) ...	A	0	1 2 3 4	(35)
Reads/looks at none of these...	0			(36)

3. (a) Is there any local or regional *daily* newspaper which you ever read or look at nowadays (it does not matter whether it is published in the morning or the evening)? ...   (37)

Yes	1	
No	2	Q. 4

   (b) IF YES TO (a) Which? What others? PROBE TO "NONE"
   (c) ASK OF EACH MENTIONED AT (b)
   How many issues of .... do you read or look at in an average week?

3 (b) WRITE IN EXACT TITLE(S)	3 (c) Issues in an average week		
	Less than one	1 2 3 4 5 6	
....	0	1 2 3 4 5 6	(38–44)
....	0	1 2 3 4 5 6	(45–51)
....	0	1 2 3 4 5 6	(52–58)
....	0	1 2 3 4 5 6	(59–65)
			Spare (66)

	Card (10/20)	Col./ Code	Skip to

4. (a) Is there any local or regional *weekly* newspaper which you ever read or look at nowadays (this includes any weekly newspaper which may be delivered free of charge to your household)?

                         (67)

        Yes 1

        No 2   Q. 5

(b) IF YES TO (a) Which? PROBE FOR EXACT TITLE. CHECK COPY FOR EXACT TITLE IF POSSIBLE. What others? (PROBE TO "NONE")

(c) ASK OF EACH MENTIONED AT (b) How many issues of .... do you read or look at in an average month?

4 (b) WRITE IN EXACT TITLE(S)	4 (c) Issues in an average month Less than one								
		1	2	3	4+				(68–74) P396
....	0	1	2	3	4	......	......	....	(78–80) Card 20 (5–6)
....	0	1	2	3	4	......	......	....	(7–13)
....	0	1	2	3	4	......	......	....	(14–20)
....	0	1	2	3	4	......	......	....	(21–27)
....	0	1	2	3	4	......	......	....	(28–34)

                         (35)

5. (a) Do you watch television at all nowadays?

        Yes ... ... A

        No 0   Q. 6

IF YES TO 5 (a), ASK 5 (b) AND 5 (c)

(b) On an average *weekday*, about how many hours do you spend watching television?

        Less than 1 hour a day 1

        1 but under 3 hours a day 2

        3 but under 5 hours a day 3

        5 hours a day or more 4

(c) Do you ever watch the BBC or ITN news on television? IF YES:

                         (36)

On average about how many days a week do you watch the news on television?

        Never watch 0

        Less than once a week 1

        1–3 days a week 2

        4–5 days a week 3

        6–7 days a week 4

			Card (20)	Col./ Code	Skip to

(a) Do you listen to the radio at all nowadays? ... ... (37)
    Yes ... ... A
    No 0   Q. 7
IF YES TO 6 (a), ASK 6 (b) AND 6 (c)

(b) On an average *weekday*, about how many hours do you spend listening to the radio?
    Less than 1 hour a day 1
    1 hour but under 3 hours a day 2
    3 hours but under 5 hours a day 3
    5 hours or more a day 4

(c) Do you ever listen to news bulletins on radio? IF YES: (38)
On average about how many days a week do you listen to the news on radio?
    Never listen 0   Q. 7
    Less than once a week 1
    1–3 days a week 2
    4–5 days a week 3
    6–7 days a week 4

(d) IF EVER LISTENS AT (c) On *weekdays*, at what times of day do you usually listen to news bulletins? Do you usually listen to them ... ... (39)
    READ OUT:
      before 9.30 a.m. 1
      between 9.30 am and 5.30 pm 2
      or after 5.30 pm 3
      none of these—Respondent does not listen on weekdays   0

Card (20)/(21)

PART 2

THE ROLE OF THE MEDIA

FOR EACH NEWSPAPER READ OR LOOKED AT ONCE A WEEK OR MORE (DAILIES), ONCE A MONTH OR MORE (WEEKLIES)

7 (a) As a .... (RESPONDENT'S POSITION, eg councillor), how important is the .... (PAPER) for keeping you up to date and well informed? SHOW CARD C

National Newspapers	Very Important	Fairly Important	Not very Important	Not at all Important	Col./Code	Skip to
	1	2	3	4	(40–46)	
	1	2	3	4	(47–53)	
	1	2	3	4	(54–60)	
	1	2	3	4	(61–67)	
	1	2	3	4	(68–74) P.396 Card 21	(78–80) (5–6)
	1	2	3	4	(7–13)	
	1	2	3	4	(14–20)	
	1	2	3	4	(21–27)	
Local Evening Newspapers						
	1	2	3	4	(28–34)	
	1	2	3	4	(35–41)	
	1	2	3	4	(42–48)	
Local Weekly Newspapers						
	1	2	3	4	(49–55)	
	1	2	3	4	(56–62)	
	1	2	3	4	(63–69)	

(b) How important is/are .... (READ FROM GRID) for keeping you up to date and well informed as a .... (RESPONDENT'S POSITION) SHOW CARD C

	Very Important	Fairly Important	Not very Important	Not at all Important	Never Look/ Listen/ Read	
Television	1	2	3	4	5	(70)
Local radio stations	1	2	3	4	5	(71)
National radio stations	1	2	3	4	5	(72)
Specialist journals	1	2	3	4	5	(73)
Magazines and periodicals	1	2	3	4	5	(74)
					Spare P. 397	(75–77) (78–80)

	Col./ Code	Skip to
Card (30)		
Record No.	(1–4)	
Card (30)	(5–6)	

ASK MANAGING DIRECTORS AND COUNCIL OFFICIALS ONLY ... ... (7)

8. Does anyone in your company/council have special responsibility for contacts with the press? ... ... No — 1
   Yes: Respondent ... ... — 2
   Press officer at head office ... ... — 3
   Personnel officer at head office ... ... — 4
   (PROMPT   Public relations officer at head office ... — 5
   FROM LIST)   Press officer at establishment ... ... — 6
   Personnel officer at establishment ... — 7
   Public relations officer at establishment — 8
   Other (specify).. — 9

ASK ALL

9. (a) When something occurs in which *you* have a particular interest or involvement, do you (does he) sometimes approach the *local evening papers* to get them to cover it or do you (does he) only speak to the local evening papers when they approach you, or do you (does he) never speak to them?

(b) REPEAT FOR "LOCAL WEEKLY PAPERS"

	(a) Local Evening	(b) Local Weekly
(SINGLE CODING ONLY)	(8)	(9)
Sometimes approaches paper ...	1	1
Speaks only when approached ...	2	2
Varies according to the paper ...	3	3
Never speaks to paper	4	4
Other (specify)...........................	5	5

IF SPEAKS TO PAPER (CODES 1–3 OR 5 AT 9 (a) OR (b)) OTHERS SKIP TO (d)

(c) How do you (does he) approach the paper or how does the paper approach you (him)? Firstly the local evening papers .... PROMPT FROM GRID.
REPEAT FOR "LOCAL WEEKLY PAPERS"

(MULTI-CODING ALLOWED)	Local Evening	Local Weekly
	(10)	(11)
Telephone/call to see the editor ...	1	1
Telephone/call to see the journalist	2	2
Editor telephones/calls	3	3
Journalist telephones/calls	4	4
Issues a press statement	5	5
Or some other way (specify)................	6	6
Varies according to the paper ...	7	7
(Not applicable)	X	X

Card (30) | Col./Code | Skip to

9. (d) IF NEVER SPEAKS TO LOCAL EVENING PAPER(S)...
Why do you (does he) never speak to the local evening papers? (PROBE FULLY)

(12)

(13)

(14)

(15)

(e) IF NEVER SPEAKS TO LOCAL WEEKLY PAPER(S) ...
Why do you (does he) never speak to the local weekly papers? (PROBE FULLY)

(16)

(17)

(18)

(19)

10. (a) Of the issues and problems that are important in this district nowadays, which *one* do you yourself see as *most* important? (PROBE FULLY)
(IF NO PROBLEM MENTIONED SKIP TO Q. 11)

(20)

(21)

(22)

(23)

(24)

(b) How have you come to know of .... (PROBLEM)?
Was it in any of these ways? SHOW CARD D Any others?
PROBE TO "NO"

(25)

From personal experience	1
From my job	2
From what people I meet say	3
From local newspapers	4
From local radio	5
From television	6
From national newspapers	7
From national radio	8
From magazines	9
Others (specify)..	0

PART 3

Attitudes to Particular Newspapers

THERE ARE TWO TYPES OF NEWSPAPER SHEET.

ONE (GREEN) IS FOR LOCAL OR REGIONAL MORNING, EVENING, WEEKLY AND SUNDAY NEWSPAPERS.

THE OTHER (PINK) IS FOR NATIONAL DAILY NEWSPAPERS (THOSE LISTED ON CARD A).

COMPLETE ONE *LOCAL OR REGIONAL* NEWSPAPER SHEET FOR:
—EACH LOCAL OR REGIONAL DAILY OF WHICH AT LEAST ONE ISSUE IS READ/LOOKED AT ONCE OR MORE IN AN AVERAGE WEEK (CODES 1–6 AT Q. 3 (b)).
—EACH LOCAL OR REGIONAL WEEKLY OF WHICH AT LEAST ONE ISSUE IS READ/LOOKED AT IN AN AVERAGE MONTH (CODES 1–6 AT Q. 4 (b)).
—EACH REGIONAL SUNDAY OF WHICH AT LEAST ONE ISSUE IS READ/ LOOKED AT IN AN AVERAGE MONTH (CODES 1–6 AT Q. 2 (b) FOR PAPERS WITH A TOWN LISTED).

COMPLETE A *NATIONAL* NEWSPAPER SHEET ONLY IF RESPONDENT READS/LOOKS AT AT LEAST ONE ISSUE OF A NATIONAL MORNING IN AN AVERAGE WEEK (CODES 1–6 AT Q. 1 (b)). IF HE READS/LOOKS AT MORE THAN ONE TITLE, USE GRID BELOW TO SELECT *ONE* TO ASK ABOUT AND RING NUMBER CHOSEN IN GRID.

No. of Nationals Read/Looked at	Last Digit of Address No.									
	1	2	3	4	5	6	7	8	9	0
One	1	1	1	1	1	1	1	1	1	1
Two	2	1	2	1	2	1	2	1	2	1
Three	3	2	1	3	1	2	1	3	2	2
Four	1	2	4	2	3	4	3	2	1	3
Five	4	5	3	1	5	3	2	1	4	2
Six	3	4	5	6	1	2	4	3	5	1
Seven	6	3	7	2	7	5	1	4	6	5
Eight	5	1	6	1	4	3	7	2	8	4
Nine	9	4	8	6	2	1	5	6	3	7

NUMBERS REFER TO THE ORDER IN WHICH THE NATIONALS READ ARE PRINTED ON THE QUESTIONNAIRE AT Q. 1.

		Card (30)	Col./Code	Skip to
	ASK AT LIVERPOOL, GLASGOW, LEEDS, BRADFORD, NEWCASTLE, WREXHAM AND DARLINGTON POINTS ... ... (OTHERS SKIP TO Q. 12)		(26)	
11.	You say that you do not read or look at the .... (WRITE IN LOCAL MORNING PAPER) nowadays/more than once a week? Why don't you read it (more often)? PROBE FULLY		(27)	
			(28)	
			(29)	
			(30)	
			(31)	
			(32)	
12.	ASK IF RESPONDENT DOES NOT READ ANY/ALL LOCAL EVENING PAPERS AT LEAST ONCE A WEEK (OTHERS SKIP TO Q. 13.) You say that you do not read or look at the .... (WRITE IN NAME OF LOCAL EVENING) nowadays/more than once a week? Why don't you read it (more often)? (IF MORE THAN ONE EVENING PAPER IN AREA RECORD REASONS FOR EACH NOT READ)		(33)	
			(34)	
			(35)	
			(36)	
			(37)	
			(38)	
			(39)	

Card (30) | Col./Code | Skip to

ASK ALL
13. (a) Is there more than one evening newspaper sold in this area so that you can make a choice? (40)
   Yes, more than one sold ... 1 — Q. 13b
   No, only one sold ... 2 — Q. 13c
   (Don't know) ... 3 — Q. 13c

(b) IF YES AT (a) Do you think you benefit at all from having more than one evening newspaper in this area? IF YES How? PROBE FULLY, RECORD ANSWERS FULLY (41)
   Yes ... 1
   No ... 2 — Q. 14

(42)

(43)

NOW SKIP TO Q. 14
(c) IF NO OR D.K. AT (a) Do you think you would benefit in any way if there were more than one evening newspaper in this area? IF YES How? PROBE FULLY, RECORD ANSWERS FULLY (44)
   Yes ... 1
   No ... 2 — Q. 14

(45)

(46)

ASK ALL
14. (a) How much influence do you think national newspapers have on the views of their readers? Would you say they have a ... PROMPT FROM GRID.
(b) REPEAT FOR LOCAL EVENING NEWSPAPERS.
(c) REPEAT FOR LOCAL WEEKLY NEWSPAPERS.

	National Newspapers	Local Evening Papers	Local Weekly Papers
	(47)	(48)	(49)
Very strong influence ...	1	1	1
Fairly strong influence ...	2	2	2
A fairly weak influence ...	3	3	3
A very weak influence ...	4	4	4
No influence at all ...	5	5	5

		Card (30)	Col./ Code	Skip to

ASK ALL

15. SHOW CARD A This is a list of all the national daily newspapers. You may have heard that some of them are in financial difficulties. It has even been suggested that some may have to close. If that happened, which *one* would you yourself most want to keep? And which after that? And which after that?

Want to keep:

	Most (50)	2nd most (51)	3rd most (52)
The Times	1	1	1
Financial Times	2	2	2
The Guardian	3	3	3
Daily Telegraph	4	4	4
Daily Express	5	5	5
Daily Mail	6	6	6
Daily Mirror/Daily Record (Scotland)	7	7	7
The Sun	8	8	8
Morning Star	9	9	9
Don't know/Don't care	0	0	0

16. Have you heard of the Press Council? (53)
    - Yes ... 1
    - No ... 2   Q. 18
    - Uncertain ... 3

    IF YES OR UNCERTAIN ASK (b)
    (b) Do you know what it does? (54)
    - Yes ... 1
    - No ... 2   Q. 17

    (c) IF YES TO (b) What does it do? PROBE FULLY, RECORD ANSWERS FULLY (55)

    (56)

    (d) How well does it perform its functions READ: (57)
    - Very well ... 1
    - Fairly well ... 2
    - Rather poorly ... 3
    - Very poorly ... 4
    - (Don't know) ... 5

    (e) Why do you say that? (PROBE FULLY) (58)

    (59)

    (60)

		Card (30)	Col./ Code	Skip to

17. Have you ever written to the Press Council? ... ... (61)
    Yes ... ... A
    No 0   Q. 18

   IF YES   (62)
   What about?

18. (a) Do you believe that the freedom of the press is now in danger?   (63)
        Yes   1
        No   2   Q. 19
        Don't know 3   Q. 19
        Other (specify fully)................................ 4

   (b) Which, if any, of these groups presents any threat to the freedom of the press? SHOW CARD E.
       IF MORE THAN ONE
   (c) Which of these groups presents the biggest threat?

	(b)	(c)
	Any Threat	Biggest
	(64–65)	(66–67)
The Libel Laws	01	01
Advertisers	02	02
Proprietors/Owners	03	03
Printing Unions	04	04
The Management	05	05
Political Parties	06	06
Journalists	07	07
The Government	08	08
Costs/Inflation	09	09
Official Secrets Act/"D" Notices ...	10	10
Others (please specify)	11	11
None	00	

PART 5   Card (30)

CLASSIFICATION DATA

		Col./Code	Skip to
		(68)	

19. (a) Were you born in this county/(region SCOT)?
    - Born in county/region ... 1
    - Not born in county/region ... A

    IF NOT BORN IN COUNTY/REGION
    (b) How long have you lived in this county/region (SCOT)?
    - 10 years or more ... 2
    - 5 but under 10 years ... 3
    - 2 but under 5 years ... 4
    - Under 2 years ... 5

ASK ALL
20. (a) Are you a member of any of these types of organisation? SHOW CARD F. IF YES Which? Any others? PROBE TO "NONE"
    FOR EACH ORGANISATION RESPONDENT IS MEMBER OF ASK (b) AND (c)
    (b) Have you attended any meetings of .... in the last 12 months? (RECORD IN GRID BELOW)
    (c) Are you an official or committee member of ....?
    (RECORD IN GRID BELOW)

	(a) Membership		(b) Attended a meeting		(c) Official or Committee member		
	Yes	No	Yes	No/D.K.	Yes	No	
Trade Union	A	2	4	5	7	B	(69)
Professional Association	A	2	4	5	7	B	(70)
Business group or club ... (eg Rotary, Chamber of Commerce)	A	2	4	5	7	B	(71)
Political Party	A	2	4	5	7	B	(72)
Parents' Association ...	A	2	4	5	7	B	(73)
Tenants' or Ratepayers' Association	A	2	4	5	7	B	(74)
Any other community or pressure group	A	2	4	5	7	B	(75)
Any public body or committee ... ... (Specify)	A	2	4	5	7	B	(76)

(d) Are you or have you ever been a ....?

	No.	Yes at present	Yes in past	
				(77)
Councillor	1	2	3	
A full-time trade union official	5	6	7	
A magistrate	9	0	X	

P. 396 (78–80)

	Card (40)	Col./ Code	Skip to
	Record No.	(1–4)	
	Card (40)	(5–6)	

21. (a) Are you a member of any of these types of organisation? SHOW CARD G. PROBE: "Any others" until "No". RECORD IN COLUMN (a) OF GRID BELOW.　(7–8)

	(a) *Member*		(b) *Run*	
	Yes	No	Yes	No
			(9)	
Sports club	A	B	1	C
A club for hobbies or other leisure activities	A	B	2	C
Youth club, scouts or guides	A	B	3	C
Charitable organisation	A	B	4	C
Voluntary welfare organisation	A	B	5	C
Military Training Group	A	B	6	C
Church club or group	A	B	7	C
Social club of any kind	A	B	8	C
Any other type of club or organisation (specify)	A	B	9	C
None of these	A		0	

(b) Do you help to organise or run any of these? (*NOT* DEPENDENT ON MEMBERSHIP) RECORD ANSWERS IN COLUMN (b) OF GRID ABOVE.

22. (a) Generally speaking, do you usually think of yourself as Conservative, Labour, Liberal (*Wales/Scotland only:* Nationalist) or what? (10)
RING ONE CODE ONLY
　　Conservative ... 1
　　Labour ... 2
　　Liberal ... 3
　　Nationalist ... 4
　　Other (specify) ... 5

　　None of these/Don't know ... Y

UNLESS NONE OR DON'T KNOW AT (a) (11)
(b) How strongly .... (PARTY) do you generally feel:
READ OUT　very strongly ... 1
　　　　　　fairly strongly ... 2
　　　　　　or not very strongly ... 3

Card (40) | Col./Code | Skip to

CLASSIFICATION SECTION

23. Sex (12)
    - Male 1
    - Female 2

24. *Age* last Birthday .... (13–14)
    (WRITE IN)

25. Activity Status (15)

26. *Age completed full-time education* (16)
    - 14 or under ... 1
    - 15 2
    - 16 3
    - 17 4
    - 18 5
    - 19 6
    - 20 7
    - 21 or over 8
    - Not yet completed full-time education 9

- Working full-time (31+ hrs.) 1
- Working part-time (10–30 hrs.) 2
- Seeking work 3
- Retired/Sick 4
- Non-working housewife ... 5
- Full-time student 6
- Other (WRITE IN) 7

27. OCCUPATION (PRESENT OR LAST MAIN PAID JOB) OF RESPONDENT
    Name/Title of job ....
    Description of activity...........
    Skill/training/qualifications/experience required for job ....
    ....
    (17–20)

    Supervision/management responsibilities (including number of people supervised) ....

    Industry/business/profession (of employer) ....
    No. of people employed at place of work............ ....
    Employment status:
    - Employee ... ... A
    - Self-employed ... ... B

TRADE UNION OFFICIAL, COUNCILLOR AND CHAIRMAN OF C. OF C. ONLY

28. (a) EXACT POSITION OF RESPONDENT (eg Secretary) OTHERS SKIP TO 29 ... ... (21–23)

    (b) NAME OF UNION/COUNCIL/CHAMBER OF COMMERCE ... ... (24–26)

    (c) AREA COVERED (eg Name of town, district, region) ... (27–29)

HEADMASTERS
29. STATUS OF SCHOOL (Secondary, independent etc)............ (30)

	Col./Code	Skip to

30. MANAGING DIRECTORS

Is your company affiliated to any employer associations (eg CBI, or the Engineering Employers Fed etc)   (32)

(31)
COMPANY: LOCALLY BASED 1
PART OF NATIONAL GROUP 2
PART OF MULTI-NATIONAL
  GROUP 3
Other (specify) ....

TIME INTERVIEW
COMPLETED ....

NAME OF
  INTERVIEWER
....

(33–35)
DURATION
OF
INTERVIEW .... MINUTES

INTER-
VIEWER ....   (36–38)
NO
DATE OF INTERVIEW
....

Record No. (1–4)
Card (5)   (5)

LOCAL OR REGIONAL NEWSPAPER SHEET

LOCAL/REGIONAL NEWSPAPER SHEET No. .... (6)
AREA CODE ....
SERIAL No. ....
OUO
NEWSPAPER TITLE (EXACT) ....
(7–12)

1. SHOW CARD J. I am going to read out some comments people have made about newspapers. I would like you to tell me how true each of them is of the .... (PAPER).
IF LAST DIGIT OF ADDRESS No. IS EVEN, READ LIST TOP TO BOTTOM.
IF IT IS ODD READ LIST BOTTOM TO TOP. RING ORDER READ.

Top to Bottom	A
Bottom to Top	B

	Very true	*Fairly true*	*Not very true*	*Not true at all*	*Don't know*	
It helps me to understand how what is happening in the country will affect my interests in the area	1	2	3	4	9	(13)
It exaggerates the sensational aspects of the news	1	2	3	4	9	(14)
It takes an interest in ordinary people's problems	1	2	3	4	9	(15)
The comments it makes on the news are usually interesting	1	2	3	4	9	(16)
It always concentrates on the bad news	1	2	3	4	9	(17)
It is afraid of offending its advertisers	1	2	3	4	9	(18)
Reading it is always enjoyable	1	2	3	4	9	(19)
It often gets its facts wrong ...	1	2	3	4	9	(20)
It has too much advertising in it	1	2	3	4	9	(21)
I would miss it a lot if it stopped being published	1	2	3	4	9	(22)
It gives fair coverage to all points of view	1	2	3	4	9	(23)
It prints too many silly or trivial stories	1	2	3	4	9	(24)
Its standard of reporting is first class	1	2	3	4	9	(25)
It sometimes goes too far in invading people's grief ...	1	2	3	4	9	(26)
It always has the latest national news	1	2	3	4	9	(27)
It is prepared to criticise *anybody* if it thinks they deserve it	1	2	3	4	9	(28)
It has too little news in it ...	1	2	3	4	9	(29)
It gives a good service to its advertisers	1	2	3	4	9	(30)
It hinders good industrial relations	1	2	3	4	9	(31)

	Card (5)	Col./ Code	Skip to

2. (a) Has anything been reported in the .... (PAPER) recently in which you have some particular interest, involvement or knowledge? (IF NO PROBE "No meeting you attended or local issue you are involved with")?

		Col./Code	Skip to
Yes		(32) A	
No		0	Q. 3

(b) What was the subject of the article or report? (Specify fully) (IF SEVERAL, ASK ABOUT MOST RECENT)

	(33)
	(34)
	(35)
	(36)

(c) What was your opinion of the way it was written? (PROBE FULLY)

Reproduced press statement	(37) 1
	(38)
	(39)
	(40)
	(42)

(d) Was the coverage ... (READ OUT)

Completely accurate	1		
Fairly accurate	2		*
Fairly inaccurate	3		*
Very inaccurate	4		*
	(43)		

(e) Did it deal fairly with the issue ... (READ OUT)

Very fairly	1	
Reasonably fairly	2	*
Rather unfairly	3	*
Very unfairly	4	*

(f) What do you think of the amount of coverage that the .... (PAPER) gave to the subject? Was it ... (READ OUT)

	(44)	
Too much	1	*
Too little	2	*
Or just about right	3	

*IF ANY ASTERISKED CODE RINGED AT (d), (e) OR (f)
(g) You have said it was not entirely accurate/fair/the right amount of coverage. How do you think this came about? (PROBE FULLY "Where do you think the fault lies?", "How do you think the article/report could have been improved?")

(45)
(46)
(47)
(48)
(49)

		Card (5)	Col./Code	Skip to

3. (a) How well does the .... (PAPER) generally treat the following topics? SHOW CARD H.
   (b) Which of these topics does it generally treat the least well?

	Very Well	Fairly Well	Fairly Badly	Very Badly	Least Well (57)
News of local industrial disputes	1	2	3	4 (50)	1
Local town redevelopment proposals...	1	2	3	4 (51)	2
Activities of the Conservative Party on the Council	1	2	3	4 (52)	3
Activities of the Labour Party on the Council ...	1	2	3	4 (53)	4
Local educational matters ...	1	2	3	4 (54)	5
News of local industry ...	1	2	3	4 (55)	6
News of local trade union activities	1	2	3	4 (56)	7

ASK OF TOPIC TREATED LEAST WELL

(c) In what ways does the .... (PAPER) generally treat this topic least well? (PROBE FULLY, eg "Are the reports or the comments at fault?", "Are they inaccurate, unfair or insufficient and for what reasons?")

(57)

(58)

(59)

(60)

(61)

IF MORE THAN ONE TOPIC TREATED VERY BADLY OR FAIRLY BADLY AT (a) ASK: OTHERS SKIP TO Q. 4

(62)

(d) Of the other topics you mentioned as generally treated either very badly or fairly badly (READ OUT) Which is treated least well?

(63)

(64)

(e) In what ways does the .... (PAPER) generally treat this topic very badly/fairly badly? (PROBE FULLY, eg "Are the reports or the comments at fault?", "Are they inaccurate, unfair, or insufficient and for what reasons?"

(65)

(66)

(67)

	Card (5)	Col./ Code	Skip to

4. (a) SHOW CARD J When it is reporting on controversial local issues, do you think .... (PAPER) often pays *too little* attention to the views of any of these sorts of people? Any others? PROBE TO "NO"

   (b) Apart from the ones on the card, are there any other *sorts of people* or *groups* to whose views the .... (PAPER) often pays *too little* attention? Any others? PROBE TO "NO"

   (c) SHOW CARD J When it is reporting on controversial local issues, do you think .... (PAPER) often pays *too much* attention to the views of any of these sorts of people? Any others? PROBE TO "NO"

   (d) Apart from the ones on the card, are there any other *sorts of people* or *groups* to whose views the .... (PAPER) often pays *too much* attention? Any others? PROBE TO "NO"

	3 (a/b) Pays too little attention (68)	3 (c/d) Pays too much attention (69)		
3 (a/c):				
Officials of the local council	1	1		
Local councillors	2	2		
Big commercial companies	3	3		
Local businessmen	4	4		
Local trade union leaders	5	5		
Religious people	6	6		
People in the higher income groups	7	7		
People in the lower income groups	8	8		
The police	9	9		
Young people	0	0		
None of these	X	X		
3 (b/d):				
Others (WRITE IN)			(70–73)	

5. (a) REFER BACK TO MAIN PROBLEM OF DISTRICT IDENTIFIED AT Q. 10 OF MAIN QUESTIONNAIRE. You mentioned earlier that the main issue or problem facing this district nowadays is .... (PROBLEM). How much attention does .... (PAPER) give to this problem? Would you say it gives it a lot of attention, some attention or no attention at all? (74)

Lot of attention	1	Q. 6
Some attention	2	
No attention at all	3	

   (b) IF SOME ATTENTION OR NO ATTENTION AT (a) Do you think the .... (PAPER) *should* give more attention to .... (PROBLEM)? (75)

Yes	1
No	2
SPARE	(76–77)
396	(78–80)

RECORD No. (1-4)
CARD (6)   (5)
SPARE (6)

	Col./Code	Skip to
	(7)	

6. (a) How are relations at present between your company/union district/school/chamber of commerce/party group/council and the .... (PAPER)?
   Very good   1
   Fairly good   2
   Not very good   3
   Very bad   4

   (b) In what way are they good/not good? ... ...   (8)

   (9)

   (10)

ASK COUNCILLORS, BUSINESSMEN AND TRADE UNION OFFICIALS ONLY OTHERS SKIP TO Q. 8   (11)

7. (a) How important is the .... (PAPER) for presenting the point of view of your party group/company/union district to the public in this area?
   Is it . . . (READ OUT)
   Very important   1
   Fairly important   2
   Not very important   3
   Not at all important   4

   (b) How satisfied are you with the way it presents the point of view of your company/union district/chamber of commerce/party group/council?   (12)
   Very satisfied   1
   Fairly satisfied   2
   Fairly dissatisfied   3
   Very dissatisfied   4

   (c) In what way are you satisfied/dissatisfied? (PROBE FULLY)   (13)

   (14)

   (15)

   (16)

   (17)

267

	Card (6)	Col./ Code	Skip to
8. (a)	ASK ALL Have you ever felt like complaining about anything that has appeared in the .... (PAPER)? IF YES PROBE "Once or more than once?" No ... ... Yes, once ... ... Yes, more than once	(18) 1 2 3	 Q. 9 (b) (b)
(b)	IF YES (CODES 2 OR 3) Have you, in fact, ever complained to anyone? IF YES PROBE "Once or more than once?" No ... ... Yes, once ... ... Yes, more than once	(19) 1 2 3	 (f) (c) (c)
(c)	IF YES TO (b) (CODES 2 OR 3 AT (b)) What did you complain about (most recently)? PROBE FULLY	(20) (21) (22) (23) (24)	
(d)	To whom did you complain? Editor ... ... Journalist ... ... Press Council ... ... Other (specify)	(25) 1 2 3 4	
(e)	What was the result of the complaint? (PROBE "Was he satisfied with the result of the complaint?")	(26) (27)	
(f)	NOW SKIP TO Q. 9 IF NO TO (b) (CODE 1 AT (b)) What did you feel like complaining about (most recently)? PROBE FULLY	(28) (29) (30) (31) (32)	
(g)	Why didn't you make a complaint to anyone? PROBE FULLY	(33) (34)	

	Col./ Code	Skip to
9. (a) Judging by what you have read in it, would you say the .... (PAPER) generally supports any one political party? IF YES Which?	(35)	
No	0	Q. 10
Yes—Conservative	1	
Labour	2	
Liberal	3	
Other (specify)...........................		
(b) IF YES TO (a) Do you think it gives fair coverage to the views of other political parties or not?	(36)	
Yes, gives fair coverage	1	
No, does not give fair coverage	2	
IF NO, DOES NOT GIVE FAIR COVERAGE AT (b) (c) To which parties' views does it not give fair coverage? Any others? PROBE TO "NO"	(37)	
To—Conservatives	1	
Labour	2	
Liberal	3	
Other parties (specify)...........................	4	
ASK ALL 10. (a) When employers and unions disagree, does the .... (PAPER) usually:	(38)	
READ OUT: *Report* both sides of things fully	1	
or—Give more space to the employer's case	2	
or—Give more space to the union's case	3	
or—Not print much about it at all	4	Q. 11
(b) UNLESS "NOT PRINT MUCH" AT (a) When it makes *comments* on disagreements between employers and unions, does the .... (PAPER):	(39)	
READ OUT: Tend to favour the employers	1	
or—Tend to favour the unions	2	
or—Try to judge fairly between them	3	
Never makes comments	4	

	Col./ Code	Skip to

11. (a) In general has the quality of the .... (PAPER) improved in recent years, declined in recent years or has it remained about the same?   (40)

    Improved ...   1
    Declined ...   2
    Remained about the same ...   3   Q. 12

IF IMPROVED/DECLINED

(b) Why, and in what way has it improved/declined in recent years? (PROBE FULLY)   (41)

(42)

(43)

(44)

(45)

12. In general, how would you rate the .... (PAPER)? Do you consider it to be ... READ OUT: (46)

    An excellent paper ...   1
    A very good paper ...   2
    A fairly good paper ...   3
    An average paper ...   4
    A fairly poor paper ...   5
    A very poor paper ...   6

13. (a) Do you know the name of the company which owns .... (PAPER)?   (47)

    No ...   1
    IF YES What is it? ....

(b) ASK ALL Do you know whether the company which owns .... (PAPER) owns any other newspapers?   (48)

    Yes—owns others ...   1
    No—does not own others ...   2
    Don't know ...   3   Q. 14

IF "YES" TO (b) ASK (c) AND (d)

(c) About how many other newspapers does it own?   (49)

    1–4 ...   1
    5–9 ...   2
    10–15 ...   3
    16–19 ...   4
    20 or more ...   5
    Don't know ...   9

(d) Does it own any other *local* or *regional* newspapers (whether daily, weekly or Sunday) which are sold *here*?   (50)

    Yes ...   1
    No ...   2   Q. 14
    Don't know ...   3   Q. 14

(e) IF YES TO (d) Which other local or regional newspapers which are sold *here* does it own? Any others? PROBE TO "NO" PROBE FOR EXACT TITLES   (51)

....

....

....

	Col./Code	Skip to
14. On average, about how long in all do you yourself spend reading or looking at a particular issue of .... (PAPER)?	(52)	
Less than 10 minutes	1	
10 minutes but under ¼ hour	2	
¼ hour but under ½ hour	3	
½ hour but under 1 hour	4	
1 hour but under 2 hours	5	
2 hours or more	6	
	P396	(78–80)

s

P396 **NATIONAL MORNING NEWSPAPER SHEET**

COMPLETE *ONE* OF THESE SHEETS IF RESPONDENT READS/LOOKS AT ONE OR MORE ISSUE OF ANY *NATIONAL MORNING* IN AN AVERAGE WEEK. IF HE READS/LOOKS AT ONE TITLE ONLY, ASK THE QUESTIONS ON THIS SHEET ABOUT THAT ONE. IF HE READS/LOOKS AT TWO OR MORE, USE THE GRID IN THE MAIN QUESTIONNAIRE TO DECIDE WHICH *ONE* TO ASK ABOUT.

Area Code ....   Record No. (1–4)

Serial No. ....   Card (40) (5–6)

Newspaper Title .... (7–12)
OUO

....
Blank (13–37)

Card (40)

1. SHOW CARD J. I am going to read out some comments people have made about newspapers. I would like you to tell me how true each of them is of the .... (PAPER).

    IF LAST DIGIT OF ADDRESS No. IS EVEN READ LIST TOP TO BOTTOM.
    IF IT IS ODD READ LIST BOTTOM TO TOP. RING ORDER READ.

Top to Bottom	A
Bottom to top	B

	Very true	Quite true	Not very true	Not true at all	Don't know	
It helps me to understand how what is happening in the country will affect my interests in the area ...	1	2	3	4	9	(38)
It exaggerates the sensational aspects of the news	1	2	3	4	9	(39)
It takes an interest in ordinary people's problems	1	2	3	4	9	(40)
The comments it makes on the news are usually interesting	1	2	3	4	9	(41)
It always concentrates on the bad news	1	2	3	4	9	(42)
It is afraid of offending its advertisers	1	2	3	4	9	(43)
Reading it is always enjoyable ...	1	2	3	4	9	(44)
It often gets its facts wrong ...	1	2	3	4	9	(45)
It has too much advertising in it ...	1	2	3	4	9	(46)
I would miss it a lot if it stopped being published	1	2	3	4	9	(47)
It gives fair coverage to all points of view	1	2	3	4	9	(48)
It prints too many silly or trivial stories	1	2	3	4	9	(49)
Its standard of reporting is first class	1	2	3	4	9	(50)
It sometimes goes too far in invading people's private grief	1	2	3	4	9	(51)
It always has the latest national news	1	2	3	4	9	(52)
It is prepared to criticise *anybody* if it thinks they deserve it	1	2	3	4	9	(53)
It has too little news in it	1	2	3	4	9	(54)
It gives a good service to its advertisers	1	2	3	4	9	(55)
It hinders good industrial relations	1	2	3	4	9	(56)

	Card (40)	Col./ Code	Skip to

2. (a) Judging by what you have read in it, would you say the .... (PAPER) generally supports any one political party? IF YES Which? (57)

No	0	Q. 3
Yes—Conservative	1	
Labour	2	
Liberal	3	
Other (specify)	4	

(b) IF YES TO (a) Do you think it *does*, or *does not*, give fair coverage to the views of other political parties?

(c) IF DOES NOT AT (b) To which parties' views does it not give fair coverage? Any others? PROBE TO "NO" (58)

Does give fair coverage to other parties	0
Does not give fair coverage:	
To—Conservatives	1
Labour	2
Liberal	3
Other (specify)	

ASK ALL

3. (a) When employers and trade unions disagree, would you say the .... (PAPER): READ OUT: (59)

Reports both sides of things fully	1	
or—gives more space to the employer's case	2	
or—gives more space to the union's case	3	
or—does not print much about it at all	4	Q. 4

(b) UNLESS "NOT PRINT MUCH" AT (a) When it makes comments on disagreements between employers and unions, does the .... (PAPER): READ OUT: (60)

Tend to favour the employers	1
or—tend to favour the unions	2
or—try to judge fairly between them	3
Never makes comments	4

	Card (40)	Col./ Code	Skip to

4. (a) Do you know the name of the company which owns .... (PAPER)? (61)
   No 1
   IF YES What is it? .... (62–65)

(b) ASK ALL Do you know whether the company which owns .... (PAPER) owns any other newspapers? (66)
   Yes—owns others 1
   No—does not own others 2   Q. 5
   Don't know 3   Q. 5

IF YES TO (b) ASK (c) AND (d)
(c) About how many other newspapers does it own? (67)
   1–4 1
   5–9 2
   10–15 3
   16–19 4
   20 or more 5
   Don't know 9

(d) Does it own any other *local* or *regional* newspapers (whether daily, weekly or Sunday) which are sold *here*? (68)
   Yes 1
   No 2   Q. 5
   Don't know 3   Q. 5

(e) IF YES TO (d) Which other local or regional newspapers which are sold *here* does it own? Any others? PROBE TO "NO" (69)
   PROBE FOR EXACT TITLES

   ....
   ....
   ....

5. On average, about how long in all do you spend reading or looking at a particular issue of .... (PAPER)? (70)
   Less than 10 minutes 1
   10 minutes but under $\frac{1}{4}$ hour 2
   $\frac{1}{4}$ hour but under $\frac{1}{2}$ hour 3
   $\frac{1}{2}$ hour but under 1 hour 4
   1 hour but under 2 hours 5
   2 hours or more 6

P396 (78–80)

PART 3:
POSTAL SURVEY AMONG EDITORS AND JOURNALISTS

SUMMARY

Introduction

As part of a programme of research for the Royal Commission on the Press, Social and Community Planning Research carried out a postal survey among editors and senior journalists in order to obtain information about their present employment and responsibilities, their education and training and their past careers; their views were also examined on certain issues such as factors affecting the freedom of the press, the Press Council, trends towards concentration of ownership and State aid to the industry.

The sample of editors was derived from the *Newspaper Press Directory* and consisted of national, provincial daily and weekly newspaper editors and editors of periodicals published at least once a month and for which an ABC circulation figure is given. The response rate was 63% after two reminders and yielded 330 completed questionnaires.

The sample of senior journalists (defined as those who had been a journalist for three or more years and were not of junior or trainee status) was drawn from the membership lists of the National Union of Journalists and the Institute of Journalists; it covered those employed on national, provincial daily and weekly newspapers or periodicals and also those working in a freelance capacity. It included cartoonists, photographers and agency journalists, but not those whose main work was in public relations, book publishing, radio or television.

The response rate for the journalists was only 43% (911 completed questionnaires), too low for reliance to be placed on the results. The low response rate seemed to be mainly due to the out of date address and employment information on the unions' record cards, though bad publicity in the trade press at the time of the mail out may also have contributed; the sample is thus likely to be deficient in the more mobile sector of the profession. Because of the low response rate, we did not feel that the results of the questions about current work and responsibilities, career and training etc, could be presented without the danger of being seriously misleading; we have therefore presented only the answers to the attitude questions; these seem to differ from those given by the editors in ways that one would expect and thus suggest that the possible unrepresentativeness of the sample has not had a distorting effect on them; however, they must be accepted with reservation.

The vast majority of editors were men; only 7% were women and most of these edited magazines. The sample of journalists responding contained only a slightly higher proportion of women (17%), mainly working on magazines or as freelance journalists.

Editors' Current Position, Reponsibilities and Conditions of Work

Most of the editors were employees, only 5% being proprietors, and most were employed by organisations whose main business was newspaper or periodical publishing. Two-thirds of them claimed to work for a company that was part of a group, 40% for one of the major national or regional publishing groups that were listed on the questionnaire.

Over a quarter of the editors worked on more than one publication; in particular, about half of the editors of provincial evening papers did so, these additional publications all being local weeklies. As would be expected from the structure of the sample, the approximate circulation size of the publications edited varied enormously from provincial weeklies and magazines with circulations of less than 10,000 to major national newspapers and mass circulation magazines with circulations in excess of 500,000.

Most of the editors had been with their present company or group for some years, half of them for more than 10 years and a quarter for more than 20 years. Editors of provincial weeklies were particularly likely to have been with their company or group for many years. Those whose company was part of a group were more likely to have been with the company or group for many years than were those in independent companies, suggestion that groups offer a career structure. However, it seems that, whether the company is part of a group or not, promotion is possible within publishing companies since overall editors had been with their present company much longer than they had been in their present position.

Only a fifth of the editors were a member of the Board of the company for which they worked and half of these were members of the Board of a subsidiary company in a group. As would be expected from this and from the wide range of circulation sizes covered, the level of responsibility carried by editors varied considerably. All the editors of national and provincial morning and most of the editors of provincial evening papers had 20 or more journalists working under them; but about half the editors of provincial weeklies and the majority of magazine editors had less than 10 journalists under them; in the case of magazines, this no doubt reflects the tendency to make use of freelance journalists.

Three-fifths of editors claimed to have full responsibility for hiring staff and most of the rest had at least some say in consultation with management. They had less complete responsibility for firing staff. Editors of weekly newspapers and magazines were less likely than other groups to have complete responsibility for hiring or firing staff.

Where the editorial budget was concerned, editors were more likely to have responsibility for controlling its spending than for fixing its amount; only 14% had complete responsibility for fixing the amount in the budget and about half had some say in consultation with management, but over a quarter had little or no say. However, half had total responsibility for spending the budget and a further third had some responsibility in conjunction with management. Editors of national and provincial morning newspapers had more responsibility in both financial spheres as well as in the control of staff than did those in other groups.

We asked editors how they divided their time between editing work, administration and writing for the publication. On average, editing work seems to take up about half of their time; about a quarter is spent on administration and a fifth on writing for the publication; but these averages hide a considerable amount of variation: editors of national and provincial daily papers seem to spend between 40% and 50% of their time on administration compared with only around 25% for weekly newspaper and magazine editors; weekly newspaper editors spend over half their time in editing work while magazine editors spend an above average proportion of their time writing.

Editors appear to work long hours; on average, they claimed to have worked 48 hours during the previous week and this was thought by the majority to be a typical week. Editors of national and provincial dailies claimed to work the longest hours, averaging over 50 hours a week. Most of editors' time seemed to be spent in the office, only about eleven hours on average being spent outside the office.

The majority of editors had a contract of employment with no fixed expiry date and in most cases the amount of notice that had to be given on either side was at least three months; in 29% of the cases six months notice had to be given and twelve or more in 11% of the cases.

The majority of editors (84%) were in a pension scheme through their employment, 92% of those whose company was part of a group compared with 66% of those in independent companies.

About a third of editors said that they did some other paid work in addition to their main employment but this seemed to contribute only small amounts to their overall income. Income from employment varied widely, reflecting the variations in levels of responsibility: almost all the small group of national newspaper editors had earned £10,000 in the last year compared with an average of £7,500 for editors of provincial mornings; this latter group, though also small, showed very much more variation and the mean is thus not a very useful figure. Editors of provincial evenings on average earned £6,500 from their employment but again there was wide variation with a fifth earning under £4,000 and a quarter earning over £8,000. The average for editors of provincial weekly newspapers was quite a bit lower at £4,250 and showed rather less variation, three-quarters earning between £3,000 and £4,900; only a fifth of them did any other paid work.

The magazines covered in the survey were very heterogeneous and this is reflected in the wide range of salaries earned; the mean was around £5,500. Half of them did other paid work and a minority (13%), earned fairly substantial amounts (over £1,000) in this way.

Just over a third of editors were current NUJ members and 8% were IOJ members. Only 20% had never been a member of the NUJ.

Editors' Education, Training and Background

Compared with those occupational groups classed as "professional" in the Registrar General's classification of socio-economic grades, the formal level of education of editors is not high, reflecting the fact that the emphasis is on in-job training rather than on preliminary qualifications. In terms of the highest qualification received in formal education, editors are most similar to the "intermediate non-manual" grade, the grade into which journalists fall. According to the Registrar General's manual, editors fall into the "employers and managerial" grade and, in comparison with these, editors have a somewhat higher level of formal education than average.

Almost two-thirds of the small group of national newspaper editors and over a quarter of magazine editors had taken a university degree but very few in the other groups had done so.

It is normally required nowadays that entrants to the profession of journalism serve a three year apprenticeship and then pass a proficiency test, but conditions of entry were less strict in the past and there are still other avenues available by which editors can reach their positions. It is, however, interesting to find that only a third of the editors covered by this survey had been indentured. Over half the editors of weekly newspapers had been indentured but only 17% of magazine editors.

Various types of courses are available for trainees in journalism but two-thirds of the editors had taken none of them. Once again, editors of weekly newspapers were the most likely to have taken these courses. Day release was the most frequently taken (14% of editors) followed by in-company courses (7%).

As we have seen, almost all the editors had some management responsibility, but only 23% had had any management training; none of the editors of national newspapers had done so but 43% of editors of provincial dailies had done so.

Although only a third of editors had been indentured, three-quarters had entered journalism before they were 25 years old. Almost half had started their career as a journalist on a weekly newspaper; about three-quarters of editors of provincial mornings or weeklies had done so compared with only a fifth of magazine editors, the majority of whom had started their career on a magazine.

Although only a third said that they had been indentured, around two-thirds indicated that they had been of trainee status at the start of their career in journalism. The majority of those who said that they had been trainees said that they had become a senior journalist by the time they were 24 years old but less than a fifth had taken the proficiency test.

In a third of the cases, editors' first post as a senior journalist had been with a weekly newspaper, while a fifth had started with a provincial daily. Just under a quarter had held their first senior post on a magazine but these were almost all currently magazine editors.

Editors' and Journalists' Opinions of Journalism as a Career

At this point we move on to consider the answers to some of the attitude questions and bring into the picture the views of the senior journalists who replied to the survey as well as those of editors. It must be remembered that the response from journalists was low and the results must be treated with caution; however, there is usually less variability of response to attitude questions and any bias in the sample is thus less likely to affect these answers than those to the factual questions.

Two-thirds of the editors said that they enjoyed their present work as a journalist "very much indeed" and a further 20% enjoyed it "quite a lot"; the majority of senior journalists also claimed to enjoy their work but less than half (47%) said that they enjoyed it "very much indeed". This pattern of editors having more favourable opinions than journalists is seen throughout the questions about journalism as a career.

When asked to say in their own words what they liked and disliked about working in journalism, both editors and journalists mentioned two aspects particularly frequently, the variety and interest of the work and the creativity and scope for initiative. Editors also quite frequently mentioned the satisfaction of producing the publication but journalists were understandably less likely to mention this. Instead they were more likely than editors to value the independence and freedom of the work. Both groups quite frequently mentioned the satisfaction of meeting members of the public, of being able to influence events and of doing what they considered to be a socially useful job.

Both the editors and journalists on national newspapers were more likely than other groups to get satisfaction from feeling that they were able to influence events. Editors of provincial newspapers, especially mornings, were particularly likely to feel that their work was socially useful.

A third of editors did not mention any dislikes about journalism as a career compared with under a fifth of journalists. Editors most frequently mentioned "poor pay" (14%) as being what they disliked about their job (particularly mentioned by editors of provincial mornings); a similar proportion of journalists (17%) also mentioned this but rather more mentioned "long and unsociable hours" (23%), particularly on provincial newspapers.

Those in both samples were asked to rate journalism as a career compared with "other" professions on a number of job attributes concerned with working conditions, the enjoyment of the work itself and the influence of the work in the community at large.

Journalism as a career was not considered to be particularly good for "security of employment", "starting salaries" or for "long term salary prospects" by either editors or journalists, journalists giving it a poorer rating than editors for both "security of employment" and "starting salaries". It was also not considered to be easy to transfer from journalism to an alternative occupation. On all these attributes very few rated journalism as "very good" and between a third and a half rated it as "poor". Views were rather more favourable about the "prospects of employment on merit", especially among editors who presumably felt that they had had personal experience that this could occur.

The picture was very different when attributes concerned with the nature of the work itself were rated; the vast majority of both editors and journalists rated journalism as "very good" or "good" on "scope for creativity", "scope for initiative", "opportunity for using one's talents", "intrinsic interest" and "degree of responsibility" though this final attribute was not rated quite as highly as the other four. In every case, journalists were rather less favourable in their opinion than editors; except on "degree of responsibility" (where the rating was lower), about 45–50% of journalists endorsed the top rating position on each attribute, compared with 60–70% for editors.

Opinions about the influence of journalism in the community were not as extreme as those on the nature of the work but were also generally favourable. The majority of editors and journalists thought it "good" or "very good" for "the value of the work to the community", for "the opportunity it gave to influence events" and for its "status", though relatively few rated it as "very good" for "status" and around a quarter in both samples rated it as "poor" in this respect.

Opinions of Editors and Journalists on Some Major Issues

Press Freedom

In examining attitudes of editors and journalists to the question of threats to the freedom of the press, some broad comparisons can be made with answers given to a very similar question in the survey undertaken in early 1976 for the Royal Commission among local influential people (councillors, council officials, head teachers, trade union leaders and managing directors in local business and industry)[1]. Almost all the editors and journalists thought that there were currently threats to the freedom of the press compared with about half the local influentials; this difference must be interpreted with caution because the forms of questioning were slightly different, but the answers indicate the existence of a considerable amount of concern on the part of those working in journalism.

Editors most frequently picked out "costs and inflation", "printing and production workers/the unions" and "the Government" as being threats to the freedom of the press; the influential sample followed the same pattern, but at a much lower level of endorsement; they also gave more emphasis to "the unions" than did the editors, selecting it more frequently as a threat and also most frequently picking it as the "biggest threat". When editors were asked which was the biggest threat, "costs and inflation" and "the Government" were the only items mentioned with any frequency. Journalists also saw "costs and inflation" and "printing and production workers" as threats but compared with the editors they saw less danger in "the Government" and more in "libel laws", "advertisers", "proprietors and owners of newspapers", "the management" and "the Official Secrets Act/'D' Notices".

When asked whether they themselves felt that their work in journalism was affected by any undesirable pressures from these sources, editors again mentioned "costs and inflation" most frequently, followed by "advertisers", "libel laws" and "printing and production workers". Journalists, on the other hand, did not feel the pressures of "costs and inflation" so strongly, but mentioned "advertisers" and "the management" just as frequently. They also felt pressures from "libel laws" and "proprietors and owners".

The Press Council

The majority of editors and journalists were able to express opinions about the way in which the Press Council performed its function. On the whole, opinion was favourable though few in either sample rated it as performing its function "very well". When asked in what ways its aims or procedures should be changed, over half of both groups had no views, the only answer given with any frequency (and by only about one in ten of both samples) was that it should have "more teeth".

Just under a fifth of the editors had been involved with the Press Council compared with only 6% of the journalists; very few magazine or weekly newspaper editors had had any dealings with the Press Council but half or more of the editors of national and provincial daily newspapers had done so. The majority of them considered that the Press Council had dealt satisfactorily with the matter and also that the outcome had been satisfactory.

Both editors and journalists expressed respect for the Press Council, the majority of both samples saying that they would regard it as an important matter if they were censured by it.

---
[1] See Part 2.

The Growing Concentration of the Press

Concern has been expressed that the tendency for ownership of newspapers to be concentrated within fewer and fewer organisations might reduce the standard of service to the public; views of editors and journalists were therefore sought on a number of aspects of this issue. Journalists appeared to be more concerned than editors: about half the editors thought there was sufficient diversity of opinion represented by the national press, while a large minority thought there should be more; over half the journalists thought that there should be more diversity.

About half of both editors and journalists did not indicate that they thought that there were any sections of the public who did not get a fair deal from the national press; the other half of each sample who thought that sections of the public were neglected mentioned a large number of minority groups, indicating a lack of consensus of opinion on the subject. The only group mentioned with any frequency (by 21% of journalists but only 8% of editors) was "left wing/trade union/Labour Party views".

When asked to say for a number of aspects of press concentration whether they were harmful or beneficial, journalists expressed more critical views than editors and were less likely to have no opinion. Over half the journalists thought it harmful that there was a lack of directly competing daily papers outside London and that there was a dominance of one company in some magazine fields (compared with 35% and 45% for editors). Around a third of journalists thought it harmful that national and provincial dailies should be owned by the same groups, that daily papers should own weekly papers in the same area and that there should be press ownership in independent radio and television; for each item, the majority of editors had no views and the remainder tended to be fairly evenly divided in their opinion as to whether the situation described was harmful or beneficial.

When asked to give their views on press monopoly law, just under half the editors and journalists expressed a preference for keeping to the present position. But whereas the remainder of the editors were equally divided between those who wanted more and those who wanted fewer restrictions than at present, the majority of the journalists who wanted a change wanted to see more restrictions than at present; only one in ten, however, wanted to go so far as to have legislation passed to force large groups to sell off certain publications.

State Assistance for the Press

Just over a quarter of editors but almost half the journalists thought there was a case for state assistance for the press. In general, the editors were against the notion of state assistance while journalists were fairly evenly divided on the subject.

When they were asked to say, from a given list, what form state assistance should take if it was decided that it was a good idea, about half of each sample picked "tax concessions" as appropriate, followed by "subsidies for paper" and "cheap loans to publishers". Relatively small proportions favoured "a special fund for new publications", "cash payments to publications in difficulties", "reallocation of advertising revenue among papers" or "a national printing corporation".

INTRODUCTION

Objectives

As part of a programme of research undertaken by the Royal Commission on the Press, Social and Community Planning Research carried out a postal survey among editors and senior journalists.

The objectives of the survey were twofold: firstly to gain an overview of certain sectors of the profession by obtaining information about the training and past careers of journalists, their present position and responsibilities, their pay and conditions of work and views on journalism as a career; the second objective was to examine their views on certain major issues of importance to the Commission, namely:

factors affecting the freedom of the press;
the Press Council;
current trends towards concentration of ownership of newspapers in fewer organisations; and
the possibility of State aid to the industry.

Method

The method of enquiry was by postal questionnaire and the sample consisted of editors of national newspapers, provincial dailies, provincial weeklies and of periodicals and of senior journalists working on the same kinds of publication or in a freelance capacity. Photographers, cartoonists and those working in news agencies were included but those working mainly in book publishing, public relations or broadcasting were not.

A "senior" journalist was defined as a journalist who had either passed the proficiency test or was aged 25 or over. Junior and trainee journalists were excluded because a separate study had already been carried out among them concentrating specifically on training and recruitment.

Details of the sampling procedure are given in Appendix 1 and only a brief description is given here.

Editors: The objective was to obtain about 400 completed questionnaires—about 200 newspaper editors and 200 editors of periodicals. On the basis of an expected 70%–75% response rate, we needed to send out about 550 questionnaires.

Since there were only 19 national newspapers, the editors of all of these were included in the sample.

There are 96 provincial daily newspapers; about half the editors of these had already been covered in the study of journalist training; all of the remaining half (51) were therefore included in this study.

There was no adequate list of editors of weekly newspapers; since some edit more than one newspaper, a list of newspapers could not be used directly as a sampling frame. However, it was considered that a list of newspapers was likely to provide the best starting point. We therefore extracted from the *Newspaper Press Directory* the names of all the weekly newspapers and their editors and punched this information on to cards. The cards were then sorted by editor's name so that duplications could be removed. There were found to be about 440 editors of weekly newspapers; 185 of these were selected at random for coverage in the survey.

In order to obtain about 200 periodical editors, a mail out of 282 was required. The *Newspaper Press Directory* lists approximately 4,100 periodicals some of which are very specialised, infrequently published and have very small circulations. It was decided to restrict the sample to those published once a month or more often and for which an ABC circulation figure was given. This yielded a universe of 564 periodicals from which 282 were selected at random.

Senior Journalists: It was decided to use NUJ and IOJ membership lists as the sampling frame; the universe thus consisted of members of these two unions.

A sample of 1,600 was required divided broadly as follows:

Working on newspapers	1,000
Working on periodicals	300
Working in a freelance capacity	300.

Allowing for a response rate of 70%, about 2,300 names would have to be selected. We wanted to ensure that there were sufficient numbers working on national, provincial daily and weekly newspapers and had no information about the distribution of senior journalists in these categories. We therefore followed a two stage procedure; the first stage was to draw from the union lists a much larger sample than was required. Taking every sixth member from the union lists but dropping those selected who were ineligible (junior and trainee journalists, retired people, those in PR etc), a sampling frame of 3,161 names was compiled on cards which we were then able to stratify by type of journalist. Full details of this analysis are given in the appendix; the table below indicates how many were found in each of the main sampling categories, what the second stage sampling fraction was and how many of each were sent questionnaires.

	Sampling frame (1 in 6 from union lists)	2nd stage sampling fraction	No. selected for mail out
Freelance journalists	508	1·2	430
Periodical journalists	445	1·0	445
Newspaper and other journalists ...	2,208	1·6	1,420
	3,161		2,295

The Questionnaire

The questionnaire was based on a list of points to be covered supplied by the Royal Commission and was discussed with them at all stages of its development. The objectives of the study, the ground to be covered and the draft questionnaires were shown by the Royal Commission to the NUJ, the IOJ, the NCTJ, the GBNE, the Newspaper Society and the Periodical Publishers Association and their comments invited.

The draft questionnaire was piloted on a small sample of 12 editors and 18 senior journalists; interviewers called at newspaper and magazine offices and arranged appointments with the editor or a senior journalist. The respondent was asked to complete the questionnaire in the presence of the interviewer and to comment on any difficulties in answering the questions. Any criticisms of or objections to questions were also noted and discussed.

Two questions were of a sensitive nature, one on income and the other on political affiliation. Both were objected to by a few respondents at the pilot stage but not to the extent that we felt they needed to be dropped from the final questionnaire. However, on the basis of the pilot and of comments received from those shown the questionnaire, the question on political affiliation was changed from the form "If there were a general election tomorrow, how would you vote?" to "How did you vote in the last three general elections?"

The first part of the questionnaire differed for editors and journalists in order to cover for each their different types of work and responsibilities. The second part, which covered their attitudes, was the same for both samples. Both questionnaires are given in Appendix 3.

The Response Rate and Problems Encountered

The questionnaires to editors were sent to the addresses of the publications given in the *Newspaper Press Directory* together with a covering letter signed by the Secretary to the Royal Commission. Up to two reminders were sent to those not replying over a period of six weeks. The first mail out took place on 31 March 1976.

A total of 537 questionnaires was sent out to editors; nine were returned indicating that the person to whom it had been sent was no longer an editor leaving 528 as the eligible sample; 330 completed questionnaires were returned, a response rate of 63%. This was lower than we had hoped but acceptable. Although we do not know the extent to which the non-responders are atypical, they would have to be very different from the responders to make a major difference to the results. The level of response was similar in all groups except editors of provincial dailies who gave a better response rate than was the case in the other groups. (Full details of the response are given in Appendix 2.)

Several problems were encountered in conducting the survey among journalists. The union lists gave home addresses rather than work addresses and these were used for the first mail out which took place on 15 April 1976. The response was very low and, for the first reminder, addresses of the publications on which, according to the union lists, they worked were used (except, of course, for freelance journalists for which we continued to use home addresses). Since some journalists were given as working on publications that had ceased publication some years previously, we suspected that in many cases the information would be out of date but felt that organisations for which journalists had worked might be more likely to know their current address and to forward their mail than would be the case if the individual had moved house.

The mail out of the questionnaires coincided with the NUJ conference and the survey received a certain amount of adverse publicity in the trade press. This undoubtedly contributed to the poor response rate though it is not possible to say how much non-response was due to this and how much to out of date information in the union records.

In total 2,300 questionnaires were mailed out; 179 were returned indicating that the person to whom it had been sent was no longer working as a senior journalist or freelance journalist; there may, of course, have been others who were ineligible in this way but who did not bother to inform us; but for purposes of working out the response rate we can only assume that the remaining 2,116 were all eligible. Only 911 completed questionnaires were returned, a response rate of 43%. This is not an acceptable level of response as even a moderate degree of difference between responders and non-responders could affect the findings. Furthermore, response was worse in some groups than others, leading to possible imbalance in the sample; a response rate of 50% or more was achieved with senior journalists working on national and provincial daily newspapers or in agencies, of 46% among freelance journalists but only 35% among those on provincial weeklies and 29% for magazine journalists. These last two groups are likely to be the most mobile, which suggests that out of date information at the sampling stage was a major factor in the poor response; this is borne out by the detailed response rate analysis set out in Appendix 2 which shows that for a *known* 8% of the names selected the information about the present status and kind of work was not correct; 9% of those apparently eligible are known to have moved from the publication and/or home address given in the union records. Others among the 44% about whom nothing is known may fall into the same category. Information sent to us in some cases when questionnaires were returned incompleted indicated that, in at least some cases, the records were some years out of date: "I've been an editor for 3 years", "He hasn't worked here for at least five years". In one case it was reported that the person to whom the questionnaire was addressed had left about 20 years ago. It therefore seems that the major bias in the sample is likely to be in those characteristics associated with job mobility. These characteristics are likely to be reflected in the information covered in the first part of the questionnaire concerned with career, training and background, work conditions, etc; we therefore cannot claim with any confidence that the information gives a true picture of senior journalists and we therefore have not presented it in this report. We feel, however, that the attitudinal information obtained from senior journalists can be regarded in a different light. Although we cannot be sure that it accurately expresses the views of senior journalists as a whole, it does represent the views of those who wished to make their opinions known to the Royal Commission. The survey among senior journalists can thus be regarded as a means of enabling a large number of senior journalists from a variety of different types of occupation to make their views known to the Royal Commission, thus expanding the basis on which evidence is collected. The answers to the second part of the questionnaire to senior journalists are therefore presented but with the reservation that they represent the views of those choosing to make their opinions known to the Royal Commission and may not accurately reflect the opinions of senior journalists as a whole.

The Report

The first part of this report describes the results of the survey among editors in two main chapters; the first covers their current work and responsibilities and their career background; the second presents their opinions on major issues affecting the press that are of interest to the Royal Commission.

The second part of this report presents the opinions of the senior journalists to journalism as a career and to the major issues affecting the press. For the reasons given above, the information on current responsibilities and career background is not presented since it may mislead rather than inform.

The editors and journalists are treated throughout as separate samples; since the basis of selection was different, they cannot be added together though they can be compared.

Weighting of Results

Since different groups within the editors' and the journalists' samples were selected with different probabilities, weights had to be applied at the analysis stage so that information for the sample of editors and for the sample of journalists could be given in total. Details of the weights attached to each group are given in Appendix 1. The weights were applied on the computer arithmetically; thus a particular respondent's answer has been multiplied by the appropriate fraction before being added to those of other respondents. The weights were determined by the group from within which the respondent was selected; those whose questionnaire indicated that they had since changed to another group (eg an editor of a provincial weekly who was now an editor of a provincial evening) would thus still be given the weight appropriate to the group to which they had apparently belonged when selected (since this determined their probability of selection) even though in the analysis they are included in the group to which they now belong. Because of the small numbers in some of the subgroups, this leads to some apparent anomalies in the percentaged results.

The percentages are based on the *weighted* numbers in each group and weighted bases are given on each table. In the first few tables, the unweighted numbers in each group are also given so that the reader may be aware of the true size of each group. This is necessary as the weighting of the weekly newspaper and magazine editors is quite extensive.

EDITORS' RESPONSIBILITIES, CONDITIONS OF WORK AND CAREER BACKGROUND

Introduction

This section of the report first gives a brief description of the personal characteristics of the sample of editors and then looks at the current position and responsibilities of editors, their conditions of work, their education, training and previous career that led up to their present position; it finally examines their opinions of journalism as a career.

The editors who answered the questionnaire ranged from those who edit a major national daily with many journalists working under them to editors of small provincial weeklies or magazines with very few or even no journalists under them; some were editors of publications owned by large groups while others edited independent publications. Clearly, responsibilities of editors in these different situations could vary widely; we therefore examined the results in terms of the type of publication edited, by whether it was owned by a group or not and by numbers of journalists under the editors.

In interpreting the tables, the very small number of editors of national newspapers, of provincial mornings and of those in the residual "other" category[1] must be borne in mind as one person can represent about 9% of the sample. In the text, we talk in terms of broad proportions in referring to these groups rather than mentioning percentages.

Personal Characteristics

Very little information on personal characteristics of respondents was asked for since it was known from earlier work that journalists tend to resent it; only sex, age and marital status were therefore obtained.

The editors completing the questionnaire were almost all men. Only 7% were women and almost all of these were editing magazines or publications in the miscellaneous "other" category.

The age range of respondents was wide but, as one would expect with a sample drawn from people in senior positions, skewed towards the older age groups. Editors of national newspapers tended to cluster in the middle age range with over half in the 40–49 age group. Editors of magazines were spread through all age groups but had a larger proportion under 40 than any of the other groups.

---

[1]This "other" category included such publications as house magazines, freesheets, trade union news sheets, etc. Since it consisted of only six editors, the group has not been included in all the tables though it forms part of the total column.

Editors of provincial dailies and weeklies also covered a wide range of ages but tended on the whole more towards the older groups than national newspaper and magazine editors.

The large majority (83%) of the sample were married.

TABLE 3.001
SEX AND AGE OF EDITORS RESPONDING BY TYPE OF PUBLICATION

	Total	National	Prov. Morning	Prov. Evening	Weekly	Magazine	Others
Base: All (Unweighted)	330	11	9	38	103	163	6
(Weighted)	689	11	17	75	244	326	13
	%	%	%	%	%	%	%
SEX: Male	91	91	100	100	94	87	49
Female	7	—	—	—	2	11	51
Not stated	2	9	—	—	4	2	—
AGE: 20–29	8	—	—	3	6	12	—
30–39	22	18	11	13	24	22	67
40–49	31	56	22	36	24	35	15
50–59	23	18	56	31	20	23	—
60 and over	13	—	11	13	21	7	18
Not stated	3	8	—	3	5	1	—

Position and Responsibilities

Types of Publication Edited

Quite a large minority (29%) of the editors worked on more than one publication; 13% worked on two or more. These publications were not always of the same type; editors were therefore classified on the basis of the first publication that they entered in the questionnaire on the grounds that this was likely to be the most important one taking most of their time.

TABLE 3.002
NUMBER OF PUBLICATIONS WORKED ON BY EDITORS

	Type of publication (Main)						
	Total	National	Prov. Morning	Prov. Evening	Weekly	Magazine	Other
Base: All (Unweighted)	330	11	9	38	103	163	6
(Weighted)	689	11	17	75	244	326	13
	%	%	%	%	%	%	%
One	71	91	75	48	69	75	100
Two	17	9	14	39	17	14	—
Three	8	—	11	10	11	6	—
Four or more	4	—	—	3	3	5	—

Just under half the national newspaper editors responding worked on a daily and just over half on a Sunday newspaper. Only one of the editors of a national daily (including London evenings) or national Sunday newspaper claimed to be involved with more than one newspaper; what type was unspecified on the questionnaire by the respondent.

A quarter of the editors of provincial mornings dealt with more than one newspaper; in the main, these additional newspapers were local weeklies though a tenth also worked on a local evening.

About half the editors of local evening newspapers worked on more than one publication, over one in ten working on three or more; these additional newspapers were all local weeklies.

Rather fewer editors of local weeklies worked on more than one publication (31%) but almost half these (14% of the editors of local weeklies) worked on three or more. The additional newspapers were almost entirely other local weeklies. Presumably in some cases these were local variants of basically the same newspaper but with different titles.

A quarter of magazine editors worked on more than one publication, mainly other magazines. Of all the magazines edited by this group, 65% were trade and technical journals and 35% other kinds of magazine. About half the magazines edited by respondents were published monthly and a third were weeklies:—

Weighted Base: all magazines edited:	430
	%
Published weekly/bi-weekly	32
Twice a month	4
Monthly	53
Quarterly	4
Annually	2
Not stated	6

Since the magazine editors were all selected via a sample of periodicals published monthly or more often, the quarterly and annual periodicals must be secondary publications on which the editors work.

TABLE 3.003
PUBLICATIONS WORKED ON BY EDITORS IN ADDITION TO THEIR MAIN PUBLICATION

	Main Publication					
	National	Prov. Morning	Prov. Evening	Weekly	Magazine	Others
Base: All (Unweighted)	11	9	38	103	163	6
(Weighted)	11	17	75	244	326	13
	%	%	%	%	%	%
Total working on more than one newspaper	9	25	52	31	25	—
Type of Additional Publication worked on:						
National	—	—	—	—	—	—
Provincial mornings	—	—	—	—	—	—
Provincial evenings	—	11	—	—	—	—
Weekly newspapers	—	14	52	29	—	—
Magazines	—	—	—	2	25	—
House magazines	—	—	—	—	—	—
Freesheets	—	—	5	1	1	—
Other	—	—	3	—	—	—
Not stated	9	—	3	7	1	—

Percentages add to more than the total working on more than one publication because some people worked on three or more.

TABLE 3.004
DETAILS OF TYPES OF PUBLICATION WORKED ON IN TOTAL BY EDITORS
CLASSIFIED ACCORDING TO TYPE OF MAIN PUBLICATION WORKED ON
(Based on total publications edited by those in each group)

	Type of Main Publication						
	Total	National	Prov. Morning	Prov. Evening	Weekly	Magazine	Others
Base (weighted): total publications edited ...	968	12	23	124	352	442	13
	%	%	%	%	%	%	%
National dailies	1	42	—	—	—	—	—
National Sundays	2	50	—	—	—	—	—
Provincial mornings	1	—	73	—	—	—	—
Provincial evenings	8	—	9	60	—	—	—
Weekly newspapers	38	—	17	33	92	—	—
Trade & tech magazines	29	—	—	—	1	63	—
Other magazines	15	—	—	—	—	34	—
House magazines	1	—	—	—	—	—	31
Freesheets	1	—	—	3	1	1	15
Others	1	—	—	2	—	*	54
Not stated	3	8	—	2	6	1	—

The approximate circulation size of the main publications edited by respondents followed the pattern that would be expected with national newspapers having the largest circulations and the weeklies the smallest; magazines covered a very wide range.

TABLE 3.005
APPROXIMATE CIRCULATION OF PUBLICATIONS EDITED
(Where respondents edited more than one, only their main publication is included in this table)

	Total	National	Prov. Morning	Prov. Evening	Weekly	Magazine	Others
Base: All (Unweighted)	330	11	9	38	103	163	6
(Weighted)	689	11	17	75	244	326	13
	%	%	%	%	%	%	%
Thousands:							
Less than 10 ...	25	—	—	3	35	25	18
10·0–19·9	16	—	14	3	18	18	33
20·0–29·9	18	—	—	8	26	15	33
30·0–39·9	9	—	—	16	12	6	—
40·0–59·9	9	9	11	20	3	11	—
60·0–79·9	5	—	11	18	1	4	—
80·0–99·9	3	—	28	—	—	4	—
100·0–149·9	4	—	22	11	—	5	—
150·0–199·9	2	—	—	8	1	2	15
200·0–500·0	2	26	14	5	—	1	—
More than 500·0	3	65	—	—	—	3	—
Don't know/Not stated	5	—	—	9	4	6	—

Current Position

The majority of the editors responding to the survey were employed; only 5% were the proprietor of the publication they edited. Half of those who were proprietors edited a weekly newspaper and a third edited a magazine.

Those in employment were in the vast majority of cases employed by an organisation whose main business was newspaper or periodical publishing; 10% of magazine editors were employed by an institution or learned society.

Two-thirds of the editors worked for a company that was part of a group. The major national regional publishing groups were listed on the questionnaire and respondents were asked to say to which group they belonged, writing in the name of their group if it was not listed; 40% worked in a company owned by one of the listed groups and 28% in other groups.

TABLE 3.006
(A) PROPORTION WORKING IN COMPANY THAT IS PART OF A GROUP BY TYPE OF PUBLICATION

	Total	National	Prov. Morning	Prov. Evening	Weekly	Magazine	Others
Base: All (Unweighted)	330	11	9	38	103	163	6
(Weighted)	689	11	17	75	244	326	13
	%	%	%	%	%	%	%
In a group	68	82	100	63	74	66	33
Independent	31	18	—	32	25	34	67
Not stated	1	—	—	5	1	—	—

(B) GROUP BELONGED TO

	All working for group	Total sample
Weighted Base	475	689
	%	%
Reed/IPC	17	12
Thomson Organisation	11	8
Pearson Longman	7	5
Associated Newspapers	6	4
United Newspapers	5	3
East Midland Allied Press	4	3
News International	3	2
Morgan-Grampian	3	2
Home Counties Newspapers	1	*
Beaverbrook Newspapers	1	*
BPM Holdings	1	1
Surrey Advertiser and County Times	*	*
D C Thomson	*	*
Others	41	28
	100	68

Over three-quarters of the editors (78%) said that their job title was "editor"; other titles were:

Managing editor 6%
Editor and director 6%
Editor-in-chief 3%
Group editor 2%
Others 5%

Only a fifth were members of the Board and half of these (10%) were members of the Board of a subsidiary company in a group.

Editors were asked whether they specialised in any particular types of work but the question proved to be rather ambiguous and so were the answers given, confusing special types of editorial work (eg leader writing) with subject specialism, including occasions when the whole publication was a specialist one. We do not feel that meaningful results can be given on this subject.

Most editors had been with their present company or publishing group for some years; half had been with it for more than 10 years and only 12% for less than two years. Editors of provincial weeklies were particularly likely to have been with the same company or group for many years while magazine editors were most likely to have joined recently. Editors were more likely to have been with their company or group for a long time in the cases where the company was part of a group, suggesting that a group provides more career opportunities.

Editors had been in their present position for considerably less time than they had been with the company; whereas half had been with their company for more than 10 years, only 17% had held their present position for that time and a third had held it for two years or less, those editing magazines being particularly likely to have taken up their position recently.

TABLE 3.007

LENGTH OF TIME (a) IN PRESENT COMPANY AND (b) IN PRESENT POSITION

	Total	Type of Publication[1]					Company is:	
		National	Prov. Morning	Prov. Evening	Weekly	Magazine	In group	Not in group
Base: All (Unweighted)	330	11	9	38	103	163	228	100
(Weighted)	689	11	17	75	244	326	476	209
	%	%	%	%	%	%	%	%
(a) Present company								
2 years or less	12	—	—	8	6	20	9	21
3–6 years	18	30	11	8	17	22	16	27
7–10 years	17	17	—	8	14	22	18	14
11–15 years	13	17	36	11	12	14	14	11
16–20 years	11	17	6	15	15	8	14	6
21–25 years	10	9	22	16	8	9	10	7
Longer	17	9	25	35	26	6	18	14
Not stated	2	—	—	—	2	—	1	—
(b) Present position								
2 years or less	32	26	22	26	23	40	30	36
3–6 years	31	38	36	36	34	28	31	32
7–10 years	18	18	—	24	16	18	17	18
11–20 years	13	18	42	11	17	10	15	9
More than 20	4	—	—	3	8	2	3	4
Not stated	2	—	—	—	2	2	4	1

The small "other" category is included in the total column but is not given separately in the table.

Responsibilities for Staff

Some (6%) of the editors had no journalists, even trainees, working under them; these were all editors of magazines or "other" types of publication. All those editing national newspapers or provincial mornings had 20 or more journalists under them and the majority of editors of provincial evenings also had 20 or more under them. Around half the editors of provincial weeklies and more than three-quarters of magazine editors, however, had fewer than 10 journalists under them.

TABLE 3.008
NUMBER OF JOURNALISTS WORKING UNDER RESPONDENT

	Total	Type of Publication					Company is:	
		National	Prov. Morning	Prov. Evening	Weekly	Magazine	In group	Not in group
Base: All (Unweighted)	330	11	9	38	103	163	228	100
(Weighted)	689	11	17	75	244	326	476	209
	%	%	%	%	%	%	%	%
None	6	—	—	—	—	10	2	16
1–2	19	—	—	—	10	33	15	29
3–5	18	—	—	—	19	23	16	24
6–9	17	—	—	10	24	16	20	10
10–19	16	—	—	6	30	10	19	10
20–49	11	30	31	33	11	5	13	5
50+	9	70	69	51	1	—	10	6
Not stated	3	—	—	—	4	3	4	1

Over half the editors (61%) claimed to have full responsibility for hiring staff under them and most of the rest had at least some responsibility in consultation with management. They had less complete responsibility for firing staff, a greater proportion in each group sharing this responsibility with management. Editors of weekly newspapers and magazines and those with relatively few journalists working under them were less likely than the other groups to have complete responsibility for hiring or firing staff. This of course reflected to a large extent the fact that editors of weekly newspapers and magazines were likely to have relatively few journalists under them. Degree of responsibility for hiring and firing staff did not vary between those whose company was part of a group and those whose company was independent.

TABLE 3.009
RESPONSIBILITY (a) FOR HIRING, (b) FOR FIRING STAFF

	Total	Type of Publication[1]					No. of Journalists[1]		
		National	Prov. Morning	Prov. Evening	Weekly	Magazine	1–9	10–19	20–98
Base: All (Unweighted)	330	11	9	38	103	163	177	50	72
(Weighted)	689	11	17	75	244	326	376	112	136
	%	%	%	%	%	%	%	%	%
(a) Responsibility for hiring									
Complete responsibility	61	100	89	95	66	47	55	68	91
Some—in consultation with management	28	—	11	3	24	40	38	28	9
Little or no responsibility	4	—	—	—	6	4	6	2	—
Not applicable (no journalists employed)	6	—	—	—	—	10	—	—	—
Not stated	1	—	—	2	4	—	1	2	—
(b) Responsibility for firing									
Complete responsibility	47	91	89	70	55	33	39	58	77
Some—in consultation with management	42	9	11	25	35	55	56	36	21
Little or no responsibility	3	—	—	—	6	2	4	4	—
Not applicable (no journalists employed)	6	—	—	—	—	10	—	—	—
Not stated	2	—	—	5	4	—	1	2	2

[1] "Other" publications and those employing no journalists omitted as breakdown groups but included in total columns.

Financial Responsibility

Only limited information of a very general kind could be obtained in a study of this kind on the complex topic of the amount of responsibility carried by editors for the financial aspects of running a newspaper. Only two aspects were covered: the amount of responsibility they had for fixing the total amount of the editorial budget and the degree of responsibility they had for controlling the spending of the budget once it was fixed.

Few (only 14%) had complete responsibility for fixing the amount of the editorial budget and the proportion varied little by type of publication. Those whose company was not part of a publishing group, however, were rather more likely than other editors to have complete responsibility. These, of course, included the small number of proprietors in the sample.

Around half (54%) had some responsibility for setting the budget in consultatation with management but over a quarter (28%) had little or no responsibility. The editors of national newspapers and provincial mornings were the most likely to have a say in setting the editorial budget while editors of weekly newspapers were the least likely.

Editors were more likely to have complete responsibility for controlling the spending of their budget than for fixing the amount in it; half had total responsibility and a further third had some responsibility in consultation with management; only 10% had no responsibility and these were mainly editors of weekly newspapers. Those most likely to have complete responsibility were once again the editors of national newspapers and of provincial mornings. There was very little difference between editors whose company was part of a group and those who were independent or between those with varying numbers of journalists under them.

TABLE 3.010

RESPONSIBILITY (a) FOR SETTING THE EDITORIAL BUDGET, (b) FOR CONTROLLING THE SPENDING OF THE EDITORIAL BUDGET

	Total	National	Prov. Morning	Prov. Evening	Weekly	Magazine
Base: All (Unweighted)	330	11	9	38	103	163
(Weighted)	689	11	17	75	244	326
	%	%	%	%	%	%
(a) Setting editorial budget						
Complete responsibility	14	9	11	10	13	14
Some responsibility in consultation with management	54	91	89	50	38	64
Little or no responsibility	28	—	—	30	44	20
No editorial budget	2	—	—	8	2	1
Not stated	2	—	—	2	3	1
(b) Control of spending editorial budget						
Complete responsibility	50	91	69	48	34	61
Some responsibility in consultation with management	35	9	31	36	38	33
Little or no responsibility	10	—	—	5	22	4
No editorial budget	2	—	—	6	2	1
Not stated	3	—	—	5	4	1

Deployment of Editors' Time

In order to obtain a broad impression as to how editors deploy their time over their various functions, they were asked to indicate approximately how much of their time they spent in the average week on three aspects of their work: writing for the publication (articles, editorials, etc.), editing, including sub-editing, layout and commissioning articles, and administration, including personnel, financial and budgetary planning. 10% of the sample felt unable to give this information; since the proportion not answering varied from group to group, this 10% has been omitted in presenting the results.

Table 3.011 shows the results for each of the three job functions side by side for the total sample (less those not answering). As can be seen, there is quite a wide variation between editors in the amount of time spent on each function but general tendencies can be observed. These are pointed up more clearly by the means given beneath each column which show that on average editors spend about a fifth of their time writing for the publication, about half doing editing work and a little over a quarter on administration.

Because of the amount of variation within sub-groups of the sample and the small size of some of the groups, comparisons between editors of different kinds of publication can best be made in terms of mean amount of time spent. Table 3.012 shows the mean amount of time spent in each of the three functions by different groups of editors. There is not a lot of difference between the editors of national newspapers and provincial dailies; all three groups tend to spend relatively little time writing for the publication and more or less equal amounts on editing work and administration.

Editors of weekly newspapers spend rather less time than editors of national and provincial dailies on administration and more on editing work while magazine editors spend more time than any of the other groups on writing.

Those whose company is part of a group do not differ very markedly in the way they deploy their time from those in independent companies.

TABLE 3.011
AMOUNT OF TIME SPENT BY EDITORS IN THREE MAIN ASPECTS OF WORK
(10% of the sample failed to answer this question and have been omitted from the % base)

	Approx % of time spent on:		
	Writing for publication	Editing/ sub-editing etc	Administration
Base (weighted): All answering question	617	617	617
	%	%	%
Amount of time spent in average week:			
None	7	*	3
1–9%	17	1	7
10–19%	26	4	21
20–29%	21	9	25
30–39%	11	10	11
40–49%	10	20	15
50–59%	5	12	9
60–79%	2	27	6
80% or more	—	16	2
Mean	21%	52%	28%

TABLE 3.012
MEAN PERCENTAGE OF TIME SPENT ON THREE MAIN ASPECTS OF WORK BY TYPE OF PUBLICATION AND GROUP MEMBERSHIP

	Mean % of time spent in average week on:		
	Writing for publication	Editing/ sub-editing etc	Administration
Editors of:	%	%	%
National newspapers	9	51	41
Provincial mornings	16	35	50
Provincial evenings	12	46	44
Weekly newspapers	16	61	24
Magazines	26	48	27
Editors whose company is:			
Part of publishing group	18	53	30
Independent	24	51	25
Mean for all editors	21	52	28

The editors were asked to say for how many hours they had worked in the previous week and how many of these hours had been spent in and out of the office. They tended to work fairly long hours; the average was 48 hours and 43% said they had worked 50 hours or more. Most (75%) said that last week was typical though 6% said that they usually worked longer hours than they had done in the last week.

Only 3% worked less than 35 hours (and thus could be classed as part-time) and these were mainly magazine editors.

Editors of national newspapers seem to work the longest hours and show little variation; their average was 58 hours and none worked less than 50 hours during the previous week. Editors of provincial dailies worked only marginally shorter hours on average (55 and 52 hours respectively) but showed more variation; editors of weekly newspapers worked marginally fewer hours again (average 49 hours) and magazine editors were a little below this on average (47 hours), showing most variability as a group.

On average, editors spend 11 hours (just under a quarter of their time) out of the office and this did not vary very much by type of publication. Hours spent in the office showed the same trend as for total hours worked with editors of national newspapers working most hours in the office and magazine editors the fewest (but with considerable variation within this latter group).

TABLE 3.013
HOURS WORKED IN THE LAST WEEK BY EDITORS

	Total hours	Hours in the office	Hours out of the office
Weighted base: All answering	655	655	655
	%	%	%
None	*	1	8
0–9	*	1	41
10–19	1	4	31
20–29	1	10	11
30–34	1	14	2
35–39	8	19	1
40–44	25	26	*
45–49	18	17	–
50–59	31	7	*
60 and over	14	2	1
Mean	48	38	11

TABLE 3.014

AVERAGE HOURS WORKED LAST WEEK BY TYPE OF PUBLICATION

	Total hours	Hours in office	Hours out of office
All editors	48	38	11
National newspapers	58	52	11
Provincial mornings	55	46	12
Provincial evenings	52	44	10
Weekly newspapers	49	41	9
Magazines	47	34	14

The hours in the second two columns do not add to those in the first because of using grouped data to calculate means.

Conditions of Work

Here again it was not possible to obtain very detailed information in a postal survey; we asked only about contracts of employment, income and union membership.

Contracts of Employment

One in ten of the editors said that they had no contract of employment (in addition to the small number who were self-employed); 8% had a contract for a fixed period of time and two-thirds had a contract with no fixed expiry date. Editors of national and provincial dailies and of magazines were most likely to have a contract, most commonly one with no fixed expiry date.

Of those who had a contract, the amount of notice that had to be given on either side to terminate it was:

One month	11%	(Base is all editors with contracts)
Three months	45%	
Six months	29%	
Nine months	1%	
Twelve months or more	11%	
Period not fixed	2%	

Those who worked for national or provincial daily newspapers have been grouped together as the numbers in each with contracts of employment was too small for separate study. On the whole, these editors tend to have longer periods of notice than weekly newspaper or magazine editors.

Overall, 84% of the editors were on a pension scheme through their employment; almost all those editing national or provincial daily newspapers were in a pension scheme but 15% of editors of weekly newspapers and of magazines were not. There was also quite a marked difference between those whose company was part of a group and those in independent companies; 27% of the latter were not in a scheme compared with only 7% of the former.

TABLE 3.015
CONTRACTS OF EMPLOYMENT, NOTICE AND PENSION SCHEMES

	Total	Type of publication			Company is:	
		National/Prov.Daily	Weekly	Magazine	In Group	Independent
Weighted base (all)	689	103	244	326	476	209
Type of contract	%	%	%	%	%	%
No contract	11	6	19	6	10	14
Fixed period	8	13	9	7	—	11
No fixed period	68	74	58	77	77	58
Not applicable (self-employed)	5	—	4	6	8	9
Not stated	8	8	10	4	5	7
Amount of notice						
Weighted base (those with contracts)	550	95	169	284	401	145
	%	%	%	%	%	%
1 month	11	2	18	11	8	21
3 months	45	28	53	45	43	49
6 months	29	25	24	34	34	16
9 months	1	6	—	1	2	—
12 months or more	11	34	5	6	12	6
Period not fixed/other	2	3	—	3	1	8
In pension scheme						
Weighted base (all)	689	103	244	326	476	209
	%	%	%	%	%	%
Yes, through employment	84	97	82	82	92	66
Yes, other	2	—	2	2	1	6
No	12	3	15	15	7	27

Income

A third of the editors did at least some paid work apart from their employment as editor; this rose to almost two-thirds of the small group of national newspaper editors and to half of the magazine editors; only 5% of editors of provincial evenings and a fifth of editors of weekly newspapers did so, however.

There was little difference between those whose company was part of a group and those working for independent companies, but those with no or few journalists working under them were more likely than those with several journalists under them to do other paid work in addition to their employment as editor.

TABLE 3.016
PROPORTION DOING OTHER PAID WORK IN ADDITION TO EMPLOYMENT AS AN EDITOR
(a) By type of publication

	Total	National	Prov. Morning	Prov. Evening	Weekly	Magazine
Base: All (Unweighted)	330	11	9	38	103	163
(Weighted)	689	11	17	75	244	326
	%	%	%	%	%	%
Do other paid work	36	65	33	5	18	53
Do not	61	35	67	92	77	44
Not stated	3	—	—	3	5	3

TABLE 3.016—continued
(b) By Group Membership and Number of Journalists Working under Editor

	Company is:		Number of Journalists			
	In Group	Independent	None	1-9	10-19	20+
Base: All (Unweighted)	228	100	21	177	50	72
(Weighted)	476	209	43	376	112	136
	%	%	%	%	%	%
Do other paid work	38	31	58	42	28	19
Do not	59	67	42	56	72	80
Not stated	3	2	—	2	—	1

Respondents were asked to say how much they earned last year from all sources under three heads: from employment, from other journalistic activities and from non-journalistic activities. They were asked about earnings "last year" since they would have had to assess their income from all sources for their income tax return for the year 1975-76.

Most were prepared to say whether they did any additional paid work but 13% refused to give information about the amount of their income during the last year. This reduced the numbers in the smaller groups to a size that makes any comparisons with other groups unreliable. The information is thus presented in the main for the sample as a whole.

The average income from employment as an editor was just over £5,000 in the last year, but the range was very wide (see Table 3.017). A third indicated that they also obtained income from other journalistic sources but more than half of these (18% of those answering) said that this came to less than £500 in the last year; only 4% of those answering said that they had earned more than £2,000 in this way.

Only 7% indicated that they had obtained income from non-journalistic sources in the last year and only 3% said that they had earned over £1,000 in this way.

Almost all the editors of national newspapers who gave income information said that they earned £10,000 or more from their employment and none of them earned less than £9,000. Most of them had also had earnings from other journalistic activities but these additional sums were all under £1,000.

Editors of provincial mornings seemed on average to earn about £7,500 from their employment but the group answering was very small and the range wide; this mean is thus unreliable. Two-fifths said that they did other journalistic work but the amounts earned were all under £500.

Editors of provincial evenings earned around £6,500 on average from their employment but again there was considerable variation, ranging from a fifth who earned under £4,000 to a quarter who earned over £8,000. Very few of them said that they had any other source of income.

Editors of weekly newspapers indicated that they earned on average about £4,250 from their employment; this group is larger than those whose income is described above and there seemed to be less variation; apart from possible bias due to non-response, this information is therefore rather more reliable.

The distribution was:

Income from employment last year by editors of weekly newspapers

Weighted base: those answering	206
	%
£2,000–£2,900	8
£3,000–£3,900	37
£4,000–£4,900	38
£5,000–£5,900	11
£6,000–£6,900	3
£7,000–£7,900	2

Almost a fifth did other paid work, almost entirely journalistic; the amounts earned this way varied considerably but in over half the cases was under £500.

TABLE 3.017
SOURCES OF INCOME AND AMOUNT (TOTAL SAMPLE)

	Total Income	Income from employment	Income from other journalistic sources	Income from other sources
Weighted base (all answering)	603	603	603	603
£	%	%	%	%
Nil	—	—	68	93
100–400	—	—	18	4
500–900	—	—	5	*
1,000–1,900	1	1	6	3
2,000–2,900	3	3	3	*
3,000–3,900	20	24	1	—
4,000–4,900	27	30	*	—
5,000–5,900	18	18	—	—
6,000–7,900	23	16	—	—
8,000–9,900	4	4	—	—
10,000 and over	4	3	—	—

TABLE 3.018
INCOME FROM OTHER JOURNALISTIC ACTIVITIES

	Total	National	Prov. Morning	Prov. Evening	Weekly	Magazine
Weighted base (all answering)	603	8	15	56	208	298
	%	No. %	%	%	%	%
Income from other journalistic activities:						
Yes	32	(5) 62	40	4	18	46
No	68	(3) 38	60	96	82	54

Note: Bases for percentages do not add up to the number in the total column because the small group of other types of editor has been omitted.

Magazine editors were also a sizeable group but the variation in income within the group was very wide. The mean was around £5,500 and the distribution was:

	Income from employment last year by magazine editors
Weighted base: those answering	302
	%
£1,000–£2,900	2
£3,000–£3,900	17
£4,000–£4,900	30
£5,000–£5,900	25
£6,000–£6,900	12
£7,000–£7,900	7
£8,000–£8,900	5
£9,000+	4

Half the magazine editors did other paid work, mainly journalistic. Again around half of those doing other journalistic work earned relatively small amounts (under £500) but 13% of magazine editors earned £1,000 or more in this way.

There was little difference in income from employment between those whose company was part of a group and those in independent companies but those with several journalists working under them tended to earn more than those with none or only a few under them:

	No. of journalists under editor			
	None	1–9	10–19	20+
Average earnings last year from employment	£3,900	£4,650	£5,000	£7,200

Union Membership

Only 20% of the editors had never been a member of the NUJ but only 36% were currently members, two-fifths having given up their membership.

Almost half the editors of national newspapers were members of the NUJ; the majority of editors of provincial evenings and mornings had been members in the past but only 15% of evening editors and none of the morning editors were currently members.

Almost a third of the editors of weekly newspapers were currently NUJ members and a further half had been in the past. 45% of magazine editors were members but only a further 21% had been members in the past and almost a third had never been members.

Almost equal proportions of those in companies that were part of a group and of those in independent companies were currently NUJ members but a larger proportion of the latter group had never been members.

Only 8% of editors were currently IOJ members and only a further 6% had been members in the past. Half of the tiny group of national newspaper editors were current members but the proportions in all the other groups were similar to that for the sample as a whole.

TABLE 3.019
UNION MEMBERSHIP AMONG EDITORS
(a) By Type of Newspaper

	Total	National	Prov. Morning	Prov. Evening	Weekly	Magazine
Base: All (weighted)	689	11	17	75	244	326
	%	%	%	%	%	%
NUJ current member	36	47	—	15	31	45
—past member	40	35	75	82	51	21
—never	20	9	11	—	12	31
Not stated	4	9	14	3	6	2
IOJ current member	8	47	—	8	11	6
—past member	6	—	—	11	8	4
—never	81	44	100	77	74	86
Not stated	5	9	—	5	8	4

(b) By Group Membership and Number of Journalists

	Company is:		No. of Journalists			
	In group	Independent	None	1–9	10–19	20+
Base: All (weighted)	476	209	43	376	112	136
	%	%	%	%	%	%
NUJ—current	37	32	30	41	35	22
—past	44	33	14	32	51	65
—never	15	32	47	26	7	5
Not stated	4	3	9	1	6	7
IOJ—current	8	7	—	7	8	10
—past	7	4	5	7	6	4
—never	79	84	86	83	75	79
Not stated	6	5	9	3	10	7

Most of the editors who were or had been members of the NUJ had been members for some years:

Member of NUJ for: % (Base: All who were or had been members)

Less than 4 years	12
5–6	9
7–8	7
9–10	10
11–15	16
16–20	20
21–25	11
26+	15

Only 2% of editors currently held office in the NUJ but 30% had done so in the past (40% of those who were or had been members).

Education, Training and Background

In this section we examine schooling, training as a journalist and how the editors entered journalism and progressed in their career.

Educational Qualifications

A quarter of the editors continued their full-time education beyond the age of 18, over a third completed it between 17 and 18 and two-fifths completed it before the age of 17.

Less than one in ten of the editors of national newspapers completed their full-time education before the age of 17, compared with two-fifths of editors of provincial mornings and half of editors of provincial evenings and weeklies. Magazine editors showed most variation with 30% completing before 17 and 30% continuing until the age of 21, reflecting the wide variety of types of periodicals, including specialist journals, covered.

15% said that they had obtained no educational qualifications during their full time education; 42% had obtained nothing beyond "O" levels (or equivalent) and a fifth had "A" levels. A further 17% had a university degree.

A fifth (19%) had obtained an educational qualification after completing their full time education, 5% obtaining "A" levels in further education and 3% a degree.

Almost two-thirds of the national newspaper editors had taken a university degree and 29% of magazine editors but very few of any of the other groups had done so.

TABLE 3.020
AGE FINISHING FULL-TIME EDUCATION AND QUALIFICATIONS OBTAINED

	Total	National	Prov. Morning	Prov. Evening	Weekly	Magazine
Base: All (weighted)	689	11	17	75	244	326
	%	%	%	%	%	%
Age finishing full-time education						
15 or under	9	—	—	3	15	8
16	31	9	42	50	38	22
17	23	30	11	35	23	21
18	12	—	22	8	11	14
19–20	6	1	14	5	6	4
21 and over	18	53	11	—	4	30
Not stated	2	—	—	—	4	1
Highest qualification gained in full-time education						
None	15	—	25	8	15	17
"O" levels	42	9	31	52	53	35
"A" levels	21	30	33	30	20	16
University degree	17	62	11	—	5	29
Other	2	—	—	7	1	2
Not stated	3	—	—	3	6	1
Gained educational qualification in further education	18	9	—	8	15	22

The following table compares the highest qualification received by editors with that of three socio-economic grades in the general public: "professional" which includes doctors, lawyers, senior teachers, qualified accountants etc, and often requires a degree or equivalent qualification; "employers and managerial" which covers those in senior positions in business, industry, public service etc; "intermediate non-manual" which includes those in occupations such as nursing, some types of teaching post and others not usually requiring a degree. According to this system, editors are classed with employers and managerial, and senior journalists with intermediate non-manual. In terms of formal general educational qualifications, it can be seen that editors are considerably less well qualified than are those in the professional socio-economic grade, but are more likely to have a qualification than are those in the employers and managerial grade. Because of the requirement that those entering journalism should have "O" levels, they are most similar in their educational qualifications to those in the intermediate non-manual grade.

	Editors %	General Public (Males) in SEG		
		Professional %	Employers and Managerial %	Intermediate Non-Manual %
No qualifications	15	3	41	20
"O" levels	42	7	20	18
"A" levels or equivalent	21	30	19	36
University degree or equivalent ...	17	53	8	17
Other	2	5	12	9
Not stated	3	—	—	—

Source: *General Household Survey*, 1972.
Figures are given for occupied males only as being most comparable to the editors' sample.

Formal Training as a Journalist

The majority of journalists are nowadays required to start their career as trainees and are indentured for three years; they are then required to take a proficiency test. Many of those who are now senior journalists or editors of some years' standing may not have had to follow this procedure or may have entered journalism at a later age by some other route.

Only a third of the editors had been indentured. Just over a third of national newspaper editors and editors of provincial dailies had been indentured compared with over half the editors of weekly newspapers but only 17% of magazine editors.

Respondents were asked to say whether, as part of their training in journalism, they had taken any of a list of types of course or any other formal training in journalism. Two-thirds said that they had taken none of them. Editors of weekly newspapers were the most likely to have taken one or more of the courses.

None of the types of course had been taken by a large proportion of editors; day release was the most frequently taken (14%), followed by in-company courses (7%) and block release courses at a college of further education (4%); all the others had been taken by tiny numbers.

TABLE 3.021
TRAINING AS A JOURNALIST

	Total	National	Prov. Morning	Prov. Evening	Weekly	Magazine
Base: All (weighted)	689	11	17	75	244	326
	%	%	%	%	%	%
Was indentured	33	38	39	35	54	17
Took: one year pre-entry course	1	—	—	—	—	1
post-graduate diploma in journalism	*	9	—	—	—	1
day release course ...	14	—	22	18	19	8
block release course ...	4	—	—	6	6	3
in-company course ...	7	18	11	5	6	7
others	8	9	—	11	14	10
none	66	65	78	64	55	74

Management Training

Almost all the editors had at least some management responsibility but only 23% had had any management training. None of the editors of national newspapers had had any; those most likely to have taken some sort of course were the editors of provincial dailies, 43% of whom had done so.

The kinds of course taken were as follows:

Weighted base: All who had taken a course	155
	%
"In-company" courses:	
Newspaper management	17
Industrial relations	1
Other	13
Not "in-company":	
General management training	36
Industrial relations	4
Other	24
"On the job" training	12
Other	12

Entering Journalism and First Job

Two-fifths of the editors had entered journalism before they were 18 years old and three-quarters entered before they were 25. It is therefore not surprising that only two-fifths had had previous employment before becoming a journalist. Magazine editors were the most likely to have entered journalism after the age of 25 and to have had previous employment. Of those who had had previous employment, only 14% had been in the newspaper industry and 6% had been involved in another writing occupation.

TABLE 3.022
AGE ENTERING JOURNALISM AND PREVIOUS EMPLOYMENT

	Total	National	Prov. Morning	Prov. Evening	Weekly	Magazine
Base: All (weighted)	689	11	17	75	244	326
Age entered journalism:	%	%	%	%	%	%
16 or under	21	18	42	37	34	11
17	20	30	—	40	25	13
18–19	13	—	36	13	17	7
20–24	20	34	22	10	14	25
25–29	10	9	—	—	2	18
30+	13	9	—	—	6	23
Not stated	3	—	—	—	2	3
Employed before became a journalist/trainee	40	18	11	18	24	60

In order to establish whether journalists tended to have had connections with the industry before entering it, editors were asked what their father's occupation was and whether at the time of entering journalism they had had close friends or relations who had been in journalism.

Over a quarter (28%) said that they had had close friends or relatives in journalism but in only 8% of the cases had their father been connected with the newspaper industry.

The occupation of editor is classified in the Registrar General's socio-economic grading system as being in the professional and managerial category. We classified their father's occupation according to the same system: on this basis, journalism appears to be a career for the socially mobile as for only 28% of the editors had their father's main occupation also been in the professional and managerial grades. Just under a quarter had been in intermediate and junior non-manual occupations (eg junior management, minor professions not requiring a degree, clerical work, small scale own account businesses such as shop owner, etc); a third had been in skilled manual occupations but only a small proportion (6%) in semi- or unskilled manual occupations. Editors of weekly newspapers were the least likely to have had their father in a professional or managerial occupation.

TABLE 3.023
PREVIOUS CONTACTS WITH JOURNALISM AND FATHER'S OCCUPATION

	Total	National	Prov. Morning	Prov. Evening	Weekly	Magazine
Weighted base: All	689	11	17	75	244	326
At time entered journalism:	%	%	%	%	%	%
Had friends/relatives in journalism	28	9	33	30	29	27
Did not	70	91	67	68	69	72
Not stated	2	—	—	2	2	1
Father's occupation was journalist	6	—	11	10	7	4
Other job in publishing industry	2	—	11	—	1	2
Not in publishing	84	91	64	77	81	89
Not stated	8	9	14	13	11	5
Socio-economic grade of father's occupation:						
Professional/managerial	28	38	33	26	19	34
Intermediate and junior non-manual	23	18	11	21	19	26
Skilled manual	32	26	36	28	39	29
Semi- and unskilled manual	6	—	6	10	7	4
Other	2	9	—	—	3	2
Insufficient information	10	9	14	15	13	5

Almost half the editors (45%) had started their career as a journalist working for a weekly newspaper; the proportion rose to about three-quarters among those currently working as editors of provincial morning and weekly newspapers but was only a fifth among magazine editors, the majority of whom had begun their career working for a magazine.

A third of the editors had learnt about their first job by writing to the editor, another third through personal contacts and a fifth through press advertisements. More than three-quarters were recruited by interview only and no more than 16% also had an entrance test.

TABLE 3.024

FIRST JOB IN JOURNALISM BY TYPE OF CURRENT PUBLICATION

	Total	National	Prov. Morning	Prov. Evening	Weekly	Magazine
Weighted base: All	689	11	17	75	244	326
	%	%	%	%	%	%
(a) Type of publication first worked on						
National daily/London evening	1	18	—	—	—	2
Provincial daily	15	35	25	42	14	10
Weekly	45	47	75	51	78	18
Trade or technical magazine	22	—	—	—	3	44
Other periodical	10	—	—	—	1	19
News agency	2	—	—	5	3	2
Other	3	—	—	3	—	3
Not stated	2	—	—	—	1	2
(b) How found out about job						
Wrote to editor	33	47	36	53	42	20
Personal contact	32	18	39	28	32	34
Press advertisement	18	9	14	11	10	27
Already worked in other capacity for publication	6	—	—	3	6	7
Through university/schools career officer	4	18	—	3	6	3
Other	5	8	11	2	2	7
Not stated	2	—	—	—	2	2
(c) How recruited						
Personal interview	77	82	89	87	72	79
Interview and entrance test	16	9	11	11	21	14
Submitted article	2	—	—	—	1	2
Other/not stated	5	9	—	—	6	5

Becoming a Senior Journalist

For those who enter the profession of journalism as trainees, there is a fairly clear demarcation between the status of trainee or junior journalist and that of senior journalist; nowadays the transition is usually marked by passing a proficiency test and by transfer to a different salary scale. However, the distinction may not always have been so clear and not all editors had followed this route to their present position.

Over a third (36%) of the editors said that they had never had trainee status; the proportion was lower among editors of provincial evenings and weeklies but higher among magazine editors.

Three-quarters of those who had been a trainee or junior journalist said that they had become a senior journalist by the time they were 24 years old; 23% had done so by the age of 21. Only 17% of those who had been a trainee (11% of all editors) had taken the proficiency test.

TABLE 3.325
PROPORTION WHO WERE NEVER A TRAINEE JOURNALIST BY TYPE OF CURRENT PUBLICATION

	Total	National	Prov. Morning	Prov. Evening	Weekly	Magazine
Weighted base: All	689	11	17	75	244	326
	%	%	%	%	%	%
Was never a trainee	36	35	47	14	21	52

TABLE 3.026
AGE THAT BECAME A SENIOR JOURNALIST AND WHETHER TOOK PROFICIENCY TEST

Weighted base: All those who were trainees	433
(a) Age became senior journalist:	%
21 or under	23
22–23	20
24	33
25–29	12
30 or over	7
Not stated	5
(b) Took proficiency test:	
Yes	17 (=11% of all editors)
No/Not stated	83

The editors were asked about their first job as a senior journalist (ie when they rose from trainee/junior status): 14% of them said that the job they were now doing was their first as a senior journalist; a third said that their first senior journalist post had been with a weekly newspaper, 23% with a magazine (these being almost entirely currently magazine editors) and 11% with a provincial evening newspaper.

Almost half said that their first senior journalist job had been as general reporter; this rose to about three-quarters in the case of editors of provincial dailies and weeklies. Almost a quarter had been executive or desk personnel (eg news editor or deputy editor) in their first senior post and 12% had been a general or feature sub-editor.

TABLE 3.027
FIRST JOB AS A SENIOR JOURNALIST

	Total	National	Prov. Morning	Prov. Evening	Weekly	Magazine
Weighted base: All	689	11	17	75	244	326
	%	%	%	%	%	%
Present work is first senior job	14	9	—	6	7	21
(a) Type of publication						
National newspaper	2	26	—	3	—	2
Provincial daily	19	30	58	51	18	11
Weekly newspaper	34	9	42	38	65	11
Trade or technical magazine	18	—	—	—	3	35
Other magazine	5	—	—	—	—	10
Other	3	17	—	—	2	6
Not stated	5	9	—	2	5	4
(b) Position held						
Executive/desk personnel	23	35	—	—	6	43
General or feature sub-editor	12	30	22	23	3	15
General reporter	47	9	78	71	75	21
Critic/feature writer	4	18	—	—	1	6
Special reporter	3	—	—	—	—	7
Sports reporter/sub-editor	3	—	—	6	5	1
Other	4	—	—	—	5	4
Not stated	4	8	—	—	5	3

Other Jobs held as Senior Journalist

In addition to the 14% whose present work was their first work as a senior journalist, a third of the editors had done no other job as a senior journalist between their first and their present job; we thus have:

14% in their first senior job;
34% in their second senior job;
52% who had held three or more senior journalist jobs.

Those who had done intermediate jobs had worked on a wide range of types of publication in them:

Weighted base: All who had done intermediate jobs	352
Had worked on:	%
National daily newspaper	14
National Sunday newspaper	11
Provincial morning newspaper	20
Provincial evening newspaper	28
Weekly newspaper	23
Trade or technical magazine	22
Other magazine	12
House publication	11
National news agency	5
Local news agency	3
In public relations	6
In a freelance capacity	24
Other	16

Work on a National Newspaper

Including those currently working on a national newspaper (2% of the sample), 11% of the editors had done so altogether. Just over half of this small group had started work on a national newspaper under the age of 25 while just under half had been older; a quarter had been over 30 but only 7% over 35 years of age.

The most common ways in which those who had worked on national newspapers had first obtained such a position were:

Weighted base: Those who have ever worked on a national newspaper	73
	%
Wrote to the editor	34
Personal contacts	16
Worked for it first in a freelance capacity	16
Invited to join by editor	12
Answered a press advertisement	5
Transferred to national from provincial paper in same group	3
Other	7
Not stated	7

The capacities in which they were employed in their first job on a national newspaper were:

	%
Executive or desk personnel	11
General or feature sub-editor	44
General reporter	23
Special reporter	10
Critic or feature writer	5
Sports reporter or sub-editor	3
Other	4

Opinions of Journalism as a Career

We now explore editors' general opinions about working in journalism and then describe their views on a number of specific aspects of journalism as a career.

General Opinions

Two-thirds of the editors said that, taking all aspects into account, they enjoyed their present work as a journalist "very much indeed" and a further 20% said that they enjoyed it "quite a lot". Editors of national newspapers were most enthusiastic about their work.

TABLE 3.028

HOW MUCH EDITORS ENJOY THEIR PRESENT WORK AS A JOURNALIST

	Total	Type of Publication					Company is:	
		National	Prov. Morning	Prov. Evening	Weekly	Magazine	In group	Independent
Weighted base: All	689	11	17	75	244	326	476	209
	%	%	%	%	%	%	%	%
Very much indeed	68	91	75	68	62	71	71	63
Quite a lot	20	9	11	21	25	17	18	24
Fair amount	3	—	14	—	4	2	2	5
Not very much	2	—	—	—	2	3	3	1
Very little	—	—	—	—	—	—	—	—
Not at all	*	—	—	—	1	—	—	1
Don't know/ Not stated	6	—	—	11	6	7	7	6

Respondents were asked to say in their own words what they liked and then what they disliked about journalism.

Two aspects were mentioned particularly frequently as being liked: the scope that journalism gave for the use of creativity and initiative (38%) and the variety, pace and excitement of the work (36%). In addition, a quarter mentioned the satisfaction of producing the publication and of seeing one's work published. Almost a fifth liked the feeling of being involved in, and perhaps being able to influence, events that editing a newspaper gave; a similar proportion enjoyed the opportunity it gave to meet all sorts of people; a tenth mentioned that they enjoyed meeting important and influential people in the course of their work; 14% liked the feeling that it was a socially useful and responsible job.

Editors of national newspapers were particularly likely to mention being involved in and influencing events as something they liked. The editors of provincial newspapers, especially mornings, were more likely than the other groups to say that they felt that their work was socially useful and responsible. Magazine editors particularly mentioned the creative aspects of the work.

Fewer editors mentioned any dislikes about their work than had mentioned likes; 15% said there was nothing they disliked and 18% did not answer the question at all.

The most frequent criticism was "poor pay" (14%), mentioned particularly by the editors of provincial morning newspapers. Long and awkward hours of work were also mentioned by one in ten; time pressures, too much administration and problems with the unions were each mentioned as disliked by 7%.

TABLE 3.029

WHAT EDITORS LIKE AND DISLIKE ABOUT WORKING IN JOURNALISM
(Spontaneous answers to open question)

	Total	National	Prov. Morning	Prov. Evening	Weekly	Magazine
Weighted base: All	689	11	17	75	244	326
Main aspects liked:	%	%	%	%	%	%
Creativity and scope for initiative	38	44	36	24	28	47
Variety and interest	36	26	22	41	38	36
Satisfaction of producing a finished product	24	9	28	23	25	22
Meeting the public	19	—	—	8	26	18
Ability to influence events	18	53	28	15	18	18
Socially useful	14	9	58	28	21	4
Independence and freedom	9	—	—	5	4	14
Meeting interesting and important people	9	9	11	3	9	10
Like to inform and educate	8	9	—	8	6	10
Travel	8	—	11	—	1	15
Stimulating colleagues	7	35	—	10	5	7
Challenging	5	18	14	5	3	5
Other answers	16	23	22	14	12	16
Main aspects disliked:						
Long and unsociable hours	10	26	—	—	12	11
Poor pay	14	—	33	8	14	15
Time pressures	7	—	—	3	10	6
Too much administration	7	9	11	21	2	9
Union interference/restrictions	7	—	11	10	7	7
Poor quality of staff	6	—	—	8	10	3
Advertising pressures	5	—	—	3	5	6
Criticism from public	4	9	—	—	5	6
Poor management	3	—	—	—	3	5
Boredom	3	—	11	—	1	4
Other answers	17	18	6	11	21	17
Nothing disliked	15	30	39	21	10	15
Not answered	18	18	—	25	21	15

In view of these mainly favourable attitudes towards their work, it is not surprising to find that 87% of editors expect to continue to work in journalism for the foreseeable future. Only 3% said that they would almost certainly change and these were almost all magazine editors.

TABLE 3.030
WHETHER EXPECTS TO CONTINUE IN JOURNALISM OR EXPECTS TO CHANGE

	Total	National	Prov. Morning	Prov. Evening	Weekly	Magazine
Weighted base: All	689	11	17	75	244	326
	%	%	%	%	%	%
Expects to continue in journalism	87	91	86	97	94	81
May change career	6	—	—	—	4	9
Almost certainly will change	3	—	—	—	1	5
Don't know/Not stated	4	9	14	3	1	4
Journalism is not main work at present	1	—	—	—	—	1

Editors' Specific Opinions about Journalism as a Career

Respondents were asked to rate journalism as a career compared with "other professions" on thirteen job attributes. The rating scale was:

Very good

Good

Poor

Very poor.

The attributes can be divided into three groups; those concerned with conditions of work, those to do with the enjoyment of the work for its own sake, and those concerned with the influence of the work on the community at large.

Conditions of Work

Only 7% rated journalism as "very good" for security of employment though over half rated it as "good"; however, 35% rated it as "poor" in this respect. The patterns of answers were very similar when editors were asked to rate journalism in terms of starting salary and of long term salary prospects; in each case, over a third rated it as "poor" and only a tiny proportion said it was "very good". In both cases, the editors of national newspapers had a more favourable view and the editors of provincial mornings a less favourable opinion than the other groups.

Opinion of the opportunities for promotion on merit were considerably more favourable with 25% saying "very good" and a further 59% rating it as "good". But on the whole it was not regarded as particularly easy to move from journalism into alternative occupations, 50% rating it as "poor" in this respect.

TABLE 3.031

JOURNALISM AS A CAREER: RATINGS ON CONDITIONS OF WORK

	Total	National	Prov. Morning	Prov. Evening	Weekly	Magazine
Weighted base: All	689	11	17	75	244	326
Security of employment	%	%	%	%	%	%
Very good	7	—	—	15	11	3
Good	54	65	89	65	61	46
Poor	31	35	—	16	25	40
Very poor	4	—	11	—	1	7
Don't know/Not stated	3	—	—	5	2	4
Prospect of promotion on merit						
Very good	25	74	39	41	29	16
Good	59	26	50	51	56	64
Poor	11	—	11	3	12	12
Very poor	2	—	—	—	2	2
Don't know/Not stated	4	—	—	5	1	5
Starting salaries						
Very good	5	47	6	8	4	4
Good	45	35	47	62	48	40
Poor	36	18	47	25	37	38
Very poor	10	—	—	—	11	14
Don't know/Not stated	4	—	—	5	1	5
Long term salary prospects						
Very good	6	38	17	3	7	4
Good	44	44	—	46	45	45
Poor	40	18	50	38	43	40
Very poor	5	—	33	3	5	6
Don't know/Not stated	5	—	—	11	1	6
Ease of movement to alternative occupations						
Very good	8	9	22	8	5	9
Good	38	9	31	25	43	39
Poor	41	35	22	52	45	36
Very poor	9	30	14	8	6	11
Don't know/Not stated	4	18	11	8	1	5

Enjoyment of the Work

As would be expected from the things that the editors said spontaneously that they liked about journalism, ratings for the items grouped under this heading were in general much higher than for those relating to conditions of work: almost all rated journalism as good for "scope for creativity", 69% rating it as "very good". Most also rated it as good for "scope for initiative", 58% rating it as "very good". Most rated journalism as being good for "degree of responsibility" though rather fewer in this case (42%) rated it as "very good". On these three attributes, the ratings by the national newspaper editors were particularly high while those from magazine editors tended to be below average.

The vast majority thought journalism was good in the extent to which it gave one an opportunity to use one's talents and 61% thought it "very good" in this respect; very similar ratings were given to the "intrinsic interest of the work".

TABLE 3.032

JOURNALISM AS A CAREER:
RATINGS ON ENJOYMENT OF THE WORK

	Total	National	Prov. Morning	Prov. Evening	Weekly	Magazine
Weighted base: All	689	11	17	75	244	326
	%	%	%	%	%	%
Scope for creativity						
Very good	69	74	75	72	67	69
Good	28	26	25	23	32	28
Poor/Very poor	1	—	—	—	—	1
Don't know/Not stated	2	—	—	5	1	3
Scope for initiative						
Very good	58	82	61	75	62	51
Good	37	18	39	20	35	44
Poor/Very poor	1	—	—	—	2	1
Don't know/Not stated	3	—	—	5	1	4
Degree of responsibility						
Very good	42	82	39	46	51	34
Good	51	18	47	51	47	56
Poor/Very poor	3	—	—	—	2	5
Don't know/Not stated	3	—	14	3	1	5
Opportunity for using one's talent						
Very good	61	56	64	62	66	56
Good	37	44	36	33	32	40
Poor/Very poor	1	—	—	—	2	—
Don't know/Not stated	2	—	—	5	—	4
Intrinsic interest of the work						
Very good	64	82	75	67	60	65
Good	33	18	25	28	40	30
Poor/Very poor	*	—	—	—	—	1
Don't know/Not stated	3	—	—	5	—	4

Influence in the Community at Large

The three items grouped under this heading also received high positive ratings though not quite as favourable as those concerned with the enjoyment of the work.

Over 90% rated journalism as good for its value to the community but the ratings were divided evenly between "good" and "very good". Editors of provincial dailies and weeklies were most likely to rate the work as "very good" in this respect while magazine editors gave the least favourable ratings.

Over four-fifths rated journalism as good for the opportunity it gives to influence events but only a third rated it as "very good" in this respect. The editors of national and provincial morning papers gave the highest ratings.

Finally, respondents were asked to rate journalism for "status"; 70% rated it as good but only 15% rated it as "very good" and 24% rated it as "poor" or "very poor".

TABLE 3.033
JOURNALISM AS A CAREER:
RATINGS ON ITS INFLUENCE IN THE COMMUNITY

	Total	National	Prov. Morning	Prov. Evening	Weekly	Magazine
Weighted base: All	689	11	17	75	244	326
	%	%	%	%	%	%
Value of work to community						
Very good	44	38	75	57	64	26
Good	47	44	25	38	35	60
Poor	5	9	—	—	1	8
Very poor	1	—	—	—	—	—
Don't know/Not stated	3	9	—	5	—	6
Opportunity to influence events						
Very good	34	47	42	26	39	32
Good	51	44	36	61	51	49
Poor	11	9	22	3	10	14
Very poor	1	—	—	3	—	2
Don't know/Not stated	3	—	—	8	—	4
Status						
Very good	15	30	17	8	16	16
Good	55	35	47	57	56	55
Poor	21	9	36	19	21	20
Very poor	3	—	—	3	4	3
Don't know/Not stated	6	26	—	13	3	6

EDITORS' OPINIONS ON SOME MAJOR ISSUES

Introduction

We look now at editors' perceptions and opinions with regard to some major issues concerning the press that were of particular interest to the Royal Commission.

Threats to Freedom of the Press

In a study among local influential people carried out in early 1976 for the Royal Commission[1], respondents were asked whether they thought the freedom of the press was now in danger; if they thought it was, then they were presented with a list of possible factors affecting press freedom and asked which they thought represented any threat and which one was the biggest threat. Pursuing this same theme, a similar question was asked of editors; the question differed in that, since it was a self-completion questionnaire and respondents could see what the next question was, the preliminary question "Do you consider that the freedom of the press is now in danger?" was not asked; respondents were simply presented with a list of factors, to which was added the category "None", and asked to say which, if any, presented any threat to the freedom of the press. The list presented was modified slightly in that "public relations people" was added and "the unions" was changed to "the printing and production work force". Nonetheless, a broad comparison between the sample of local influential people and the sample of editors can be made.

The local influential people included local councillors and officials, head teachers, managing directors in local business and industry and local trade union leaders; it is therefore particularly relevant to compare their views with those of editors of provincial daily and weekly newspapers.

Just over half (52%) of the sample of local influential people thought that the freedom of the press was in danger but 92% of the editors indicated that they thought so by marking at least one of the listed items as presenting a threat. This difference must be interpreted with caution since the variation in question form is particularly likely to have an influence on these proportions, but it is very large and suggests that editors have greater awareness of pressures on the press.

The editors endorsed more items than did the local influential people; this is probably partly due to the different form of questionnaire administration, self-completion giving them longer to think over the list, but may also reflect again their greater awareness of the pressures to which the press is subject. The items most frequently given by the editors as presenting a threat to the

---
[1] See Part 2.

freedom of the press were "costs and inflation" (59%), "printing and production workers" (50%, plus an additional 2% mentioning "the unions" as such under other answers) and "the Government" (47%). These were also the three items mentioned most frequently by the local influential people but with a rather different emphasis: to them, "the printing unions" were most frequently seen as a threat and were also selected most frequently as presenting the biggest threat. When the editors were asked which items presented the biggest threat, "the Government" (23%) and "costs and inflation" (20%) were selected much more frequently than "printing and production workers" (8%).

TABLE 3.034
THREATS TO THE FREEDOM OF THE PRESS

	Any Threat							Biggest Threat	
	Editors						Local Influentials	Editors	Local Influentials
	Total	National	Prov. Morning	Prov. Evening	Weekly	Magazines			
Base: All	689	11	17	75	244	326	350	689	350
	%	%	%	%	%	%	%	%	%
Costs/inflation	59	70	64	70	54	59	27	20	10
Printing and production workers/Trade unions	52	65	64	55	47	55	40	10	16
The Government	47	44	72	64	47	41	25	23	10
Libel laws	39	62	28	56	41	34	6	5	1
Advertisers	32	35	—	11	22	46	9	4	1
Political parties	30	26	22	43	32	26	19	7	4
Proprietors/owners	26	44	11	13	17	36	18	2	4
Journalists	25	26	47	46	25	18	12	3	1
The management	20	26	—	11	13	27	6	2	*
Official Secrets Act/'D' Notices	19	62	14	31	12	21	10	*	1
Public relations people	11	35	—	11	12	10	N/A	1	N/A
Others	5	9	—	8	11	1	3	3	2
None/No threat	3	—	—	—	4	3	45	4	45
Don't know/Not answered	5	9	14	—	5	6	3	16	2

Quite large proportions of both the editors and the local influential people considered that "the proprietors or owners" of the newspapers, and "political parties" presented a threat to the freedom of the press but similar proportions of editors also thought that the "libel laws" and "advertisers" were a threat while relatively few members of the local influential sample selected these items.

The editors of national and provincial daily papers were particularly likely to mention "costs and inflation" as being a threat; the editors of provincial dailies mentioned "the Government" and "journalists" more frequently than other groups while magazine editors particularly mentioned "advertisers".

The editors were then asked whether their own work in journalism was affected by any undesirable pressures from any of these sources. Again, "costs and inflation" was the most frequently mentioned by all groups (32% overall). followed by "advertisers" (15%), the "libel laws" (14%) and "production and printing workers" (12%).

It is interesting to note the relatively greater importance of "advertisers" in this context but they were *only* mentioned by editors of weekly newspapers (13%) and of magazines (21%) whereas the "libel laws" were mentioned more by the national and provincial daily editors and "printing and production workers" by all groups.

TABLE 3.035

UNDESIRABLE PRESSURES PERCEIVED BY EDITORS ON THEIR WORK

	Total	National	Prov. Morning	Prov. Evening	Weekly	Magazine
Weighted base: All	689	11	17	75	244	326
	%	%	%	%	%	%
Costs and inflation	32	26	33	31	30	33
Advertisers	15	—	—	—	13	21
Libel laws	14	18	22	31	13	12
Printing and production workers	12	18	17	8	14	11
The Government	9	9	6	21	9	6
The management	8	—	—	—	6	13
Journalists	6	9	11	10	12	2
Proprietors/owners	6	—	—	—	5	8
Public relations people	5	—	—	—	3	7
Political parties	3	—	—	11	6	1
Others	4	18	—	—	8	9
None	20	26	11	21	21	20
Don't know / Not stated	22	38	39	24	27	16

Political Affiliation

Pressure on editors might also arise if their own political views differed markedly from those of their publication. They were therefore asked how they had voted in the last three general elections and whether their views were to the left or right of those of the publication they edited.

A fifth of the editors did not answer the question on how they voted, making it impossible to examine differences between subgroups. Based on those answering, the distributions at the three elections compared with the voting behaviour of the population as a whole are given below and are with those in social classes AB. These comprise the top two grades—professional and managerial—of the social classification system devised by the Institute of Practitioners in Advertising and widely used in readership and market research. In this system, editors would be classified as AB.

The proportion of editors voting for each of the three main political parties has remained remarkably constant over the three elections. This is in contrast with the pattern among the general voting public which shows a small decline in the proportion of Labour voters, a somewhat larger decline in the proportion of Conservative voters, and more than a doubling in the size of the Liberal vote.

The trend among voters in the social classes AB (professional and managerial) has been away from the Conservative Party (although still supported by 63%) but with very little gain in the number of votes cast for the Labour Party. Again the Liberal vote has more than doubled in size. In fact, looking at all the elections, the voting pattern among editors has more closely resembled that of the voting public as a whole than that of social class AB, particularly in the numbers supporting the Labour Party. However, a majority supported the Conservative Party in the most recent election as in the previous two elections.

TABLE 3.036
HOW EDITORS VOTED IN THE LAST THREE GENERAL ELECTIONS

	1970			February 1974			October 1974		
	Editors	All voters[1]	Social class AB[1]	Editors	All voters[1]	Social class AB[1]	Editors	All voters[1]	Social class AB[1]
Weighted base: All answering who voted	490			513			512		
	%	%	%	%	%	%	%	%	%
Conservative	53	46	79	50	38	67	52	36	63
Labour	27	43	10	25	37	10	27	39	12
Liberal	20	8	10	22	19	20	20	18	22
Other	†	2	1	2	6	3	1	7	3
Not voting (Based on all answering)	7	28	†	5	22	†	4	27	†

Source: The British General Election of October 1974, David Butler and Dennis Kavanagh.

[1] Figures not available.

† Figures not available.

The question asking respondents to say how their own political views compared with those of their publication bore little fruit; 16% did not answer the question and the proportion was particularly high among editors of national and provincial daily papers; 41% said that their publication did not express views; these were almost entirely the editors of weekly newspapers and magazines; 19% said that their views were the same as those of their publication and 11% said it depended on the issue, leaving only tiny proportions saying whether their views were to the left or the right of their publication: 10% said that their views were to the left and 4% that their views were to the right of the publication they edited.

Views on the Press Council

All except 15% of editors were prepared to express an opinion of the way in which the Press Council performed its function and, on the whole, opinion was favourable; 70% said that it performed at least "fairly well" though only 15% said "very well". Magazine editors were the most likely to have no opinion on the subject (26%) but were also the most critical with 22% saying that it performed its function "rather" or "very poorly".

When asked in what ways, if any, the aims or procedures of the Press Council should be changed, almost two-thirds had no views on the subject. The only change wanted by any sizeable proportion was that the Press Council should have "more teeth" (14%); 3% went further and thought it ought to have punitive powers backed by law.

TABLE 3.037
VIEWS ON THE PRESS COUNCIL

	Total	National	Prov. Morning	Prov. Evening	Weekly	Magazine
Weighted base: All	689	11	17	75	244	326
	%	%	%	%	%	%
(a) Press Council performs its function:						
Very well	15	30	28	38	19	7
Fairly well	55	53	58	57	68	45
Rather poorly	11	9	—	5	7	16
Very poorly	4	—	—	—	3	6
Don't know/Not stated	15	8	16	10	3	26
(b) Ways in which aims and procedures of the Press Council should be changed:						
More teeth	14	18	11	11	14	15
Punitive powers	3	—	—	3	4	2
Should set standards	2	18	—	—	1	2
Should give publicity to findings and activities	3	—	11	—	3	2
Should not be changed	5	—	11	8	10	2
Other answers	10	18	10	15	5	10
Don't know/Not stated	65	47	58	65	65	68

Less than a fifth (17%) of editors had been involved in any way at all in a complaint made to the Press Council. Hardly any magazine editors (5%) and only 12% of editors of weekly newspapers had been involved in any such complaint but around half the provincial evening editors and two-thirds of the editors of national and provincial morning newspapers had had some such involvement.

Of those who had been involved with the Press Council, over half said that they considered the way the matter was dealt with was "very satisfactory" and a further third said it was "fairly satisfactory"; only 13% expressed dissatisfaction. The majority also thought that the outcome was "very satisfactory"; when asked why they said this, most commented that they felt that the findings from the enquiry had been fair but some said that they were satisfied because they had been in the right and the findings had been in their favour.

On the whole, editors exhibited respect for the Press Council; when asked how important it would be to them if they were censured by the Press Council, 43% said it would be "very" and a further 33% "fairly" important. Editors of provincial dailies were the most likely to say that it would be very important to them.

TABLE 3.038
IMPORTANCE ATTACHED TO BEING CENSURED BY PRESS COUNCIL

	Total	National	Prov. Morning	Prov. Evening	Weekly	Magazine
Weighted base: All	689	11	17	75	244	326
	%	%	%	%	%	%
Very imporant	43	35	58	58	46	37
Fairly important	33	47	17	29	35	33
Rather unimportant	11	—	14	11	8	13
Completely unimportant	5	—	—	—	4	7
Depends on circumstances	3	—	11	—	3	4
Other answers	1	—	—	—	1	1
Not stated	4	18	—	2	3	5

The Growing Concentration of the Press

Concern has been expressed that the tendency for ownership of newspapers to be concentrated within a smaller number of organisations may result in a less good service to the public. The views of editors were sought on a number of aspects of this issue; they were firstly asked their views on the amount of diversity of opinion represented at present by national newspapers.

About half thought there was sufficient diversity but a large minority (44%) thought that there should be more; 17% thought there should be a lot more diversity. The magazine editors were the most likely to say that there should be more diversity. Over a third of the editors of national newspapers failed to answer this question.

There were no differences between those whose company was part of a group and those in independent companies.

TABLE 3.039
VIEWS ON DIVERSITY OF OPINION REPRESENTED BY THE NATIONAL PRESS

	Total	National	Prov. Morning	Prov. Evening	Weekly	Magazine
Weighted base: All	689	11	17	75	244	326
	%	%	%	%	%	%
Too much diversity	2	—	—	—	3	2
Sufficient	49	35	64	57	58	40
Should be a little more	27	18	36	35	20	31
Should be a lot more	17	9	—	3	17	23
No opinion/Not stated	7	38	—	5	2	4

When the editors were asked whether they felt that any sections of the community or political viewpoints did not get a fair deal from the national press, almost half of them gave no answer or actually entered "none"; the proportion was similar across all groups of editors.

Those naming one or more types of people whose views were not adequately represented listed a large number of different minority groups. The only group to be mentioned by more than 2–3% were "Labour Party/left wing views/trade unions", mentioned by 16% (8% of the sample).

Editors were then asked to say, for a number of aspects of press concentration, whether they thought it was harmful or beneficial or whether they had no views on the subject. Over a third (35%) thought that the lack of directly competing daily papers outside London was harmful; only 6% thought it beneficial though almost half of the small group of provincial morning editors thought so. Over half the editors had no views.

A quarter thought that the ownership of provincial dailies and national dailies in the same group was harmful but 15% thought it beneficial; again, over half had no views. Editors of provincial mornings and evenings were most likely to say that this was beneficial.

When asked what they thought about daily papers owning weekly papers in the same areas, over half again had no opinion but the remainder were more or less equally divided with a fifth saying it was beneficial and a fifth saying it was harmful. Editors of provincial dailies were particularly likely to say it was beneficial while editors of weeklies were only a little more likely to say it was beneficial than they were to say it was harmful, showing a diversity of views.

TABLE 3.040
VIEWS ON DIFFERENT ASPECTS OF PRESS CONCENTRATION

	Total	National	Prov. Morning	Prov. Evening	Weekly	Magazine
Weighted base: All	689	11	17	75	244	326
	%	%	%	%	%	%
(a) Lack of directly competing newspapers outside London						
Harmful	35	26	25	30	24	45
Beneficial	6	9	47	10	5	2
No views/Not stated	59	65	28	60	71	53
(b) Ownership of provincial dailies and national dailies in same group						
Harmful	25	18	11	10	24	29
Beneficial	15	18	36	40	16	7
No views/Not stated	60	64	55	50	60	64
(c) Daily papers owning weekly papers in the same area						
Harmful	20	9	11	8	21	24
Beneficial	21	9	47	48	28	8
No views/Not stated	59	82	42	44	51	68
(d) Press ownership in independent television and radio						
Harmful	21	18	11	18	15	26
Beneficial	21	35	47	33	29	11
No views/Not stated	58	47	42	49	56	63
(e) The dominance in some magazine fields of a single company						
Harmful	45	26	28	32	32	61
Beneficial	2	—	22	3	1	2
No views/Not stated	53	74	50	65	67	37

The overall picture of opinion was very similar on the subject of ownership by the press in independent television and radio: over half had no views and the remainder were equally divided into a fifth thinking it beneficial and a fifth considering it harmful. All the groups of newspaper editors, however, tended to consider it beneficial rather than harmful while the reverse was true of magazine editors.

Although over half, again, had no opinion on the question of the dominance in some magazine fields of a single company, almost all of those with views considered it harmful. Magazine editors were particularly likely to consider it harmful.

Finally, on the topic of press concentration, a series of five different attitudinal positions was set out and editors were asked to indicate which one represented their own position most closely. Almost half (46%) favoured the continuation of the present position, described as follows:

> a general prohibition on mergers involving larger press groupings, while the Monopolies Commission has agreed to some purchases of weekly groups by large national groups.

The national and provincial daily editors were particularly likely to opt for the present position.

The remainder of the editors were equally divided between those wanting less restriction and those wanting more:

Less: (Base: All)
No legal restrictions on press concentration 11%
Some restriction but a relaxation of the present press monopoly law 14%

More:
A toughening of the present law so as to prevent any mergers except those between two small groups... ... 22%
Legislation to force the largest press groups to sell off certain publications 3%

The balance of opinion was towards less restriction among national and provincial daily editors while magazine editors tended to favour more restriction; weekly editors were evenly divided.

Thus, overall, it seems that editors are fairly happy with the present situation as regards the concentration of press ownership or have no particular views on the subject.

TABLE 3.041
POSITIONS FAVOURED IN THE FIELD OF PRESS MONOPOLY LAW

	Total	National	Prov. Morning	Prov. Evening	Weekly	Magazine
Weighted base: All	689	11	17	75	244	326
	%	%	%	%	%	%
No legal restrictions	11	21	11	8	13	10
Some restriction but a relaxation of the present law	14	9	—	20	17	12
Continuation of present position	40	53	61	62	45	42
Toughening of law to prevent most mergers ...	22	9	14	3	22	27
Legislation to force large groups to sell off certain publications	3	—	—	—	1	5
Not stated	4	8	14	5	2	4

State Assistance for the Press

The final topic covered by the questionnaire was whether or not editors thought there was a case for state assistance for the press and, if there was, what form it should take.

Only 27% thought there was a case for state assistance though editors of national newspapers and of magazines were rather more in favour of it than other groups.

The relatively small proportion who thought there was a case for state assistance mainly gave as their reason that it would preserve the number and variety of newspapers and avoid closures (51% of those in favour); comparatively small numbers gave other reasons; the main ones were:

	(Weighted base: All in favour: 187)
It would assist the freedom of the press	15%
To limit/end dependence on advertisers	9%
It would assist minority publications	7%
To allow the installation of new technology	6%

The much larger proportion who declared themselves to be against state help for the press gave two main reasons for their attitude:

	(Weighted base: All against: 455)
It would be a threat to the freedom of the press	52%
It would encourage the inefficient papers	24%

No other answer was given by more than 2%.

Editors were given a list of possible forms in which state help might be made available and asked to indicate which they considered to be preferable if it was decided that state assistance was desirable. They were allowed to pick more than one form.

Three forms of state aid stood out as being very much preferred over the other four on the list and only one other received any number of endorsements:

Tax concessions	56%
Subsidies for paper	25%
Cheap loans for publishers	25%
Special fund to launch new publications	12%

Editors of national and provincial morning newspapers were least in favour of tax concessions but, together with provincial evening newspaper editors, were more in favour of cheap loans to publications than were other groups.

TABLE 3.042
EDITORS' VIEWS ON STATE ASSISTANCE TO THE PRESS

	Total	National	Prov. Morning	Prov. Evening	Weekly	Magazine
Weighted base: All	689	11	17	75	244	326
	%	%	%	%	%	%
(a) *Is there a case for state assistance*						
Yes	27	44	22	24	21	33
No	66	56	78	76	71	60
Don't know/Not stated	7	—	—	—	8	7
(b) *What form should it take*						
Tax concessions	56	18	31	61	66	52
Subsidies for paper	25	9	11	18	26	28
Cheap loans to publishers	25	53	31	40	21	23
Special fund for new publications	12	9	11	10	4	20
Cash payments to publishers in difficulties	6	—	—	3	6	8
Re-allocation of advertising revenue among newspapers	5	9	—	—	5	6
A national printing corporation	3	9	—	3	2	4
Don't know/Not stated	21	38	47	15	16	23

THE VIEWS OF SENIOR JOURNALISTS

Introduction

Since the response rate to the mail out to senior journalists was only 43%, we do not feel that we can present the data on jobs, salaries, conditions of work etc with any confidence that they present a true picture. We therefore present only the results of the opinion section of the questionnaire—and only these with the reservation that they may not accurately reflect the views of all senior journalists. However, in order to put into perspective the views of the senior journalists who replied to the survey, some description of them is required. It must be borne in mind that, because of the low response rate, this information is only a description of those journalists who chose to take part in the survey or who happened to be still at the address given in the unions' records; it cannot be taken as giving a picture of all senior journalists.

The composition of the sample in terms of type of publication or type of work done was:

	Before weighting	After weighting to correct for differential selection
Base: All replying to survey	911	1,272
	%	%
On a national daily newspaper (including London evenings)	20	18 } 22
On a national Sunday newspaper		4
On a provincial morning newspaper	9	10
On a provincial evening newspaper	19	21
On a weekly newspaper	14	15
On a trade or technical magazine	13	5 } 10
On other type of magazine		5
National or international news agency	4	3 } 4
Other news agency		1
As a freelance journalist	19	16
Other	1	1
Not answered	2	2

TABLE 3.043
SEX AND AGE OF SENIOR JOURNALISTS REPLYING TO SURVEY

	Total[1]	National	Prov. Morning	Prov. Evening	Weekly	Magazine	Agency	Freelance
Base: All (Unweighted)	911	180	85	170	126	114	34	175
(Weighted)	1,272	276	131	262	192	116	52	207
Sex:	%	%	%	%	%	%	%	%
Male	83	91	92	87	80	61	94	71
Female	17	8	7	12	19	38	6	28
Age:								
Under 30	32	16	31	38	52	43	32	20
30–39	28	33	27	26	19	24	38	36
40–49	19	25	23	19	14	15	9	19
50–59	14	17	16	12	10	13	15	14
60 or over	6	9	2	4	5	4	6	10

[1] The small "other" category has been left out of the breakdown though it is included in the total. There are also some who did not give information about the type of publication on which they worked who appear in the total column but not in any of the subgroups; the breakdown group bases therefore do not add to the total column in this and subsequent tables.

(Compare with Table 3.001)

Of those journalists who were in employment (ie excluding freelance journalists), 75% worked for a company that was part of a group of companies. The job titles of those in employment were:

Weighted base: All in employment 1,065

	%
Executive or desk personnel (eg news editor, deputy or assistant editor)	19
General or feature sub-editor	16
General reporter	22
Specialist correspondent	13
Critic or feature writer	10
Sports reporter/sports sub-editor	10
Photographer	9
Other	13
Not answered	3

(Percentages add to more than 100 as some respondents had more than one title)

The majority of the senior journalists replying to the survey were men; only 17% were women. There was a higher proportion of women in the freelance category or working on magazines than in the other groups.

On average, the senior journalists who replied were younger than the editors; three-fifths were under 40 years of age. Those working on weekly newspapers and magazines had larger proportions in the under 30 age bracket than did any of the other groups.

Senior Journalists' Opinions of Journalism as a Career

Senior journalists were asked the same questions as the editors about their opinions of journalism as a career; the replies of the two samples can therefore be compared.

General Opinions

As with the editors, the majority of the journalists claimed that they enjoyed their present work as a journalist "quite a lot" or "very much indeed"; but whereas two-thirds of editors said that they enjoyed their work "very much indeed", less than half (47%) of the journalists gave it the most favourable rating. In every group of journalists, the replies to this question were less favourable than those given by the editors.

Journalists working for provincial evening or weekly newspapers or for news agencies had less favourable opinions of their present work than other groups; those working in a freelance capacity or for national or provincial morning newspapers had the most favourable opinion.

TABLE 3.044
HOW MUCH JOURNALISTS ENJOY THEIR PRESENT WORK AS JOURNALISTS

	Total	National	Prov. Morning	Prov. Evening	Weekly	Magazine	Agency	Freelance
Weighted base: All	1,272	276	131	262	192	116	52	207
	%	%	%	%	%	%	%	%
Very much indeed	47	54	50	39	40	48	29	59
Quite a lot	31	30	33	31	31	33	36	26
A fair amount	15	12	5	22	19	12	32	9
Not very much	3	1	6	4	4	2	3	1
Very little	1	1	1	2	1	—	—	—
Not at all	*	1	—	1	—	—	—	1
Don't know/Not stated	3	1	6	2	5	5	—	3

(Compare with Table 3.028)

The two things most frequently mentioned as being liked about working in journalism by the editors were also most frequently mentioned by the senior journalists, though the order was reversed:

	Senior Journalists	Editors
Variety and interest of the work	46%	36%
Creativity and scope for initiative	39%	38%

The senior journalists were less likely than the editors to mention the satisfaction of producing a finished product but more frequently mentioned that they liked the independence of the work. Similar proportions in each sample mentioned other aspects of the work such as meeting the public, the ability to influence events, the work being socially useful and having stimulating colleagues.

TABLE 3.045
WHAT JOURNALISTS LIKE AND DISLIKE ABOUT WORKING IN JOURNALISM

	Total	National	Prov. Morning	Prov. Weekly	Evening	Magazine	Agency	Freelance
Weighted base: All	1,272	276	131	262	192	116	52	207
Main aspects liked	%	%	%	%	%	%	%	%
Variety and interest	46	47	66	51	45	40	48	35
Creativity and scope for initiative	39	44	37	35	28	59	32	42
Meeting the public	23	13	31	25	34	17	18	21
Independence and freedom	21	15	27	21	24	24	5	21
Ability to influence events	19	26	14	21	20	13	21	10
Satisfaction of producing a finished product	12	15	12	15	12	14	3	9
Socially useful	11	13	11	14	9	12	—	6
Stimulating colleagues	11	20	7	9	8	6	15	9
Flexible hours	10	11	5	8	14	12	15	8
Like to inform and educate	9	6	11	8	10	12	6	11
Travel	8	12	6	4	—	22	15	10
Challenging	7	9	6	8	7	4	6	6
Meeting interesting and important people	7	7	9	6	5	15	—	7
Other answers	16	23	11	11	16	15	23	20
Main aspects disliked								
Long and unsociable hours	23	16	34	25	38	10	22	11
Poor pay	17	10	14	21	29	13	3	19
Poor quality staff	9	13	6	9	8	7	12	6
Poor management	9	8	8	15	9	4	3	6
Boredom	8	8	7	9	11	4	12	8
Distortion of stories	8	10	12	7	4	8	9	10
Time pressures	7	7	2	4	5	11	—	5
No career structure	6	7	6	7	6	6	6	1
Lack of security	5	8	1	2	1	4	9	8
Union interference	4	7	—	6	4	2	—	3
Intrusion of privacy	4	4	4	3	6	2	3	3
Advertising pressures	3	2	4	5	4	5	—	3
Criticism from the public	3	4	5	4	3	2	—	2
Other answers	14	12	18	18	10	16	9	12
Nothing disliked	9	12	13	6	9	9	12	7
Not answered	8	8	6	6	5	16	9	11

(Compare with Table 3.029)

In keeping with their less enthusiastic rating of journalism as a career, the senior journalists were rather more likely than the editors to mention things that they disliked about journalism. Only 17% said there was nothing they disliked or gave no answer compared with 33% of editors.

Again, the two items most frequently mentioned by the editors were also most frequently mentioned by journalists, and by a larger percentage in each case:

	Senior Journalists	Editors
Long and unsociable hours	23%	10%
Poor pay	17%	14%

None of the other aspects of the work was mentioned as being disliked by 10% or more of the journalists.

The journalists in the different groups of the sample did not differ a great deal in their likes and dislikes about journalism. Those working on national newspapers were rather more likely than others to say that they enjoyed having the opportunity to influence events but were less likely to mention pleasure in meeting the public as something they liked; they were also below average in their mention of both long and unsociable hours and poor pay as things disliked.

Journalists working on provincial morning papers particularly mentioned the variety and interest of the work and were above average in liking to meet the public but they were also above average in the frequency with which they mentioned long and unsociable hours as something disliked. Those working on provincial evenings were also more likely than any except those on provincial mornings to mention the variety and interest of the work; on the negative side they stood out in that 15% of them mentioned poor management as something disliked, compared with 9% for the sample as a whole. The journalists on weekly newspapers were above average in the proportion mentioning meeting the public as an aspect they liked but below average in frequency of mentioning creativity and scope for initiative. They mentioned the two main dislikes of long and unsociable hours and poor pay more frequently than any of the other groups.

Magazine journalists had the highest proportion of all groups mentioning creativity and scope for initiative as something they liked and had the lowest proportion saying that they thought the hours long and unsociable. Over a fifth of them mentioned travel as something they liked about the work compared with 8% for the sample as a whole.

The small group of agency journalists differed from journalists as a whole in two respects: very few mentioned the independence and freedom as an aspect of the work that they liked (5% compared with 21% for the total sample) and very few (3%) of them mentioned poor pay as something they disliked.

The freelance journalists were the least likely of all the groups to mention the variety and interest of the work and the ability to influence events as things liked. Not surprisingly, a relatively small proportion of them mentioned long and unsociable hours as something disliked.

As with the editors, the majority of the senior journalists (79%) expected to continue in journalism; those working on magazines were the most likely to think they might change.

TABLE 3.046
WHETHER JOURNALISTS EXPECT TO CONTINUE IN JOURNALISM

	Total	National	Prov. Morning	Prov. Evening	Weekly	Magazine	Agency	Freelance
Weighted base: All	1,272	276	131	262	192	116	52	207
	%	%	%	%	%	%	%	%
Expect to continue	79	84	87	78	79	67	82	74
May change career	12	9	9	12	13	18	12	10
Almost certainly will change	3	3	2	2	5	6	3	3
Don't know/Not stated	4	4	1	5	3	7	3	4
Journalism not main work at present	2	—	—	—	—	2	—	9

(Compare with Table 3.030)

Specific Opinions about Journalism as a Career

We now examine journalists' ratings of various aspects of journalism compared with "other professions" under the same three headings as were used in describing editors' opinions.

Conditions of Work

The senior journalists had a somewhat poorer opinion of journalism compared with other professions than the editors on all the attributes to do with conditions of work except "long term salary prospects" on which both samples had very similar views. Around half the journalists rated journalism as poor or very poor for security of employment, starting salary, long term salary prospects and ease of movement to alternative occupations. Over a third rated it as poor or very poor for prospects of promotion on merit compared with only 13% of editors.

There was quite a lot of variability of opinion on conditions of work between the various subgroups of journalists. The national newspaper journalists were particularly likely to rate journalism as good for prospects of promotion on merit and for both starting salary and long term salary prospects. Those on provincial mornings were likely to think that security of employment and starting salaries were good to an above average extent. Those on provincial evenings were even more likely than those on provincial mornings to rate journalism as good for security of employment but were less likely than the sample as a whole to rate it as good for prospects of promotion on merit, long term salary prospects or ease of movement to other professions.

Those journalists working on weekly newspapers had a poor opinion of starting salaries in the profession, 72% rating journalism as poor or very poor in this respect. On the other attributes, their views were similar to those for the sample as a whole.

The magazine journalists did not rate journalism as highly as most groups did on security of employment but were rather above average in their opinion of starting salaries. The freelance journalists had the poorest opinion of all the groups on the security of employment of journalism with only a quarter rating it as good or very good in this respect; but they had the most favourable view on the ease of movement to other professions.

The agency journalists differed considerably from most of the other groups in their ratings of conditions of work; they were more likely to give favourable ratings to security of employment, prospects of promotion on merit, starting salary and long term salary prospects.

Journalists' views did not differ much by age except in the rating given for starting salaries; only 34% of those under 30 rated journalism as good or very good in this respect compared with 47% of those aged 30–39 and 55% of those aged 40 and over.

Enjoyment of the Work

As did the editors, the vast majority of journalists rated journalism as good or very good on all the attributes concerned with aspects of the enjoyment of the work; only tiny proportions rated it as poor or very poor on any of them. But on every attribute fewer journalists than editors chose "very good" as the scale position representing their views.

There was little variation of opinion between the various groups of journalists on these attributes. Agency journalists were rather more likely than others to rate journalism as very good for scope for initiative and both agency and provincial morning journalists were above average in the extent to which they rated it as very good for degree of responsibility; both editors and journalists gave a less good rating to journalism on this attribute than on any of the others in the group.

TABLE 3.047
JOURNALISM AS A CAREER: RATINGS ON CONDITIONS OF WORK BY JOURNALISTS

	Total	National	Prov. Morning	Prov. Evening	Weekly	Magazine	Agency	Freelance
Weighted base: All	1,272	276	131	262	192	116	52	207
	%	%	%	%	%	%	%	%
Security of employment:								
Very good	7	6	9	9	7	3	18	2
Good	43	41	51	59	49	38	45	22
Poor	40	46	30	29	37	53	35	45
Very poor	8	6	7	2	5	3	—	26
Don't know/Not stated	2	1	2	2	2	4	2	5
Prospects of promotion on merit:								
Very good	11	12	13	5	11	12	26	11
Good	51	60	47	45	50	47	51	51
Poor	29	21	31	40	30	31	20	23
Very poor	6	4	7	9	8	6	—	5
Don't know/Not stated	4	3	2	1	1	4	3	10
Starting salaries:								
Very good	7	12	13	6	2	6	6	5
Good	39	50	38	34	24	46	51	39
Poor	35	30	37	39	42	32	24	31
Very poor	16	7	11	20	30	15	17	15
Don't know/Not stated	3	2	1	2	1	1	2	10
Long term salary prospects:								
Very good	8	16	13	5	3	10	6	4
Good	41	50	34	28	40	44	68	44
Poor	40	30	44	52	44	38	26	34
Very poor	8	2	8	12	12	5	—	8
Don't know/Not stated	3	2	1	2	1	3	—	10
Ease of movement to alternative occupations:								
Very good	8	7	7	7	6	6	15	10
Good	37	34	37	28	45	39	30	43
Poor	37	40	39	39	35	39	41	29
Very poor	16	16	14	25	13	10	11	10
Don't know/Not stated	3	3	2	1	1	6	3	8

(Compare with Table 3.031)

TABLE 3.048

**JOURNALISM AS A CAREER:
RATINGS ON ENJOYMENT OF THE WORK**

	Total	National	Prov. Morning	Prov. Evening	Weekly	Magazine	Agency	Freelance
Weighted base: All	1,272	276	131	262	192	116	52	207
	%	%	%	%	%	%	%	%
Scope for creativity:								
Very good	49	50	50	49	48	54	50	47
Good	44	43	44	45	47	41	48	43
Poor	4	4	5	5	2	3	—	6
Very poor	1	1	1	—	2	1	—	—
Don't know/Not stated	2	2	—	1	1	2	2	3
Scope for initiative:								
Very good	45	44	48	41	45	45	53	43
Good	45	49	43	48	42	46	36	46
Poor	7	5	6	8	9	8	6	6
Very poor	1	—	2	2	3	—	—	—
Don't know/Not stated	2	2	1	2	1	2	5	4
Degree of responsibility:								
Very good	29	30	41	24	25	29	38	30
Good	59	58	51	67	63	57	54	54
Poor	8	8	7	7	10	11	6	7
Very poor	1	1	—	2	1	2	—	2
Don't know/Not stated	3	3	1	1	1	2	2	7
Opportunity for using one's talents:								
Very good	45	41	43	42	44	45	52	52
Good	49	52	51	50	50	51	45	40
Poor	3	2	5	4	4	1	3	3
Very poor	1	2	—	2	1	1	—	1
Don't know/Not stated	2	3	1	1	1	3	—	4
Intrinsic interest of work:								
Very good	51	58	52	46	43	46	50	58
Good	44	38	43	50	51	50	48	36
Poor	2	1	1	1	4	2	—	2
Very poor	*	1	1	1	—	—	—	—
Don't know/Not stated	2	2	2	2	2	3	2	4

(Compare with Table 3.032)

Influence in the Community at Large

Between two-thirds and four-fifths of the journalists rated journalism as good or very good in terms of "value to the community", "opportunity for influencing events" and "status" but, again, their ratings were less favourable than were those given by the editors, mainly due to lower proportions rating journalism as very good and higher proportions rating it as good; in each case, only a minority rated it as poor, though the minority amounted to 30% where "status" was concerned.

Differences between groups of journalists were small; magazine journalists seemed to have a poorer opinion of the value of journalism to the community than did other groups and also were a little less likely to rate it as good for opportunity to influence events. Those on provincial evenings and agency journalists had a slightly better opinion of the status of journalism than did other groups.

TABLE 3.049

JOURNALISM AS A CAREER:
RATINGS ON ITS INFLUENCE IN THE COMMUNITY

	Total	National	Prov. Morning	Prov. Evening	Weekly	Magazine	Agency	Freelance
Weighted base: All	1,272	276	131	262	192	116	52	207
	%	%	%	%	%	%	%	%
Value of work to the community:								
Very good	27	23	28	34	31	15	27	27
Good	58	59	65	55	57	63	59	52
Poor	10	11	7	9	6	15	9	12
Very poor	3	4	—	1	5	3	—	4
Don't know/Not stated	3	3	—	1	1	4	5	6
Opportunity for influencing events:								
Very good	20	20	13	22	24	18	21	18
Good	58	59	63	59	61	51	54	55
Poor	15	16	17	14	12	23	23	11
Very poor	4	4	4	2	2	3	—	7
Don't know/Not stated	3	2	4	2	2	4	2	8
Status:								
Very good	10	13	8	8	9	10	6	11
Good	56	56	70	48	51	60	74	57
Poor	26	25	16	33	33	20	18	20
Very poor	4	2	4	7	5	3	—	5
Don't know/Not stated	4	4	2	4	2	7	2	7

(Compare with Table 3.033)

Journalists' Opinions on Some Major Issues

Threats to Freedom of the Press

On the whole, the senior journalists had similar views to the editors on the issue of press freedom; over 90% of each sample picked one or more of the listed items as constituting a threat to the freedom of the press and each most often named "costs/inflation" and "printing and production workers" as threats, very similar proportions of both samples picking out these items. The journalists, however, were more likely than the editors to consider "libel laws", "advertisers" "proprietors/owners of the newspapers", "the management" and "Official Secrets Act/'D' Notices" to be threats to press freedom; they were less likely to think of "the Government" as a threat; perhaps surprisingly, they were only marginally less likely than editors to consider journalists to be a threat.

When asked to indicate what they considered to be the biggest threat, 20% of journalists mentioned "costs and inflation"—the same proportion as for editors; fewer journalists, however, picked "the Government" as the biggest threat, the item that was mentioned most frequently by editors in this context. Approximately equal proportions of journalists (about a tenth) named as the biggest threat each of the following: "printing and production workers", "the Government", "libel laws", "advertisers" and "proprietors/owners of newspapers", indicating considerable diversity of opinion on the subject.

Journalists in different groups did not differ much in their views as to what constituted threats to the freedom of the press. Those on national newspapers were rather less likely to mention "advertisers", but more likely to mention "print and production workers" and "the Official Secrets Act/'D' Notices". Journalists on provincial evenings and weeklies were less likely than other groups to see "printing and production" workers as a threat but those on weekly newspapers were more likely to think of "political parties" in this way.

The younger journalists differed from older journalists in several respects; they were more likely to see as threats "advertisers", "proprietors and owners" and "the management" and were less likely to blame "costs and inflation".

TABLE 3.050
THREATS TO THE FREEDOM OF THE PRESS

	Any Threat								Biggest Threat
	Total	National	Prov. Morning	Prov. Evening	Weekly	Magazine	Agency	Freelance	Total
Weighted base: All	1,272	276	131	262	192	116	52	207	1,272
	%	%	%	%	%	%	%	%	%
Costs/inflation	56	59	62	54	51	52	71	53	20
Printing and production workforce/trade unions	55	64	55	46	46	56	68	61	13
Libel laws	45	50	46	48	39	35	54	41	10
Advertisers	45	35	41	49	51	52	36	48	5
Proprietors/owners	44	45	37	45	45	48	39	44	9
Official Secrets Act/'D' Notices	40	50	39	42	36	32	45	33	2
The Government	38	36	41	38	42	33	39	38	11
The management	36	30	39	39	36	47	45	34	5
Political parties	29	24	34	27	40	29	36	28	5
Journalists	20	20	26	21	24	23	15	16	1
Public relations people	16	12	21	17	19	14	9	18	*
Others	2	1	5	2	2	2	—	3	1
None/No threat	2	1	2	1	1	3	3	3	3
Don't know/Not answered	3	3	5	1	2	5	—	5	14

(Compare with Table 3.034)

When asked whether they themselves felt that their work in journalism was affected by any undesirable pressures from any of the same list of sources, roughly equal proportions of journalists mentioned "costs and inflation", "advertisers" and "the management" (about a fifth in each case) whereas "costs and inflation" was mentioned by a third of editors and the other two items by much smaller proportions.

TABLE 3.051
UNDESIRABLE PRESSURES PERCEIVED BY JOURNALISTS ON THEIR WORK

	Total	National	Prov. Morning	Prov. Evening	Weekly	Magazine	Agency	Freelance
Weighted base: All	1,272	276	131	262	192	116	52	207
	%	%	%	%	%	%	%	%
Advertisers	21	12	21	28	31	28	3	16
The management	20	13	22	25	23	25	21	16
Costs/inflation	20	21	15	17	20	22	20	24
Libel laws	15	22	21	16	11	4	18	11
Proprietors/owners	14	12	13	16	17	13	6	13
Printing and production workers	12	18	6	10	13	8	—	13
Public relations people	9	3	14	7	11	12	6	9
Journalists	6	5	8	6	5	4	3	6
Official Secrets Act/'D' Notices	5	7	3	6	2	1	15	5
Political parties	3	2	2	2	6	2	—	5
The Government	3	4	5	2	3	1	3	4
Others	1	1	1	1	2	2	—	2
None/No pressures	30	30	27	29	27	35	47	30
Don't know/Not answered	12	12	13	13	13	15	6	12

(Compare with Table 3.035)

Political Affiliation

Journalists, being junior to editors, might suffer more than editors from pressure to conform to the political views of their publication. The journalists who replied to the survey were more willing than editors to answer the questions about voting in the last three elections; only about one in twenty failed to answer the questions compared with four in twenty of the editors.

Overall, the journalists showed less support for the Conservative Party and more support for the Labour Party than did the editors. They also showed increasing support for the Liberal Party over the last three elections.

TABLE 3.052
HOW JOURNALISTS VOTED IN THE LAST THREE GENERAL ELECTIONS

	1970	*February* 1974	*October* 1974
Weighted base: All answering who voted	981	1,076	1,072
	%	%	%
Conservative	39	36	34
Labour	43	40	38
Liberal	14	20	25
Other	2	2	3
Can't remember	1	1	*
Not voting (based on all answering)	17	11	11

(Compare with Table 3.036)

Journalists did not differ very markedly in voting behaviour by type of publication worked on nor by age; those working in agencies or on provincial morning newspapers were least likely to have supported the Labour Party while those on weekly newspapers were most likely to have done so.

A fifth of the journalists said that their publication did not express political views but the proportion was much smaller among those working on national or provincial morning newspapers and considerably higher among those on weekly newspapers or periodicals (39% and 61% respectively).

If we look only at newspaper journalists, the majority of whom were able to compare their own political position with that of the publication on which they worked, we find that a fifth of them said that their views were the same as those of their newspaper; a further third said that it depended on the issue, indicating that they sometimes disagreed with the views of their newspaper but not consistently. Almost half (45%) felt that their views were either to the left or to the right of the newspaper on which they worked and four-fifths of these felt they were to the left of their newspaper. There were no very marked differences by type of newspaper when the reduced size of the sub-samples is taken into account.

TABLE 3.053
NEWSPAPER JOURNALISTS' COMPARISON OF THEIR OWN VIEWS WITH THOSE OF THEIR PUBLICATION

	Total	*National*	*Prov. Morning*	*Prov. Evening*	*Weekly*
Weighted base: All indicating paper has views	677	255	110	198	114
	%	%	%	%	%
Depends on the issue	33	31	39	34	30
Views about the same	21	23	21	17	22
I am well to left of paper	10	11	11	12	6
I am somewhat to left	26	25	20	29	32
I am somewhat to right	8	8	7	7	10
I am well to right	1	2	2	1	—

Views on the Press Council

About a fifth (18%) of the journalists were unable to express an opinion on the Press Council, a proportion that was only a little higher than was the case with editors (15%). As with the editors, opinion among the remainder was largely positive though relatively few (9%) went so far as to say that it performed its function "very well".

Magazine journalists were much less likely than other groups to have any views on this subject (42%); views of the different groups of journalists did not differ much in other ways though it seems that those on national newspapers had a somewhat less favourable view than other groups.

As was the case with the editors, a large proportion (59%) of the journalists were not able to say in what ways the Press Council's aims and procedures should be changed; the only answer given with any frequency was again that it should have "more teeth" (10%).

TABLE 3.054
VIEWS ON THE PRESS COUNCIL

	Total	National	Prov. Morning	Prov. Evening	Weekly	Magazine	Agency	Freelance
Weighted base: All	1,272	276	131	262	192	116	52	207
	%	%	%	%	%	%	%	%
(a) Press Council performed its function:								
Very well	9	8	11	11	10	7	9	9
Fairly well	52	48	63	57	57	33	42	46
Rather poorly	15	20	15	14	12	14	20	16
Very poorly	6	9	2	8	3	4	3	8
Don't know/Not stated	18	15	8	10	18	42	26	22
(b) Ways in which aims and procedures of the Press Council should be changed:								
More teeth	10	11	14	11	9	3	21	10
Punitive power	8	13	6	11	6	5	3	4
Should set standards	4	4	6	5	2	4	—	3
Should give publicity to findings and activities	4	4	2	3	8	2	—	3
Others	18	23	14	21	7	18	—	15
Should not be changed	6	7	9	7	5	3	12	2
Don't know/Not stated	59	52	52	52	65	71	64	68

(Compare with Table 3.037)

Whereas 17% of the editors had been involved in some way with a complaint made to the Press Council, only 6% of the journalists had had this experience; two-thirds of this tiny proportion said that the matter had been dealt with satisfactorily. There were no notable differences between subgroups.

When asked how important it would be to them if they were censured by the Press Council, journalists gave answers that, overall, were very similar to those given by the editors with over two-thirds considering that it would be at least fairly important to them (39% "very important").

TABLE 3.055
IMPORTANCE ATTACHED TO BEING CENSURED BY PRESS COUNCIL

	Total	National	Prov. Morning	Prov. Evening	Weekly	Magazine	Agency	Freelance
Weighted base: All	1,272	276	131	262	192	116	52	207
	%	%	%	%	%	%	%	%
Very important	39	43	45	37	42	32	39	35
Fairly important	31	26	37	38	31	25	32	31
Rather unimportant	13	12	7	16	17	12	9	12
Completely unimportant	6	7	1	4	4	8	3	10
Depends on circumstances	5	6	7	2	4	2	12	5
Other answers	1	3	—	1	2	—	—	—
Not stated	5	4	2	2	1	22	5	7

(Compare with Table 3.038)

The Growing Concentration of the Press

Journalists appeared to be more concerned than editors about possible undesirable effects from the growing concentration of newspapers within a few large companies. When they were asked their views on the diversity of opinion represented by the national press, the journalists were more likely to think that there should be a lot more than there is at present (29%, compared with 17% for editors).

Journalists on provincial mornings were more likely than other groups to feel that there was sufficient diversity of views in the national press while the freelance journalists and those on national newspapers were the most likely to think that there should be more diversity; the differences were not marked, however.

TABLE 3.056
VIEWS ON DIVERSITY OF OPINION REPRESENTED BY THE NATIONAL PRESS

	Total	National	Prov. Morning	Prov. Evening	Weekly	Magazine	Agency	Freelance
Weighted base: All	1,272	276	131	262	192	116	52	207
	%	%	%	%	%	%	%	%
Too much diversity	1	1	1	3	2	—	3	—
Sufficient diversity	38	33	48	38	44	42	38	31
Should be a little more diversity	26	32	22	23	24	25	36	24
Should be a lot more diversity	29	29	23	33	23	25	20	36
No opinion/Not stated	6	5	5	3	6	7	3	9

(Compare with Table 3.039)

When journalists were asked whether they thought that any sections of the community or political viewpoints did not get a fair deal from the national press, answers followed a similar pattern to those given by editors; almost half (48%) either said "none" or gave no answer; the answers given by the remainder were spread across a large number of different types of people and there was little general consensus of opinion; however, a rather larger proportion of journalists than of editors felt that left wing/trade union/Labour Party views were under-represented (21% of journalists compared with 8% of editors); those on national newspapers were particularly likely to mention this (31%). Other groups mentioned by more than 2% or 3% were:

Black people/immigrants 8%

Minority views 7%

When asked to say for a number of specific aspects of press concentration whether they thought it harmful or beneficial, journalists exhibited more unfavourable opinions than editors and were less likely to say that they had no opinion. Over half the journalists thought it harmful that there was a lack of directly competing newspapers outside London (55%) and a dominance in some magazine fields of one company (59%), compared with 35% and 45% respectively for editors; the other three items, the ownership of provincial dailies and national dailies by the same group, daily papers owning weekly papers in the same area and press ownership in independent television and radio, were each thought to be harmful by between a fifth and a quarter of editors but by a third of journalists.

Magazine journalists were less likely than other groups to have an opinion on the propositions concerned specifically with newspapers but both they and the freelance journalists were particularly likely to have an opinion on the dominance in some magazine fields of one company, and think the situation harmful. There was little variation between the other groups of journalists.

TABLE 3.057
VIEWS ON DIFFERENT ASPECTS OF PRESS CONCENTRATION

	Total	National	Prov. Morning	Prov. Evening	Weekly	Magazine	Agency	Freelance
Weighted base: All	1,272	276	131	262	192	116	52	207
	%	%	%	%	%	%	%	%
(i) The lack of directly competing newspapers outside London								
Harmful	55	58	59	65	52	40	47	51
Beneficial	7	9	6	5	9	4	9	5
No views/Not stated	37	32	35	30	39	56	44	44
(ii) Ownership of provincial dailies and national dailies in same group								
Harmful	34	32	33	39	29	26	23	41
Beneficial	22	21	15	25	27	16	35	15
No views/Not stated	44	48	52	36	43	58	42	44
(iii) Daily papers owning weeklies in same area								
Harmful	33	31	27	41	41	20	20	34
Beneficial	19	14	20	25	19	17	35	16
No views/Not stated	47	55	53	33	40	63	45	50
(iv) Press ownership in independent television and radio								
Harmful	30	31	26	34	24	32	21	34
Beneficial	24	20	26	28	31	13	24	19
No views/Not stated	46	49	49	38	45	54	55	47
(v) Dominance in some magazine fields of one company								
Harmful	59	62	47	59	49	64	44	71
Beneficial	2	2	—	1	3	1	3	2
No views/Not stated	39	37	52	40	48	35	53	27

(Compare with Table 3.040)

When asked to give their views on press monopoly law by picking one of five positions, 43% of the journalists wanted to continue with the present position, a similar proportion to that of editors (46%), but, whereas 25% of editors wanted fewer restrictions than at present, only 16% of journalists wanted any relaxation of the present laws; conversely, 36% of journalists wanted more restrictions than at present, compared with 25% of editors. Journalists on national and provincial morning newspapers were the least likely to want to see further restrictions while magazine and freelance journalists were most in favour of them.

TABLE 3.058
POSITIONS FAVOURED IN THE FIELD OF PRESS MONOPOLY LAW

	Total	National	Prov. Morning	Prov. Evening	Weekly	Magazine	Agency	Freelance
Weighted base: All	1,272	276	131	262	192	116	52	207
	%	%	%	%	%	%	%	%
No legal restrictions	5	7	2	4	3	3	6	8
Some restriction but a relaxation of the present law	11	11	12	9	13	7	21	8
Continuation of present position	43	52	53	43	47	39	30	28
Toughening of law to prevent most mergers	25	21	19	29	25	25	25	28
Legislation to force large groups to sell off certain publications	11	6	7	10	8	17	6	18
Not stated	6	3	7	5	4	9	12	10

(Compare with Table 3.041)

State Assistance for the Press

Rather more journalists than editors thought there was a case for state assistance for the press (44% compared with 27%). In fact, whereas editors were mainly against state assistance, the opinion of journalists was fairly evenly divided. National newspaper and agency journalists were most in favour with over half thinking that there was a case for it.

The main reasons given for favouring state support were:

	Weighted base: All in favour 557 %
It would avoid closures/preserve variety	57
It would assist the freedom of the press	14
It would assist the launching of new newspapers	8
It would end the dependence on advertising revenue	7
It would allow the installation of new technology	6

Those who were not in favour of state assistance gave two main reasons, that it would be a threat to the independence and freedom of the press and that it would encourage inefficient papers (65% and 21% respectively of those not in favour).

Respondents were then asked to say, from a given list, what form state assistance should take if it were decided that there was a case for it. They were allowed to tick as many items as they liked and overall journalists selected rather more forms as acceptable than did the editors.

As with the editors, "tax concessions" was the form most frequently selected (by 50% of journalists compared with 56% of editors). The second most popular method among journalists was "subsidies for paper", endorsed by 36% compared with 25% of editors; the third method, "cheap loans to publishers", was selected by equal proportions of journalists and editors (a quarter of each sample) but the remaining items, though endorsed by small proportions, were nonetheless each endorsed by a larger proportion of journalists than of editors.

There were no marked differences between the different groups of journalists in the proportion endorsing each item and the order of frequency with which they were endorsed was virtually the same for each group. Exceptions were that national journalists appeared to give slightly greater emphasis to "cheap loans to publishers" than most of the other groups; weekly newspaper journalists were more in favour of "cash payments to publishers in difficulties" than any other group and selected this more frequently than a "special fund to launch new publications". Freelance journalists, on the other hand, were more in favour than other groups of a "special fund to launch new publications", endorsing this item more frequently than "cheap loans to publishers".

TABLE 3.059

JOURNALISTS' VIEWS ON STATE ASSISTANCE TO THE PRESS

	Total	National	Prov. Morning	Prov. Evening	Weekly	Magazine	Agency	Freelance
Weighted base: All	1,272	276	131	262	192	116	52	207
	%	%	%	%	%	%	%	%
(a) *Is there a case for state assistance*								
Yes	44	55	40	42	39	37	52	39
No	46	39	49	48	50	51	33	47
Don't know/Not stated	11	7	11	10	10	12	15	14
(b) *What form should it take*								
Tax concession	50	48	54	52	53	41	59	49
Subsidies for paper	36	37	35	37	39	36	34	31
Cheap loans to publishers	26	33	28	22	22	21	30	24
Special fund to launch new publications	18	15	15	20	15	19	18	28
Cash payments to publishers in difficulty	12	11	13	12	22	5	9	12
Re-allocation of advertising revenue among newspapers	10	7	9	9	11	9	9	14
A national printing corporation	10	11	7	13	9	8	6	11
Don't know/Not stated	14	9	13	11	14	21	18	21

(Compare with Table 3.042)

APPENDICES

Appendix 1: Further Details of Sampling Method

The Universe of Editors

The table below gives the total number of editors known or estimated to be in each category, the number selected for mail out and the weighting fractions applied to the returned questionnaires at the analysis stage to correct for the differential probabilities with which the selection for mail out was made within each group.

Type of Editor	Estimated Total No.	No. Selected for Mail Out	Weighting Fraction
National Newspapers	19	19	1·0
Provincial Daily Newspapers	96	51	1·9
Provincial Weekly Newspapers	440	185	2·4
Periodicals[1]	564	282	2·0
	1,119	537	

[1] Only periodicals published once a month or more frequently and for which an ABC circulation figure was given in the *Newspaper Press Directory* were included.

The Universe of Senior Journalists

The universe comprised senior journalists who were NUJ or IOJ members. As a first stage every sixth name was selected from the unions' records, deleting those who were trainees or retired, or who were employed in public relations, book publishing or broadcasting. This procedure yielded 3,161 senior journalists and indicated that there are approximately six times this number (18,966) of senior journalists in total. This figure must be regarded with some caution, however, since the union records were found not to be always up to date.

The names, addresses and publications of the 3,161 senior journalists were written on to cards and they were then sorted by type of publication so that the sample could be designed to ensure that there were sufficient numbers working on national, provincial daily and provincial weekly newspapers for separate analysis. It was found that the proportion falling into each of these categories was close enough to obviate any need for differential sampling within them; since the occupational details in the union records for some journalists indicated only that they worked for a provincial newspaper company with no indication of type of newspaper, some could not be properly classified. These are given in the table below as "other provincial". There was thus an advantage in sampling newspaper journalists as a single group.

For the second stage of the sampling it was, therefore, decided to divide the journalists into just three groups: newspaper journalists of all kinds and agency journalists, periodical journalists and freelance journalists.

The second stage sampling procedure thus consisted of combining the cards for national and provincial daily and weekly newspapers, "other provincial" journalists, journalists working on other types of newspaper (eg freesheets) or in news agencies, into one stratified group; 1,420 of these were to be selected for inclusion in the sample and 788 rejected, a sampling fraction of 1·6. To get around the problem of fractional selection, firstly every third card was rejected from the set and then every thirty-first from the remainder to arrive at the desired number of 1,420.

Only 445 periodical journalists were selected in the first stage of the sampling procedure so all of these were taken at the second stage for the mail out. There were 508 freelance journalists and 430 of these were selected at the second stage by rejecting every seventh card (a sampling fraction of 1·2).

In total, 2,295 senior journalists were selected for the mail out in the second stage of the sampling procedure.

The table below gives the full details of the analysis of the 3,161 senior journalists selected from the NUJ and IOJ lists at the first stage of the sampling procedure and indicates how they were grouped for the second stage selection. It gives the number of each type of senior journalist found in the 3,161 selected at stage 1 of the sampling procedure, the number selected for mail out and the weighting fractions used at the analysis stage. Since all the newspaper and agency journalists were grouped together at the second stage, they all have the same sampling fraction and thus the same weighting fraction at the analysis stage to correct for the different probabilities of selection.

Type of Senior Journalist	No. at 1st Stage of Sampling	% in each Category	No. Selected for Mail Out	Weighting Fraction
	No.	*%*	*No.*	
Newspaper and Agency Journalists	2,208	70	1,420	1·6
Nationals	*571*	*18*	*370*	
Provincial dailies	*773*	*24*	*497*	
Provincial weeklies	*665*	*21*	*426*	
Other provincial	*59*	*2*	*127*	
Other newspapers	*19*	*1*		
Agency	*131*	*4*		
Periodical Journalists	445	14	445	1·0
Freelance Journalists	508	16	430	1·2
TOTAL	3,161	100	2,295	

Appendix 2: Response Rate Analyses

Editors

	TOTAL		Nationals		Provincial dailies		Provincial weeklies		Magazines	
	No.	%	No.	%	No.	%	No.	%	No.	%
Total number of questionnaires mailed out	537	100	19	100	51	100	185	100	285	100
Ineligible (ie no longer working as editor)	9	2	—	—	—	—	—	*	8	3
Total assumed to be eligible	528	100	19	100	51	100	184	100	274	100
Completed questionnaires	330	63	11	58	47	92	103	56	169	62
Non-response:										
Written or telephoned refusal	28	5	2	11	2	4	7	4	17	6
Returned, not known by Post Office	3	1	—	—	—	—	2	1	1	*
No answer after three requests	167	31	6	32	2	4	72	39	87	32

Journalists

	TOTAL		Nationals		Provincial dailies		Provincial weeklies		Magazines		Freelance		Agency and others	
	No.	%	No.	%	No.	%	No.	%	No.	%	No.	%	No.	%
Total number of questionnaires mailed out	2,295	100	370	100	493	100	426	100	445	100	430	100	127	100
Ineligible (see below for details)	179	8	12	3	24	5	26	6	56	13	49	12	12	9
Total assumed to be eligible	2,116	100	358	100	473	100	400	100	389	100	381	100	115	100
Completed questionnaires	911	43	180	50	255	54	126	32	114	29	175	46	61	53
Non-response:														
Written or telephoned refusal	87	4	13	4	19	4	19	4	19	5	18	5	4	5
Returned, not known by Post Office	1	*	—	—	—	—	—	—	—	—	—	—	1	1
Not known at publication address	116	5	14	4	37	8	13	3	41	11	—	—	11	10
Moved from job/home and no forwarding address	80	4	6	2	7	1	37	9	16	4	10	3	4	3
Misunderstood instructions and thought questionnaire did not apply	8	*	—	—	—	—	1	*	5	1	2	*	—	—
No answer after three requests	941	44	145	41	155	33	209	52	194	50	176	46	35	30

Journalists

	TOTAL	Nationals	Provincial dailies	Provincial weeklies	Magazines	Freelance	Agency and others
	No.	No.	No.	No.	No.	No.	No.
Details of Ineligibility[1]: Retired/Not working	44	7	8	7	7	12	3
Now an editor	72	1	5	11	40	13	2
In PR/Advertising	19	2	2	1	3	9	2
In TV/Radio	18	—	3	—	3	11	1
Other ineligible category	9	—	1	2	1	3	2
Junior/Trainee	11	—	4	3	3	1	—
Deceased	6	2	1	2	1	—	—

[1] This information was not entered on the union record cards.

Appendix 3: The Questionnaires

Royal Commission on the Press

April, 1976

The Royal Commission on the Press has been appointed to inquire (among other things) "into the factors affecting the maintenance of the independence, diversity and editorial standards of newspapers and periodicals".

As part of the inquiry the Royal Commission is carrying out a survey among editors, senior journalists and freelance journalists. The purpose of the survey is to provide information not available from other sources about the background, past career and present work of editors and journalists and to obtain their views on certain general issues of importance to the Royal Commission. The Royal Commission has asked Social and Community Planning Research (SCPR), an independent non-profit research institute, to carry out the survey. The service work for the survey is being carried out by Centre for Sample Surveys, an organisation associated with SCPR.

Trade unions and other associations have been informed about the purpose of the survey and their suggestions and comments have been taken into account in designing the questionnaire.

We should like to ask for your help in this survey, which will form the basis of recommendations by the Royal Commission on journalists' career opportunities and conditions of work. We would appreciate it if you would complete the questionnaire and return it in the stamped addressed envelope provided.

You may feel that some of the questions are rather personal but we assure you that all of them are necessary to provide us with the overall view of journalists' work that we need. We also give a categorical assurance that all the answers you provide will be treated as strictly confidential. The results of the survey will be presented only as aggregates and *no individuals* will be identified.

If you have any queries, please contact SCPR at 01-278-6943 and ask for Miss Morton-Williams or Mr. Stowell.

Thank you very much for your co-operation.

Yours sincerely,

P. McQUAIL,
Secretary

P.415 CONFIDENTIAL

SURVEY AMONG EDITORS

Social and Community Planning Research, an independent research institute, is carrying out this survey at the request of the Royal Commission on the Press. We would be very grateful if you would complete this questionnaire and return it in the pre-paid addressed envelope provided.

The survey is part of a programme of research for the Commission and covers editors and senior journalists. A survey of trainee/junior journalists has already been undertaken.

This questionnaire is designed for editors of newspapers, magazines and periodicals. Editors' names have been obtained by reference to the *Newspaper Press Directory* but this may be out of date. When this is the case we would like the present editor to complete the questionnaire and to accept our apologies for putting the wrong name.

If for any reason you feel that the questionnaire does not apply to you, please fill in the box below and return the questionnaire in the envelope provided.

This questionnaire does not apply to me because ..

How to complete the questionnaire

To answer most questions all you have to do is to put a tick in one or more of the boxes provided but sometimes you are asked to write in your answer.

If you feel that the answer categories provided do not fit your particular case, please write in your answer at the side.

Sometimes you will see an arrow and a question number beside an answer box, eg .... →Q 10. This means that if you have ticked that box you should skip to question 10, leaving out the intermediate questions.

Confidentiality

In order to preserve confidentiality, we do not ask for your name or that of any publications for which you work on the questionnaire. It is therefore necessary to have a serial number on the questionnaire so that we can check that questionnaires have been returned and avoid sending unnecessary reminders. We undertake to ensure that your name will not be linked with your questionnaire.

CONFIDENTIAL   (1–4)
                                                              Card No. 1   (5)
THIS SECTION DEALS WITH YOUR PRESENT
WORK AS AN EDITOR—   ....   (6–10)

1. Are you currently employed or are you the proprietor/owner of a publication?

   Employed 1   (11)
   Proprietor/owner 2

   NOTE: *If you are a proprietor/owner, questions refer to the publication you own.*

2. By what sort of organisation are you currently employed?
   Newspaper/periodical publisher 1   (12)

   Other (PLEASE WRITE IN) ....
   ....
   ....

3. (a) How many publications (with different titles) are produced by the company that employs you? (*If your company is part of a group, do not include publications produced by other companies in the group.*)

   (WRITE IN) ....

   (b) On how many publications do you work in your employment?
   (WRITE IN) ....

   (c) On what types of publication do you work in your employment?
   (*If you work on more than one, please enter separately.*)

	1st	2nd	3rd	
National morning or London evening newspapers	1	1	1	(13–15)
Other morning newspapers (including Scottish morning)	2	2	2	
National Sunday newspapers	3	3	3	
Evening newspapers other than London ...	4	4	4	
Local or regional weekly newspapers ...	5	5	5	
Trade or technical magazine	6	6	6	
Other magazine	7	7	7	
House magazine	8	8	8	
Free sheet	9	9	9	
Other (PLEASE WRITE IN)	0	0	0	

   ....
   ....
   ....

   Please list any others on which you work in your employment.   (16)
   ....
   ....

4. **IF YOU WORK ON A MAGAZINE OR FREESHEET**
   How frequently is it published? (*If you work on more than one, please enter separately*)

	1st	2nd	3rd	
Weekly/bi-weekly	1	1	1	(17–19)
Twice a month	2	2	2	
Monthly	3	3	3	
Other (SPECIFY)	4	4	4	

   TO BE ANSWERED BY ALL EMPLOYED ON A NEWSPAPER/PERIODICAL
5. What is the approximate circulation of the publication(s) on which you work in your employment? (*Please write in*)
   1st .... (20)
   2nd .... (21)
   3rd .... (22)
   .... (23)

   TO BE ANSWERED BY ALL IN EMPLOYMENT
6. (a) Does the company by which you are employed belong to a group?

Yes	1	(24)
No	2	

   IF YES:
   (b) To which group does it belong?

Pearson Longman	1	(25)
Thomson Organisation	2	
Beaverbrook Newspapers	3	
Associated Newspapers	4	
News International	5	
United Newspapers	6	
Reed International/IPC	7	
Scottish and Universal Newspapers	8	
B.P.M. Holdings	9	
D. C. Thomson	0	

Home Counties Newspapers	1	(26)
East Midland Allied Press	2	
Morgan-Grampian	3	
Surrey Advertiser & County Times	4	
Other (*Please write in*)	5	

7. (a) What is your job title? (*Please write in*) .... (27)

   (b) Do you specialise in any particular type of work? .... (28)

   (c) Are you a member of the Board?

Yes, Board of main company	1	(29)
Yes, Board of subsidiary company	2	
No, not Board member	3	

8. (a) How long have you been with your present employer/publishing group? ....years (30)

   (b) And how long have you held your present position? ....years (31)

9. (a) Do you have a contract with your employer/publishing group for a fixed period of time (eg a 2-year or 5-year contract) or do you have a contract with no fixed expiry date?
Contract for fixed period of time 1 (32)
Contract with no fixed expiry date 2
Other (SPECIFY)............3
Not applicable (eg self-employed) ....4 ⟶(c)

(b) How much notice does either side have to give for termination of your contract? ....months (33)

(c) Are you in a pension scheme?
No 1 (34)
Yes, through employment 2
Yes, other (SPECIFY)............3

10. (a) Have you had any management training?
Yes 1 (35)
No 2

IF YES:
(b) Please give details and dates: (36)

(37)

11. How many journalists (including trainee journalists) do you have working under you?
(*Please write in number*)............ (38–39)

12. (a) What responsibility do you have for fixing the total amount of the editorial budget?
Total responsibility for fixing amount 1 (40)
Some responsibility, in consultation with management 2
Little or no responsibility for fixing amount 3
Other (PLEASE WRITE IN) 4

(b) And what responsibility do you have, once the total amount is fixed, for controlling the spending of the editorial budget?
Total responsibility for controlling spending 1 (41)
Some responsibility, in consultation with management 2
Little or no responsibility for controlling spending 3
Other (PLEASE WRITE IN)............4

13. (a) Do you have responsibility for the hiring of journalists under you?
   Yes, full responsibility ...1 (42)
   Yes, some responsibility, in consultation with management ...2
   No, little or no responsibility ...3
   Other (PLEASE WRITE IN) ...4

   (b) And do you have responsibility for the firing of journalists under you?
   Yes, full responsibility ...1 (43)
   Yes, some responsibility, in consultation with management ...2
   No, little or no responsibility ...3
   Other (PLEASE WRITE IN) ...4

14. (a) In an average week, about what proportion of your time do you spend on the different categories of work listed below?
   %
   Writing for the publication (inc. articles & editorials): ... (44–45)
   Editing (inc. sub-editing, layout & commissioning articles): ... (46–47)
   Administration (inc. personnel, financial & budgetary planning): ... (48–49)

   (b) About how many hours did you spend *last week* working on your job?
   (*Please give hours for last week even if not typical*)
   Inside the office ... hours (50–51)
   Outside the office ... hours (52–53)
   TOTAL ... hours (54–55)

   (c) Was this a typical week?
   Yes ...1 (56)
   No ...2
   IF NO, COMMENT:

15. Do you do any other paid work (including work outside journalism) either regularly or from time to time?
   Yes ...1 (57)
   No ...2

16. About how much did you earn last year from all sources?
   (*ie before tax and other deductions*)
   (*If you're unsure an estimate will be sufficient*)
   From employment ... £ (58–60)
   From other journalist activities (including broadcasting) £ (61–63)
   From non-journalist activity (including public relations) £ (64–66)
   TOTAL ... £ (67–69)

Spare (70)

TO BE ANSWERED BY EVERYONE
This section asks you about your education and training as a journalist and about your previous experience.

17. (a) At what age did you finish your full-time education? .... years (71)

(b) What is the highest educational qualification you gained in your *full-time* education? (*Please tick under* (b) *below*)

(c) Did you get any other qualifications after finishing full-time education? (*Please tick under* (c) *below*)

	(b) Full-time	(c) Part-time	
None...	1	1	(72–73)
University degree or above	2	2	
"A" levels/higher or senior leaving certificate	3	3	
"O" levels/Matriculation/GCE	4	4	
Other (SPECIFY)	5	5	

18. (a) As part of your training in journalism did you take any of the following:
    None of these 1 (74)
    One year pre-entry course 2
    Post-graduate diploma in journalism 3
    Day release courses 4
    Block release courses at college of further education 5
    An in-company course run by a publishing group 6
    Any other formal training (please give details) 7
    ....
    ....

(b) Were you indentured as an apprentice or trainee journalist or did you get into journalism in some other way?
    Was indentured 1 (75)
    Got into journalism another way 2

19. (a) Did you have any paid employment before you became a journalist or a trainee journalist? (other than temporary jobs)
    Yes 1 (76)
    No 2

(b) IF YES: Please describe your main employment before entering journalism: (77)
    Job title..
    What you did..

415 (78–80)

2 (1–4) (5)

361

20. (a) How old were you when you first became a journalist or trainee journalist?
   ....years (6–7)
   (b) Was your first job as a journalist with:
   National morning or London evening newspaper 1 (8)
   Other morning newspaper (including Scottish morning) 2
   National Sunday newspaper 3
   Evening newspaper other than London 4
   Weekly newspaper 5
   Trade or technical magazine 6
   Other magazine 7
   A house publication 8
   A local radio station 9
   National or regional radio or television 0

   A national or international news agency 1 (9)
   A local news agency 2
   A freesheet 3
   Other (SPECIFY)..4

21. (a) How did you learn about your first job as a journalist?
   Wrote to the editor 1 (10)
   Through University/School Careers Officer 2
   Through National Council for Training of Journalists
   literature 3
   Through personal contacts 4
   Through press advertisement 5
   Was already working for publication but not as a journalist 6
   Other (WRITE IN)..7
   (b) How were you recruited?
   By interview only 1 (11)
   By entrance test only 2
   By both an interview and an entrance test 3
   Other (WRITE IN)..4

22. (a) At the time you entered journalism did you have any close friends or
   relations who were or had been in journalism?
   Yes 1 (12)
   No 2
   (b) What is your father's occupation? (*If he has changed careers or is retired
   or dead, please describe his main occupation during his working life*) (13–14)
   ....
   ....

23. (a) How old were you when you became a senior journalist? (*ie passed
   from trainee/junior journalist status*) ....years (15)
   Was never a trainee 1
   (b) Did you take the proficiency test before becoming a senior journalist?
   Yes 1 (16)
   No 2

24. (a) When you *first* became a senior journalist, what sort of work did you do? (*Please tick one box under (a) below*)

(b) What position did you hold then? (*Please tick under (b) at foot of page*)

(c) Apart from your *first* job as a senior journalist and your present job, which *other* types of organisation or publication have you *ever* worked for? (*Please tick all that apply under (c) below*)

	(a) First work as a senior	(c) Other work ever done	
My present work is what I first did as a journalist	0		(17–18)
On a national morning or London evening newspaper	1	1	
On another morning newspaper (including Scottish mornings)	2	2	
On a national Sunday newspaper	3	3	
On an evening newspaper other than London	4	4	
On a weekly newspaper	5	5	
On a trade or technical magazine	6	6	
On other type of magazine	7	7	
On a house publication	8	8	
On a freesheet	9	9	
With a local radio station	1	1	(19–20)
On national or regional radio or television	2	2	
With a national or international news agency	3	3	
With a local news agency	4	4	
As a freelance journalist	5	5	
Other (WRITE IN)	6	6	
I have not done any other types of work		7	

(b) Position held in first work as senior journalist:

	(b)	
Executive or desk personnel (eg news editor/deputy or assistant editor)	1	(21)
General or feature sub-editor	2	
General reporter	3	
Specialist reporter/correspondent	4	
Critic or feature writer	5	
Sports reporter/sports sub-editor	6	
Photographer	7	
Other (WRITE IN)	8	
Not applicable (eg freelance)	9	

> IF YOU HAVE *NEVER* BEEN EMPLOYED BY A NATIONAL OR LONDON EVENING NEWSPAPER, PLEASE GO TO Q.26.

FOR THOSE WHO HAVE OR ARE EMPLOYED BY A NATIONAL NEWSPAPER (*INCLUDING LONDON EVENINGS AND SUNDAYS BUT EXCLUDING SCOTTISH NEWSPAPERS*)

25 (a) How old were you when you obtained your *first* job on a national newspaper? ....years (22)

(b) How did you obtain your first job on a national newspaper? (*Please write in full details*)
.... (23)

(c) In what capacity were you employed in your first job on a national newspaper?
Executive or desk personnel (eg news editor, assistant or deputy editor) 1 (24)
General or feature sub-editor 2
General reporter 3
Specialist reporter/correspondent 4
Critic/feature writer 5
Sports reporter/sports sub-editor 6
Photographer 7
Other (SPECIFY) 8

FOR EVERYONE
This section is about your views on working in journalism.

26. Taking *all* aspects into account, how much overall do you enjoy your present work as a journalist?
Very much indeed 1 (25)
Quite a lot 2
A fair amount 3
Not very much 4
Very little 5
Not at all 6

27. What do you like about working in journalism? (*Please write in*) (26)

(27)

28. What do you dislike about working in journalism? (*Please write in*) (28)

(29)

29. Compared with other professions, in general how would you rate journalism as a career on each of the criteria listed below?
(Tick one box for each item)
Compared with other professions, journalism is:

	Very good	Good	Poor	Very poor	
(i) For security of employment	1	2	3	4	(30)
(ii) For scope for creativity	6	7	8	9	
(iii) For prospects of promotion on merit	1	2	3	4	(31)
(iv) For scope for initiative	6	7	8	9	
(v) For starting salary	1	2	3	4	(32)
(vi) For long-term salary prospects	6	7	8	9	
(vii) For degree of responsibility	1	2	3	4	(33)
(viii) For ease of movement to alternative occupations	6	7	8	9	
(ix) For value of work to community	1	2	3	4	(34)
(x) For opportunity for using one's talents	6	7	8	9	
(xi) For intrinsic interest of work	1	2	3	4	(35)
(xii) For opportunity for influencing events	6	7	8	9	
(xiii) For status	1	2	3	4	(36)

30. (a) Do you expect to continue working in journalism for the foreseeable future or do you expect to change?
Expect to continue in journalism 1 (37)
May change career 2
Almost certainly will change 3
Don't know 4
Journalism is not my main work at present 5

31. Please give the following information about your union membership:
(a) Are you or have you been a member of the NUJ or IOJ?

	NUJ	IOJ	
Yes, now a member	1	1	(38–39)
Yes, in part	2	2	
No, never	3	3	

(b) How long were you or have you been a member?
Years.......... (40–41)

(c) Have you ever held office in either the NUJ or the IOJ

Yes, now	1	1	(42–43)
Yes, in past	2	2	
No, never	3	3	

32. (a) How did you vote in the last three general elections?

	Oct. 1974 election	Feb. 1974 election	1970 election	
Conservative	1	1	1	(44–46)
Labour	2	2	2	
Liberal	3	3	3	
Other (SPECIFY)	4	4	4	
Don't know	5	5	5	
Did not vote	6	6	6	

IF YOU CURRENTLY WORK ON A NEWSPAPER OR PERIODICAL:

(b) Would you say your views are to the Left or to the Right of those of the publication you work on?
I am well to the Left 1 (47)
Somewhat to the Left 2
About the same 3
Depends on the issue 4
Somewhat to the Right 5
Well to the Right 6
The publication does not express views 7

THE FOLLOWING QUESTIONS SEEK YOUR VIEWS ON A NUMBER OF GENERAL ISSUES.

33. (a) How well would you say the Press Council performs its functions? (48)
    - Very well 1
    - Fairly well 2
    - Rather poorly 3
    - Very poorly 4
    - Don't know 5

    (b) In what ways (if any) should the aims or procedure of the Press Council be changed? (49)

    (50)

34. (a) Have you ever been involved in any way at all in a complaint made to the Press Council?
    - Yes ....A (51)
    - No ....0 →Q.35

    IF YES:
    (b) Did you consider the way it was dealt with was:
    - Very satisfactory 1
    - Fairly satisfactory 2
    - Not really satisfactory 3
    - Not at all satisfactory 4

    (c) And did you consider the outcome to be:
    - Very satisfactory 1 (52)
    - Fairly satisfactory 2
    - Not really satisfactory 3
    - Not at all satisfactory 4

    (d) Why do you say that? (53)

35. How important would it be to you if you were censured by the Press Council?
    - Very important 1 (54)
    - Fairly important 2
    - Rather unimportant 3
    - Completely unimportant 4
    - Other answer (WRITE IN) 5

36. (a) Which, if any, of the following, present any threat to the freedom of the press? (*Tick all that apply under* (a) *below*)

(b) Which *one* presents the biggest threat? (*Tick one under* (b) *below*)

(c) Do you yourself feel that *your* work in journalism is affected by any undesirable pressures from any of these sources? (*Tick all that apply under* (c) *below*)

	(a) Any threat	(b) Biggest	(c) Pressures you	
The Libel Laws	1	1	1	(55–57)
Advertisers	2	2	2	
Proprietors/owners	3	3	3	
Printing and production workforce	4	4	4	
The management	5	5	5	
Political parties	6	6	6	
Journalists	7	7	7	
The Government	8	8	8	
Costs/inflation	9	9	9	
Official Secrets Act/'D' Notices	0	0	0	
Public relations people	1	1	1	(58–60)
Other (SPECIFY)	2	2	2	
None	3	3	3	

37. (a) What is your view of the amount of diversity of opinion represented at present by *national* newspapers?

There is too much diversity	1
There is sufficient diversity	2
There should be a little more diversity	3
There should be a lot more diversity	4
Don't know	5

(61)

(b) Are there any sections of the community or any political viewpoints that you feel do not get a fair deal from the national press? (*Please give full details*)

(62)

(63)

38. Would you say that each of the following aspects of press concentration is harmful, beneficial or have you no views? (*Please put one tick in each row*)

	Harmful	Beneficial	No views	
(i) The lack of directly competing daily papers outside London	1	2	3	(64)
(ii) The ownership of provincial dailies and national dailies in the same group	1	2	3	(65)
(iii) Daily papers owning weekly papers in the same areas	1	2	3	(66)
(iv) Press ownership in independent television and radio	1	2	3	(67)
(v) The dominance in some magazine fields of a single company	1	2	3	(68)

39. (a) Which of the following positions would you favour in the field of Press Monopoly law? (*Please tick one box only*) (69)
   No legal restrictions on press concentration 1
   Some restriction, but a relaxation of the present press monopoly law 2
   Continuation of the present position under which there is a general prohibition on mergers involving larger press groupings, while the Monopolies Commission has agreed to some purchases of weekly groups by large national groups 3
   A toughening of the present law so as to prevent any mergers, except those between two small groups 4
   Legislation to force the largest press groups to sell off certain publications 5

40. (a) Do you think there is a case for State assistance to the press? (*examples of possible forms of State assistance are given at* (c) *below*) (70)
   Yes 1
   No 2
   Don't know 3

   (b) Why do you say that? (*Please write in*) (71)

   (72)

   (c) If it was decided that State assistance was desirable, what forms should it take? (*Please tick as many as you like*) (73)
   Subsidies for paper 1
   Cheap loans to publishers 2
   Tax concessions 3
   Cash payments to publishers in difficulties 4
   Reallocation of advertising revenue among newspapers 5
   A national printing corporation 6
   A special fund to launch new publications 7
   Other (SPECIFY) 8

   PERSONAL DETAILS
   The following details are required for analysing the survey since journalists' views may differ according to their sex, age or marital status.
   (a) Sex (74)
      Male ... ...
      Female ... ...
   (b) Age last birthday (*Write in box*) ... ... (75–76)
   (c) Marital status (77)
      Married ... ...
      Single ... ...
      Widowed ... ...
      Divorced/separated ... ...

We are very grateful indeed for your co-operation. If you would like to make any further comments to the Commission or to comment on any of the questions in the questionnaire, space is provided below.

PLEASE RETURN THE QUESTIONNAIRE IN THE ENVELOPE PROVIDED

P.415   CONFIDENTIAL

SURVEY AMONG SENIOR JOURNALISTS

Social and Community Planning Research, an independent research institute, is carrying out this survey at the request of the Royal Commission on the Press. We would be very grateful if you would complete this questionnaire and return it in the pre-paid addressed envelope provided.

The survey is part of a programme of research for the Commission and covers editors and senior journalists. A survey of trainee/junior journalists has already been undertaken.

This questionnaire is designed for SENIOR JOURNALISTS. (Editors have a different version and are being sampled separately). It applies to all types of journalist (including deputy and assistant editors, sub-editors, reporters, photographers, cartoonists etc) working on newspapers, periodicals, in news agencies or in a freelance capacity. Your name was selected from NUJ or IOJ membership lists which indicated that you were in one of these categories. It is possible, however, that the records may be out of date; the questionnaire does not apply to you if you are now a full editor or if your work is *mainly* in public relations or as a radio or television journalist. In this case, please complete the box below and return the questionnaire in the envelope provided and accept our apologies for troubling you.

The questionnaire does not apply to me because . . .

How to complete the questionnaire

To answer most questions all you have to do is to put a tick in one or more of the boxes provided but sometimes you are asked to write in your answer.

If you feel that the answer categories provided do not fit your particular case, please write in your answer at the side.

Sometimes you will see an arrow and a question number beside an answer box, eg .... →Q.10. This means that if you have ticked that box, you should skip to question 10, leaving out the intermediate questions.

Confidentiality

In order to preserve confidentiality, we do not ask for your name or that of any publications for which you work on the questionnaire. It is therefore necessary to have a serial number on the questionnaire so that we can check that questionnaires have been returned and avoid sending unnecessary reminders. We undertake to ensure that your name will not be linked with your questionnaire.

CONFIDENTIAL   (1–4)

                                   Card No. 1   (5)

                                   (6–10)

1.   Are you *in employment* as a journalist or working only as a *freelance* journalist? *Please tick one box*
     In employment as a journalist ... .1 →*GO TO NEXT QUESTION*   (11)
     Only freelance work as a journalist ....2 →*GO TO QUESTION* 14

     QUESTIONS 2–13 ARE FOR THOSE *IN EMPLOYMENT* AS A JOURNALIST (FREELANCE JOURNALISTS GO TO QUESTION 14 ON PAGE 5)

2.   By what sort of organisation are you employed?
     Newspaper/periodical publisher ... .1 →*GO TO NEXT QUESTION*   (12)
     National or international news agency ... ...2 →*GO TO QUESTION 6*
     Other news agency ... ...3 →*GO TO QUESTION 6*
     Other (PLEASE WRITE IN) ... .4 →*GO TO NEXT QUESTION*

3. (a) How many publications (with different titles) are produced by the company that employs you? (*If your company is part of a group, do not include publications produced by other companies in the group*) (*WRITE IN*)..............
   (b) On how many publications do you work in your employment? (*WRITE IN*)..............
   (c) On what types of publication do you work in your employment? (*If you work on more than one, please enter separately*)

	1st	2nd	3rd	
National morning or London evening newspapers	1	1	1	(13–15)
Other morning newspapers (inc. Scottish morning)	2	2	2	
National Sunday newspapers	3	3	3	
Evening newspapers other than London	4	4	4	
Local or regional weekly newspapers	5	5	5	
Trade or technical magazine	6	6	6	
Other magazine	7	7	7	
House magazine	8	8	8	
Freesheet	9	9	9	
Other (PLEASE WRITE IN)	0	0	0	

Please list any others on which you work in your employment.
.... (16)

IF YOU WORK ON A MAGAZINE OR FREESHEET

4. How frequently is it published? (*If you work on more than one, please enter separately*)

	1st	2nd	3rd	
Weekly/bi-weekly	1	1	1	(17–19)
Twice a month	2	2	2	
Monthly	3	3	3	
Other (SPECIFY)	4	4	4	

TO BE ANSWERED BY ALL EMPLOYED ON A NEWSPAPER/PERIODICAL

5. What is the approximate circulation of the publication(s) on which you work in your employment? (*Please write in*)
   1st .... (20)
   2nd .... (21)
   3rd .... (22)
   .... (23)

TO BE ANSWERED BY ALL IN EMPLOYMENT

6. (a) Does the company by which you are employed belong to a group?
   Yes 1 (24)
   No 2
   IF YES
   (b) To which group does it belong?
   Pearson Longman 1 (25)
   Thomson Organisation 2
   Beaverbrook Newspapers 3
   Associated Newspapers 4
   News International 5
   United Newspapers 6
   Reed International/IPC 7
   Scottish and Universal Newspapers 8
   B.P.M. Holdings 9
   D. C. Thomson 0
   Home Counties Newspapers 1 (26)
   East Midland Allied Press 2
   Morgan-Grampian 3
   Surrey Advertiser & County Times 4
   Other (*Please write in*) 5

7. What is your job title?
   (*Please tick all that apply*)
   Executive or desk personnel (eg news editor/deputy or assistant editor) 1 (27)
   General or feature sub-editor 2
   General reporter 3
   Specialist correspondent 4
   Critic or feature writer 5
   Sports reporter/sports sub-editor 6
   Photographer 7
   Other (SPECIFY) 8

8. (a) How long have you been with your present employer/publishing group? ....yrs (28)

   (b) And how long have you held your present position? ....yrs (29)

9. (a) Do you have a contract with your employer/publishing group for a fixed period of time (eg a 2-year or 5-year contract) or do you have a permanent contract which has no fixed expiry date?
   Contract for fixed period of time 1 (30)
   Permanent contract 2
   Other (SPECIFY) 3

   (b) How many months' notice do either side have to give for termination of your contract? ....months (31)

   (c) Are you in a pension scheme?
   No 1 (32)
   Yes, through employment 2
   Yes, other (WRITE IN) 3

10. (a) About how many hours did you spend *last week* working on your job?
    (a) Inside the office ....hrs (33–34)
    (b) Outside the office ....hrs (35–36)
    (c) In total ....hrs (37–38)

    (b) Was this a typical week?
    Yes 1 (39)
    No 2
    IF NO, Comment ....

11. Do you do any other paid work (including work outside journalism) either regularly or from time to time?
    Yes 1 (40)
    No 2

12. About how much did you earn last year from all sources? (i.e. before tax and other deductions)
    From employment £.......... (41–43)
    From other journalistic activities (including broadcasting) £.......... (44–46)
    From non-journalistic activities (including public relations) £.......... (47–49)
    TOTAL £.......... (50–52)

PLEASE SKIP TO QUESTION 17 AT THE TOP OF PAGE 6

THIS PAGE IS FOR FREELANCE JOURNALISTS ONLY

13. (a) For how long have you been working as a freelance journalist? ....years (53)
    (b) Which of these types of media do you write for at all? (*Tick all that apply*)
    (c) Which one or two do you *mainly* write for? (*Tick one or two*)

	(b) Write for at all	(c) Mainly write for	
National morning or London evening newspapers	1	1	(54–55)
Other morning newspapers (including Scottish mornings)	2	2	
National Sunday newspapers	3	3	
Evening newspapers other than London	4	4	
Weekly newspapers	5	5	
Trade or technical magazines	6	6	
Other magazines	7	7	
House publications	8	8	
Radio and/or television	9	9	
National or international news agencies	0	0	
Other news agencies	x	x	
Other (SPECIFY)	y	y	

14. What sort of journalistic work do you mainly do? (*Please write in full details and indicate if you specialise in particular topics*) (56–57)

    ....
    ....
    ....

15. (a) About how many hours a week do you spend on average on journalistic work? (include broadcasting but not public relations) ....hours (58–59)
    (b) Do you do any paid work that is outside journalism?
        Yes 1 (60)
        No 2
    (c) About how much did you earn from each source last year?
        Work in journalism £.......... (61–63)
        Work outside journalism £.......... (64–66)
        TOTAL £.......... (67–69)

16. Are you a member of a pension scheme?
    Yes, for employees 1 (70)
    Yes, for self-employed 2
    No 3

TO BE ANSWERED BY EVERYONE
This section asks you about your education and training as a journalist and about your previous experience.

17. (a) At what age did you finish your full-time education? ....yrs. (71)
    (b) What is the highest educational qualification you gained in your *full-time* education? (*Please tick under* (b) *below*)
    (c) Did you get any other qualifications after finishing full-time education? (*Please tick under* (c) *below*)

	(b) Full-time	(c) Part-time	
None	1	1	(72–73)
University degree or above	2	2	
'A' levels/higher or senior leaving certificate	3	3	
'O' levels/Matriculation/GCE	4	4	
Other (SPECIFY)	5	5	

18. (a) As part of your training in journalism did you take any of the following: (74)
   - None of these ...1
   - One year pre-entry course ...2
   - Post-graduate diploma in journalism ...3
   - Day release courses ...4
   - Block release courses at college of further education ...5
   - An in-company course run by a publishing group ...6
   - Any other formal training (please give details) ...7

   (b) Were you indentured as an apprentice or trainee journalist or did you get into journalism in some other way? (75)
   - Was indentured ...1
   - Got into journalism another way ...2

19. (a) Did you have any paid employment before you became a journalist or a trainee journalist? (other than temporary jobs) (76)
   - Yes ...1
   - No ...2

   (b) IF YES: Please describe your main employment before entering journalism.
   - Job title .... (77)
   - What you did ....

   415 (78–80)

   (1–4)
   (2) (5)

20. (a) How old were you when you first became a journalist or trainee journalist? ......years (6–7)
   (b) Was your first job as a journalist with: (8)
   - National morning or London evening newspaper ...1
   - Other morning newspaper (including Scottish morning) ...2
   - National Sunday newspaper ...3
   - Evening newspaper other than London ...4
   - Weekly newspaper ...5
   - Trade or technical magazine ...6
   - Other magazine ...7
   - A house publication ...8
   - A local radio station ...9
   - National or regional radio or television ...0

   - A national or international news agency ...1   (9)
   - A local news agency ...2
   - A freesheet ...3
   - Other (SPECIFY) ...4

21. (a) How did you learn about your first job as a journalist? (10)
   - Wrote to the editor ...1
   - Through University/School Careers Officer ...2
   - Through National Council for Training of Journalists literature ...3
   - Through personal contacts ...4
   - Through press advertisement ...5
   - Was already working for publication but not as journalist ...6
   - Other (WRITE IN) ...7

   (b) How were you recruited? (11)
   - By interview only ...1
   - By entrance test only ...2
   - By both an interview and an entrance test ...3
   - Other (WRITE IN) ...4

22. (a) At the time you entered journalism did you have any close friends or relations who were or had been in journalism? (12)
Yes 1
No 2

(b) What is your father's occupation? (*If he has changed careers or is retired or dead, please describe his main occupation during his working life*) (13–14)

....
....

23. (a) How old were you when you became a senior journalist? (15)
(*i.e. passed from trainee/junior journalist status*) ....years
Was never a trainee 1

(b) Did you take the proficiency test before becoming a senior journalist?
Yes 1 (16)
No 2

24. (a) When you *first* became a senior journalist, what sort of work did you do?
(*Please tick one box under (a) below*)

(b) What position did you hold then? (*Please tick under (b) at foot of page*)

(c) Apart from your *first* job as a senior journalist and your present job, which *other* types of organisation or publication have you *ever* worked for?
(*Please tick all that apply under (c) below*)

	(a) First work as a senior	(c) Other work ever done
My present work is what I first did as a senior journalist ...	0	
On a national morning or London evening newspaper ...	1	1
On another morning newspaper (inc. Scottish mornings) ...	2	2
On a national Sunday newspaper ...	3	3
On an evening newspaper other than London ...	4	4
On a weekly newspaper ...	5	5
On a trade or technical magazine ...	6	6
On other type of magazine ...	7	7
On a house publication ...	8	8
On a freesheet ...	9	9
With a local radio station ...	1	1
On national or regional radio or television ...	2	2
With a national or international news agency ...	3	3
With a local news agency ...	4	4
As a freelance journalist ...	5	5
Other (WRITE IN)	6	6
I have not done any other types of work ...		7

(17–18)

(19–20)

(b) Position held in first work as senior journalist: (b)
Executive or desk personnel (e.g. news editor/deputy or assistant editor) 1 (21)
General or feature sub-editor 2
General reporter 3
Specialist reporter/correspondent 4
Critic or feature writer 5
Sports reporter/sports sub-editor 6
Photographer 7
Other (WRITE IN).. 8
Not applicable (e.g. freelance) 9

IF YOU HAVE *NEVER* BEEN EMPLOYED BY A NATIONAL OR LONDON EVENING NEWSPAPER, PLEASE GO TO Q.26.

FOR THOSE WHO HAVE OR ARE EMPLOYED BY A NATIONAL NEWSPAPER (*INCLUDING LONDON EVENINGS AND SUNDAYS BUT EXCLUDING SCOTTISH NEWSPAPERS*)

25. (a) How old were you when you obtained your *first* job on a national newspaper? ....years (22)

    (b) How did you obtain your first job on a national newspaper? (*Please write in full details*) (23)

    (c) In what capacity were you employed in your first job on a national newspaper?
    Executive or desk personnel (e.g. news editor, assistant or deputy editor) 1 (24)
    General or feature sub-editor 2
    General reporter 3
    Specialist reporter/correspondent 4
    Critic/feature writer 5
    Sports reporter/sports sub-editor 6
    Photographer 7
    Other (SPECIFY) 8

FOR EVERYONE
This section is about your views on working in journalism.

26. Taking *all* aspects into account, how much overall do you enjoy your present work as a journalist?
    Very much indeed 1 (25)
    Quite a lot 2
    A fair amount 3
    Not very much 4
    Very little 5
    Not at all 6

27. What do you like about working in journalism? (*Please write in*) (26)

    ─────── (27)

28. What do you dislike about working in journalism? (*Please write in*) (28)

    ─────── (29)

29. Compared with other professions, in general how would you rate journalism as a career on each of the criteria listed below?
(*Tick one box for each item*)
Compared with other professions, journalism is:

	Very good	Good	Poor	Very poor	
(i) For security of employment ...	1	2	3	4	(30)
(ii) For scope of creativity	6	7	8	9	
(iii) For prospects of promotion on merit	1	2	3	4	(31)
(iv) For scope for initiative	6	7	8	9	
(v) For starting salary	1	2	3	4	(32)
(vi) For long-term salary prospects	6	7	8	9	
(vii) For degree of responsibility ...	1	2	3	4	(33)
(viii) For ease of movement to alternative occupations ...	6	7	8	9	
(ix) For value of work to community ...	1	2	3	4	(34)
(x) For opportunity for using one's talents ...	6	7	8	9	
(xi) For intrinsic interest of work...	1	2	3	4	(35)
(xii) For opportunity for influencing events ...	6	7	8	9	
(xiii) For status	1	2	3	4	(36)

30. (a) Do you expect to continue working in journalism for the foreseeable future or do you expect to change?
    Expect to continue in journalism 1 (37)
    May change career 2
    Almost certainly will change 3
    Don't know 4
    Journalism is not my main work at present 5

31. Please give the following information about your union membership:
    (a) Are you or have you been a member of the NUJ or IOJ?

	NUJ	IOJ	
Yes, now a member ...	1	1	(38–39)
Yes, in part	2	2	
No, never	3	3	

(b) How long were you or have you been a member?
    Years............ (40–41)
(c) Have you ever held office in either the NUJ or the IOJ?

Yes, now	1	1	(42–43)
Yes, in past	2	2	
No, never	3	3	

32. (a) How did you vote in the last three general elections?

	Oct. 1974 election	Feb. 1974 election	1970 election	
Conservative ...	1	1	1	(44–46)
Labour ...	2	2	2	
Liberal ...	3	3	3	
Other (SPECIFY)	4	4	4	
Don't know	5	5	5	
Did not vote ...	6	6	6	

IF YOU CURRENTLY WORK ON A NEWSPAPER OR PERIODICAL:
(b) Would you say your views are to the Left or to the Right of those of the publication you work on?
    I am well to the Left 1 (47)
    Somewhat to the Left... 2
    About the same 3
    Depends on the issue 4
    Somewhat to the Right 5
    Well to the Right 6
    The publication does not express views 7

THE FOLLOWING QUESTIONS SEEK YOUR VIEWS ON A NUMBER OF GENERAL ISSUES.

33. (a) How well would you say the Press Council performs its functions?
   - Very well 1
   - Fairly well 2
   - Rather poorly 3
   - Very poorly 4
   - Don't know 5

   (48)

   (b) In what ways (if any) should the aims or procedure of the Press Council be changed?

   (49)

   (50)

34. (a) Have you ever been involved in any way at all in a complaint made to the Press Council?
   - Yes ....A
   - No ....0 →Q. 35

   (51)

   IF YES:

   (b) Did you consider the way it was dealt with was:
   - Very satisfactory 1
   - Fairly satisfactory 2
   - Not really satisfactory 3
   - Not at all satisfactory 4

   (c) And did you consider the outcome to be:
   - Very satisfactory 1
   - Fairly satisfactory 2
   - Not really satisfactory 3
   - Not all all satisfactory 4

   (52)

   (d) Why do you say that?

   (53)

35. How important would it be to you if you were censured by the Press Council?
   - Very important 1
   - Fairly important 2
   - Rather unimportant 3
   - Completely unimportant 4
   - Other answer (WRITE IN) 5

   (54)

36. (a) Which, if any, of the following, present any threat to the freedom of the press? (*Tick all that apply under* (a) *below.*)

(b) Which *one* presents the biggest threat? (*Tick one under* (b) *below.*)

(c) Do you yourself feel that *your* work in journalism is affected by any undesirable pressures from any of these sources? (*Tick all that apply under* (c) *below.*)

	(a) Any threat	(b) Biggest	(c) Pressures you	
The Libel Laws	1	1	1	(55–57)
Advertisers	2	2	2	
Proprietors/owners	3	3	3	
Printing and production workforce	4	4	4	
The management	5	5	5	
Political parties	6	6	6	
Journalists	7	7	7	
The Government	8	8	8	
Costs/inflation	9	9	9	
Official Secrets Act/"D" Notices	0	0	0	
Public relations people	1	1	1	(58–60)
Other (SPECIFY)	2	2	2	
None	3	3	3	

37. (a) What is your view of the amount of diversity of opinion represented at present by *national* newspapers?

There is too much diversity 1	(61)
There is sufficient diversity 2	
There should be a little more diversity 3	
There should be a lot more diversity 4	
Don't know 5	

(b) Are there any sections of the community or any political viewpoints that you feel do not get a fair deal from the national press? (*Please give full details.*)

(62)

(63)

38. Would you say that each of the following aspects of press concentration is harmful, beneficial or have you no views? (*Please put one tick in each row.*)

	Harmful	Beneficial	No views	
(i) The lack of directly competing daily papers outside London	1	2	3	(64)
(ii) The ownership of provincial dailies and national dailies in the same group	1	2	3	(65)
(iii) Daily papers owning weekly papers in the same areas	1	2	3	(66)
(iv) Press ownership in independent television and radio	1	2	3	(67)
(v) The dominance in some magazine fields of a single company	1	2	3	(68)

39. (a) Which of the following positions would you favour in the field of Press Monopoly law? (*Please tick one box only.*)

    No legal restrictions on press concentration 1   (69)
    Some restriction, but a relaxation of the present press monopoly law 2
    Continuation of the present position under which there is a general prohibition on mergers involving larger press groupings, while the Monopolies Commission has agreed to some purchases of weekly groups by large national groups 3
    A toughening of the present law so as to prevent any mergers, except those between two small groups 4
    Legislation to force the largest press groups to sell off certain publications 5

40. (a) Do you think there is a case for State assistance to the press? (*examples of possible forms of State assistance are given at (c) below*)
    Yes 1   (70)
    No 2
    Don't know 3

(b) Why do you say that? (*Please write in.*)   (71)

    (72)

(c) If it was decided that State assistance was desirable, what forms should it take? (*Please tick as many as you like*).

    Subsidies for paper 1   (73)
    Cheap loans to publishers 2
    Tax concessions 3
    Cash payments to publishers in difficulties 4
    Reallocation of advertising revenue among newspapers 5
    A national printing corporation 6
    A special fund to launch new publications 7
    Other (SPECIFY) 8

....

41. PERSONAL DETAILS
The following details are required for analysing the survey since journalists' views may differ according to their sex, age or marital status.
(*a*) Sex
    Male ... ...   (74)
    Female ... ...

(*b*) Age last birthday. (*Write in box.*) ... ...   (75–76)

(*c*) Marital status
    Married ... ...   (77)
    Single ... ...
    Widowed ... ...
    Divorced/separated ... ...

We are very grateful indeed for your co-operation. If you would like to make any further comments to the Commission or to comment on any of the **questions in** the questionnaire, space is provided below.

PLEASE RETURN THE QUESTIONNAIRE IN THE ENVELOPE PROVIDED

Printed in England for Her Majesty's Stationery Office by Oyez Press Limited
Dd. 290770   K28   8/77